The ABCs of Architectural and Interior Design Drafting

with an Introduction to AutoCAD® 2000

Tony Cook

Gwinnett Technical College

Robin Prater

Gwinnett Technical College

Prentice
Hall

Upper Saddle River, New Jersey
Columbus, Ohio

DMS

Library of Congress Cataloging-in-Publication Data

Cook, Tony, 1959-
   The ABCs of architectural and interior design drafting: with an Introduction
to AutoCAD 2000 / Tony Cook, Robin Prater
       p. cm.
   Includes index.
   ISBN 0-13-086637-7
   1. Architectural drawing--Data processing. 2. Interior decoration--Data processing.
3. AutoCAD. 4. Computer-aided design. I. Prater, Robin. II. Title.

NA2728.C684 2001
720′.28′402855369--dc21   00-059850

Vice President and Publisher: Dave Garza
Editor in Chief: Stephen Helba
Executive Editor: Debbie Yarnell
Associate Editor: Michelle Churma
Production Editor: Louise N. Sette
Production Supervision: Karen Fortgang, *bookworks*
Design Coordinator: Robin G. Chukes
Cover Designer: Jeff Vanik
Cover art: ©FPG
Production Manager: Brian Fox
Marketing Manager: Jimmy Stephens

This book was set in Times Roman by STELLARViSIONs and was printed and
bound by Courier Kendallville, Inc. The cover was printed by Phoenix Color Corp.

10 9 8 7 6 5 4 3 2 1
ISBN: 0-13-086637-7

Preface

Drafting is one of the most powerful tools available for translating ideas from the brain of the creator to the reality of a completed product. Too often, drafting is seen as territory belonging strictly to architects and engineers. The purpose of this book is to demystify the art and science of drafting. The techniques covered will be valuable to a variety of fields including interior design, landscape architecture, surveying, and construction.

This book aims to provide the maximum comfort level possible for the nontechnical student, so if you do not have a background in drafting or computer-aided design, relax. We realize that we are asking you to step slightly out of your field to gain a valuable asset. This book will give you the tools you need to communicate your ideas. Each new concept is accompanied with step-by-step instructions as well as illustrations. The examples were purposely chosen to hold the interest of a variety of students. Our approach differs from that of many classic drafting textbooks in that the emphasis is on architecture, interior design, and landscape design rather than on machine parts. Our purpose is not to make you an expert in all the fields covered but rather to provide you with a good working knowledge of the fundamentals of both manual and computer-aided drafting.

The text is divided into three sections: the basics of manual drafting, an introduction to architectural drawings, and a beginner's guide to AutoCAD®. Our aim is to provide a versatile text that can be used in a variety of classroom settings. Each section stands on its own. An advanced drafting class could begin with Section II and use Section I for review. An AutoCAD® class might choose to begin at Section III and use Sections I and II for reference material. Many examples are cross-referenced between board drafting and AutoCAD®. For example, the construction of an ellipse will be covered as a manual drafting technique as well as be included in the AutoCAD® section of the text.

Special Features of the Text

We have tried to provide as many ways to understand the material as possible. Each chapter contains review questions as well as fundamental exercises to underline the basic principles of that particular chapter. These fundamental exercises are then supplemented with drawing assignments aimed at deepening the student's understanding of the material.

You will find a continuity of examples between the chapters. For example, the same residence is used for drawing floor plans and interior elevations, for inserting text, for using various AutoCAD® commands to draw furniture and fixtures, and for illustrating the use of blocks and layers. This allows the student to focus on the concept being introduced instead of being distracted by trying to interpret an unfamiliar set of plans.

In addition, concepts are cross-referenced between chapters. If a command is mentioned that is covered in detail in another chapter, the chapter and section number are generally provided. Appendices supplement the information and provide information for further in-depth work.

Where appropriate, tips are provided for more efficient drafting whether manually or with AutoCAD®. The notes and reminders are placed outside the body of the text to draw attention to a sentence that might otherwise be overlooked. The tips are also easier to find when flipping through a chapter for a review.

Examples within each chapter are also set apart from the rest of the text. Boxed examples allow students to find their place quickly as they work between the text and their computer.

Each section covering an AutoCAD® command provides ready access to instant information about ways to enter that particular command. The methods are spelled out at the beginning of each section and highlighted with bullets.

If you are left-handed, look for the special hints provided just for you.

Background of the Authors

Tony Cook (ACI) is the Drafting Program Director at Gwinnett Technical College. He has been a drafting and CAD instructor since 1985. He has a 2-year drafting diploma from Valdosta Tech and a Bachelor of Architectural Engineering Technology degree from Southern Polytechnic State University. His industry experience includes working 3 years in residential construction along with 5 years in an architectural/interior design firm that specialized in medical buildings, educational facilities, and public utilities buildings.

Robin Prater is a registered professional engineer with Bachelor of Civil Engineering and Master of Civil Engineering degrees from Georgia Institute of Technology. Her years of experience in industry include projects ranging from offshore platforms to coal preparation plants. Since 1995 she has taught classes in blueprint reading, drafting, AutoCAD®, and other related subjects at Gwinnett Technical College in Lawrenceville, Georgia. She has worked with AutoCAD® and residential design for more than five years.

Acknowledgments

Having just completed the writing of a textbook, both authors have a new appreciation for the importance of acknowledgments. Without the help of a team behind us, this book would never have been completed.

We would like to thank W. Eric Lawrence (AIA, Dean of Continuing Education) for reviewing sections of the text with an eye toward architectural integrity. In addition, a thank you goes out to Todd Cook (Architect) and Georgia Perimeter College for their generosity in supplying several drawings as text illustrations. Donald Mobley (Autodesk® Training Center Manager, Gwinnett Technical College) also spent many valuable hours reviewing the text for accuracy. Thank you all for your time and efforts.

On the publishing side, we have Carole Horton to thank for starting us on the road to publishing. Steve Helba and Michelle Churma provided us with valuable insights along the way.

Thank you to Gwinnett Technical College and the drafting students who helped us in preparing some of the graphics in this text. Many of our other students provided the inspiration for this text. We tried very hard to imagine we were speaking directly to our students as we were writing. The excitement of seeing you begin to accomplish things you never dreamed you were capable of is one of the best parts of teaching.

And now we come to the two persons who absolutely enabled us to write this book. Thank you, Kathy Cook and Cordell Prater, for your many hours of support. We've read these words before in other prefaces but we had no idea how heartfelt they can be.

Contents

Section I □ Universal Drafting for Everyone

Section III □ AutoCAD for Beginners

Universal Drafting for Everyone

Introduction to Drafting Fundamentals

1.1 The History and Origins of Drafting

Before the earliest cultures developed systems of written and verbal language, individuals were moved to scratch pictures on cave walls to communicate with one another. In Egypt, these pictures evolved into hieroglyphics (see Figure 1.1), and the world's first graphic communication system was born. As civilizations advanced, drawing developed in two different directions, artistic and technical. The emphasis of technical drawing or drafting shifted to the construction of buildings and other structures. Certainly, the Egyptians did not lay out their pyramids and vast cities without detailed working drawings (see Figure 1.2).

The Greeks developed elaborate systems of architecture, which were later expanded by the Romans. Buildings such as the Parthenon in Athens (see Figure 1.3) were built to precise specifications for the proportions and geometry of the structure. Each column was spaced at an exact distance, and the dimensions of the columns and entablature were determined by precise formulas.

The Roman military engineer Vitruvius (ca. 90–ca. 20 B.C.), left written evidence of the use of technical drawings in his treatise on architecture, *De Architectura,* or *The Ten Books on Architecture.* The book states, "The architect must be skillful with the pencil and have a knowledge of drawing so that he readily can make the drawings required to show the appearance of the work he proposes to construct." Vitruvius also discusses working with drafting instruments as well as developing plan, elevation, and perspective views of a building.

The achievements of the Romans were tremendous. They are credited with developing concrete, which allowed advances in vaulting and domes. Sections of the Roman Forum and Colosseum are still in existence today (see Figure 1.4).

Firmly rooted in architecture, the graphic language continued to develop through the ages. As people began to satisfy needs beyond basic food and shelter, they used drafting to prototype products and inventions (see Figure 1.5). Drafting expanded into hundreds of new fields.

FIGURE 1.1 Egyptian hieroglyphics. Courtesy of PhotoDisc, Inc.

FIGURE 1.2 The Egyptian pyramids at Giza. Courtesy of PhotoDisc, Inc.

FIGURE 1.3　The Parthenon on
the Acropolis at Athens, Greece.
Courtesy of SuperStock, Inc.

FIGURE 1.4　Remains of the
Roman Forum and Colosseum.

FIGURE 1.5　A flying machine in
a drawing by Leonardo da Vinci.

1.2　The Function of Drafting in Our World

How would you describe drafting in today's world? *Drafting* is graphic communication that is essential to designing, laying out, and developing ideas. Drafting makes these ideas reality through the use of sketches, board drawing, and computer-generated images (see Figure 1.6). In other words, drafting is the art and skill of drawing.

Today, almost everything with which you come in contact needed some form of drawing to be built or constructed. The clothes you wear, the furniture you sit on, and the car you drive all needed drawings to become a reality. In this country you cannot even begin constructing a house without first taking a set of drawings to the local building department for approval. Consider the following areas where drafting is utilized:

Construction Related

Architecture

Interior Design

FIGURE 1.6   Drafters at work.
Courtesy of IBM Corp.

Structural Engineering

Civil Engineering/Site Plans/Mapping/Surveying/Road and Bridge Design

Mechanical/Heating and Air Conditioning/Plumbing

Fire Protection

Landscaping

Electrical Engineering/Power and Lighting Plans

Manufacturing

Automated Manufacturing

Apparel Design

Furniture Design

Mechanical Engineering

Machine Tool Assembly

Sheet Metal Assembly

Plastic Design

Automobile Design

Aeronautical Design

Electronic Design

Computer Science

Telecommunications

Nuclear Engineering

Military Engineering

The list is endless and is constantly changing as technology advances. The terms *designing* and *engineering* will always be associated with drafting. Engineers and designers use drafting during the early stages of creating a product. They sketch, design, and come up with preliminary plans that are generally rough in the beginning. As they get closer to refining their ideas they use a more precise level of drawing. Engineers and designers work with drafters on projects. The primary job of the drafter is to take the architect/engineer/designer's drawings and prepare them for a builder or manufacturer to use to make the desired products.

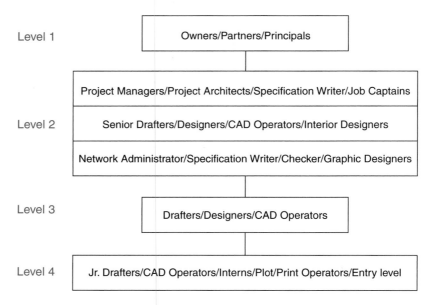

1.3   The Utilization of Drafting by Architectural and Related Firms

A typical architectural or engineering firm employs people with many job descriptions. The following flowchart (see Figure 1.7) shows the hierarchy in a typical organization.

Although the terms *drafter* and *CAD* (computer-aided design) *operator* are listed separately, most offices expect their employees to be able to perform both functions. As you look through the chart be aware that all four levels use drafting skills.

Architects and engineers work as a team to put together construction drawings and specifications for commercial buildings. An architect is hired to design and oversee the construction of a project. In turn, the architect hires an engineering team to handle the building components outside the architect's expertise. There are five basic services an architect performs for a client under a standard agreement:

1. *Schematic design phase*—The architect makes preliminary drawings to get a concept of the project and its extents.
2. *Design development phase*—The architect produces refined design with more detailed drawing than in the previous phase.
3. *Construction document phase*—The architect makes production/working drawings and writes specifications for the building contractor to construct the building.
4. *Bidding and negotiation phase*—The architect helps the owner compare the different contractors' bids and helps select one for the job of building the structure.
5. *Construction phase*—The architect oversees the construction of the building, making sure that the contractor builds according to the working drawings and specifications.

Building components such as heating and air conditioning, plumbing, fire protection, electrical, and structural elements are included with the architectural drawings. The architect must hire engineers to prepare a full complement of drawings and specifications in order to complete his or her obligation to the owner. The architect is not normally responsible for services such as interior design or landscape design; however, some firms do have these departments and for an additional charge will provide these services. Otherwise, landscaping and interior design are contracted out separately.

A full set of construction drawings would have the following index:

Civil

C-1 Site Plan, Plot, and Topography

C-2 Profile Sections and Site Details

Architectural

A-1 Architectural Site Plan

A-2 Floor Plans with Details and Wall Legends

A-3 Reflected Ceiling Plan and Details

A-4 Exterior Elevations and Roof Plan

A-5 Wall Sections and Building Sections

A-6 Door Schedule, Window Schedule, and Details

A-7 Finish Schedule with Interior Elevations

A-8 Miscellaneous Details and Elevations

Structural

S-1 Foundation Plans and Footing Details

S-2 Framing Plans for Floors and Roofs

S-3 Structural Wall Sections and Details

Mechanical/Heating and Air Conditioning

M-1 Floor Plans Showing Duct Layout

M-2 Details and Schedules for Equipment

Mechanical/Plumbing

P-1 Floor Plans Showing Plumbing Pipe Layouts

P-2 Equipment Schedules and Riser (3D pipe) Diagrams

Fire Protection Plan

FP-1 Floor Plans with Fire Sprinkler Layouts

Electrical

E-1 Electrical Site Plan

E-2 Floor Plan with Lighting and Switch Layouts

E-3 Floor Plan with Power and Outlet Layouts

E-4 Equipment Schedules and Details

Additional drawings may be added or deleted depending of the complexity of the project. This list gives you a good idea of how many different types of drafting are involved whenever a building is constructed. Each field has its own need for drafters and engineers.

Interior designers and drafters use many of the same drawings as architectural professionals but with slightly different applications. Being able to appreciate and understand architectural drawings is a valuable asset for an interior design professional. Floor plans, elevations, and finish schedules provide information required to enhance and make features aesthetically pleasing on the inside of a building. Color schedules are used to mix and match paint, wallpaper, window treatments, and carpet. Furniture layouts and lighting may also be included in the scope of work.

Landscape architects and designers primarily use site plans to perform their duties. Their job is to plan the layout of plants and trees as well as to blend human-made structures with nature so the resulting mix is pleasing to the eye. The site plan is used to place the plants and trees in their proper location along with walkways, gardens, and ponds. Plant schedules are also coordinated with the site plan.

FIGURE 1.8 Prototype batter's helmet for baseball and softball with a flip-off mask. (Designed by Mike Hamilton. Drawn by Doug Maddox.)

Drafting in Manufacturing

The drawings used by manufacturing groups run through stages similar to those in the building construction fields. The initial design phase aims at refining the design to the point at which basic drawings can be utilized to construct a prototype or model of the desired product (see Figure 1.8). Once a real-life model is put together, it can be evaluated and tested to see if the product will work. At this point the product may be accepted, improvements may be made, or the entire project may be scrapped. If the bugs are worked out, then the working or construction drawings can be drafted. This set of plans can then be used to patent or to mass-produce the product.

Drafting in Electronics-Related Fields

The electronics industry also uses drafting as a design tool, and most of the drafting is now computerized. Special CAD programs are designed to aid in the layout of integrated circuits and printed circuit boards (see Figure 1.9). In a product such as a cell phone, even the case holding the electronic components is designed using a CAD program.

FIGURE 1.9 Drawing of an integrated circuit.

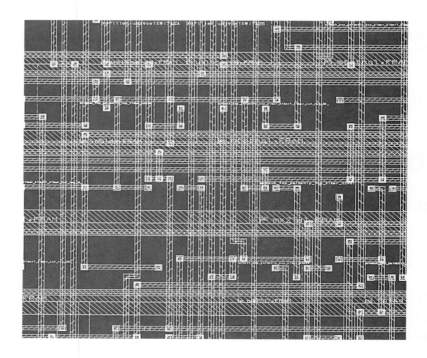

1.4   Board Drafting versus Computer-Aided Design (CAD)

In the last few decades the computer has spawned a major revolution in drafting. Computers were around for several years before they had any impact on drafting; however, the development of CAD software changed things considerably. The early software programs were cumbersome and fairly elementary, whereas today's CAD packages have brought computers to the forefront of drafting technology (see Figure 1.10).

In the late 1970s, most schools and colleges had only drawing boards in their labs. The only way students got to see CAD back then was by taking a field trip to a manufacturing company with a large engineering department.

By the early 1980s, schools were setting up a few labs with CAD, but it was far from smooth sailing. In its infancy, CAD had quite a few problems. The CAD software locked up the computers daily, and with limited computer memory, drawing was slow. Many industry people did not want to upgrade from drawing boards to computers because of the cost of the software and equipment. A number of bugs were still showing up in the software packages. Toward the end of the 1980s, the computers improved and so did the software, and the cost of the CAD packages became more affordable. AutoCAD emerged as the leading software for drafting. Today, very few companies and schools are without CAD, a powerful and productive tool.

Will Board Drawing Disappear?

A drafter is expected to learn both board and CAD skills. When you encounter the term *drafter,* you need to think of a person skilled in both CAD and board drawing. Board drawing remains a valuable tool for instruction, and elements of board drawing skills are still needed to help build a fundamental understanding of drafting basics (see Figure 1.11).

FIGURE 1.10   A CAD workstation.

FIGURE 1.11   A drawing board station.

FIGURE 1.12   A drafter doing a
freehand sketch in the field.

There are several skills that most industry professionals believe should be taught on a drawing board: freehand sketching, lettering, reading scales, and geometric construction (see Figure 1.12). There is a real art and skill to board drawing that not everyone can manage, but fortunately the computer can compensate to some degree. Interestingly, it is extremely rare for an individual who is a really good board drafter not to be an exceptional CAD operator.

Board Essentials

Freehand sketching and lettering are the most free-form skills in drafting and two of the most difficult to master. There was a company in Atlanta in the early 1980s that gave a drafting skills test to prospective employees. The only thing on the test was a sheet of lettering. The company reasoned that an individual who had mastered lettering could learn to master anything else involved in drafting.

Today, some people claim that a portable notebook computer loaded with CAD software is replacing lettering and sketching. Freehand sketching is normally done out of the office while visiting a field or job site. Much of the time you are standing up holding a pad of grid paper with a pencil and eraser. Now, it is possible to take the notebook computer to the field, but imagine standing up balancing your computer while trying to punch keys and drag the cursor. The pencil begins to sound more enticing. Plus, sketching commands in most current software packages do not give you the control to sketch easily and effectively.

Most sketches are brought back to the office to be redrawn to scale using the equipment of your choice. It is important that the sketch be easy to understand because someone else back at the office who was not on the field visit may have to do the drawing. That person will be counting on your sketch to be accurate and readable.

This concept applies to lettering as well as sketching. Any notes taken in the field must be clear and concise. Your lettering skills will be counted on to produce information that others can comprehend.

Engineers and designers often use the technique of freehand sketching for their preliminary ideas. Most find it much easier and faster, initially, to sketch on paper. The ideas are then turned over to a drafter to draw the design to scale using a computer or a drawing board. Interior designers find this technique particularly useful. A quick sketch at the job site can ensure that their ideas reflect their clients' desires. This can save time and money later on in the project.

1.5   Scales and Geometric Constructions

Two other skills that are better learned on the drawing board are reading scales and geometric construction. It is possible to learn them using a computer, but the drafter then relies on the computer software to do a lot of thinking and problem solving. This leaves the drafter in the dark as to how the skill is accomplished. When a difficult geometric or scaling problem comes along that the computer will not handle, the drafter is at a loss as to where to start.

Think back to when you were a child learning to add, subtract, multiply, and divide. Did a teacher hand you a calculator and show you how to press the buttons? You might have wished for this to happen, but it did not. You learned, your parents learned, and your grandparents learned by writing numbers down and using the tool called the brain. This type of training helps develop a problem-solving ability that is very helpful. Once the basics are mastered, calculators become time-saving tools for solving difficult problems.

Learning to draft utilizes the same process. Mastering the basics on the board enhances CAD use for more difficult problems. Walk through a business that uses drafting. Look at the computer stations and notice the drafting scales beside them. Every once in a while a drafter needs a scale. Believe it or not, the scale is not for laying on a computer screen. Computer-aided drafting is just a tool—a time saver—and not a replacement for thinking. When the drafter is faced with a problem the computer may not be able to do, then the brain must take over.

1.6   CAD Is the Workhorse

Today, CAD drives the drafting industry and has worked its way into most fields (see Figure 1.13). The advantages of CAD are clear. Even people who hated the thought that a computer would replace the majority of board drawing have come around to accepting CAD as a valuable tool.

Here are some of the advantages of computer-aided drafting:

1. *Revisions*—Remember; almost all drawings get changed. Changes on a computer are done with ease as well as being neater and less time consuming.

2. *Speed*—Most drawing is much faster on a computer. Time is a big factor when crunch time comes and the drawing must get completed. Once a drawing has been completed using CAD, the finished product can be easily transmitted to most areas of the globe.

3. *Consistency*—Human beings can work as a team. They can even try to copy each other's style of lettering and line work, but when many people work on the same project, it is easy to distinguish different styles when the set of drawings is done. With CAD you can make every drawing look like the same person drew it. Duplication and copying is an exact science with CAD software. Drawings are easy to read and use for construction.

4. *Neatness and layouts*—With a computer-generated drawing, components of a job can easily be moved and oriented into any position. Smearing is a thing of the past. If an original drawing gets torn or ripped, you just print out another copy from a floppy disk or hard drive.

5. *Storage*—Putting drawings on floppy disks, CDs, and tape backups has helped reduce the size of the storage space needed in an office. A box of floppy disks takes up much less room than a large flat file drawer for 24 ″ × 36 ″ sheets.

6. *Precision*—No one can draw on the board more accurately than the computer or change the entire scale of a drawing in a matter of seconds. Think of a computer as a big calculator that you can set up to be as exact as the drawing requires.

FIGURE 1.13   CAD workstations showing different displays. Courtesy of Hewlett-Packard Co.

1.7 Summary

Although the drawing board is no longer the primary focus of drafting in today's world, it still retains value. The competencies and skills learned at the drafting board provide valuable lessons that complement rather than compete with CAD skills. A good board drafter as well as a good CAD operator need to possess similar skills: speed, accuracy, neatness, making revisions without complaining, and using industry standards. When you encounter the term *drafter*, think of an individual proficient in CAD as well as in board drawing. This book will endeavor to teach you how to do both well.

REVIEW QUESTIONS

1. Why were hieroglyphics developed by early humans?
2. What were some of the earliest civilizations to use drawings to build structures?
3. The Romans were credited with the development of what construction material?
4. What advanced structural forms did the Romans use?
5. Define *drafting* in today's terms.
6. List eight industries or professions that use drafting.
7. What development has made the largest impact on the drafting field?
8. Why did it take so long for most companies to start using CAD?
9. Name four skills in drafting that should be taught on the drawing board.
10. What are some advantages to sketching by hand?
11. List the advantages of CAD over board drawing.
12. Make a list of the drawings that an architect uses on a set of construction documents.
13. Develop your own definition or description of drafting.
14. List five objects that needed design drawings to be drafted in order to be built or constructed.
15. Why would an interior designer need to utilize drafting skills?
16. Why would a landscape designer need drafting skills?
17. What does the acronym CAD stand for?

RESEARCH ASSIGNMENTS

1. Research ancient Greek architecture and list five different structures from that time as well as two contributions the Greeks made to architecture.
2. Make a list of five architects of the past and include their more famous buildings or structures.
3. Research ancient Roman architecture and make a list of famous structures still standing today.
4. Research the Renaissance period of architecture in Europe and list some of its architects and the structures they designed.
5. List three modern-day architects or interior designers and include photocopies of their work.
6. Research the terms *architect, engineer, landscape architect,* and *interior designer,* and explain the differences among the four.

○ ○

Learning the Basic Tools and Terminology of Drafting

2.1 Drafting Equipment from A to Z

The first step in learning to draft manually is to assemble your tools. A wide variety of items are available, so you will need to decide how extensive your kit needs to be. The details given in this chapter should help you in your decision. A list of typical equipment needs follows:

- Drafting board and/or table (see Figure 2.1)
- Chair
- Drafting tape
- Drafting pencils, mechanical pencils, or automatic pencils
- Leads, lead sharpener (if using lead holder)
- Erasers, erasing shield, and dusting brush
- Triangles (30°-60°-90°, 45°-45°-90°, adjustable)
- T square, parallel rule, or drafting machine
- Scales (triangular architect's, triangular engineer's)
- Dividers, compass
- Protractor
- Lettering guides and other templates
- Irregular curves (French curves and/or flexible curves)
- Technical pen set and drafting ink
- Dry cleaning pad or drafting powder
- Carrying case or box

FIGURE 2.1 A manual drafting station. Courtesy of Alvin & Co.

Drafting Furniture

Drafting Boards and Tables

Drafting tables are generally referred to by the dimensions of the top of the table (see Figure 2.2). Standard sizes range from 24″ × 36″ (610 × 915 mm) to 42″ × 84″ (1067 × 2134 mm). If you are buying a table, you should base your decision on the size drawings with which you plan to work, the space available for the table, and the cost you can afford. It is important that the surface of the table be hard and smooth. Imagine trying to draft precisely on a surface that is wavy or ridged. Materials range from soft- and hardwoods to Masonite or particleboard with a vinyl veneer. Some tops come ready to use, whereas others must first be covered. Vinyl is often used for this purpose. Covering material needs to be smooth and of the proper density for drawing, otherwise you will be able to inscribe the cover as you draw, leaving ridges that will create difficulties for future drawings. The covering material also should be self-healing so that small holes made by instruments such as a compass will close up. The left edge is generally considered the working edge or the edge on which the T square slides, so this edge must be straight. It can be tested with a framing square or a T-square blade that is true.

When you have decided on your basic table, you can look at the bells and whistles. It is very important to be able to adjust the position of the drafting table to fit your comfort level. A one-hand tilt control as well as a one-hand or -foot height control are very desirable features. The capability of positioning the board in the vertical position is also advantageous. In addition, many professional drafting tables come equipped with electrical outlets and drawers in which to store tools or drawings.

If you do not want to invest in a drafting table, a drafting board may be a good alternative (see Figure 2.3). Some drafting boards come with a base that acts as a support and allows the board to be tilted. A drafting board is a good accessory to have even if you have a full-sized drafting table because of the portability of the board. Boards range from as small as 9″ × 12″ for sketching and field work to as large as 48″ × 72″. Choose a board that is slightly larger than the sheet size that you plan to use most often. For example, a 20″ × 24″ board will work well for 17″ × 22″ drawings. The criteria for selecting a drafting board are similar to those for choosing a drafting table: the board must have a smooth surface without warpage, and the ends must be square and true. Traditionally, boards were made of a softwood such as basswood and were either solid or hollow, often with a metal edging. One reason for this choice was to allow the drafter to use thumbtacks to anchor drawings to the board. This practice eventually left evidence in the form of tiny holes that could interrupt the smooth flow of a penciled line. Today, most drafters choose to use drafting tape to attach their drawings to the board. Boards, just like tables, now come in a variety of surfaces such as particleboard with a vinyl veneer, Masonite, or the traditional wood.

FIGURE 2.2   A professional drafting board.

FIGURE 2.3   A drafting board with a parallel ruler. Courtesy of Keuffel & Esser Co.

Drafting Chairs

Investing in a good-quality drafting chair can save you many aches and pains down the road. Take time to find a chair that fits your body style. Some drafters prefer to use a stool rather than a chair. Seats should be padded or contoured and of sturdy construction. Select a fabric that allows air to circulate. Height adjustment is also important.

Lamps

Adequate lighting is critical to successful drafting. Lamps may be attached to the drafting table or placed on a table nearby. Most drafting lamps are adjustable so that they can be positioned according to the needs of the drafter. It is difficult to draw accurately in a shadow. Lamps may be either incandescent or fluorescent. If fluorescent is used, you may want to experiment with lamps of a different spectra.

Drafting Pencils, Leads, and Sharpeners

Drafting Pencils

What is more inspirational than a handful of newly sharpened pencils? It makes you want to jump in and start drawing. Drafting pencils can be distinguished from regular pencils by their lack of an eraser on the end. The grade of the pencil is marked on one end. As with regular pencils, keeping a sharp point requires a continual process of sharpening. After several trips to the sharpener, the pencil becomes awkwardly short. For this reason, many professional drafters do not use drafting pencils but look to alternatives.

Mechanical and Automatic Pencils

The first improvement in drafting pencils was the mechanical pencil or lead holder (see Figure 2.4). A long piece of lead, approximately the same diameter as a drafting pencil lead, is inserted manually into the holder. Grips at the end of the tube keep the lead from slipping out. As the lead wears away, the drafter presses a button on the top of the mechanical pencil to release the grips so more lead can be pulled from the holder. Mechanical pencils overcome the problem of shortening pencils, but they must still be sharpened using special sharpening tools.

The next generation of pencils was the automatic pencil. The lead in these pencils is advanced by increments with the push of a button or tab. Automatic pencils are designed for thin leads that do not need sharpening. They are available in widths of 0.3, 0.5, 0.7, and 0.9 mm. These pencils generally have a small eraser hidden in the end button. Pretend this eraser does not exist. If it wedges down in the pencil, it will plug the hole and lead will not drop down in the base of the barrel when refills are needed.

Drafting Leads

The lead used for drafting is made of graphite with enough kaolin (clay) added to produce the hardness required for each particular grade. Leads come in 18 grades ranging from 9H, which is the hardest, to 7B, which is the softest (see Figure 2.5). If you look at a cross section of the leads you will notice that the harder grades have a smaller diameter than the softer grades. The softer grades need a larger diameter to give them enough strength to be useful. You can generally divide the eighteen grades of lead into three categories. Grades 9H up to 5H are considered "hard" grades; 4H and 6H leads are commonly used for a light linetype referred to as construction lines. Grades 3H, 2H, H, F, HB, and B are considered "medium" in hardness. The grades most commonly used for line work on architectural drawings are H and 2H. The softer grades in this category, such as F and HB, are better suited to technical sketching and other freehand work such as arrow-

FIGURE 2.4 Examples of mechanical and automatic pencils. Courtesy of C.B. White.

Leads for Vellum or Paper

9H
Hardest Lead

8H

7H

6H

5H

4H
Construction Lines

3H

2H

H
For Normal Lines

F

HB

B

2B

3B

4B

5B

6B

7B
Softest Lead

Leads for Construction Lines

Non-Print Blue   Non-Photo Blue

Leads for Film or Polyester

E0   E1   E2   E3   E4   E5
Soft   Harder

FIGURE 2.5   Lead diameters and examples of their common usage.

heads. The third category ranges from 2B to 7B, the softest grade. These leads are more suited for artwork than technical drafting. They smudge easily and are very difficult to keep sharp.

Special leads are also available through drafting supply stores. Polyester or plastic leads are useful for drawing on the polyester drafting film commonly referred to as Mylar. Normal drafting lead does not adhere as well to this type of drafting media and is easily smudged. The plastic leads are usually labeled with an S or E. The grades available are equivalent to F, 2H, 4H, and 5H. Some companies produce a combination lead for use on both vellum and polyester film.

Colored leads serve a variety of purposes. Red and yellow leads are often used for corrections; however, these colors will appear on prints as black (or blue). If you have information that you wish to place on a drawing but not have it appear on a print, blue lead is a good choice. Blue lead will not reproduce on a diazo (blueprint) machine; it will however reproduce on a photocopy if special photo blue lead is not used. Some drafters prefer to use blue lead for guideline and construction lines.

Sharpeners

Drafting pencils may be sharpened with the same type of pencil sharpeners used for regular pencils. The leads used in lead holders (mechanical pencils) can be sharpened with a pencil pointer made for lead only (see Figure 2.6a). Sanding blocks are another method of sharpening pencils or lead (see Figure 2.6b). With a sanding block the lead can be sharpened to a conical, wedge, or elliptical shape (see Figure 2.7).

Erasers, Erasing Shields, and Dusting Brushes

Erasers

Now that you have selected your drafting pencils, you will most likely find yourself in need of some good erasers. Erasers are commonly found in two basic shapes, rectangular and stick. The stick erasers are good

FIGURE 2.6   (a) A pencil pointer and (b) a sanding block. Courtesy of Alvin & Co.

(a)   (b)

FIGURE 2.7 Conical, wedge, and elliptical leads.

Cone Shape   Wedge Shape   Elliptical Shape

for erasing in tight areas because they are small in diameter. Erasers also come in a variety of compositions that are tailored for different media and drawing instruments, so before you select an eraser, you need to know whether you will be drawing in pencil or pen and on vellum or polyester film. Proper selection can make the eraser your best friend instead of your worst enemy.

White Pencil Eraser. A white pencil eraser is a good general-purpose eraser for pencil on paper. It contains a small amount of pumice, which is an abrasive material sometimes added to make the eraser more effective.

Pink Pencil Eraser. Pink pencil erasers have less pumice than the white pencil erasers. They work well at erasing pencil marks off most types of office papers.

Soft Green and Soft Pink Pencil Eraser. These types of erasers contain no pumice, so they are useful for working with delicate papers. The erasing characteristics of the two colors are the same. The eraser is manufactured in two colors just to satisfy individual preferences.

Gray Ink Eraser. Gray ink erasers are designed to remove ink from paper. They contain a fair amount of pumice and are firm to the touch. Use care when using this type of eraser; it can easily erase a hole right through your sheet of vellum.

Red Pencil Eraser. This is the firmest of all pencil erasers and, not surprisingly, contains the largest amount of pumice. As with the gray ink eraser, use care when using this type of eraser.

Kneaded Eraser. At the other end of the spectrum is the kneaded eraser. This eraser is soft, pliable, and nonabrasive. It is a great stress reliever because it can be kneaded and shaped into any size you need. The kneaded eraser is used mostly for pencil and charcoal. In addition, it is a useful tool for shading. Many drafters also use the kneaded eraser for cleaning up smudges on drawings and work surfaces.

Caution: When erasing on polyester film, take care not to rub off the matte finish. If the matte finish is removed, ink and pencil will no longer adhere to the surface of the medium. Wipe the film with a paper towel after erasing to remove any oil residue on the surface. Otherwise, the ink will run when reapplied to the portion of the film that has been erased.

Vinyl Eraser. The vinyl eraser contains no abrasive material and is used on polyester drafting film (Mylar) to erase ink or plastic lead.

India Ink Erasing Machine Refill. The India ink refill eraser is used for removing India ink from vellum or polyester film. A solvent dissolves the binding agents between the ink and the vinyl, allowing the ink to be removed. This substance is specially made for ink and consequently does not work well with pencil.

Electric Erasers. Electric erasers use a motor to spin a stick eraser around at high speeds to facilitate erasing. You do not need to press down hard with an electric eraser; it does the job for you. Electric erasers are available in models with or without a cord. Some students think using the electric eraser is one of the highlights of manual drafting.

Erasing Shields. An erasing shield is a thin metal or plastic sheet covered with holes of different shapes and sizes (Figure 2.8). These holes allow you to isolate the particular mark you wish to erase without accidentally erasing nearby lines and symbols. Slightly bend one corner to make the erasing shield easier to pick up when it is lying flat.

FIGURE 2.8 An erasing shield with tooled openings. Courtesy of C.B. White.

FIGURE 2.9 Wooden dusting brushes. Courtesy of C.B. White.

Dusting Brush. Using your hand to sweep away eraser dust and graphite particles can leave oily residue from your skin and smudge your drawing. A dusting brush (see Figure 2.9) solves this problem. The fine bristles on the brush clear away unwanted particles without smearing your drawing.

Triangles

Triangles, made of shaped transparent plastic, are used as straightedges to draw lines. They are produced in two standard shapes, which are referred to by the size of the angles at the three corners of the triangle. The first of these triangles, shown in Figure 2.10a, has angles of 30°, 60°, and 90° and is called a 30°-60°-90° triangle. The other standard triangle (see Figure 2.10b) has angles of 45°, 45°, and 90° and is called a 45°-45°-90° triangle. The bigger the number of an angle, the larger the angle. Therefore, the 60°angle is larger than the 30° angle. Also, the three angles of a triangle must always add up to 180° (30° + 60° + 90° = 180°) (45° + 45° + 90° = 180°). The designation of these triangles refers only to the shape of the triangle; both shapes of triangles are available in a variety of sizes depending on the size of your drawing

Using the two shapes of triangles individually and in combination allows the drafter to draw lines at any 15° increment (see Figure 2.11). Adjustable triangles (see Figure 2.12) are also available. These triangles come with a built-in protractor that allows the drafter to adjust the edge of the triangle to draw a line at any angle.

FIGURE 2.10 A 30°-60°-90° triangle and a 45°-45°-90° triangle. Courtesy of C.B. White.

(a)   30°-60°-90°

(b)   45°-45°-90°

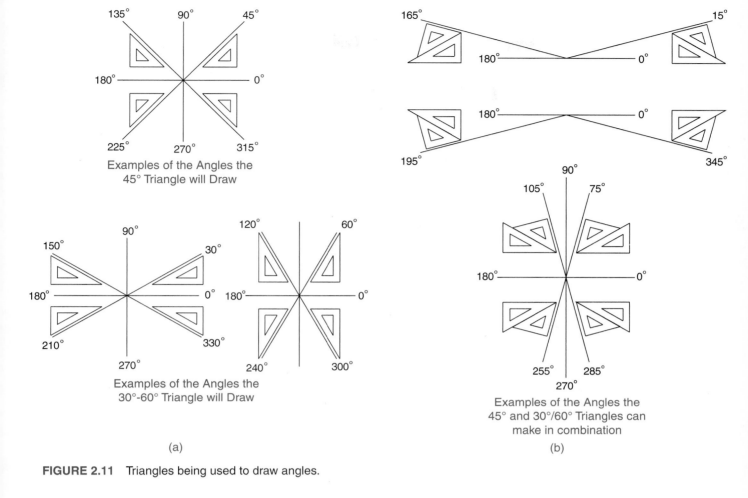

Examples of the Angles the
45° Triangle will Draw

Examples of the Angles the
30°-60° Triangle will Draw

Examples of the Angles the
45° and 30°/60° Triangles can
make in combination

(a)

(b)

FIGURE 2.11 Triangles being used to draw angles.

FIGURE 2.12 An adjustable drafting triangle. Courtesy of C.B. White.

T Squares, Parallel Rules, and Drafting Machines

T squares

In many minds, the T square is the piece of equipment that seems to symbolize drafting. Notice how often the symbol is displayed on the corner of a business card or in a letterhead. The T square (see Figure 2.13) consists of a long strip, called the *blade*, that is fastened tightly at right angles to a shorter piece known as the *head*. The long edges of the blade are the working edges of the T square. They must be perfectly straight and free of any nicks. These edges are usually made out of transparent plastic about ⅜″ wide. This allows the drafter to see what is surrounding the line being drawn.

Treating the T square gently is very important. If the blade becomes nicked or the head loose, the T square will be of very little value. Never use your T square to drive a tack into the board or to cut paper. Check periodically to make sure that the head remains at a 90° angle to the blade. Place the head against a straight edge such as a framing square or a drafting board that has been tested and found true. If the T square wiggles, it needs to be adjusted or replaced. To check the trueness of the blade carefully draw a line along one edge of the blade. Use a hard pencil so the line will be clearly defined. Turn the blade over and draw a line along the same edge. The two lines should coincide (see Figure 2.14). If they do not, the space between the lines will be twice the error of the blade. Again, the T square should be corrected or replaced.

Parallel Rules

Parallel rules or bars (see Figure 2.15) are mounted directly on the drafting board or table using a system of cables running through pulleys attached at the four corners of the board. The parallel bars slide up and down the board on the cable enabling the drafter to draw horizontal parallel lines. Vertical lines and angled lines can be drawn using the parallel bar with triangles (see Figure 2.16). As with a T square, the edges must be kept straight and nick free.

Parallel bars are particularly suited to drawing lines reaching almost the full length of the board. Many architectural drawings fall into this category. A T square may have a tendency to deflect when extremely long lines are drawn. The bar and any triangles must be kept securely in place while drawing. More sophisticated parallel bars are equipped with a locking device to ensure that the bar does not move. Parallel bars can be used even when the board is in the vertical position.

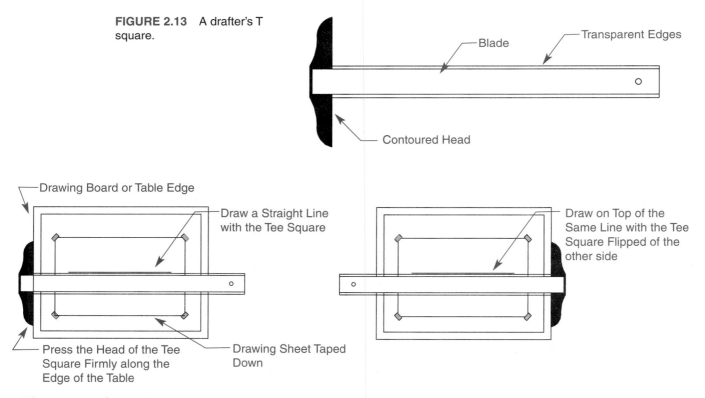

FIGURE 2.13 A drafter's T square.

Blade

Transparent Edges

Contoured Head

Drawing Board or Table Edge

Draw a Straight Line with the Tee Square

Draw on Top of the Same Line with the Tee Square Flipped of the other side

Press the Head of the Tee Square Firmly along the Edge of the Table

Drawing Sheet Taped Down

FIGURE 2.14 One method for checking the trueness of a blade.

(a)   (b)

FIGURE 2.15 Parallel rules. Courtesy of Alvin & Co.

Darken the line then slide down to darken the next line   Slide the Parallel Bar in this direction

Slide this direction

Slide this direction

Example for Horizontal Lines

Right-handers Example. Darken from left to right keeping the triangle from dragging across the lines.

Left-handers Example. Darken from right to left keeping the triangle from dragging across the lines

FIGURE 2.16 Drawing lines with parallel rules.

Drafting Machines

A drafting machine attaches directly to the drawing board and combines the function of triangles and parallel bars. The main body of the machine (see Figure 2.17) consists of a vertical and a horizontal bar clamped to a circular control that allows the angle of the machine to be rotated. While the two bars remain at 90° to each other they can be rotated in order to draw lines at any angle. The center control contains a protractor and vernier plate that allows the rotation of the bars to be measured to within 5′ (minutes). The two bars of the drafting machine serve the combined function of a straightedge and a scale.

The main body of the drafting machine is mounted in either an arm system or a track system. The aptly named arm system (see Figure 2.18) functions just as your arm does using two sections connected by an elbow to position the drafting machine at the desired location on the board. The track system (see Figure 2.19) attaches the main body of the drafting machine to a vertical track that traverses the length of the board on a horizontal track mounted at the top of the board. The body of the drafting machine can be moved up and down along the vertical bar and from side to side using the horizontal bar. A locking device on both bars allows the drafting machine to be fixed at any location on the board.

FIGURE 2.17 Close-up of a drafting machine.

FIGURE 2.18   A drafting machine mounted on a drafting table. Courtesy of Keuffel & Esser Co.

FIGURE 2.19   A track drafting machine mounted on a drafting table. Courtesy of Vemco Corporation

Both the arm and the track drafting machines work well. The arm drafting machine is more compact and slightly less expensive than the track drafting machine; however, the track drafting machine can be used with the board in a vertical position. Because the drafting machine must be able to be situated at any position across the drafting board, both types of machines come in sizes relative to the size of the drafting board. Drafting machines tailored for left-handed drafters are available.

Operating the Drafting Machine Controls

The controls of a drafting machine allow movement horizontally, vertically, and at an angle. Models of drafting machines will vary slightly, so have your instructor demonstrate the controls for your particular machine. In a track drafting machine, horizontal and vertical locks are usually located on the vertical track. The rotation control for both arm and track drafting machines will be on the center control with the protractor and vernier. The protractor and vernier scale allow you to set the angle of the bars with precision. First, try setting the bars to a specified whole degree. Place your hand on the center knob and use your thumb to depress the index thumbpiece. This releases the head and allows the bars to rotate. As you experiment with this control, notice that the head automatically relocks every 15°. You will have to press the index thumbpiece to continue rotating the machine. Pay attention to the protractor and vernier scales as you rotate the drafting machine (Figure 2.20). Each tick mark or increment of the protractor represents 1° of rotation, with every 10° is marked with a number. The zero mark on the vernier plate will line up with the degree of rotation. If the zero mark on the vernier scale lines up exactly with one of the tick marks on the protractor scale, the drafting machine will have been rotated that many whole degrees (see Figure 2.21).

Always be aware whether you are measuring an angle off the position of the vertical or the horizontal bars. The horizontal bar rotates from a base position at 0°, so the readings for the horizontal bar come directly off the protractor and vernier scales. The vertical bar, however, has a base position at ninety degrees. To position the vertical bar you must determine the angle change from 90°. Figure 2.22 shows examples of measuring angles for both the horizontal and vertical bars. The trick is always to determine whether you are working with the horizontal bar, which references to 0°, or the vertical bar, which references to 90°.

After experimenting with rotating your drafting machine to various angles you should be able to see how easy it is to measure whole angles. Now let's learn how to read angles to an accuracy of 59 (minutes). [As a reminder, 1 degree equals 60 minutes (1° = 60′), and there are 60 seconds in each minute (1′ = 60″)]. On the vernier scale, positive angles read upward, and negative angles read downward from zero. Each tick mark on the vernier scale represents 5′. In the illustration shown in Figure 2.23, the zero on the vernier plate is resting between 9° and 10°, therefore, the drafting machine has been rotated at an angle greater than 9° and less than 10°. Use the vernier scale to narrow this reading down further. Look upward on the vernier scale above the zero mark and find the location where the tick marks on the vernier and the protractor scale line are most closely aligned. In Figure 2.23, this occurs at 25′ on the vernier scale, so the correct reading for this angle is 9°25′. A negative angle is read the same way, except the vernier scale is aligned using the lower half of the scale.

FIGURE 2.20   Close-up of a protractor and vernier on a drafting machine.

The Twenty Degree is reached when the Zero mark lines up.

FIGURE 2.21   Protractor and vernier set at 20°.

90°

The vertical guide now is set to 120°

120°

30°

Rotate counterclockwise to 30° tick

0°

(a)

90°   60°

The vertical guide now is set to 60° as 30° is subtracted from 90°

0°

−30°

Rotate clockwise to 30° tick to draw a 330° or −30° angle

(b)

FIGURE 2.22   A vernier measuring an angle from the horizontal and the vertical.

FIGURE 2.23   A vernier reading of 9°25′.

9°25′ on the Vernier

FIGURE 2.24   Architectural and engineering scales.

FIGURE 2.25   The four basic shapes of drafting scales.

Scales

Because objects are rarely drawn full size, scales or rulers play an important role in drafting. Typical scale types are mechanical, engineering, and architectural. Units are either metric (millimeters) or English (inches). Figure 2.24 shows typical scales used for engineering and architectural drawings. Scales come in four basic shapes, which are illustrated in Figure 2.25. Some two-bevel scales are equipped with attachments so they can be used as arms on a drafting machine. Triangular scales combine many scales on one instrument, which gives them an advantage over the other styles of scales. Directions for reading architectural and engineering scales are provided in Section 2.3.

Compass and Dividers

Compass

The compass is used for drawing circles and arcs (see Figure 2.26). One leg of the compass has a needle point, and the other contains lead for drawing. This lead must be kept sharp in order for your drawings to remain accurate. A conical or wedge point may be used. The lead is sharpened in the same way as is the lead for a mechanical pencil. An adjusting screw is the most common device for opening and closing the legs of the compass. Some less expensive models swing the compass open and shut with a metal arc. These tend to become loose over time.

FIGURE 2.26   A compass in use. Courtesy of C.B. White.

FIGURE 2.27 A compass and divider set.   **FIGURE 2.28** A protractor.

If you plan to do much drafting, it is well worth the extra investment to purchase a high-grade instrument. Professional compass sets usually come with removable ends, an extender bar, and an adapter for ink pens.

A compass set and dividers are often packaged together in a specially lined and divided case (see Figure 2.27). A compass adapter will allow the drafter to use an automatic pencil or an ink pen with the compass.

Dividers

A divider is similar to a compass, except both ends are needle points. It may have a center wheel for adjustments, or it may simply use pivot adjustment under friction. Whichever method is used, the divider must be easily adjusted with one hand and remain steady in the new position. Dividers are used for transferring dimensions and dividing a distance into some number of equal parts.

Protractor

Drafters not using a drafting machine will want to include a protractor (see Figure 2.28) in their drawing kit. Protractors are circular instruments marked off in 360°. They can accurately be used to measure angles to within a tolerance of 0.5°.

Lettering Guides and Other Templates

Lettering guides and templates make life easier for the drafter. They are sheets of plastic with various shapes and symbols cut out for tracing. Lettering guides are available in many sizes and styles of lettering. Other templates range from circles and ellipses to architectural floor plan symbols. Specialized templates exist for almost any discipline, whether it be electrical, plumbing, or even computers. The most common architectural templates are at ¼″ = 1′ scale and provide door swings, plumbing fixtures, appliance symbols, roof pitches, circles, cabinets, and electrical symbols (see Figure 2.29) Furniture templates are very useful for interior de-

FIGURE 2.29 Examples of architectural templates. Courtesy of C.B. White.

sign. Templates with a scale of ⅛″ = 1′ are also readily available for commercial as well as residential applications.

If you plan to use ink with your template, buy one with risers built in to keep the template slightly above the drawing. Otherwise, capillary action may cause the ink to run under the template and create a smear. If your template does not have risers, a few layers of tape under the template may serve the same purpose.

Irregular Curves

The curves required in drafting are not always circles or portions of circles. Irregular or French curves (see Figure 2.30), made out of transparent plastic, provide a solution to the problem of drawing curves that do not have a constant radius (i.e., circles or arcs). French curves come in a variety of shapes, but the one constant is that none of the curves on the template have a constant radius. Shapes such as parabolas, hyperbolas, ellipses, and logarithmic spirals are used to construct the French curves.

Flexible curves are another answer to the problem of drawing irregular shapes (see Figure 2.31). Made out of plastic with a flexible core, they allow the drafter to bend them into the desired shape. The core holds the curve in place so the line can be drawn.

Technical Pen Sets and Drafting Ink

Technical Drafting Pens

Technical drafting pens work on the principle of capillary action. A needle acts as a valve to allow ink to flow out of the main body of the pen through a small tube that monitors the amount of ink. Different sized needles are used to draw lines of different width. For this reason, technical pens are usually purchased in a set (see Figure 2.32).

Price range varies for technical pens and is partly determined by the choice of points for the needle part of the pen. Points should be selected based on how you intend to use them. Stainless steel points are well suited for vellum but wear out quickly when used on polyester film (Mylar). Tungsten carbide points are a good choice for polyester film (Mylar) and can also be used on vellum. The longest lasting points are jewel points, which can be used with excellent results on either polyester film or vellum. Jewel points provide the smoothest flow of ink for polyester film.

Careful cleaning and maintenance are critical to keeping technical pens in good working order. Triangles with a special edge for inking are useful accessories when working with technical pens.

Drafting Ink

Drafting ink has its own set of requirements for usefulness. It must dry quickly, not clog the pen, adhere well to the drafting media, and provide even color for reproducing. Select ink that is recommended for the surface on which you plan to draw. Ink must be kept tightly sealed so that it does not dry out or become thick. Some inks can be thinned with a combination of four parts aqua ammonia to one part distilled water.

FIGURE 2.30 Examples of French curves.

FIGURE 2.31 A flexible curve. Courtesy of C.B. White.

FIGURE 2.32 A set of drafting pens and ink. Courtesy of C.B. White.

2.2 Drafting Media and Title Blocks

Drafting Media

The goal of most drafting projects is to produce a finished drawing that is accurate and professional in addition to being easily reproducible. Choosing the right drafting media is key to reaching this goal. Factors to take into consideration when selecting drafting media include transparency, durability, smoothness, erasability, dimensional stability, and cost.

Transparency becomes an important consideration primarily because of reproduction processes. Rarely does the original of a manual drawing get anywhere near a job site. The original usually stays safely in a file drawer while the various trade professionals use sets of copies. Traditionally, the originals have been copied using a diazo process commonly referred to as *blueprinting*. This process requires that light pass through the material being reproduced. If drawings are to be reproduced using a photocopy process, transparency is not important.

Durability becomes an issue when the drawing will be used and handled over a period of time. The amount of use will determine the amount of durability required. If the drawing becomes wrinkled with constant use, it may become difficult to read. Certain types of media are more resistant to crumpled edges and torn corners than others.

The smoothness of the paper is critical to producing sharp, crisp lines that are easily read. Drafting media should be easy to draw and letter on without disproportionate effort. Imagine trying to draw a straight line across a surface that is even slightly bumpy or wavy. The smoothness of the paper also determines how the media will accept ink and pencil.

Whenever humans are involved in drafting, erasability becomes a consideration. A paper that erases easily allows the drafter to make changes without leaving behind telltale marks. A medium that does not erase easily may tempt the drafter to work so hard at getting rid of unwanted lines that the paper becomes worn through or torn. If a residue is left behind on the medium, it may "ghost" through and appear when the drawing is reproduced.

Some media may expand or contract as the temperature or the humidity changes. This can play havoc with figures drawn carefully to scale. The ability of a medium to maintain its size in spite of the ambient conditions is referred to as *dimensional stability*. Media used for drafting should always have good dimensional stability.

The final criterion for selecting drafting media is, as with most things, cost. Transparency, durability, smoothness, erasability, and dimensional stability come at a price. The drafter must decide how to maximize these factors for a price that is affordable. The two most common drafting media are vellum and polyester film.

Vellum

Vellum is commonly used in drafting because it is one of the least expensive papers with good smoothness and good transparency. It is specifically designed to accept either ink or pencil. The erasability of vellum is good, although some brands are better than others. The two most widely used weights of vellum are 1000H and 2000H (see Figure 2.33)

There are some trade-offs to using vellum. It is not as dimensionally stable as some other materials and so it is affected by humidity and other atmospheric conditions. In addition, vellum must be handled carefully because it is not the most durable of the drafting media. Frequent handling can cause the material to deteriorate. In spite of these slight flaws, lead on vellum is still the most prevalent combination used in manual drafting today.

Polyester Film (Mylar)

Polyester film is a plastic material commonly referred to by the trademark name Mylar. It is more expensive than vellum but possesses excellent characteristics of transparency, durability, smoothness, erasability, and

FIGURE 2.33 A table of paper weights.

Typical Vellums

1000H Vellum
Contains 10 lbs
of rag or cloth

2000H Vellum
Contains 20 lbs
of rag or cloth.

Typical Film Sizes Range from 3mils–9mils

Film can be found
as thin as .003"
or 3 mils

Film can be found
as thick as .009"
or 9 mils

dimensional stability. Regular graphite lead will smear when used on polyester film, so it is better to use ink or special polyester leads.

Polyester film is produced with a single- or double-matte surface. The matte surface gives a texture to the film so that it will accept ink or polyester lead. With the single-matte style, one side has a matte surface that can be drawn on, whereas the other side is slick and will not accept drawing. This is the most common type of polyester film. The double matte style is surfaced on both sides and is slightly more expensive than the single matte.

You need to take the following precautions when drawing on polyester film. Avoid getting any moisture on the surface of the film. Moisture interferes with the adhesion of ink or lead to the polyester film, giving the appearance that the area was skipped when lines are drawn. Dirt can also interfere with the adhesion of ink to polyester film. The ink may appear to flow nicely but will flake or wear away with time. So keep your hands clean and dry when working on polyester film. If the surface becomes soiled, clean it with a cleanser formulated for use on polyester film. Make sure the surface is completely dry before you begin drawing.

Erasing on polyester film takes a certain amount of technique. If you are not careful, you can erase not only the ink you applied but also the factory-applied matte surface. If the matte surface is destroyed, the film will not accept ink or lead on that spot on the drawing. Always erase at right angles to the line you are changing, using a light touch without too much pressure. Ink erasers leave an oil residue that needs to be wiped before more ink is reapplied.

Sheet Sizes for Drafting Media

Drafting media come in either rolls or precut sheets. Figure 2.34 shows the most common sizes for precut sheets. The sheet size chosen for various types of jobs will usually be standardized within a particular office.

FIGURE 2.34   ANSI specifications for sheet sizes.

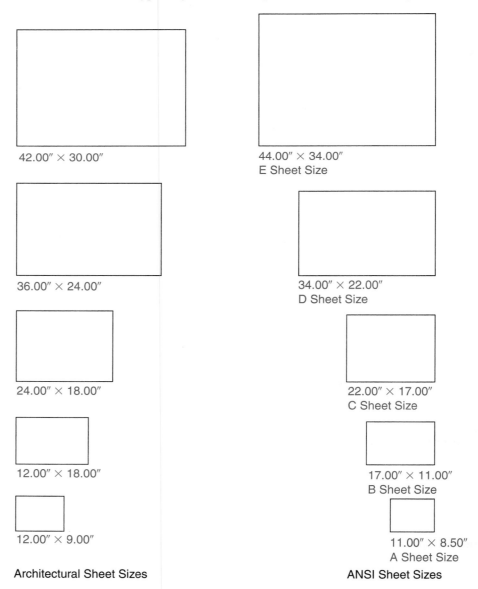

42.00″ × 30.00″

44.00″ × 34.00″
E Sheet Size

36.00″ × 24.00″

34.00″ × 22.00″
D Sheet Size

24.00″ × 18.00″

22.00″ × 17.00″
C Sheet Size

12.00″ × 18.00″

17.00″ × 11.00″
B Sheet Size

12.00″ × 9.00″

11.00″ × 8.50″
A Sheet Size

Architectural Sheet Sizes

ANSI Sheet Sizes

Attaching Drafting Media to the Drafting Board

Although other systems exist, drafting media are most often attached to the board using drafting tape. This tape is specially prepared to hold the paper down without damaging the board or destroying the paper when it is removed. To remove the tape, pull it off slowly in the direction of the edge of the paper, pulling from the outside can cause the paper to tear. Drafting tape is also manufactured in the shape of round dots that are easily removed.

It is best if your drafting board is larger than the sheet size on which you are working. This will allow you to place your paper so that you can use your T square or drafting machine to reach any section of the sheet (see Figure 2.35). If using a T square, place the paper close to the edge of the board with the head of the T square. This will minimize errors resulting from the flex of the T square. Allow enough room at the bottom of the board to support your arm as well as to provide room for the T square or drafting machine.

Title Blocks and Borders

Borders on architectural drawings are usually thick solid lines around the outside of the entire sheet. Typically they are indented ⅜″ to ½″ on the top, bottom, and right sides of the sheet. The left side of the border is indented ¾″ to 1½″ to allow room for binding (see Figure 2.36). Borders are not required, but they provide an excellent frame for the drawing as well as adding a professional looking finish.

The placement of the title block on a drawing will vary with different disciplines. Architectural title blocks are typically found on either the right side or the bottom of the sheet. Both the title block and border can be preprinted on the drafting media for an additional charge. Borders and title blocks are often created in AutoCAD to suit a particular individual's or company's requirements.

The information provided in the title block will vary slightly from company to company. The following items may be included in the title block:

- Name of the project
- Name, address, and phone number of firm
- Name and address of the client
- Drawing name
- Drawing number (Example: Sheet 2 of 10)
- Job or file number
- Scale of the drawing
- Designer or architect
- Drawn by
- Checked by
- Date completed
- Revisions with dates

FIGURE 2.35 Paper positioned correctly on a drafting board.

Fig. II   Form 1. Title Block

Fig. III   Form 2. Title Block

Fig. IV   Form 3. Title Block

Fig. I   Size A Sheet (8.50″ × 11.00″)

Sheet Sizes

**American National
Standard**
A –   8.50″ × 11.00″
B – 11.00″ × 17.00″
C – 17.00″ × 22.00″
D – 22.00″ × 34.00″
E – 34.00″ × 44.00″

International Standard
A4 – 210 mm ×   297 mm
A3 – 297 mm ×   420 mm
A2 – 420 mm ×   594 mm
A1 – 594 mm ×   841 mm
A0 – 841 mm × 1189 mm
   (25.4 mm = 1.00″)

Fig. V   Size B Sheet (11.00″ × 17.00″)

Fig. VI   Size C Sheet (17.00″ × 22.00″)

Fig. VII   Form 4. Title Block

Fig. VIII   Form 5. Title Block

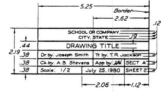

Fig. IX   Form 6. Title Block

Fig. X   Form 7. Parts List or Material List

Fig. XI   Form 8. Revision Block

FIGURE 2.36   ANSI standards for title blocks.

2.3 Reading Architectural, Engineering, and Metric Scales

Rulers measure the actual size of an object in the "real" world. A scale, on the other hand, allows you to measure the size that the object is drawn to represent. Thus, instead of measuring the actual length of a line on a drawing and then multiplying by a scale factor, you can read the number directly off your scale. The work is done for you. The scale of a drawing should always be noted either in the title block or as a note in the body of the drawing. This section discusses using three types of scales: architectural, engineering, and metric.

Architectural Scales

Architectural scales are available in several different shapes, as discussed in Section 2.1. The triangular scale is the most versatile because it combines eleven scales on one piece of equipment. Learning to use a scale is best done as a hands-on experience.

Take a minute to pick up your scale and look it over. The type of numbers on the ends distinguish the architect's scale from other scales. Architect's scales have a fraction at the end of each scale. One edge contains a full-size scale that measures just like a traditional ruler (see Figure 2.37). It is marked with a 16 at the end because each inch is further subdivided into sixteenths. All the other edges contain two scales. One scale is read from left to right, and the other scale is read from right to left. The scales that share an edge are always multiples of each other. For example, ¼ is twice ⅛. With the exception of the full-size scale, the numbers at the end of the scale represent the number of inches on the scale that represent a foot. Thus, the ⅜ at the end of one scale stands for ⅜ inch = 1 foot. Each foot of the actual object will take up ⅜" on your drafting paper when it is drawn to this scale.

The incremental markings between the zeros represent feet and half feet, depending on which scale you are using. Turn your scale over until you find the ⅛" and ¼" scales (Figure 2.38). Most residential drawings are drawn at a ¼" = 1' scale. Commercial architectural drawings are generally drawn using the ⅛" = 1' scale. Notice that each edge contains two rows of numbers. On the ⅛" and ¼" scales, the top set of numbers go from zero on the left to 92 on the right. The bottom set of numbers start at zero on the right and go to 46 on the left. The numbers on the top correspond to the ⅛" scale. The zero is closest to the ⅛" designation, and the numbers get larger as you move to the right. The bottom numbers correspond to the ¼" scale, since the zero on the bottom right is closest to that designation.

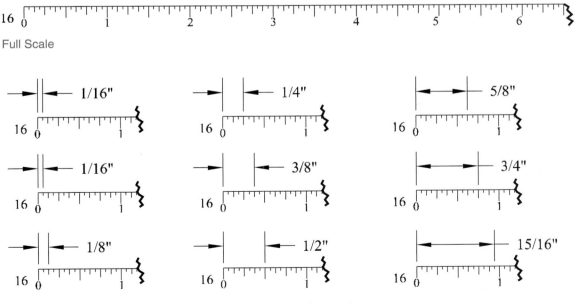

If this scale is used as 1″ =1″, then every tick mark will represent ¹⁄₁₆″.

FIGURE 2.37 Full scale.

FIGURE 2.38 Architectural scales ⅛″ = 1.0′ and ¼″ = 1.0′.

The left side is the ⅛″ =1′-0″ scale.

The right side is the ¼″ =1′-0″ scale.

Every tick mark to the left of the zero represents 2″ on this scale.

Every tick mark to the right of the zero represents 1″ on this scale.

Every tick mark to the right of the zero represents 1′ on this scale.

Every long tick mark to the left of the zero represents 1′ on this scale.

This line measures 2′-8″ at this scale.

This line below measures 4′-5″ at this scale.

The next step is to determine the significance of each tick mark for each particular scale. Every tick mark between the two zeros serves a double duty. On one scale, every tick mark will represent a full foot. On the other scale, every *other* tick mark represents a foot, making the marks in between equal to a half foot, or 6″. Let's look at the ⅛″ = 1′ scale. (see Figure 2.38). Remember, we are using the top numbers for that scale. Notice that the first tick mark is labeled with a zero. The next three tick marks bear no labels on the top and are followed by a tick mark labeled with a four. Thus, each tick mark represents a foot using the ⅛″ = 1′ scale. Now, examine the ¼″ = 1′ scale (see Figure 2.38). Looking at the numbers on the bottom, notice that the far right tick mark is labeled with a zero. Moving to the left, the next three ticks marks are not labeled on the bottom. The next tick mark to the left is labeled with a two. Thus, each tick mark represents a half foot or 6″. The full foot marks fall on the tick marks that are slightly longer. All the scales except the full scale work in this manner. Experiment with using the other scales.

Now let's look at the portion of your scale outside the zeros. Each divided portion to the left and right of the two zeros represents one foot subdivided into inches and portions of inches. The number of subdivisions depend on the room available. The 3″ = 1′ scale has room for many more divisions than the 3⁄32″ = 1′ scale. Take a look at the 3″ = 1′ scale (Figure 2.39). Space is available to actually label 3, 6, and 9″ on the scale. The tick marks get slightly shorter at each subsequent division until the smallest increment, which represents ⅛″. Now look at the 3⁄32″ = 1′ scale (Figure 2.40). The section to the left of zero is divided into only six sections, so each subdivision represents 2″. Take time to check out the other scales and find out how they are divided into inches at the ends.

The best way to measure with a scale is to position the instrument in such a way that it does not have to be picked up to complete the measurement. Moving the scale introduces a chance for error. Figures 2.39 and 2.40 show some examples of measuring with various scales.

Engineer's Scales

Engineer's scales are used for reading and constructing drawings such as plot plans, landscape designs, and topographic maps. The triangular engineer's scale contains six scales labeled 10, 20, 30, 40, 50, and 60. Notice that there are more divisions on the 60 scale than on the 10 scale. This is because the 60 scale is divided into sixty increments along each inch, whereas the 10 scale is divided into only ten increments per inch.

The drafter has the option of using each scale in several ways. For example, the 20 scale can represent 1″ = 20′, 1″ = 200′, 1″ = 20 miles, and so forth. The engineer's scale is graduated in decimals rather than feet and inches, so there are ten divisions between numbers on the scale. Figures 2.41a–e show some examples of measuring with the engineering scale.

The right side is the 3″ = 1′-0″ scale.

Every long tick mark to the right of the zero represents 1″ on this scale.

Every long tick mark to the right of the zero represents 1″ on this scale.

This line measures 1′-10 1/2″ at this scale.

FIGURE 2.39 Architectural scale 3″ = 1.0′.

FIGURE 2.40 Architectural scales 3/32″ = 1/0′ and 3/16″ = 1.0′.

The left side is the 3/32″ =1′-0″ scale.

The right side is the 3/16″ =1′-0″ scale.

Every tick mark to the left of the zero represents 2″ on this scale.

Every tick mark to the right of the zero represents 1″ on this scale.

Every tick mark to the right of the zero represents 1′ on this scale.

Every long tick mark to the left of the zero represents 1′ on this scale.

This line measures 2′-8″ at this scale.

This line below measures 4′-5″ at this scale.

Metric Scales

Metric scales are divided into sections of ten just like engineering scales. The numbers at the end of a metric scale indicate the proportion of the drawing to the actual object being drawn. For example, a 1:2 scale is a half scale. Each line would be drawn at half of its original size. Figures 2.42a–c show some examples of measuring using a metric scale. Most mechanical drawings use millimeters or centimeters, whereas architectural drawings use meters. Metric scales are used in many countries and are very flexible, just like the engineer's scale. Architectural drawings that use metric are almost nonexistent in the United States.

An example of the engineer's 10 scale. Notice the 10 on the left-hand side, which indicates the number of scale increments per inch.

If you use the scale as 1″=10′, then each short tick mark represents 1′, and each long tick mark represents 10′.

This line measures 43' at the 1"=10' scale.

(a)

An example of the engineer's 40 scale. Notice the 40 on the left-hand side, which indicates the number of scale increments per inch.

If you use the scale as 1″=40′, then each short tick mark represents 1′, and each long tick mark represents 10′.

This line measures 37' at the 1"=40' scale.

(b)

An example of the engineer's 60 scale. Notice the 60 on the left-hand side, which indicates the number of scale increments per inch.

If you use the scale as 1″=60′, then each short tick mark represents 1′ , and each long tick mark represents 10′.

This line measures 57' at the 1"=60' scale.

(c)

FIGURE 2.41 Measuring with engineer's scales.

If you use the scale as 1″=1″ (full scale), then each short tick mark represents 0.1″, and each long tick mark represents 1″.

If you use the scale as 1″=100′, then each short tick mark represents 10′, and each long tick mark represents 100′.

This line measures 3.3″ at full scale.

(d)

This line measures 430′ using the 1″=100′ scale.

(e)

FIGURE 2.41 *continued*

An example of the metric scale. The .05 and 1:20 on the left-hand side indicate the number of scale increments per one meter.

This line measures 78 mm at full scale.

An example of the metric scale. The .01 and 1:100 on the left-hand side indicate the number of scale increments per one meter.

It takes 1000 mm to make 1 meter.

It takes 100 cm to make 1 meter

This line measures 42 mm at full scale.

(a)

An example of the metric scale. The .03 and 1:33 1/3 on the left-hand side indicate the number of scale increments per one meter.

This line measures 1120 mm at full scale.

(b)

FIGURE 2.42 Measuring with metric scales. *continued on next page*

An example of the metric scale. The .025 and 1:40 on the left-hand side indicate the number of scale increments per one meter.

This line measures 740 mm at full scale.

The metric scales are blown up very large for the reader to see.

(c)

FIGURE 2.42   *continued*

2.4 Freehand Drawing

Many people mistakenly think that sketching is an artistic skill requiring a natural skill or ability. For a drafter, freehand sketching can be quite different from what an artist might do. An artist sketches to bring life to a picture, giving great attention to shades and shadows and sometimes even adding colors, whereas a drafter makes sketches that are heavily geared toward explaining and communicating to colleagues. Drafters are normally exposed to sketching in two ways:

1. In the office, sketching is a quick method for a boss or coworker to organize, detail, design, and plan out drawings. This type of sketching occurs in both the design process and in the working drawing stage. The sketches are not necessarily analyzed on how pretty they are (unless they are being shown to a client) but more on how clear and understandable they are to read. This type of sketching is used to share ideas and to help develop the working drawings.

2. In the field or on a job site being able to sketch well is a must. This type of sketching is used by an individual to bring back details or ideas to the office. These sketches must be clear enough to be read by the office staff in order for them to develop the sketches into detailed scaled drawing. Remember, it can be very embarrassing not to be able to read or interpret your own sketch.

Basic Tools for Freehand Sketching

- Blueline grid pads of paper or translucent sketch paper
- Soft leads and blue lead
- Color markers/pencils
- Erasers

One of the most important tools a drafter can bring to a job site for sketching is a pad of gridded vellum. The paper comes in a wide range of sizes. Two of the most common sizes used in technical sketching are the 8 × 8 gridded boxes ($\frac{1}{8}''$ × $\frac{1}{8}''$ actual box size) and 10 × 10 gridded boxes ($\frac{1}{10}''$ × $\frac{1}{10}''$ actual box size). The grids are highlighted in 1″ bold blue boxes with the smaller boxes inside them (see Figure 2.43).

The gridded vellum gives the drafter instant vertical and horizontal guidelines or construction lines and, it is hoped, a sense of a controlled sketching environment. When students are first learning to sketch, the guidelines are invaluable, but as they get better and more confident it is common for them to use rolls of white or yellow transparent tissue vellum. A lot of professionals (including instructors) use this medium to sketch out examples quickly.

The drawing techniques for sketching can vary just like in board drawing. Generally, softer leads work better. The drawback is that smearing will increase as the leads get softer. Varying line weights is important when sketching, so pick a lead that is versatile enough to draw thick and thin lines easily. Start off with HB or F to see

FIGURE 2.43 Gridded vellum.

8 X 8 Grid (8 boxes per inch along the horizontal and vertical lines)

10 X 10 Grid (10 boxes per inch along the horizontal and vertical lines)

how they work. Some drafters and designers will draw and sketch with H lead all the time, relying on hand pressure to get the thick lines. Blue lead can also be used to lay out or construct sketches just like on normal drawings. The drafter or designer then darkens the sketch with the soft lead. If the designer wants the sketch to take a more artistic form, then color markers or pencils can be used to give the drawing a more realistic feel.

Sketching to Communicate Ideas

The first thing to learn is to treat a sketch just like a drawing. Pull the pencil to draw, keep the pencil vertical and bear down hard to get thick lines and ease off the pressure to get thin lines. While learning to sketch it is acceptable to lay out and plan out the sketch in blue lines, just as when drawing with all your tools. This will give you a much nicer looking sketch.

Sketching without a scale tends to give students a bit of a challenge. The grid paper can be used as a scale in a number of ways.

1. An easy method to use is to count boxes in order to stay proportional. Simply look at the object to be drawn and evaluate the proportions of the length, width, and height of the object. Establish an overall size for the length, width, or height by a box count (see Figure 2.44). Get your overall sizes

FIGURE 2.44 A house gridded on paper.

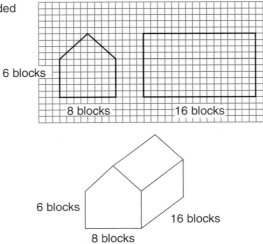

6 blocks

8 blocks   16 blocks

6 blocks

16 blocks

8 blocks

Assign each dimension a number of blocks.

FIGURE 2.45 Elevation with gridded windows.

set and work within the limits to sketch out the smaller items using smaller boxes (see Figure 2.45). Most students can use this method well with a little practice.

2. Using the grid as a real scale is another method. If the gridded vellum is divided into eight boxes per inch, then it can be used for many architectural scales (see Figure 2.46).

This method of sketching can be used instead of drawing because it is accurate as long as you sketch neatly.

3. Another method is to use a visual measuring stick for proportions. Some drafters use their thumb or pencil to measure for scaling a sketch. A person up against a wall can also be used as a scaling guide.

Having to sketch rather than draw can be an uneasy feeling. Take the tools away from a new drafting student and the challenge begins. A student forgets that sometimes tools and computers cannot be hauled everywhere a drafter needs to go, so some basic freehand survival skills are needed. Being a drafter rather than an artist does have some advantages, especially when it comes to sketching. An artist may draw one line with several strokes of a pencil, whereas a drafter needs to draw that line with one long stroke (see Figure 2.47). Approach your sketch just like a drawing. It needs to be clear, and readable line splits and split ends are not acceptable for a drafter.

The grid method of sketching works extremely well for horizontal and vertical lines. The challenge comes when angled lines, arcs, and circles are needed. It is normal for sketched circles and lines to be less than perfect, but there is no excuse for the sketch to look sloppy.

Angled lines should be sketched in one continuous stroke. Locate where the endpoints need to go. A couple of points in between the two ends may be added if needed (see Figure 2.48). Simply draw the angled line pulling through the points. Do not think too much about it. Just do it. It gets easier with practice.

FIGURE 2.46 Gridded paper scales.

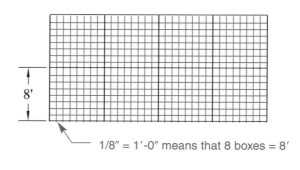

8'

1/8″ = 1'-0″ means that 8 boxes = 8'

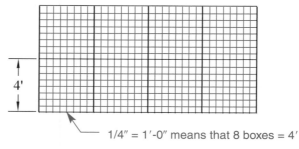

4'

1/4″ = 1'-0″ means that 8 boxes = 4'

FIGURE 2.47 The difference between an artist's sketch line and a drafter's sketch line.

Artist Sketch Line: multiple strokes tend to make the line rougher and give it more character

Drafter's Sketch Line: one continuous stroke makes the line clearer to read.

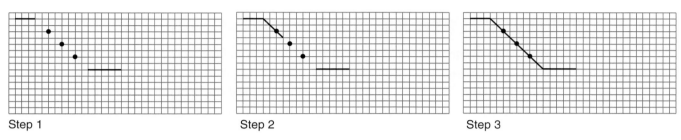

Step 1   Step 2   Step 3

FIGURE 2.48 Sketching an angled line.

FIGURE 2.49 Sketching a circle.

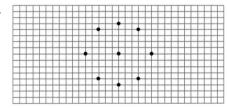

Once you reach a good comfort level on angled lines then it is time to tackle circles and arcs. Circular motions seem to be fairly easy and natural on small shapes, but as they grow in size the circle form becomes harder to hold true. Using grid boxes will help plot you plot the bigger circles and arcs.

Start out by marking the center, then the four quadrant points (see Figure 2.49). Some good drafters can sketch a great circle using these four points and drawing through the grid proportionally. When you are in the learning stages laying out three points between the quadrants may help a great deal (see Figure 2.50). Using this method allows you to make a much smoother circle when you sketch. As you gain competency you may bypass sketching points and using grid paper. It is a little like taking the training wheels off a bicycle. Start off with small shapes and sizes, and progress to bigger and more difficult shapes.

Beginning students have a tendency to want to use their triangles and circle templates on their sketches to make them look better. Remember that if the instructor wanted the sketches to look better then students would be allowed to use all their tools. The purpose of sketching is to learn to draw with bare minimum tools. Do not fear sketching. Embrace it for what it is: a fast method for gathering, designing, and sharing ideas. Practice can make a drafter or designer an exceptional sketcher, so be patient. Learning to sketch will take time, patience, and a good eraser.

FIGURE 2.50 Completing the circle sketch.

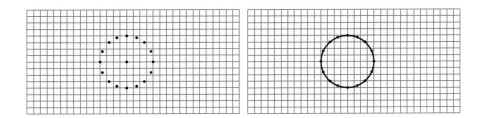

REVIEW QUESTIONS

1. Make a list of equipment to include in your own personal drafting kit.
2. What features should you look for in a top-quality drafting table?
3. Name three criteria for making a decision about the type and size of drafting table to buy.
4. What is the difference between a 9H drafting lead and a 7B drafting lead? What grades of lead are most commonly used for line work on architectural drawing?
5. Why would a drafter use blue lead for a drawing?
6. Why should you use a drafting brush rather than simply brushing away the eraser dust with your hand?
7. List the six factors that influence the choice of drafting media. Briefly summarize why each of these elements is important.
8. Compare vellum with polyester film.
9. List 10 pieces of information that might be placed on a title block.
10. What is the difference between a ruler and a scale?
11. Explain the advantage of using grided vellum when you sketch.

EXERCISES

Scales exercises should be done on 8″ × 11″ sheets.

Exercise 2.1

Reproduce the patterns shown in Figure 2.51 using freehand sketching methods (i.e., use no triangles, drafting machines, etc.).

Exercise 2.2

Try your hand at sketching the drawings in Figures 2.52 freehand.

Exercise 2.3

Practice reading the angle shown on the vernier and protractor settings in Figure 2.53.

Exercise 2.4

Use your architect's scale to complete the following exercise. Use each of the eleven scales to draw a line that measures 1′9″.

FIGURE 2.51 Exercise 2.1.

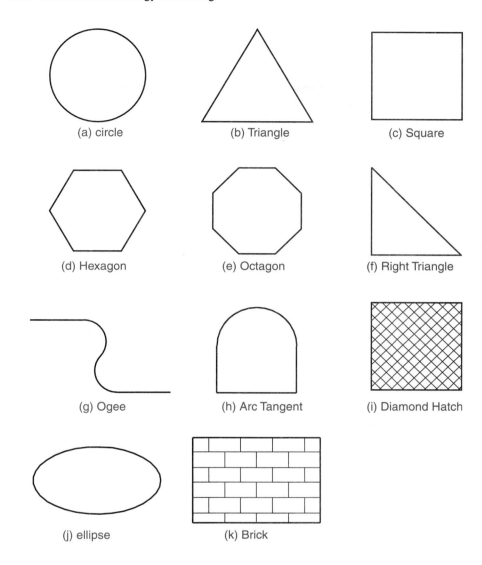

(a) circle (b) Triangle (c) Square

(d) Hexagon (e) Octagon (f) Right Triangle

(g) Ogee (h) Arc Tangent (i) Diamond Hatch

(j) ellipse (k) Brick

Exercise 2.5
Read the architect's scale illustrated in Figure 2.54. What are the lengths of the lines being measured?

Exercise 2.6
Use your architect's scale to draw a line of the length specified using the given scale.

Problem	Length of Line	Scale
1	0'-7 ½"	3"=1'−0"
2	1'-3"	3"=1'−0"
3	10'-5"	¼"=1'−0"
4	1'-9"	¼"=1'−0"
5	4'-6"	⅛"=1'−0"
6	1'-9"	⅛"=1'−0"

(a)

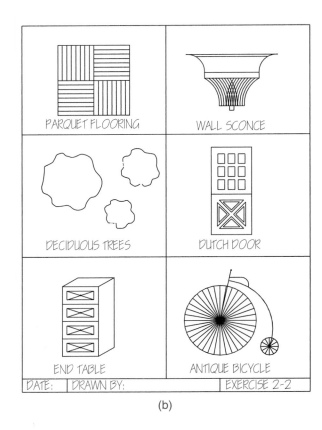

(b)

FIGURE 2.52 Exercise 2.2.

Exercise 2.7

Use an engineer's scale to measure 36′ on each of the six scales. What if you wanted to measure 360′?

For Exercises 2.8 through 2.11, use an architectural scale to draw a line of the assigned distance for the given scale. Use thin vertical lines as the endpoints.

Exercise 2.8

Draw the following distances using a ¹⁄₁₆″ = 1′-0″ scale

- 48′
- 16′-6″
- 12″
- 25′-9″

Exercise 2.9

Draw the following distances using a 3″ = 1′-0″ scale.

- 4 ″
- 1′-9″
- 10 ½″
- 2′-2¼″

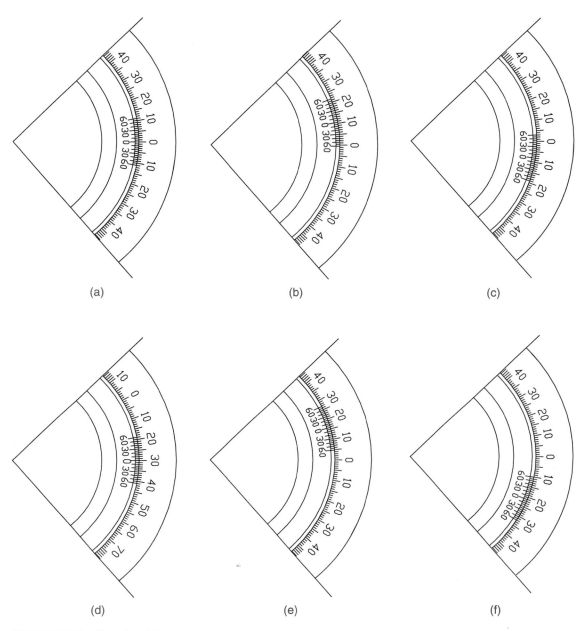

FIGURE 2.53 Exercise 2.3.

Exercise 2.10

Draw the following distances using a 1½″ = 1′-0″ scale.

- 4″
- 1′-9″
- 10½″
- 2′-2¼″

FIGURE 2.54   Exercise 2.4.

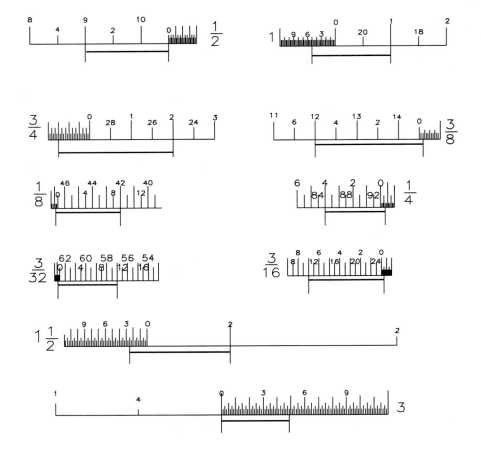

Exercise 2.11

Draw the following distances using a ¼ ″=1′-0″ scale.

- 31′-3″
- 5′-9″
- 12″
- 21′-10″

For additional practice, repeat Exercises 2.8 through 2.11 for the following scales:

- ½″=1′-0″
- 1″=1′-0″
- ¼″=1′-0″
- ¾″ = 1′-0″
- ³⁄₁₆″ = 1′-0″
- ⅜″ = 1′-0″
- ³⁄₃₂″=1′-0″
- Full scale

Manual Drafting Skills: A Masterly Art

Manual drafting skills come naturally to some and can be acquired by those who practice and do not give up in the early stages. In a few weeks, beginners will start to get the hang of it with a little practice and patience. Some persons may never become great board drafters but may learn enough skill to be competent at it when they occasionally step away from CAD. As discussed earlier, there is much value to board drawing and lettering, so do not take it for granted. It just may sneak up and take a bite out of you in the workplace.

3.1 How to Make Your Lines Look Good

Lead Drawing Techniques

The technique of good line work is not a secret but it does take a little bit of getting used to. First, select a good automatic drawing pencil with a 0.5-mm lead width (see Figure 3.1). The old-fashioned lead holders require a little more skill to master and less upkeep, so try the automatic pencil first. Another factor that seems to help in the beginning is picking a pencil with a wide barrel at the base. The wider the base, the more control you will have. Think of first graders starting to learn to write with large pencils. Large pencils are much easier to control.

The next step is to hold the pencil using a comfortable grip so the hand will not tire out quickly. The grip must allow you to draw with the pencil perpendicular to the paper or vellum. This is not a natural writing position so it will take some getting used to. Some teachers demonstrate a standard method of holding the pencil (see Figure 3.2). You may need to experiment a little in the beginning to find a comfortable grip that fits your hand.

FIGURE 3.1 Two types of drafting pencils. Courtesy of Alvin & Company, Inc.

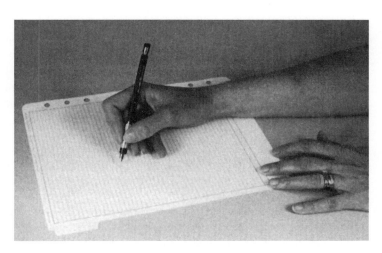

FIGURE 3.2 Correct hand position. Courtesy of C. B. White.

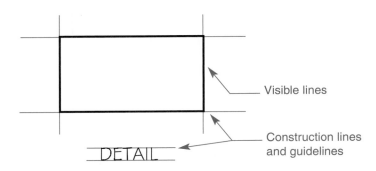

FIGURE 3.3   Pencil lead chart.

FIGURE 3.4   Drawing with construction lines.

Choosing the Right Lead

Once you have selected a good grip, then the next step is picking the right lead to use (see Figure 3.3). For construction layouts blue nonprint lead is the best to use, but some drafters use 6H lead because that was what they were taught when they first learned years ago. Blue lead is better because it does not print when reproduced in blueline prints using a diazo process.

After the construction lines are drawn on the sheet then it is time to use H or 2H lead for darkening lines (see Figure 3.4). The H is a softer lead, so it is easier to make wide dark lines with it, but the drawback is that it will smear more than the harder 2H lead. The 2H lead is acceptable to use for darkening a drawing; however, it does require a lot more pressure bearing down on the paper with the pencil to get wide dark lines. Most instructors want you to try using the H lead and learn some techniques to avoid smearing your lines.

Helpful Hints for Achieving Good Line Quality

Drawing bold thick lines may require at least two hard passes with the 0.5-mm pencil to darken the lines. Thin lines can be drawn with one hard pass over the construction lines. Remember that both lineweights need to be of the same darkness. The only difference should be the width of the lines.

Perfecting your line work can take some time and practice, but there are some things that can help. The automatic pencils are sold in different widths, namely, 0.9 mm, 0.7 mm, 0.5 mm and 0.3 mm. The 0.9 mm is the largest, and the 0.3 mm is the smallest. If you do not mind changing pencils as you draw, this can be a shortcut to developing good line work. A combination of a 0.7 mm for the thick lines and a 0.5 mm for the thinner lines will vary the line width using only one pass at a time when darkening.

If smearing is a problem, locate the source of the smearing. It can be only one of two things. Either the bottom of the hand (below the little finger) is dragging, or some of the drafting tools are dragging across the sheet. If the problem is the hand, then avoid sliding it on the paper/vellum as much as possible. It is fine to rest the hand on the paper, but just keep from sliding it.

The triangles and scales are supposed to slide on the paper, so use a drafting powder pad or can and sprinkle the powder on top of the paper (see Figure 3.5). The dry cleaning pad creates a gap between the paper and the tools and reduces the smearing. Another way to cut down on smearing is to brush the graphite off the sheet of paper, but remember to brush in the direction the lines are running (see Figure 3.6). Brush every 5 minutes or so.

Drawing in a pattern can help cut down on smearing by keeping the equipment from dragging back and forth across darkened lines. Horizontal lines should be drawn from left to right and from top to bottom of the page. Left-handed drafters should draw horizontal lines from right to left (see Figure 3.7). You may draw vertical lines from either direction, but just keep from crossing over them with the triangle (see Figure 3.7). Circles, angled lines, and other shapes need to be darkened last along with the border lines and title block to prevent unnecessary smearing. Practicing these techniques can make a major difference in the neatness of a drawing.

FIGURE 3.5 Applying powder to a drawing.

(a)

(b)

FIGURE 3.6 Proper brushing technique.

Brush in the direction the lines are running.

Brush in the direction the lines are running.

Brush in the direction the lines are running.

FIGURE 3.7 Drawing lines with a triangle.

Darken the line, then slide down to darken the next line.

Horizontal Lines

Slide the parallel bar in this direction.

Slide in this direction.

Right-Handers: Darken from left to right, keeping the triangle from dragging across the lines.

Slide in this direction.

Vertical Lines

Left-Handers: Darken from right to left, keeping the triangle from dragging across the lines.

3.2 The Alphabet of Lines

The purpose of drafting is to communicate ideas. Lines, symbols, lettering, and dimensions form the "language" of a drawing. The drafter has a choice of linetypes to convey the necessary information. Over the years, particular types of lines have acquired special meanings. These lines are referred to as the *alphabet of lines* (see Figures 3.8, 3.9, and 3.10).

Alphabet of Lines for Architectural Drawing

Thicker/Wide lines
Line width around ⅟₃₂″ or about the same width as a 0.7-mm drawing pencil

Visible or Object Line
Thick continuous line

Cutting-Plane Line
Thick line with ¼″ segments and ⅛″ gaps

Viewing-Plane Line
Thick line with ⅛″ segments and ⅟₁₆″ gaps

Short Freehand Break Line
Thick rough line drawn freehand across short distances

Thin lines
Line width around ⅟₆₄″ or a little wider than a 0.3-mm pencil

Long Break Line
Thin line with jagged Z shape that varies in size depending on space limitations

Hidden Lines
Thin line with ⅛″ segments and ⅟₁₆″ gaps

Center Lines
Thin line with ⅛″ segments and ⅟₁₆″ gaps

Section or Hatch Lines
Thin continuous line

Dimension Lines
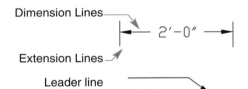
2′-0″

Extension Lines

Leader line
Used when pointing to parts of the drawing

FIGURE 3.8　Alphabet of lines for architectural drawing.

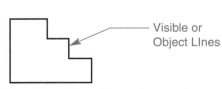

Visible or Object LInes

These lines represent edges or intersections of planes perpendicular to your line of sight.

A cutting-plane or viewing-plane line must be used here to indicate that a cut is being made.

Hatch lines indicate solid material in here.

Section Cut

Visible or Object LIne
Center LIne
Hidden LIne

Front View of a Pipe　Side View of a Pipe

A Mechanical Use of Hidden Lines (See the architectural examples in the partial floor plan.)

Freehand break lines indicates a small interruption in the drawing.

FIGURE 3.9　Examples of mechanical uses of the alphabet of lines.

Long break line indicates an interruption in a drawing spread a long way.

This hidden line indicates a recessed wall so chairs can slide under the counter.

CLOSET

TOILET ③

This shows a change in the ceiling height.

Bar in the closet on which to hang clothes

MICRO WAVE

②

KITCHEN

Dimension line

14'- 0"

Visible lines show walls and edges and other surfaces.

Wall-mounted cabinets above the finished floor

WASHER

DRYER

①

REFG.

C.O. 3'-6"   PAN

Hatching for wood wall

Wall-mounted cabinets above the finished floor

This hidden line indicates that the opening does not go all the way up to the ceiling.

FIGURE 3.10   Examples of architectural uses of the alphabet of lines.

Construction Lines and Guidelines

Construction lines are used to lay out drawings. If drawn properly, they are so light that they can barely be seen when the drawing is held at arm's length. Typically, construction lines are drawn with a sharp 4H or 6H lead with very little pressure applied by the drafter. These lines are used for preliminary work, so they should not be able to be reproduced. For this reason, some drafters prefer to use blue lead for construction lines because it does not reproduce in a diazo process.

Guidelines and construction lines differ only in purpose. Guidelines are used to provide a boundary or guide for lettering. Much like the writing tablets used in kindergarten, guidelines keep your letters uniform and level. Just like construction lines, guidelines should be drawn very lightly so that they do not reproduce. Neither guidelines nor construction lines should need to be erased.

Visible or Object Lines

Visible or object lines form the principal lines of a drawing. They are relatively thick lines (see Figure 3.9) that form the outlines of the object being drawn. These lines should stand out in comparison with other lines on the drawing. On an architectural plan, object lines are used to draw the outline of the walls. They are thicker than the lines used for dimensions or notes (see Figure 3.10). Occasionally, this rule will be ignored and all the lines will be drawn with the same weight or thickness. In this case, shading can be used to emphasize the importance of the walls (see wood hatching in Figure 3.10). The lead chosen for outline or object lines is in the range of 2H, H, or F.

Dashed or Hidden Lines

Dashed lines are used on a drawing to indicate features that are not visible in the view being shown. For example, in an architectural drawing, a dashed line would be used to show the location of closet rods, under-counter appliances, electrical circuit runs, cased openings, sky lights, overhead cabinets, ceiling fans, roof overhangs, and so on; footings below the ground, existing contours, and other features being blocked from view; cabinet door swings, window swings, and all kinds of bracing and reinforcing for steel. Hidden lines are placed on drawings only when they provide useful insights. (See Figure 3.10 for some hidden line uses in architectural drawing.)

Dashed lines are of medium thickness, intermediate between thick object lines and thin dimension lines. The ideal proportions are ⅛″ to ⅜″ long dashes with ¹⁄₁₆″ to ⅛″ spaces in between. When manually drafting, make your dashes and spaces as close to these sizes and as uniform as possible without measuring each pencil mark.

Dimension and Extension Lines

Dimension and extension lines are used together to clarify the size of the object being shown. The extension lines show the extent of a dimension. In other words, they show that the dimension is being measured from point A to point B. The extension lines should not connect with the object lines of the drawing. A small space should always be left between the extension line and the object being dimensioned.

The dimension lines are drawn along the length being measured at right angles to the set of extension lines (see Figure 3.11). A number indicating the measurement for the dimension is placed near the center of the dimension line, either slightly above the line or inserted in a broken line (see Figure 3.11). Dimensions are given in either feet and inches or in millimeters and meters. One system of units should be used consistently throughout a set of drawings.

Both dimension and extension lines are relatively thin, but this does not mean they are to be drawn lightly. Use an H or 2H lead to make the lines thin but dark. The intersection of the extension and dimension lines can be marked with either an arrowhead, a slash, or a dot (see Figure 3.11). The placement of the dimension and extension lines plays a critical part in the readability of a drawing. They should be spaced as evenly around the drawing as possible. Avoid the appearance of crowding whenever possible.

Leader Lines

The purpose of a leader line is to connect notes to their related feature on a drawing. Leader lines can be drawn either as a freehand curve or as a straight line and shoulder drawn with a straightedge (see Figure 3.12). The end of the line terminates in a dot or an arrowhead pointing to the feature being discussed. In architectural drafting, arrowheads are often an expression of individuality (see Figure 3.13), but once again, it is important to be consistent in your choices. Use the same type of leader line and arrowhead throughout a set of drawings.

FIGURE 3.11 Examples of dimensioning.

Mechanical Dimensioning

— 2.1231 — Closed Arrows

Architectural Dimensioning

3'-4" Slashes or Ticks

3'-4" Dots

3'-4" Open Arrows

Straight Leader

Curved Leader

1/8"

FIGURE 3.12 Examples of architectural style leader lines with open arrowheads.

FIGURE 3.13 Arrowheads should be around 1/8″ (.125) long and about 1/3 as wide. Arrowheads are drawn freehand.

Center Lines

The centerline is used to mark the center of an object such as a column or a beam. It is also used to indicate the finished floor line on a building. A centerline consists of a long line alternating with a short dash. Figure 3.14 shows some typical proportions for this type of line.

Break Lines

Break lines are used to indicate that a portion of an object has not been shown on the drawing. For example, you may have a long object of uniform cross section that will not fit on the page at the scale being used. The solution would be to show the object with break lines at the center indicating that a section was left out in order to fit the ends on the drawing. Figure 3.15 illustrates a long break line. The short break line is merely a thick wavy freehand line. It is used when the distance required is relatively short. Imagine how difficult it would be to draw a line of this type over several inches without imparting an amateurish feel to the drawing. When a longer break is required, a long break line, consisting of a straight line broken periodically by a freehand jagged line, is used. The long break line is more common on architectural drawings.

FIGURE 3.14 Example of centerline use in an architectural drawing.

FIGURE 3.15 Example of break line usage.

Special Lines Used on Architectural Drawings

Some architectural drawings may also contain lines and symbols with special meanings. The key to understanding these variations is found in the drawing legend (see Figure 3.16a). Look at the legend and then find where all the special lines occur in the site plan (see Figure 3.16b). Without the legend you would be at a loss to understand the drawing.

Most architectural plans also have a symbols legend. It is a reference that explains how the drawing details will be organized and laid out on the drawing sheets. The example in Figure 3.16c is a basic one. Depending on the particular architectural firm the symbols legend will vary somewhat, so always look carefully at the legends in all drawings. The American Institute of Architects (AIA) has set standards that an architect can use as guidelines. These guidelines can be formed in a book or CD ROM called *Architectural Graphic Standards.*

(a)

(b) *continued on next page*

FIGURE 3.16   (a) Site legend and (b) site plan; (c) examples of symbols used in drawing.

2"x6" RAFTER @ 16" O.C.

1/2" DECKING BOARD

NO. 15 FELT

ASPHALT SHINGLES

1/2" VINYL FASCIA

1/2" VINYL SOFFIT

CORNICE BOARD

5/8" ANCHOR BOLT 48" O.C.

SEALANT

STRIKE JOINTS FLUSH

EXT. LATEX PAINT

FILL CELLS SOLID FROM FINISHED FLOOR TO FOOTING

2"x6" JOIST @ 16" O.C.

2"x6" BLOCKING

INSULATION

1/2" GYP BOARD

2"x8" PRESSURE-TREATED TOP PLATE

8" U BLOCK W/ 2 #6 REBAR CONT. FILLED SOLID W/ CONCRETE

8" CMU

1/2" E.J.

4" CONCRETE SLAB 6X6 10/10 W.W.F.

V.B.

4" GRAVEL

EARTH

8"x16" FOOTING W/ 2 #6 REBAR CONT.

7'-11½"

2'-2"

2'-0"

4 **WALL SECTION**
A-2

SCALE: 3/4" = 1' - 0"

(c)

FIGURE 3.16 *continued*

SLAB TO SLOPE 1" PER FT MIN.

RAMP

EXTERIOR LIGHTS

ROOF OVERHANG

ELECTRICAL WIRING

INTERIOR LIGHTS

OPEN FOR HEAT PUMP

TYP. PASS-THRU WINDOW

OPTIONAL OR PLANTERS

FLASHING

BOOTH #1

BOOTH #2

BOOTH #3

45'-4"

10'-8"

6'-4"(TYP)

1 **FLOOR PLAN**
A-2

SCALE: 1/4" = 1' - 0"

2
A-2

COUNTY FAIR GROUNDS

4" CMU: (RECESSED)

6'-0"

2'-10"

6'-0"

3'-4"

BULL NOSE

2 **FRONT ELEVATION**
A-2

SCALE: 1/4" = 1' - 0"

(b) *continued*

3/4" SMOOTH BAR

1" X 1/4" SMOOTH BASE

1/8" ALUMINUM SHELF & BRACES

2'-8"

2'-8"

A **WINDOW ELEVATION DETAIL**

SCALE: 1/4" = 1'-0"

3.3 Tackling Different Styles of Lettering

There are two things that most drafters hate and lettering is both of them. It is one of the most difficult skills to master. Until a level of competency is reached, lettering will always detract from (see Figure 3.17) drawings. The longer a drafter puts off learning to letter decently the more of a burden it becomes.

Variations among Lettering Styles

Lettering styles can vary drastically, with some being quite interesting. Depending on the drafting field there may not be many choices of lettering styles. Mechanical drafting uses ANSI (American National Standards Institute) for guidelines to drawings. The lettering styles for mechanical drawings are restricted, with single-stroke Gothic being recommended, since it is the most legible and readable style of lettering. The letters may

FIGURE 3.17 Example of poor lettering. Being sloppy and inconsistent is unacceptable in all drafting fields.

ABCDF

FIGURE 3.18 Examples of mechanical lettering styles. Courtesy of *Architectural Drawing and Light Construction* by Edward J. Muller.

ABCDEF
GHIJKLM
NOPQRS
TUVWXYZ
01234
56789
Sloped Style at 72° Angle

ABCDEF
GHIJKLM
NOPQRS
TUVWXYZ
01234
56789
Vertical Styles

THE BASIC LETTER FORM

be either vertical or sloped (see Figure 3.18). These styles are very basic and easy to read with few accents or characters and are widely accepted in other drawing and engineering fields.

Lettering in Architecture and Related Construction Fields

Architecture has a more freestyle approach to lettering. An artistic flare is put into lettering to give individuals more control over how their lettering should look. There are many architectural styles of lettering. Some are shown in Figures 3.19 and 3.20. If a drafter develops a good style it is even possible to use it on CAD drawings. The image of the letter can be put in a font file and loaded into a software package.

FIGURE 3.19 CAD architectural lettering styles.

ABCDEF
GHIJKLM
NOPQRS
TUVWXYZ
01234
56789
CITYBLUEPRINT
lettering style

ABCDEF
GHIJKLM
NOPQRS
TUVWXYZ
01234
56789
STYLUS BT
lettering style

ABCDEF
GHIJKLM
NOPQRS
TUVWXYZ
01234
56789
COUNTRYBLUEPRINT
lettering style

FIGURE 3.20 Architectural lettering styles. Courtesy of *Architectural Drawing and Light Construction* by Edward J. Muller.

No. 1 EXTENDED

ABCDEFGHIJKLMNO
PORSTUVWXYZ···
1234567890 ¹₂ ³₄

WIDE LETTERS WITH LITTLE
SPACE BETWEEN. NOTICE
THE CENTER STROKES.

Extended lettering

No. 2 INCLINED

ABCDEFGHIJKLMOPQR
STUVWXYZ 123456789

INCLINED LETTERS ARE COMMON
FOR ENGINEERING DRAWINGS···
VERTICAL LETTERS ARE COMMON
FOR ARCHITECTURAL DRAWINGS

Inclined lettering

No. 3 TRIANGLE...

ABCDEFGHIJKLMNOPQR
STUVWXYZ 1234567890

VERTICAL STROKES ARE DONE
WITH THE HELP OF A TRIANGLE.
NOTICE THE SLIGHT EXTENSIONS.

Triangle lettering

Keys to Good Lettering

There are three major components to good lettering.

- **Uniformity:** Always use horizontal guidelines to keep the heights the same. In the beginning use vertical guidelines to gauge the widths of your letters. Spaces between words should be about the width of the widest letter, like a W or O.

- **Legibility:** Keep the letters clear and distinct. If the letters are hard to read, then the person reading the drawing must guess at the words.

- **Consistency:** Once you have chosen a style, then you must try and match each individual letter or number each time it is made. Keep the slope consistent on sloped letters, and keep vertical letters as straight up and down as possible. Never allow them to slope back to the left (see Figure 3.21).

An angle of 68° is the maximum slope allowed for lettering (see Figure 3.22). Guides can be used to establish this angle.

The Ames lettering guide is a very useful tool that helps the drafter lay out all the construction lines dealing with lettering (see Figure 3.23). This lettering guide is the most popular tool for lettering drawings because of the speed with which it can be used. Other templates tend to slow you down. Using all uppercase letters is standard for working drawings. However, some designers use lowercase letters for presentation drawings. There are minimum standard heights for lettering (see Figure 3.24) .

Fractions in mechanical drawing are shown stacked with a horizontal line (see Figure 3.25). The overall fraction height is always two times the height of the letter that is being used. Fractions in architectural lettering use an angled slash or solidus (see Figure 3.26). This style allows the height of the fractions to fit within normal lettering guidelines.

Lettering Tip:
When learning to letter, stick to short exercises and concentrate on making good letters. Short assignments tend to bring out the best in a beginner.

Always use guidelines for consistancy.

Try to make each letter look the same. Always be consistant with the letter shapes and strokes.

FIGURE 3.21   Lettering hints.

Never slope your letters back to the left. This is unacceptable in any drafting field.

Always use guidelines for consistancy.

Sloped style should be between 90° and 68°.

FIGURE 3.22   Sloped lettering style.

VERIFY ALL DIMENSIONS ON THE FLOOR PLAN.
Use 1/8"-tall letters for notes as a minimum.

WALL SECTION DETAIL
Use 1/4"-tall letters for titles as a minimum.

FIGURE 3.23   The Ames lettering guide. Courtesy of Alvin & Co.

FIGURE 3.24   Examples of lettering heights.

$$\frac{1}{4} \quad \frac{1}{2} \quad \frac{7}{8}$$

FIGURE 3.25 Examples of mechanical fractions.

1/4   1/2   7/8   3/16   1/4

(a)   (b)

FIGURE 3.26 Examples of architectural fractions.

Crafting Your Skill

One problem that shows up in beginner's work is weak lines and weak letters. Remember that originals must be printed or reproduced and will require dark lines to generate good prints. Do not be afraid to bear down hard when drawing lines and letters. Carve them out with meaning. Yes, the lead will break on the end of the pencil frequently, but soon the combination of the right amount of pressure and holding the pencil at a 90° angle will develop good, consistent dark lines and letters. If the lead breaks, have a scrap piece of paper beside the drawing and scribble off the sharp edges of the lead. Remember to reset the lead so that the tip is about $\frac{1}{16}''$ long.

Being consistent is a goal for all quality drafters, but even the best drafters have occasional bad days when it comes to lettering and line work, even when they have achieved a good level of consistency. Don't be hard on yourself when you have a bad day.

3.4 Ink Drafting

When it comes to ink drawing throw out all the rules that pertain to pencil drafting. Inking tends to make board drawing much slower and meticulous. New tools with new rules create a whole new set of skills to develop and learn (see Figure 3.27).

Inking Tools, Equipment, and Resources

The medium best suited for inking is polyester film (Mylar). Technical Rapidograph pens in a variety of widths are a must for doing the best inking job. Make sure to get fast-drying latex ink for film. It cuts the drying time down by at least half.

General drafting tools such as a triangle, circle template, and French curve are manufactured for inking. As a rule, look at the base of these tools for risers that raise up the edges where the tip of the ink pen glides along. If the risers are present, the tool has been altered for inking pens (see Figure 3.28).

FIGURE 3.27 An ink pen.

Risers on the bottom of a template for inking

Inking edge sticks out on the triangles

FIGURE 3.28 Inking-aided equipment.

If the ink touches anything other than the film it will run everywhere and leave a mess. If you intend to do some ink drawing in the future, buy the tools made for inking, because they work with lead drawings also. A compass adapter can hold an ink pen or pencil, so be sure to include one in your drafting kit along with special ink erasers made for erasing on film.

Drawing Film Basics

Film comes in a variety of thicknesses for durability and transparency for printing—as thin as 3 mils (0.003″) or as thick as 9 mils (0.009″). The surface of the film is matted (treated) to make the ink adhere to the plastic better. Make sure the surface is clean and oil free. A mild thinner or alcohol can be rubbed on the surface to clean it. Lay out construction lines with blue lead as usual, then when it is time to ink just draw right on top of the blue.

The big advantage of inking on film is that the lines go down smoothly without your having to apply much pressure to the pen. This is easier on the hand. Erasing ink on paper or vellum is a challenge because the paper tears when you try to erase. Film can be erased and look great. Knowing that mistakes are fixable, the drafter will ink faster and draw with more confidence. A print made from a polyester original looks great and is much sharper and crisper than a pencil-on-paper drawing. The transparency of the film gives it a superior print quality.

One thing to remember on ink drawings is that it is more critical to keep the surface as clean as possible. Any bit of dirt that the pen picks up will cause the lines to vary in thickness. Use a paper towel to wipe the end of the pen to keep it clean. Ink erasers will also leave an oil residue on the film. After using an ink eraser make sure to wipe the area that has been erased with a damp paper towel to remove the oil from the surface in order to keep the ink from running when reapplied.

Ink Pens

Ink pens come in different widths, which makes it very easy to change pens when you need a thick line (visible) versus a thin one (center) (see Figure 3.29). Read the instructions that come with the pens. The instructions will show the pen widths, will give disassembly directions, and will describe the correct methods for caring for and cleaning the pens. The pens come with either a steel tip or a jewel tip depending on how much money a person wants to spend and how long the pens need to last.

A good tip to remember is to keep the pens full of ink. Air bubbles create internal pressure, which causes pens to drip and skip when they are used (see Figure 3.30).

Ink Lettering Woes

An instrument called the Leroy Lettering Device performs ink lettering. The manual one, which comes only in a right-handed model, takes a little getting used to. The automatic Leroy has a keyboard and is easier to use no matter which hand you prefer using. However, most offices prefer freehand ink lettering on working drawings done by hand.

Learn to letter with pencil and paper first before trying to freehand with ink. Once you have style and have developed some consistency, then it is time to try the ink. Ink pens require little or no pressure at all and

Keep ink filled to the mark found on the chamber.

Plastic Ink Chamber

Air Bubbles in the Chamber

Ink

FIGURE 3.29　An exploded view of an ink pen.

FIGURE 3.30　Formation of air bubbles in an ink pen.

show every tiny shake and jerk that occurs in the hand. The trick to ink lettering is to relax and let the hand make the letters you have practiced over and over. No real pressure is being applied, so let the hand take control and flow freely and quickly. If you have already mastered lead lettering, then the inking will come quickly.

Tips for Left-Handed Drafters

A left-hander will find it rough going no matter if the lettering is in lead or in ink. The problem that cannot be avoided is dragging the hand across the letters as the lettering is done from left to right. The left-handed drafter has to become very creative in dealing with this problem. Some possible solutions follow

1. Cock the hand above or below the lines of letters.
2. Use a piece of paper to rest the hand on to keep from smearing.
3. Overextend the pen or pencil out from the hand.
4. Rotate the sheet at an angle.
5. Brush the graphite away frequently.

Some individuals prefer ink drafting once they get used to the timing of letting the ink dry and planning out a fast path for the drawing. If a drafter loves to draw, then inking is just another hurdle to jump.

REVIEW QUESTIONS

1. Why should a beginner choose a wide-barrel drawing pencil?
2. Automatic drawing pencil leads come in how many different widths?
3. What leads are used by a drafter to produce dark wide lineweights?
4. Smearing is caused by the drafter's hand or by the equipment. How can a drafter prevent smearing?
5. List and define the different line types in the standard alphabet of lines.
6. List the symbols used on architectural drawings or elevation callouts and section callouts. Name two methods used to draw dark thick lines.
7. How are architectural lettering styles different from those of other drafting professions?
8. List the major points to good lettering.
9. What is the maximum angle of slope used in lettering?
10. Guidelines for lettering are drawn with which tool?
11. When is it acceptable to use lowercase letters on drawings?
12. What is the minimum letter height used for notes and dimensions? For titles?
13. Sketch an example of how architectural and mechanical fractions are lettered.
14. In the alphabet of lines which ones are drawn to be thick/wide?
15. List some reasons why an alphabet of lines is necessary.
16. Sketch out the alphabet of lines and write the name beside each line.
17. Ink can be used on both paper and polyester. What are the advantages of using it on polyester?
18. If you have a sheet of single-matte polyester film, which side do you draw on? Why?.
19. Make a list of special drawing equipment used for ink drafting.
20. What are some of the tools that a drafter can use for lettering?
21. Illustrate the three methods that can be used to mark the intersection of dimension and extension lines.
22. Why should you use guidelines when lettering?
23. What is the most legible and readable style of lettering?

EXERCISES

Lettering exercises using all uppercase letters and guidelines.

Exercise 3.1

Using a lettering style of your choice, letter the alphabet A–Z and numbers 1–20 three times. Use ¼″ tall guides for letters and ¼″ spacing between your rows.

Exercise 3.2

Repeat Exercise 3.1 using a 68° slope to your letters, and ⅛″-high letters and ⅛″ spacing between your rows.

Exercise 3.3

Using ¼″-tall letters and ¼″ spacing between your rows, make a list of your 10 favorite movies, numbering them from 1 to 10.

Exercise 3.4

Using ⅛″-tall letters and using ⅛″ spacing between your rows, make a list of 12 singers or musical groups/bands, numbering them from 1 to 12.

Exercise 3.5

Using ¼″ sloped letters list 20 of your favorite songs.

Exercise 3.6

Letter five of your favorite quotes using ¼″-tall lettering.

Exercise 3.7

Pick 10 television shows and letter their names using ¼″-tall sloped letters and numbering them from 1 to 10.

Exercise 3.8

Using the title block in Figure 3.31 as a guide, design a title block of your own using similar information in it.

FIGURE 3.31   Exercise 3.8.

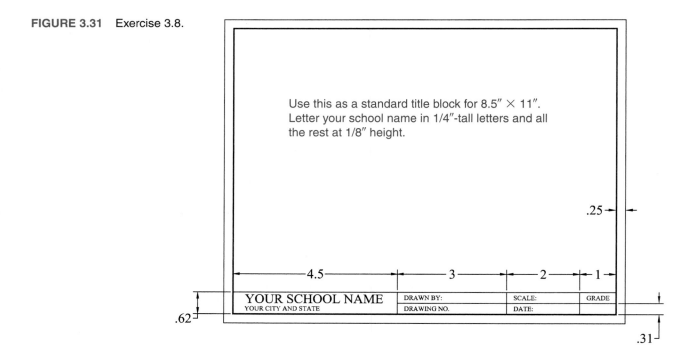

Exercise 3.9

Practice your uppercase lettering on an 8.5″ × 11″ sheet of vellum using the lettering layout in Figure 3.32.

Exercise 3.10

Practice your uppercase lettering on an 8.5″ × 11″ sheet of vellum using the lettering layout in Figure 3.33.

Exercise 3.11

Practice drawing your thick lines on an 8.5″ × 11″ sheet of vellum using the same format as in Figure 3.34.

Exercise 3.12.

Practice drawing your thin lines on an 8.5″ × 11″ sheet of vellum using the same format as in Figure 3.35.

FIGURE 3.32 Exercise 3.9.

(Use ¼″ height.)
ABCDEFGHIJKLMNOPQRSTUVWXYZ
ABCDEFGHIJKLMNOPQRSTUVWXYZ
1234567890   1234567890   1234567890
"THE ARCHITECT'S SCALE IS ONLY AS
ACCURATE AS ITS USER"

(Use ⅛″ height.)
ABCDEFGHIJKLMNOPQRSTUVWXYZ
ABCDEFGHIJKLMNOPQRSTUVWXYZ

1234567890   1234567890   1234567890

"THE ARCHITECT'S SCALE IS ONLY AS
ACCURATE AS ITS USER"

ABCDEFGHIJKLMNOPQRSTUVWXYZ
ABCDEFGHIJKLMNOPQRSTUVWXYZ

1234567890   1234567890   1234567890

"THE ARCHITECT'S SCALE IS ONLY AS
ACCURATE AS ITS USER"

(Use ⅛″ height.)
ABCDEFGHIJKLMNOPQRSTUVWXYZ
ABCDEFGHIJKLMNOPQRSTUVWXYZ

1234567890   1234567890   1234567890

"THE ARCHITECT'S SCALE IS ONLY AS
ACCURATE AS ITS USER"

ABCDEFGHIJKLMNOPQRSTUVWXYZ
ABCDEFGHIJKLMNOPQRSTUVWXYZ

1234567890   1234567890   1234567890

"THE ARCHITECT'S SCALE IS ONLY AS
ACCURATE AS ITS USER"

(Use ¼″ height.)
ABCDEFGHIJKLMNOPQRSTUVWXYZ
ABCDEFGHIJKLMNOPQRSTUVWXYZ
1234567890   1234567890   1234567890
"THE ARCHITECT'S SCALE IS ONLY AS
ACCURATE AS ITS USER"

FIGURE 3.33　Exercise 3.10.

(Use ¼″ height.)

BDPRS AEFHILT CGOQ IJKMNUVWYZ

38 96 O7 S 5ZX 38 96 O7 S 5ZX 38 96 O7 S 5ZX

STAY WITH ONE STYLE SO YOU WILL

BE MORE CONSISTENT.

(Use ⅛″ height.)

BDPRS AEFHILT CGOQ IJKMNUVWYZ　　　　BDPRS AEFHILT CGOQ IJKMNUVWYZ　　　　BDPRS AEFHILT CGOQ IJKMNUVWYZ

38 96 O7 S5ZX　　　38 96 O7 S5ZX　　　38 96 O7 S5ZX　　　38 96 O7 S5ZX

STAY WITH ONE STYLE SO YOU WILL　　　STAY WITH ONE STYLE SO YOU WILL

BE MORE CONSISTENT.　　　BE MORE CONSISTENT.

(Use ⅛″ height.)

BDPRS AEFHILT CGOQ IJKMNUVWYZ　　　　BDPRS AEFHILT CGOQ IJKMNUVWYZ　　　　BDPRS AEFHILT CGOQ IJKMNUVWYZ

38 96 O7 S5ZX　　　38 96 O7 S5ZX　　　38 96 O7 S5ZX　　　38 96 O7 S5ZX

STAY WITH ONE STYLE SO YOU WILL　　　STAY WITH ONE STYLE SO YOU WILL

BE MORE CONSISTENT.　　　BE MORE CONSISTENT.

(Use ¼″ height.)

BDPRS AEFHILT CGOQ IJKMNUVWYZ

38 96 O7 S 5ZX 38 96 O7 S 5ZX 38 96 O7 S 5ZX

STAY WITH ONE STYLE SO YOU WILL

BE MORE CONSISTENT.

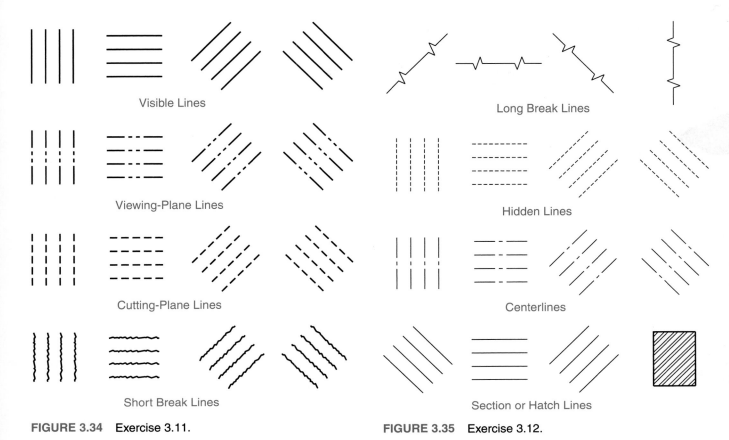

FIGURE 3.34 Exercise 3.11.   **FIGURE 3.35** Exercise 3.12.

DRAWING ASSIGNMENTS

1. Construct drawings 3.1–3.5 in Figure 3.36 at full scale to give you some practice using inches and fractional parts of an inch. Use the sample title block shown earlier. Do not dimension your drawings, but center them inside the title block drawing area. Haver your instructor demonstrate techniques for centering drawings.

2. Construct architectural drawings 3.6–3.11 in Figures 3.37 using the asigned scales.

3. Do site drawing assignment 3.12 in Figure 3.38.

FIGURE 3.36   Drawing Assignment 1.

3.6
Scale ½″ = 1′-0″

3.7
Divide the window into four
equal sections, then divide the
glass into four equal sections.
Scale ¾″ = 1′-0″

3.8
Choose any dimensions
that are not given, and
custom-design the rest of
the cabinet.
Scale ¾″ = 1′-0″

3.9
Draw this table with a basic
overall size of 3′ × 6′.
Choose the radius of the
circles and fillets.
Scale 1″ = 1′-0″

3.10
Some wall dimensions are given. Use a 4″ thick-
ness for your walls. Research the dimensions that
are not given to you by looking in the *Architectural
Graphic Standards* or a manufacturer's catalog.
Scale ¼″ = 1′-0″

3.11
This deck has 6″ wide deck boards.
Scale ¼″ = 1′-0″

FIGURE 3.37   Drawing Assignment 2.

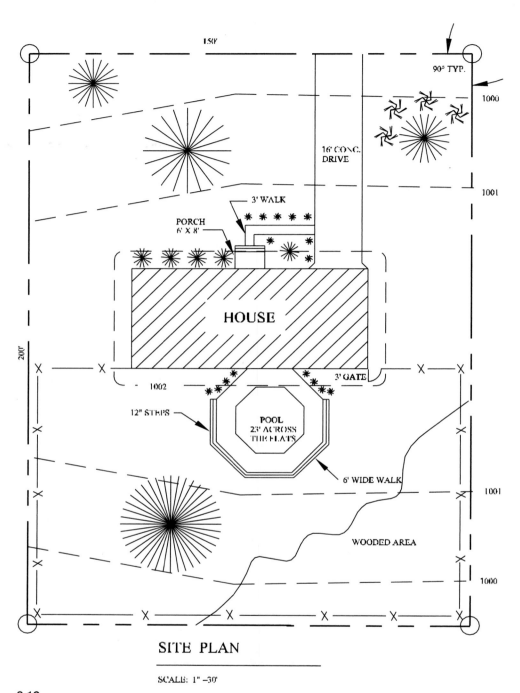

SITE PLAN

SCALE: 1″ –30′

3.12

Redraw this site plan at a Scale 1″ = 20′. You can freehand the contours, plants, and trees. The house is 35′ × 80′ and should be 65′ back from the road and 15′ from both side property lines as a minimum.

FIGURE 3.38   Drawing Assignment 3.

CHAPTER 4

○ ○

Drawing Basic Shapes and Patterns

4.1 Mastering Geometric Constructions

Take a moment to look at a technical drawing. Use a floor plan layout, a landscape design, or even the assembly drawings for a tool such as a drill press. Break these drawings down into their most basic elements and you will find geometric shapes. In some ways, learning geometric constructions is similar to learning to form the alphabet before writing words and sentences. Geometric constructions allow you to become familiar with your drafting instruments. The skills that you develop become the stepping stones for more complex projects.

Accuracy is a key factor in successful geometric construction. Keep leads sharp in both your pencil and your compass. A variation on the old carpenter's rule works well here: measure twice, draw once. Construction lines should be drawn as lightly as possible or with nonprint blue lead. Remember the rule about drawing construction lines so lightly that they can hardly be seen if the drawing is held at arm's length. You do not want your technique to show through to your clients, only the results.

The Terminology of Geometric Constructions

Points and Lines

A point represents a position in space or on a drawing. In drafting, this location is shown as the intersection of two lines (see Figure 4.1). A dot or a period should never be used to indicate a point. A dot big enough to be seen easily will also be big enough to be inaccurate. Instead, use a short crossbar on a line or a cross to show the location of a point.

Now that you have mastered points, let's move on to lines. Simply put, a line connects two points. A line may be either straight or curved. Remember, though, that the shortest distance between two points is a straight line. Sometimes a line is drawn and the beginning and end are not defined. (Think of a rainbow.) In this case, the endpoints are not marked. If the endpoints are significant, they are marked with a crossbar (see Figure 4.2).

By definition, parallel lines never intersect, since they remain an equal distance apart along the length of the lines. Parallel lines can be either straight or curved (see Figure 4.2). The symbol used to indicate parallel lines is //. Two lines are called perpendicular if they intersect or form at 90° (see Figure 4.2). The symbol for perpendicular is ⊥. As shown in Figure 4.2, a small box will sometimes be shown at the intersection of two lines that are perpendicular to each other.

Angles

When two lines intersect, they form an angle. The lines are referred to as the *legs* of the angle. The point at which the lines meet is called the *vertex*. Angles come in three basic varieties: right, acute, and obtuse (see Figure 4.3). A right angle is formed when two lines meet at 90°. If the lines meet at less than 90°, the angle is called *acute*. Angles of greater than 90° are called *obtuse*. The symbol for an angle is ∠.

FIGURE 4.1 Point styles.

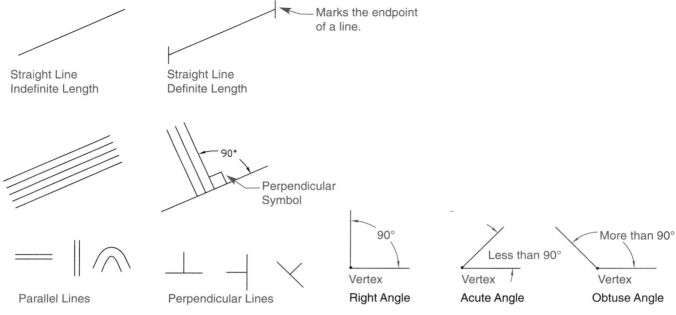

FIGURE 4.2 Line conventions.

FIGURE 4.3 Angle terminology.

Polygons

A polygon is defined as any plane figure that is bounded by straight lines. If all the sides and angles are equal, the figure is a regular polygon (see Figure 4.4). Triangles, octagons, and quadrilaterals are types of polygons.

Triangles

Mathematically, a triangle is a two-dimensional or plane figure with three sides and three interior angles. The three interior angles always add up to 180°. If you use straight lines to connect three points that are not in a straight line, you form a triangle. Give it a try.

Like angles, triangles come in different flavors (see Figure 4.5). In a *right triangle*, one of the interior angles is 90°. The longest side is called the *hypotenuse* of the triangle. The two other sides are called the *legs* of the triangle. In a right triangle, the square of the hypotenuse is equal to the sum of the squares of the two legs.

An *equilateral triangle* has three equal sides and three equal angles. An *isosceles triangle* has two sides of equal length and two equal angles. None of the sides or angles are equal on a *scalene triangle*.

Quadrilaterals

A quadrilateral is a plane figure bounded by four straight sides. Depending on whether the sides are equal and/or parallel, the figure can also be defined as a square, a rectangle, a rhombus, a rhomboid, a trapezoid, or a trapezium (see Figure 4.6).

Circles and Arcs

A circle is a closed curve with all points on the circle the same distance away from the center point (see Figure 4.7). The shortest distance from the center of the circle to a point on the circle is called the *radius*. The distance across the circle through the center is called the *diameter*. The diameter is twice the length of the ra-

FIGURE 4.4 Regular polygons.

FIGURE 4.5 Types of triangles.

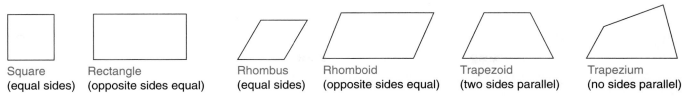

Square
(equal sides)

Rectangle
(opposite sides equal)

Rhombus
(equal sides)

Rhomboid
(opposite sides equal)

Trapezoid
(two sides parallel)

Trapezium
(no sides parallel)

FIGURE 4.6 Types of quadrilaterals.

FIGURE 4.7 Components of a circle.

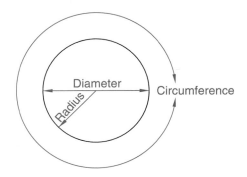

dius. The distance around the circle is referred to as the *circumference*. A circle can be divided into 360 segments called degrees.

An arc is simply a piece or section of a circle.

Tangents

In geometric constructions, a tangent can be thought of as a point of touching (see Figure 4.8a). The tangent point may be the spot at which one line ends and another line begins (see Figure 4.8d). If two circles or arcs touch at only one point, that point is a tangent point (T.P.) (see Figure 4.8c). A straight line touching a circle at only one point is another example of tangency (see Figure 4.8a).

FIGURE 4.8 Examples of tangency.

CONSTRUCTION: Parallel Lines

Given: Line AB, distance X (see Figure 4.9a)
Problem: Draw a line parallel to line AB at a distance X.
Solution I—Using a Compass:

Note: This methods works for curved as well as for straight lines.

1. Measure the distance X with your compass. Place the pointed end of the compass on one endpoint and adjust the lead until it lines up with the other endpoint. This setting will determine the radius of the arcs you will draw in the next step.

2. Keeping the compass on the same setting, place the point of the compass anywhere on the line AB. Lightly draw an arc. Repeat this process until you have a series of arcs along the line (see Figure 4.9b).

3. Draw a line tangent to the series of arcs. In other words, draw a line that just touches each of the arcs at a single point.

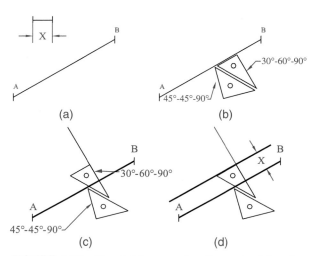

FIGURE 4.10   Parallel line construction using triangles.

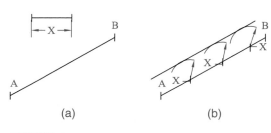

FIGURE 4.9   Parallel line construction using a compass.

Solution II—Using Triangles (see Figure 4.10):

1. Align the shortest leg of your 30°-60°-90° triangle with the line AB (see Figure 4.10b).
2. Place the hypotenuse of the triangle against the hypotenuse of your 45°-45°-90° triangle (or the edge of your T square).
3. Holding the 45°-45°-90° triangle firmly in place, slide the 30°-60°-90° triangle upward so the edge intersects line AB. Keep the edges of the triangles together. Draw a construction line along the edge of the 30°-60°-90° triangle (see Figure 4.10c).
4. Mark the distance X from line AB along the construction line drawn in step 3.
5. Check to make sure the triangles are still aligned with line AB. Slide the 30°-60°-90° triangle up until the short edge is distance X from line AB. Draw your parallel line (see Figure 4.10d).

Given: Line AB, point C (see Figure 4.11a)
Problem: Draw a line parallel to line AB through point C.
Solution:

1. Place the point of your compass on point C and draw an arc that intersects anywhere along line AB. Call this point D (see Figure 4.11b).
2. Leaving your compass at the same setting, put the point on point D (the intersection of line AB and the arc drawn in step 1). Draw an arc that passes through point C and intersects line AB. Call this point E. (see Figure 4.11c).

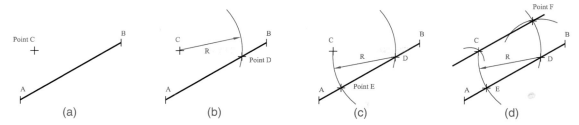

FIGURE 4.11 Parallel line construction.

3. Place the point of your compass on point E (the intersection of the line AB and the arc drawn in step 2). Adjust the compass until the lead passes through point C.

4. Move your compass to point D and draw an arc. This arc will intersect the arc drawn in step 1. Call this intersection point F (see Figure 4.11d).

5. Draw a line through points C and F. This line will be parallel to line AB and will pass through point C. The problem is solved.

CONSTRUCTION: Perpendicular Lines

Given: Line AB, point C (on line AB) (see Figure 4.12a)
Problem: Construct a line perpendicular to line AB at point C.
Solution I:

1. Place the point of your compass on point C. Draw an arc that intersects line AB on either side of point C. Call the two intersections points D and E (see Figure 4.12b).

2. Adjust your compass to a larger setting. Draw an arc with the point of the compass on point D. Repeat on point E. The two arcs should intersect at a point we will call point F (see Figure 4.12c).

3. A line drawn through points F and C will be perpendicular to line AB (see Figure 4.12d).

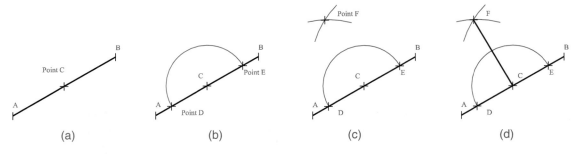

FIGURE 4.12 Perpendicular line construction (Solution I).

Solution II (see Figure 4.13):

1. Use your compass to draw a circle that intersects line AB at point C and one other location (point D) (see Figure 4.13b). The center of this circle must be away from line AB. Mark the center of the circle with a cross.

2. Draw a construction line through point D and the center of the circle. Continue the line until it intersects the opposite side of the circle (point E) (see Figure 4.13c).

3. A line drawn through points E and C will be perpendicular to line AB (see Figure 4.13d).

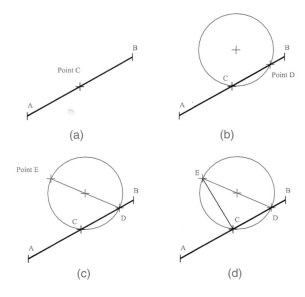

FIGURE 4.13 Perpendicular line construction (Solution II).

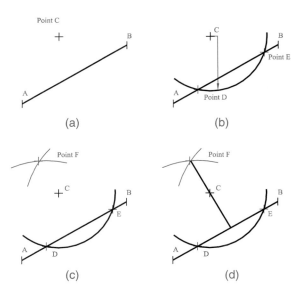

FIGURE 4.14 Perpendicular line construction with point not on line.

Given: Line AB, point C (not on line AB) (see Figure 4.14a)
Problem: Construct a line perpendicular to line AB and passing through point C.
Solution:

1. Place your compass point on point C. Swing an arc that intersects line AB in two places. Call these intersections points D and E (see Figure 4.14b).

2. Adjust your compass to draw a larger arc. Draw arcs with points D and E as the centers of the arcs. The two arcs should intersect. Call this intersection Point F (see Figure 4.14c).

3. A line drawn through points F and C will be perpendicular to line AB (see Figure 4.14d) .

CONSTRUCTION: Bisecting a Line

Given: Line AB (see Figure 4.15a)
Problem: Divide line AB into two equal parts.
Solution I—Using a Compass:

1. Place the point of your compass on one endpoint of the given line AB. *Lightly* draw an arc that intersects the line anywhere between the midpoint of the line and the other endpoint (see Figure 4.15b).

2. Now, use your compass to construct another arc of the same radius but with the center of the arc being at the other endpoint of line AB (see Figure 4.15c). (In other words, keep your compass at the same setting that you used for Step 1.) Notice that the two arcs intersect at two points not on line AB. One point is above the line, and the other is below the line. Call those intersections points C and D.

3. Draw a construction line through points C and D (see Figure 4.15d). The point at which this line intersects your original line AB is at the midpoint of line AB. You have divided the line into two equal parts.

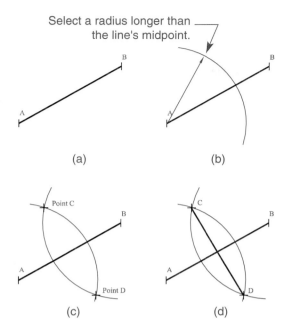

Select a radius longer than the line's midpoint.

(a) (b)

(c) (d)

FIGURE 4.15 Bisecting a line. (Solution I)

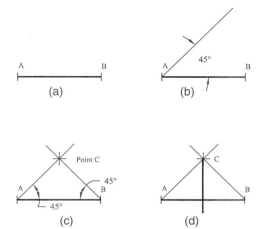

(a) (b)

Point C

(c) (d)

FIGURE 4.16 Bisecting a line using triangles.

Solution II—Using Triangles (see Figure 4.16):

Note: This method may be used with any equal angles; 45° angles were chosen because they are easy to draw using a standard triangle.

1. Align your drafting machine or T square with the given line AB. Use your 45°-45°-90° triangle to draw a construction line at a 45° angle to line AB through point A (see Figure 4.16b).

2. Draw a similar line through point B. The two lines should form a triangle with line AB as the base. Define the point of the triangle as point C (see Figure 4.16c).

3. Use your triangle to draw a line running perpendicular to line AB and through point C. This line will divide line AB into two equal segments (see Figure 4.16d).

CONSTRUCTION: Construction: Dividing a Line into Any Number of Equal Segments

Given: Line AB (see Figure 4.17a)
Problem: Divide line AB into any number of equal segments,
   For this example you will divide the line into seven equal segments.
Solution:

1. Draw a construction line that connects to the given line AB at an acute angle (labeled line AC in this example). (see Figure 4.17b.)

2. Use a scale or ruler to divide the construction line into seven equal spaces (see figure 4.17c). You do not need to use the entire length of the construction line. Find any number (on any scale) that conveniently divides into 7. For example, if 21 fit on the line, you would place tick marks at 3, 6, 9, 12, 15, 18, and 21.

3. Draw a construction line connecting the open endpoint of line *AB* and the last tick mark on the construction line *AC*.

FIGURE 4.17   Dividing a line into an equal number of segments.

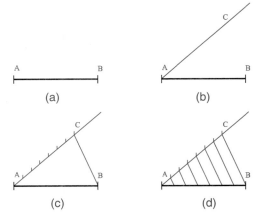

4. Draw lines parallel to this new line and intersecting each of the divisions marked on line *AC*. The intersections of these parallel lines and line *AB* will be the seven equal divisions required to solve the problem.

CONSTRUCTION: Dividing a Line into Proportional Parts

Given: line *AB* (see Figure 4.18a)
Problem: Divide line AB into proportional parts.
    For this example, divide the line into 2, 3, and five proportional parts
Solution:

1. Add the numbers of proportions together, $2 + 3 + 5 = 10$.

2. Draw a construction line that connects to the given line AB at an acute angle (labeled line AC in this example). (see Figure 4.18b)

3. Use a scale or ruler to divide the construction line into 10 equal spaces (see Figure 4.18c). You do not need to use the entire length of the construction line. Find any number (on any scale) that conveniently divides into 10. Place tick marks at the proportional locations. This first mark will be at 2. The next mark will be at 5, three spaces past the 2.

4. Draw a construction line connecting the open endpoint of line AB and the last tick mark on the construction line AC (see Figure 4.18d).

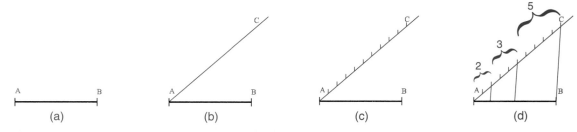

FIGURE 4.18   Dividing a line into proportional parts.

5. Draw lines parallel to this new line and intersecting each of the divisions marked on line AC. The intersections of these parallel lines and line AB will be the proportional divisions required to solve the problem.

CONSTRUCTION: Divide a Space into Equal Parts

Given: Space between two lines (see Figure 4.19a)
Problem: Divide the space into a number of equal parts.
　　　　For this example, you will divide the space into five equal parts.
Solution:

1. Place your scale across the two lines at an angle. Find a scale that will allow you to place the zero on one line and a 5 (or multiple of 5) on the other line. Place a tick mark at each of the increments between 0 and 5 (see Figure 4.19b).

2. Take the scale away (see Figure 4.19c). Draw a series of four lines parallel to the initial lines and through each of the divisions marked in step 1 (see Figure 4.19d). This will divide the space into five equal parts.

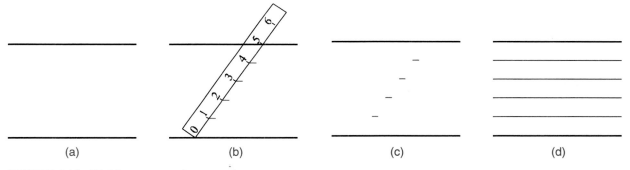

(a)　　　　　　　　(b)　　　　　　　　(c)　　　　　　　　(d)

FIGURE 4.19　Dividing a space into equal parts.

CONSTRUCTION: Adding or Subtracting Lines

Given: Line AB of length X, line CD of length Y (see Figure 4.20a)
Problem: Add line AB to line CD.
Solution:

1. Draw a construction line in the desired position for the finished line. Assign one end of the line to be the endpoint of your new line (AB) + (CD). Mark this point with a cross or crossbar (see Figure 4.20b).

2. Use your compass to measure the length of the given line AB by placing the pointed end of the compass on one end of the line and adjusting the lead end of the compass to rest on the other endpoint of the line.

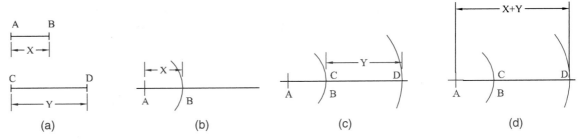

FIGURE 4.20   Adding lines.

3. Without adjusting the compass opening, place the pointed end of the compass on the endpoint of the new line. Lightly draw an arc intersecting the previously drawn construction line. You have just transferred the length of line AB to your construction line (see Figure 4.20b).

4. Now, position your compass on the given line CD, just as you did for line AB in step 2.

5. Using this new compass position, place the pointed end of the compass on the intersection of the construction line and the arc drawn in step 3. Draw another arc intersecting the construction line (see Figure 4.20c).

6. Darken the section of your construction line between the point defined in step 1 and the arc drawn in step 5. This is your new line of length (AB) + (CD) (see Figure 4.20d).

Given: Line AB of length X, line CD of length Y (see Figure 4.21a)
Problem: Subtract line AB from line CD.
Solution:

1. Draw a construction line in the desired position for the finished line. Assign one end of the line to be the endpoint of your new line (AB) – (CD). Mark this point with a cross or crossbar (see Figure 4.21b).

2. Use your compass to measure the length of the given line CD by placing the pointed end of the compass on one end of the line and adjusting the lead end of the compass to rest on the other endpoint of the line.

3. Without adjusting the compass opening, place the pointed end of the compass on the endpoint of the new line. Lightly draw an arc intersecting the previously drawn construction line. You have just transferred the length of line CD to your construction line (see Figure 4.21b).

4. Now position your compass on the given line AB, just as you did for line CD in step 2.

FIGURE 4.21   Subtracting lines.

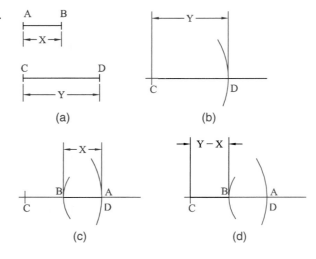

5. Using this new compass position, place the pointed end of the compass on the intersection of the construction line and the arc drawn in step 3. Aiming your compass toward the beginning endpoint of your new line, draw an arc intersecting the construction line (see Figure 4.21c).

6. Darken the section of your construction line between the point defined in step 1 and the arc drawn in step 5 (see Figure 4.21d). This is your new line of length AB − CD.

CONSTRUCTION: Draw an Arc or Circle through Three Points

Given: Point 1, point 2, and point 3 (see Figure 4.22a)
Problem: Construct a circle (or arc) that contains the three given points.
Solution:

Note: Follow the same steps for constructing arcs.

1. Draw two lines to connect the three points. For example, draw a line from point 1 to point 2 then another line from point 2 to point 3 (see Figure 4.22b).

2. Construct the perpendicular bisectors for the two lines (see Figures 4.14 and 4.22c).

3. Notice that the two bisectors intersect. This will be the center of your circle. Call it point 4 (see Figure 4.22d).

4. Place the point of your compass on point 4. Adjust the compass so that the lead touches points 1, 2, or 3. If you have done the previous steps correctly, points 1, 2, and 3 will all be the same distance from point 4, the center of your circle. Use your compass to draw this circle (see Figure 4.22e).

    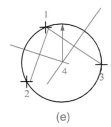

(a)   (b)   (c)   (d)   (e)

FIGURE 4.22 Constructing an arc or circle through three points.

CONSTRUCTION: Bisect an Angle

Given: Angle ∠SUN (see Figure 4.23a)
Problem: Bisect or divide the given angle into two equal angles, that is, divide the angle in half.
Solution:

1. Place your compass point on the vertex of the angle, the point where the two legs of the angle come together. Swing an arc at any location that intersects both legs of the angle. Label these intersections points A and B (see Figure 4.23b).

2. Place your compass on point A and swing an arc. Use any size arc that is convenient. Keep your compass at the same setting and draw an arc with the compass point on point B. Notice that the two arcs intersect at a location we will call point C (see Figure 4.23c).

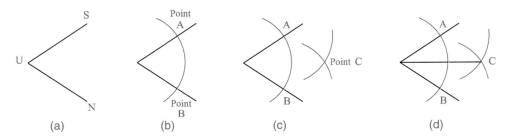

FIGURE 4.23   Bisecting an angle.

3. A straight line drawn through point *C* to the vertex of the angle will bisect or divide the angle in half (see Figure 4.23d).

CONSTRUCTION: Transfer an Angle

Given: ∠ABC, location A′B′ (see Figure 4.24a)
Problem: Transfer ∠ABC to a new location at A′B′.
Solution:

1. Place your compass point on point B. Strike an arc at any location along ∠ABC. Make sure the arc passes through both legs of the angle (see Figure 4.24b).

2. Duplicate the arc with your compass point on point B′. Designate the intersection of line A′B′ and the arc as point 1 (see Figure 4.24c).

FIGURE 4.24   Transferring an angle.

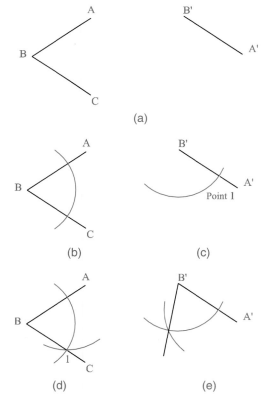

3. Use your compass to measure the chord length between the intersections of the arc in step 1 and the legs of ∠ABC. Place the point of your compass on the intersection on one leg while adjusting the lead of the compass until it goes through the other intersection. Keeping your compass on the same setting, place the sharp end on point 1 and strike an arc (see Figure 4.24d).

4. Draw a line from point B′ to the intersection of the two arcs drawn in steps 2 and 4 to complete the transfer of the angle to its new location (see Figure 4.24e).

CONSTRUCTION: Fillets

Given: Right angle ∠XYZ, radius R (see Figure 4.25a)
Problem: Construct a fillet of radius R tangent to ∠XYZ.
Definition: A fillet is basically a rounded interior corner.
Solution:

Note: This method works only for right-angle fillets.

1. Adjust your compass to the distance given for the radius R. Keep the compass on this setting for the entire construction.

2. Place the point of your compass on the vertex of ∠XYZ. Draw an arc of radius R that passes through each of the legs of the angle. These intersections are labeled points 1 and 2 in Figure 4.25b.

3. Leaving your compass on the same setting, draw an arc whose center is point 1. Draw another arc with a center at point 2. Notice that the two arcs intersect at the point labeled point 3 in Figure 4.25c.

4. Place the point of your compass on point 3 and draw an arc of radius R tangent to the legs of ∠XYZ (see Figure 4.25d).

(a)

(b)

(c)

(d)

FIGURE 4.25 Constructing a right-angle fillet.

Given: ∠ABC, radius R (see Figure 4.26a)
Problem: Construct a fillet of radius R tangent to ∠ABC.
Solution:

1. Construct a line parallel to each leg of ∠ABC at a distance R (see Figures 4.9 and 4.26b).

(a)

(b)

(c)

(d)

FIGURE 4.26 Constructing a fillet of any angle.

2. The two lines should intersect. Place your compass point on this intersection and draw an arc of radius R tangent to the legs of ∠ABC (see Figure 4.26c).

3. Darken the visible lines (see Figure 4.26d) to complete the drawing.

CONSTRUCTION: Round—Two Circles

Given: Circle 1 of radius X, circle 2 of radius Y, radius R (see Figure 4.27a)
Problem: Construct a round of radius R tangent to circles 1 and 2.
Solution:

1. Placing the point of your compass on the center of circle 1, draw an arc of radius R – X (see Figure 4.27b).

2. With the point of the compass on the center of circle 2, draw an arc of radius R – Y (see Figure 4.27c).

3. Locate the intersection of the two arcs drawn in steps 1 and 2. This point is labeled Z in Figure 4.27c. Use this point as the center of your round. Construct an arc of radius R that is tangent to the two circles (see Figure 4.27d).

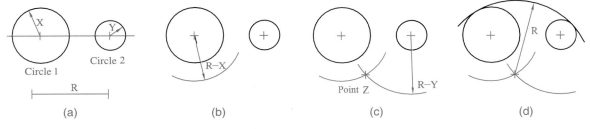

FIGURE 4.27   Constructing a round between two circles.

CONSTRUCTION: Drawing Triangles

Given: Three lines of lengths A, B, and C (see Figure 4.28a)
Problem: Draw a triangle with sides of lengths A, B, and C.
Solution:

1. Lightly draw a construction line to assemble your triangle on. Use your compass to measure the longest of the three lines, line C. Mark off that length on the construction line. This will define side C (see Figure 4.28b).

2. Measure length B with your compass. Place the point of your compass on one end of line C and draw an arc.

3. Measure length A with your compass. Place the point of your compass on the end of line C that you did not use in step 2. Draw an arc (see Figure 4.28c). This arc should intersect the arc drawn in step 2.

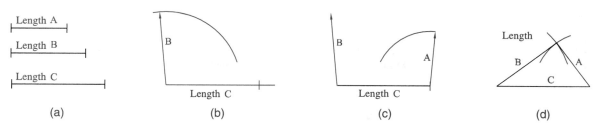

FIGURE 4.28   Constructing a triangle with three given sides.

4. Draw a line from each endpoint of line C to the intersection developed in step 3. These lines define sides A and B of your triangle (see Figure 4.28d).

Given: Length L (see Figure 4.29a)
Problem: Draw an equilateral triangle with sides of length L.
Solution:

1. Draw a construction line to begin building your triangle. Set your compass to measure length L. Mark this distance on your construction line with an arc. This will define the first side of your equilateral triangle. This line is labeled AB in Figure 4.28b.

2. Keeping your compass on the same setting, strike an arc from each end of the line defined in step 1. The two arcs should intersect.

3. Draw lines from each end of line AB to the intersection of the arcs drawn in step 2 (see Figure 4.29c). These lines define the other two sides of the triangle.

FIGURE 4.29   Constructing an equilateral triangle.

(a)   (b)   (c)

CONSTRUCTION: Drawing Squares

Given: Length J, location of center (see Figure 4.30a)
Problem: Construct a square with sides of length J.
Solution:

1. Lay out the center of the square with perpendicular construction lines.

Note: The radius of a circle is equal to half the diameter.

2. Next lay out a circle with diameter J. First, bisect the line of length J. This will give you the radius for your circle.

3. Place your point on the center laid out in step 1. Draw a circle of radius J/2 (see Figure 4.30b).

4. Use your triangle to draw four construction lines tangent to the circle (see Figure 4.30c). Two of the lines will be horizontal, and two will be vertical.

5. Check the four lines drawn in step 4 to make sure they are of equal length. If so, darken the four lines to define your square (see Figure 4.30d).

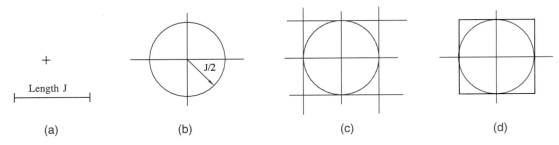

FIGURE 4.30   Constructing a square given the length of the sides.

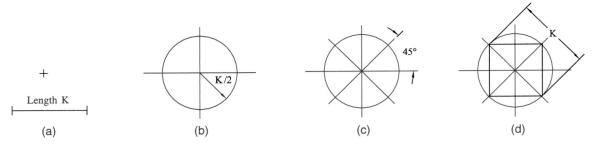

FIGURE 4.31   Constructing a square given the diagonal distance.

Given: Length K, location of center (see Figure 4.31a)
Problem: Construct a square with a diagonal distance between corners of length K.
Solution:

1. Lay out the center of the square with perpendicular construction lines.

Note: The radius
of a circle is equal to
half the diameter.

2. Next, lay out a circle with diameter K. First, bisect the line of length K. This will give you the radius for your circle.

3. Place your point on the center laid out in step 1. Draw a circle of radius ½K (see Figure 4.31b).

4. Use your 45°- 45°- 90° triangle to draw four construction lines. The lines will go from the center of the circle (the intersection of the circle with the horizontal and vertical lines) to the outside of the circle (see Figure 4.31c).

5. Draw horizontal and vertical lines between the intersections of the 45° lines and the circle (see Figure 4.31d).

6. Check the four lines drawn in step 5 to make sure they are of equal length. If so, darken the four lines to define your square.

CONSTRUCTION: Enlarge or Reduce a Rectangle

Given: Rectangle EFGH (see Figure 4.32a)
Problem: Enlarge or reduce rectangle EFGH proportionately.
Solution:

1. Draw a straight line from corner to corner. Extend the line beyond the triangle (see Figure 4.32b).

2. Use the diagonal to find the correct proportions by which to enlarge or reduce the triangle.

(a)　　　　　　　(b)　　　　　　　(c)　　　　　　　(d)

FIGURE 4.32　Enlarging or reducing a rectangle.

Lines projected horizontally and vertically from the diagonal will define a rectangle of the correct size (see Figures 4.32c and d).

CONSTRUCTION: Octagons

Given: Circle of diameter A (see Figure 4.33a)
Problem: Draw an octagon with the distance across the *flats* (the distance between opposite sides) of length A.
Solution:

1. Use construction lines to draw a circle with a diameter of length A (see Figure 4.33a).
2. Draw horizontal lines tangent to the top and bottom of the circle (at 90° and 270° (see Figure 4.33b).
3. Draw vertical lines tangent to both sides of the circle (at 0° and 180°).
4. Use your 45°-45°-90° triangle to draw four lines tangent to the circle at 45° and −45° to horizontal (see Figure 4.33c).
5. The intersection of these eight lines forms an octagon (see Figure 4.33d). Darken in the eight lines to finish the octagon (see Figure 4.33a).

(a)　　　　　　　(b)　　　　　　　(c)　　　　　　　(d)　　　　　　　(e)

FIGURE 4.33　Constructing an octagon around a circle. Circumscribed example.

Given: Square with sides of length B (see Figure 4.34a)
Problem: Draw an octagon with the distance across the flats of length B.
Solution:

1. Use construction lines to draw diagonal lines between opposite corners on the square. The intersection of these lines will define the center of the square.

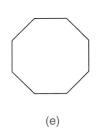

FIGURE 4.34 Constructing an octagon around a square.

2. Adjust your compass so the point is on one corner of the square and the lead is at the center of the square. Keeping your compass at this setting, draw an arc that intersects the two sides of the corner. Repeat this step at each corner of the square (see Figures 4.34b and c).

3. The arcs drawn in step 2 should intersect the square at eight points. Connect these points to form an octagon (see Figures 4.34d and e).

CONSTRUCTION: Pentagons

Given: Circle of diameter K
Problem: Construct a pentagon inscribed in the given circle (see Figure 4.35).
Solution:

1. Using construction lines, draw intersecting horizontal and vertical lines longer than length K. With the compass point at the intersection of these two lines, draw a circle of diameter K (see Figure 4.35a).

2. Define point 0 as the center of the circle. Define point 1 as the right-side intersection between the circle and the horizontal line. Define point 2 as the left-side intersection of the circle and the horizontal line. (See Figure 4.35b)

3. Bisect the distance between points 0 and 1. Define that midpoint as point 3 (see Figure 4.35b).

FIGURE 4.35 Constructing a pentagon inside a circle.

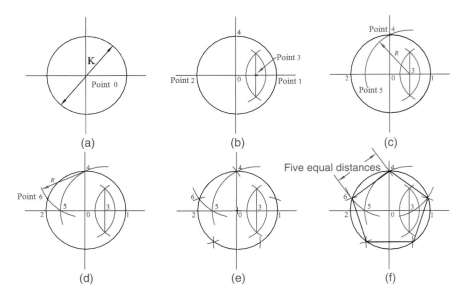

4. Define point 4 as the top intersection between the circle and the vertical line (see Figure 4.35c).

5. Place your compass point on point 3. Draw an arc passing through point 4 and the horizontal line. Define the intersection of this arc and the horizontal line as point 5 (see Figure 4.35c).

6. Place your compass point on point 4. Draw an arc that passes through point 5 and the edge of the circle (see Figure 4.35d). Define the intersection of this arc with the circle as point 6.

7. The distance between points 4 and 6 defines the length of one side of your pentagon. Adjust your compass to span these two points. Work your way around the circle marking off this distance around the circumference of the circle (see Figure 4.35e). You should end up back at point 4 having marked five intersections around the circle (including points 4 and 6). Connect these five points to form a pentagon (see Figure 4.35f).

CONSTRUCTION: Hexagons (five methods)

Given: Circle of diameter D
Problem: Construct a hexagon of distance D across the corners. (The corners of the hexagon will be on the circle.)
Solution I (see Figure 4.36):

1. Lightly draw a circle of diameter D (see Figure 4.36a). (Remember, you should set the compass to the length of the radius of the circle, not the diameter. You may need to bisect the length D in order to determine the radius.)

2. Keeping your compass on the same D/2 setting, place the point of your compass on the circle. Strike an arc through the circle (see Figure 4.36b).

3. Move the point of your compass to the intersection of the circle and the arc drawn in step 2. Strike another arc through the circle.

4. Continue striking arcs and moving to the intersection until you work your way around the circle. When you get back to the original point, you should have intersected the circle at six points (see Figure 4.36c).

5. Connect these six points to form the sides of the hexagon.

FIGURE 4.36   Constructing a hexagon (Method I). Inscribed example.

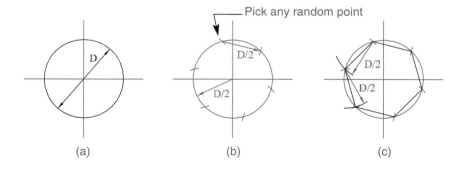

(a)   (b)   (c)

Solution II (see Figure 4.37):

1. Use construction lines to draw intersecting horizontal and vertical lines. Draw a circle of diameter D whose center is on the intersection of the horizontal and vertical lines at point 1 (see Figure 4.37a). (Remember to use the radius to set your compass. Since the radius is one-half the length of the diameter, you could find the radius length by bisecting the length D.)

2. Define point 2 as the top intersection of the circle and the vertical line. Define point 3 as the bottom intersection of the circle and the vertical line (see Figure 4.37b).

FIGURE 4.37   Constructing a hexagon (Method II).

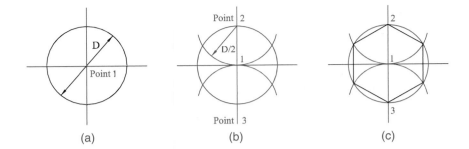

3. Keeping the same compass set on D/2, place the point of your compass on point 2. Strike an arc through the center of the circle and two points on the circle (see Figure 4.37b).

4. Place the compass point on point 3. Strike an arc through the center and the circumference of the circle.

5. The arcs drawn in steps 2 and 3 intersect the circle at four points. These four points plus points 2 and 3 define the corners of the hexagon. Connect these six points to form the hexagon (see Figure 4.37c).

Solution III (see Figure 4.38):

1. Use construction lines to draw intersecting horizontal and vertical lines. Draw a circle of diameter D whose center is on the intersection of the horizontal and vertical lines (see Figure 4.38a). (Remember to use the radius to set your compass. Since the radius is half the length of the diameter, you could find the radius length by bisecting the length D.)

2. Define point 1 as the left intersection of the circle with the horizontal line. Define point 2 as the right intersection of the circle with the horizontal line (see Figure 4.38b).

3. Use your 30°-60°-90° triangle to draw a construction line that begins at point 1 and runs 60° to the horizontal (see Figure 4.38b). Draw another line starting at point 1 and running −60° to the horizontal (see Figure 4.38b). These two lines form two sides of the hexagon. Darken the lines between point 1 and the circle.

4. Draw lines starting at point 2 and running at 60° and −60° to the horizontal. These two lines form two more sides of the hexagon. Darken the lines between point 2 and the circle (see Figure 4.38c).

5. Use horizontal lines to connect the ends of the lines drawn in steps 3 and 4 and form the final two sides of the hexagon (see Figures 4.38d and e).

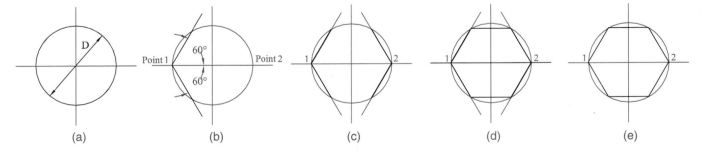

FIGURE 4.38   Constructing a hexagon (Method III). Inscribed example.

Solution IV (see Figure 4.39):

1. Use construction lines to draw intersecting horizontal and vertical lines. Draw a circle of diameter D whose center is on the intersection of the horizontal and vertical lines (see Figure 4.39a). (Remember to use the radius to set your compass. Since the radius is half the length of the diameter, you could find the radius length by bisecting the length D.)

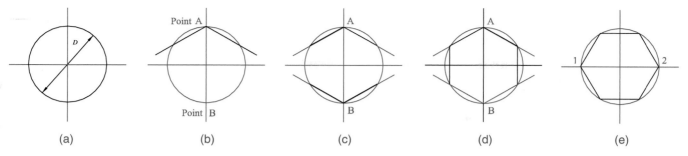

FIGURE 4.39 Constructing a hexagon (Method IV). Inscribed exam-

2. Define point A as the intersection of the top of the circle and the vertical line. Define point B as the intersection of the bottom of the circle and the vertical line (see Figure 4.39b).

3. Use your 30°-60°-90° triangle to draw two lines starting at point A and running at −30° to horizontal. One line will go toward the left, the other toward the right (See Figure 4.39b). These lines form two sides of the hexagon. Darken the lines between point A and the circle.

4. Draw two lines starting at point B and running at 30° to the horizontal (see Figure 4.39c). These lines form two sides of the hexagon. Darken the lines between point B and the circle.

5. Complete the hexagon by using two vertical lines to connect the ends of the lines drawn in steps 3 and 4 (see Figures 4.39d and e).

Given: Circle of diameter M
Problem: Construct a hexagon of distance M across the *flats* (the distance between *opposite* sides) (see Figure 4.40).
Solution:

1. Use construction lines to draw intersecting horizontal and vertical lines. Draw a circle of diameter M whose center is on the intersection of the horizontal and vertical lines (see Figure 4.40a). (Remember to use the radius to set your compass. Since the radius is half the length of the diameter, you could find the radius length by bisecting the length M).

2. Lightly draw two vertical lines tangent to the circle on the left and right sides (see Figure 4.40b).

3. Use your 30°-60°-90° triangle to draw four construction lines tangent to the circle at 30° to the horizontal (see Figure 4.40c).

4. The intersections between the four lines from step 3 and the two lines from step 2 form six points (see Figure 4.40d). Connect these six points and darken the lines to form the hexagon (see Figure 4.40e).

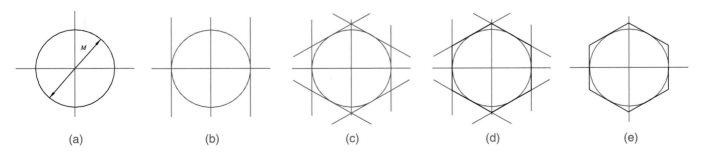

FIGURE 4.40 Constructing a hexagon with a given distance across the flats. Circumscribed example.

CONSTRUCTION: Concentric-Circle Ellipse

Given: Lengths A and B (see Figure 4.41a)
Problem: Construct an ellipse with major diameter A and minor diameter B.
Solution:

1. Use construction lines to draw intersecting horizontal and vertical lines. Define the intersection of the two lines as Point 0 (see Figure 4.41b). Draw all the lines in this method as very light construction lines.

2. Draw a circle of radius A/2 whose center is at point 0.

3. Draw a circle of radius B/2 whose center is at point 0.

4. At this point, the circles are divided into four quadrants. Next, use your 30°-60°-90° triangle to divide the circles into 12 equal sections. Draw lines through the center (point 0) at ±30° and ±60° to the horizontal (see Figure 4.41c).

5. Define the top intersection of the smaller circle the vertical line as point 12 (think of a clock face). Define the intersection of the bottom of the circle with the vertical line as point 6. Define the intersection of the right side of the circle with the horizontal line as point 3. Define the intersection of the left side of the circle with the horizontal line as point 9 (see Figure 4.41c).

6. Because the two concentric circles correspond to the lengths given for the major and minor axes of the ellipse, points 3, 6, 9, and 12 will form four points on your ellipse.

Note: For extremely large ellipses, you may wish to divide the circles into more than 12 sections.

7. Now your need to define eight more points on the ellipse. Work with one radial line at a time. Start at the center of the circles. Move out along the line until you reach the smaller of the two circles. Draw a horizontal line outward from the intersection of the small circle with the radial line. Now, continue on the radial line until you reach the intersection of the larger circle with the radial line. Draw a vertical line downward from this point until it intersects the horizontal line just drawn. The intersection of the horizontal and vertical lines from this step forms a point on the ellipse (see Figure 4.41d).

8. Repeat step 7 until you have worked your way around the entire ellipse (see Figure 4.41e). Remember that you do not have to do anything at points 3, 6, 9, or 12. They are already defined.

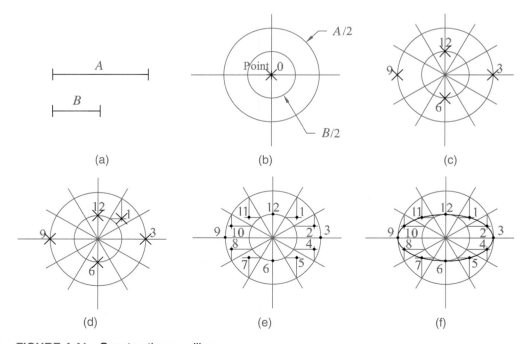

FIGURE 4.41 Constructing an ellipse.

9. Lightly connect the intersections defined in steps 7 and 8 to get a rough outline of your el-lipse. Include Points 3, 6, 9, and 12 in the ellipse (see Figure 4.41f).

10. Use a flexible curve or a French curve to darken in the ellipse with a smooth, continuous line.

CONSTRUCTION: Reverse or Ogee Curve (S-Curve)

Given: Points A and B
Problem: Draw an S-curve between points A and B (see Figure 4.42).
Solution:

Note: The S-curve in this example is symmetrical. The method for construct-ing asymmetrical S-curves is beyond the scope of this text.

1. Lightly draw a straight line between Points A and B.

2. Divide line AB into four equal sections (see Figure 4.42a). (*Hint:* Bisect the line, then bisect each of the halves.)

3. Draw a line 90° to the horizontal beginning at point A and intersecting the line marking the nearest quarter section of line AB. This point of intersection is labeled point C in Figure 4.42b.

4. Draw another line at −90° to the horizontal beginning at point B and intersecting the line marking the nearest quarter section of line AB. This point of intersection is labeled point D in Figure 4.42b.

5. Using points C and D as centers, draw in the S-curve of radii CA and DB (see Figure 4.42c).

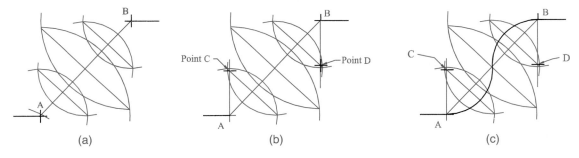

(a)   (b)   (c)

FIGURE 4.42   Constructing a reverse or ogee curve.

4.2 Getting Started with One-View Drawings

Once you have mastered the fundamentals of geometric construction, you are ready to move on to more com-plex figures. The key to mastering this skill is to teach your eye to recognize basic patterns within the figure. Find an element that you know how to construct and start from there.

For example, look at Figure 4.43. At first glance it is rather intimidating. But look again. You know how to draw a circle with a given diameter. You have also inscribed hexagons within a circle of given diameter. (The same process as drawing a hexagon when the distance from opposite corners is defined.) Once the cir-cle and hexagon are drawn, recognize that the three lines through the center of the circle simply connect the

FIGURE 4.43   One-view drawing.

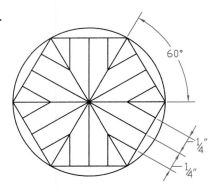

points of the hexagon. You are left with having to draw three parallel lines within each pie-shaped section. The lines are equally spaced, so one way to approach the problem would be to divide each side of the hexagon into four equal parts. This can be accomplished in several ways. You could use the method illustrated in Figure 4.17. Alternatively, you could bisect each side and then bisect each half. Either way, once each side is proportioned into four equal parts, notice that the center line connects with the center of the circle. Once that line is defined, all you need to do is draw a line on either side that is parallel and starts at the appropriate division point. Repeat this procedure for each piece of the "pie," and before you know it you are done.

The illustration just provided should give you an idea of the basic approach to take in solving one-view drawings. Rarely will you be given a geometric construction that stands alone. Just relax and find the pieces. Remember, you can never solve a jigsaw puzzle unless you pick up the first piece and begin. Each piece works with the previous pieces to form your finished design.

REVIEW QUESTIONS

1. Why should you never use a dot or a period to represent a point in drafting?
2. When should the endpoints of a line be marked? How should they be marked?
3. Define a parallel line. What symbol is used to represent that two lines are parallel?
4. At what angle do two lines intersect if they are perpendicular to each another? What symbol is used to indicate this?
5. What term is used to refer to an angle of less than 90°?
6. Name three types of polygons. What makes them polygons?
7. What is the sum in degrees of the three angles inside a triangle? (*Hint:* Use your drafting triangles as a visual aid.)
8. What is the difference between an isosceles triangle and an equilateral triangle? Define both.
9. Define the terms *radius, diameter*, and *circumference*. You may want to use a sketch.
10. What is a quadrilateral?
11. Can a line and a circle be tangent to each another? How about two circles?

EXERCISES

EXERCISE 4.1

Divide an 11″ × 17″ sheet into six equal spaces.

Part A: In the top three spaces, going from left to right, construct the following geometric techniques.

First construction: Draw a 2.375″ horizontal line and divide it into seven equal spaces.

Second construction: Draw a 1.875″ line and bisect it.

Third construction: Draw an acute angle of 72° and bisect it.

Part B: In the bottom three spaces, going from left to right, construct the following geometric techniques.

Fourth construction: Draw a square with 1.5″ legs. Draw a circle tangent to the four sides.

Fifth construction: Draw a line 2.125″ long and divide it into three proportional parts.

Sixth construction: Draw an ellipse with a major diameter of 1.75″ horizontally and a minor diameter of 0.875″ vertically.

EXERCISE 4.2

Divide an 11″ × 17″ sheet into six equal spaces.

Part A: In the top three spaces, going from left to right, construct the following geometric shapes.

First construction: Inscribe a hexagon inside a circle with a radius of ⅝″.

Second construction: Circumscribe a hexagon about a circle with a radius of ⅞″.

Third construction: Circumscribe an octagon about a circle with a radius of ¾″.

Part B: In the bottom three spaces, going from left to right, construct the following shapes.

Fourth construction: Construct an equilateral triangle with 1″ sides, and bisect the interior angles. Do the lines intersect at one point or two?

Fifth construction: Construct an isosceles triangle with 0.5″ base and 1.5″ sides. Bisect the sides to find the center of the triangle.

Sixth construction: Inscribe a pentagon using a 1.25″-diameter circle as a base. Locate the center by bisecting the angles.

EXERCISE 4.3

Place the geometric constructions shown in Figure 4.44 on an 8½″ × 11″ sheet of vellum. Work the problems as shown.

(a)
Draw an arc tangent to the given circle and line using a .75″ radius.

(b)
Draw an arc tangent to the given circles using a .625″ radius.

(c)
Transfer the given 72° angle to the horizontal line to the right using a compass and a straightedge.

(d)
Draw a triangle with the three given lines using your compass and a straightedge.

FIGURE 4.44 Exercise 4.3.

ASSIGNMENTS

1. Draw the one-view drawings in Figure 4.45 using the scales listed with the assignment.

4.1
Scale: Full

4.2
Scale: Full

4.3
Scale: Full

4.4
Scale: Full

4.5
Scale: ⅛" = 1'-0"

FIGURE 4.45   Drawing assignment 1.

4.6
Scale: ¹⁄₁₆″ = 1′-0″

FIGURE 4.45 *continued*

○ ○

Introduction to Drawing Conventions

The purpose of any drawing is to convey information. The different types of drawings used in drafting can be broken down into two categories: artistic or pictorial (illustrating what the human eye might see) and technical or working drawings that are used in building or manufacturing. Both have their functions in drawing and are used across all fields of drafting.

Pictorial or artistic drawings can be used to give a nontechnical person or client a good idea of what the project will look like when it is completed, just as three-dimensional models make useful sales tools for marketing construction projects (see Figure 5.1).

If you have ever purchased a piece of furniture that had to be assembled, you have probably seen another type of pictorial drawing. A drawing (exploded pictorial) is usually provided to show the purchaser how to put together the various pieces into a fully assembled product. These three-dimensional drawings show width, length and depth, but because paper is two dimensional, some distortion will occur (see Figure 5.2).

Technical drawings are geared toward building or manufacturing and are very detailed and exact. They show measurements and many different views and sectional cuts in order to show how to produce, manufacture, or build. Parts lists, bills of materials, and all types of schedules can also be used to get the desired end result. People also refer to technical drawings as *working drawings*. They build on one another like a technical manual, explaining and showing every aspect that is required. The major characteristic of these drawings is their true flat two-dimensional views. No depth is shown in the individual views (see Figure 5.3).

FIGURE 5.1 A 3D model of a house. Courtesy of Doug Maddox.

FIGURE 5.2 Exploded isometric of a pressure gun assembly. Courtesy of Innovative Penning Systems.

FIGURE 5.3 Example of a house elevation drawing.

The advantage in using technical drawings is that flat views make it easy to dimension. Dimensioning is much clearer to read in flat views, which makes them easier for the builder to read and understand.

The drafting world needs both types of drawing to complement each other. Neither one is more important than the other; they merely serve different functions. The following chart shows the types of drawings that fall under the two different categories while Figure 5.4 provides examples for you to compare.

Technical/Working	Artistic/Pictorial
Orthographics—Elevations	Axonometric
Auxiliary views	Isometric
Sections	Dimetric
Plan views	Trimetric
	Oblique
	Perspectives
	One-point
	Two-point
	Three-point
	True 3-D Computer-generated drawing

FIGURE 5.4 Examples of technical and pictorial drawings.

This chapter explains the different types of drawing and some of their characteristics. Later chapters will explain how to actually draw working drawings and pictorials.

5.1 Orthographic Drawings

The orthographic drawing is the backbone of technical drafting. Almost all forms of working drawings originate from the orthographic concept. Most schools spend a lot of time teaching orthographic drawing because once the fundamental concepts are grasped they can easily be applied to other fields of drafting.

The standard orthographic principles are largely mechanically based and are explained using a flat plane view approach. For example, look at the dice in Figure 5.5 in pictorial form. Each side is a flat surface with dimples. There are six total sides with six different dimple patterns to distinguish the sides (see Figures 5.6 and 5.7). Almost everyone is familiar with dice and knows the dimple pattern of the dots.

So far the dice have been shown in pictorial form or as a three-dimensional concept. The orthographic views are drawn looking at one surface at a time. Each surface has a different orthographic view showing only the true flat two-dimensional surface (see Figure 5.8). If the drawing was going to be used in typical orthographic form, then the views would be laid out as in Figure 5.9.

Now let's look at a different example using a stairway and letters (see Figure 5.10). The hidden lines represent corners or edges blocked by solid material in front of the viewing plane.

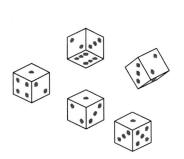

FIGURE 5.5 Pictorial drawings of dice.

FIGURE 5.6 Dice surfaces.

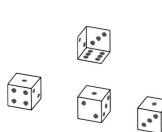

FIGURE 5.7 The six different surfaces of dice.

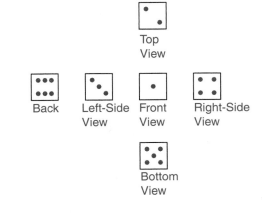

FIGURE 5.8 The six orthographics/elevations of dice.

FIGURE 5.9 An example of how orthographic views would be flipped out using third-angle projection. This alignment is not followed in architectural drawing.

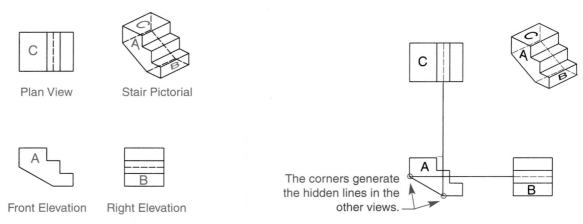

Plan View   Stair Pictorial

Front Elevation   Right Elevation

FIGURE 5.10 Isometric and orthographic representations of stairs.

The corners generate the hidden lines in the other views.

FIGURE 5.11 A blowup of Figure 5.10.

The example in Figure 5.11 shows how standard orthographic views are laid out. An architectural version of these views would leave out the hidden lines, and the view alignment would be left up to the drafter for balance and readability.

A good example of how an architect uses the flat orthographic view is in an elevation view. Let's visualize the pictorial example and then look at the same example in elevation or orthographic form.

First, go to a door and open it to about a 45° angle. Stand back about 5 ft and look at the door and the wall (see Figure 5.12) This is a pictorial showing all three dimensions of the door—height, width, and depth. Once you have the picture locked into your brain, shut the door, return to the same spot, and look again (see Figure 5.13). This time when you look, notice that the depth perception has been taken away because the door is shut and your eyes are perpendicular to the door. This is the difference between the orthographic view and its cousin the elevation.

One of the major differences is in hidden line use. In architectural elevations the hidden lines can be used to show how doors or windows open or pivot (see Figure 5.14). They can also show forms below the ground such as footing and basement outlines (see Figure 5.15).

Although the orthographic view and elevations are both two-dimensional flat views they differ in the view alignment. The mechanical orthographic has a very strict set of guidelines for laying out views and showing lines. The architectural elevations have a lot more freedom in layouts with no rigid format to follow. Architects treat elevations almost like artistic drawings, using shading and dressing up the views for aesthetic purposes even though they are technical drawings (see Figure 5.16).

Most drafters enjoy drawing elevations, trying to bring a two-dimensional drawing to life. It may take you a little while to grasp the pictorial and orthographic concepts and relationships. The real fun begins when you are learning to draw a three-dimensional space from flat views and vice versa (see Figure 5.17).

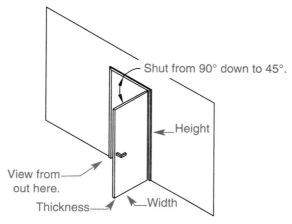

Shut from 90° down to 45°.

Height

View from out here.

Thickness   Width

FIGURE 5.12 A pictorial drawing of a door.

FIGURE 5.13 A door elevation.

FIGURE 5.14 Door and window elevations with hidden lines.

Cabinet Door
Elevation

Window
Elevation

FIGURE 5.15 Front elevation with hidden lines showing a basement below.

FRONT ELEVATION
Scale: 1/ 4" = 1'-0"

FIGURE 5.16 Hatched elevation of a church.

FRONT ELEVATION

Plan View

Pictorial

Front Elevation

Right Elevation

FIGURE 5.17 Pictorial and elevations of a basic shape of a house.

5.2 Auxiliary Views

Once you have mastered orthographics, you have laid the foundation for the rest of the technical drawings. Next are auxiliary views, which use the same basic principles as the orthographic with a slight twist. Auxiliary views are flat two-dimensional drawings that are projected off angled surfaces (see Figure 5.18). Auxiliary views provide a length and width just like orthographics, but these views are projected off the inclined surface of the orthographic to avoid the distortion a side view would give (see Figure 5.19).

Auxiliary views can be split into two types: primary and secondary. The primary auxiliary is used when a view is needed off a single inclined surface (see Figure 5.20). A secondary auxiliary view is used for multiangled surfaces. It is not used often but does occur from time to time (see Figure 5.21). The secondary auxiliary view is a two-dimensional flat view that is flipped and aligned off the primary auxiliary.

Auxiliary views are heavily rooted in mechanical drawing but occasionally one will pop up in an architectural offshoot. You will most likely see it used in architectural drawing in elevations of bay windows or some other angled walls where true views and true dimensions are needed (see Figure 5.22). If you were trying to follow the mechanical layouts, the same drawing would look like Figure 5.23—flipped and aligned off the plan view. Architectural drafters are free to align the views to meet their needs.

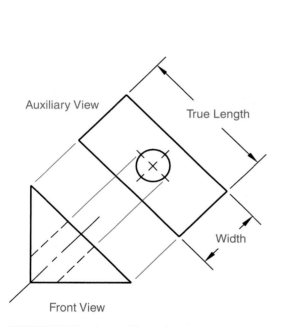

FIGURE 5.18   An auxiliary view.

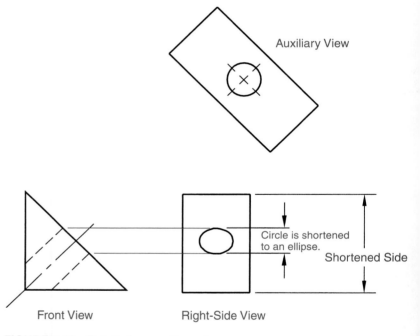

FIGURE 5.19   Detail of an auxiliary view.

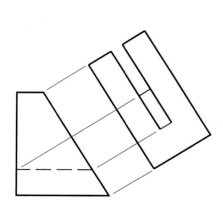

FIGURE 5.20   Example of a primary auxiliary view.

FIGURE 5.21   Example of a primary and a secondary auxiliary view.

FIGURE 5.22 Plan with bay elevation.

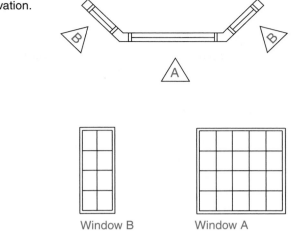

Window B   Window A

Window Elevations

FIGURE 5.23 Plan with bay elevation orthographically aligned.

5.3 Section Views

Section views are the final piece in the technical drawing puzzle. The two-dimensional theme is continued in section drawing, but this type of drawing represents a cut through one or more objects. The task of a section drawing is to make it easier to read something that is complicated or blocked from sight.

Section views make unnecessary the hidden lines found in orthographics because you are no longer on the outside looking in, being blocked by solid material; instead you are cutting through to the inside with nothing blocking your vision at the critical viewing position (see Figure 5.24).

Section drawing is very common in most drafting fields. There are many types of sections, and most relate to the placement of the cutting-plane line (see Figure 5.25).

The key to reading sections is to imagine yourself behind the cutting plane looking in the same direction as the arrowhead is pointing (see Figure 5.26). Not all sections need cutting-plane lines such as the broken-out, removed, revolved, and rotated; however, it is very rare for an individual in architecture not to use a section callout or cutting-plane line. The cutting-plane line placement is extremely important. It allows the person reading the drawing to know exactly where the section is taken from.

Orthographic Views

Orthographic with the
Section View Below

The viewer is looking
at the object after the
cut is made.

The viewer is on the
outside of the object
looking at an orthographic
or an elevation

FIGURE 5.24　Example of sections.

Architectural drawings use many sections to explain materials and to show how they are assembled or put together. In architecture, most sections are cut vertically through walls or buildings. Plan views are usually sections that are cut horizontally (see Figure 5.27). For example, a floor plan is a section on a horizontal plane cut about 4′ above the finished floor. A wall section is a vertical section or cut that goes all the way through from top to bottom showing the footing in the ground and the roof assembly on the very top of the wall (see Figure 5.28).

Building sections are typically cut all the way across the building, showing walls in section, but they can include interior and exterior elevations of objects not in the direct path of the cutting-plane line (see Figure 5.29). Sections can be very small, representing cuts through door frames or counters or cabinets or any detail that might need explaining to the builder to get it constructed according to the designer's vision (see Figure 5.30).

Here are some tips for understanding sections in architectural drawing.

1. Learn the material's hatching symbols and look on all drawings for a hatching legend just in case someone is using atypical hatch patterns (see Figure 5.31).

2. Visit real-life examples so you can learn how construction materials are attached together. During construction is the best time because when the project is finished too much is covered up.

3. Look at models or even put a model together to learn how a building goes together.

4. Get some practice, and do not hesitate to ask a mentor for advice. There is nothing that can replace years of experience in the profession.

Section drawings are beneficial and irreplaceable when it comes to taking the mystery out of the construction and assembling of buildings.

The cutting plane line goes all the way across the object on a full section.

Full Section

In a half section the cutting-plane line stops at the half-way point and comes out at a 90° angle.

Half section

In the offset section the cutting plane-line changes paths at 90° angles.

In the aligned section the cutting-plane line angles with the part. The section view measurements are also taken along the cutting-plane line.

Offset Section

Aligned Section

These types of sections have no cutting-plane lines. They are rotated internally 90° and show the shape.

Rotated/Revolved Sections

These sections do not require cutting-plane lines and are found very close to the area from which they are taken.

Broken-Out Section

FIGURE 5.25   Example of various sections.

The cutting-plane line slices through at this location.

Visualize looking right behind the cutting-plane line and pick out the edges that are visible.

This represents what is seen in the section. Hidden lines beyond are ignored.

FIGURE 5.26   Isometric section.

FIGURE 5.27   Isometric house plan with a horizontal cut made just below the ceiling.

ASPHALT SHINGLES

TWO LAYERS OF
15# ROOFING FELT

5/8" PLYWOOD
EXTERIOR GRADE
PLYWOOD

INSULATION STOP

METAL EAVE
TRIM

1 x 6 WOOD
FASCIA

2" CONT METAL
VENT STRIP

1 x 12 WOOD
SOFFIT

1 x 6 WOOD
TRIM 12 TYPICAL

2 x 12 STRINGER
CUT FROM A 2 x 6
AT EACH TRUSS

3 1/2"

3'-0"

NOTE: CAULK ALL JOINTS IN
WOOD RUNNING TRIM

NEW 4" SPLIT FACE
CMU

EXISTING BRICK

PROVIDE SIMILAR
REINFORCING AT EXISTING
WALLS AS NEW WALLS
EXCEPT OMIT DOWELS
AT THE FOOTING.

GRADE

WOOD TRUSS AS DESIGNED
AND FABRICATED BY TRUSS
MFR.

ANCHOR TRUSSES TO NAILERS
WITH HURRICANE TYPE CLIPS

2—2x6 WOOD PRESSURE TREATED

R30 INSULATION

EXTERIOR GYPSUM
SOFFIT BOARD

RB623 WOOD
BASE MOULDING
INVERTED AND
QUARTER ROUND
MOULDING

5/8" DIA. x 10"
LONG ANCHOR
BOLTS AT 2'-0"
O.C. MAX.

NEW CONCRETE BOND
BEAM REINFORCED
WITH 1 # 5 BAR
TOP AND BOTTOM
AND FILLED WITH
CONCRETE

NEW 8" CMU

PROVIDE INSPECTION HOLE
AT MID—HEIGHT OF WALL
AND BOTTOM TO ASSURE
THAT CONCRETE FLOWS
TO BOTTOM OF WALL

EXISTING 8" CMU

BASE FINISH AS
SCHEDULED

FLOOR FINISH AS
SCHEDULED

EXISTING
CONCRETE SLAB

1'-7"

EQ.   EQ.   EQ.

8'-0"

1'-0"

3" CLR.

3" CLR.

2'-0"

CONCRETE FOOTING

WALL SECTION

FIGURE 5.28

FIGURE 5.29

BUILDING SECTION
Scale: 1/4" = 1'-0"

SECTION THRU SHELVING
Scale: 1 1/2" = 1'-0"

CABINET SECTION
Scale: 3/4" = 1'-0"

FIGURE 5.30
continued on next page

FIGURE 5.30   *continued*

8" CMU

REINFORCED CMU LINTEL—
REINFORCE WITH 2 #5 BARS
AND FILL SOLID WITH
CONCRETE

CAULK EACH
SIDE

H.M. FRAME—FILL
SOLID WITH MORTAR

HEAD
Scale: 1 1/2" = 1'-0"

5/8" G.W.B. EACH SIDE
ON 3 5/8" METAL STUDS

CAULK EACH SIDE

2 METAL STUD CHANNELS
BACK TO BACK AT HEAD

METAL DOOR FRAME

HEAD
Scale: 1 1/2" = 1'-0"

5/8" G.W.B. EACH SIDE
ON 3 5/8" METAL STUDS

CAULK EACH SIDE

METAL DOOR FRAME

PROVIDE JAMB ANCHORS,
3 EACH SIDE. ATTACH
TO METAL STUDS WITH
SELF—DRILLING, SELF—TAPPING
SCREWS

JAMB
Scale: 1 1/2" = 1'-0"

FIGURE 5.31   Typical hatching
symbols for section and plan
view.

Earth   Sand   Gravel   Concrete

Concrete   Reinforced   Brick
Block   Conc. Block

Wood Stud   Metal Stud

5.4 Pictorial Drawings

Pictorial drawings are some of the easiest ones to understand. A person sees a pictorial and can visualize what the project looks like. Most drafters really enjoy pictorial drawings and do not seem to be able to get enough of this type of drawing. However, pictorial drawing normally makes up only a small part of drawing in most architectural offices compared with the multitude of working drawings that must be done on projects.

When learning about pictorials, it is best to start with the easiest and work your way into the more complicated because each type lays down a foundation for the following one.

Oblique Drawings

The oblique drawing style of pictorial is the easiest to use and draw (see Figure 5.32). Some individuals in the field also refer to it as a cabinet drawing. It borrows some features from two-dimensional drawings and uses an angled line for depth. One major drawback to oblique drawings is that although it may be one of the simplest to draw, it is one of the most deceptive to view because of the combined principles. Most drafters counteract the distortion by changing the scale of the depth.

The face that appears to be closest to the viewer represents the two-dimensional part (true measurement) of the oblique, along with any surface that is parallel to the front face (see Figure 5.33). These faces are measured just like an orthographic would be.

Distortion on an oblique occurs along the angled lines. Circles on this surface become ellipses (see Figure 5.34). The combination of true and distorted surfaces makes the oblique unique to the pictorial world.

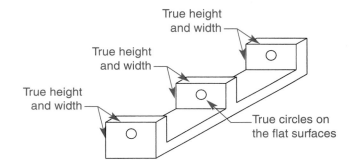

True height and width

True height and width

True height and width

True circles on the flat surfaces

FIGURE 5.32 Oblique example.   **FIGURE 5.33** Oblique example.

FIGURE 5.34 Oblique example.

Distortion along the angled and top surface

Ellipses rather than circles occur on the angled surfaces.

Axonometric Drawings

In axonometric drawing there is no true two-dimensional surface. All the surfaces are on angles in this kind of pictorial. There are three types of axonometric drawings: isometric, dimetric, and trimetric. The angles used determine the type.

1. Isometric drawing is one of the most commonly used pictorials today in manual drawing. The surfaces are created with vertical lines (90°) and 120° equal interior angles (see Figure 5.35). Dimensions and measurements are taken along the interior angles in isometric drawing (see Figure 5.36).

2. Dimetric drawing follows the same principle with some minor changes. The *di* in dimetric means 2, and in this case it means that two of the interior angles are equal instead of all three, as in the isometric. It does not matter which two of the angles are equal (see Figure 5.37).

   Another difference in dimetric drawing is that some techniques allow the drafter to adjust the scales along the depth in order to make the drawing more proportional and less distorted to the viewer. The changing of the angles and of the depth scale is an attempt to make the viewing closer to real life (see Figure 5.38).

3. In trimetric axonometric drawing the three central interior angles are unequal (see Figure 5.39). Just as in dimetric drawing the scale along the angled lines can be adjusted to cut down on distortion to make the pictorial more like real-life viewing. All three scales should be proportionally different.

Axonometric and oblique drawings do not show objects the way the human eye sees them; you must use a perspective to achieve this effect.

Isometric Construction Box

FIGURE 5.35   Iso box with interior angles.

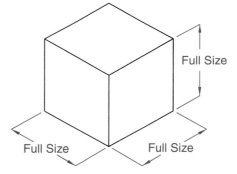

FIGURE 5.36   Measurements can be taken along the interior angles or along parallel angles of an iso box.

FIGURE 5.37   Dimetric box with interior angles. Any two angles can be equal to form a dimetric.

FIGURE 5.38   Measurements along a dimetric box.

FIGURE 5.39 Trimetric box. All three interior angles must be different to form a trimetric.

150°

100°   110°

Full Size

Adjusted Scale

Adjusted Scale

Perspective Drawings

Perspective drawing is the most complicated pictorial but the benefit is that this type of drawing emulates what the human eye would see. Architectural perspectives are a big selling tool when marketing a design (see Figure 5.40).

A good perspective looks as if an artist did the work instead of a drafter. This sometimes leads people to confuse a drafter with an artist. A perspective drawing is done with tools and is not a freehand sketch, so it is not as hard as it might seem. Euclid, the father of geometry, developed basic principles for perspective drawing more than 2000 years ago. Perspectives can be categorized into three groups: one-point, two-point, and three-point.

One-Point Perspectives

The best way to understand a one-point perspective is to see a real-life example. Find a building that has a long narrow hallway and stand at one end. Look down the hall and notice what is happening (see Figure 5.41). The doors look as if they get smaller the farther down the hallway you look, and the ceiling seems to drop lower. Your eyes cause this illusion, and it can be duplicated on paper by using one point of convergence where all the corners meet. The same phenomenon occurs outdoors. Look down a long straight road or down

FIGURE 5.40 Rendered perspective of a building. Courtesy of *Architectural Drawing and Light Construction* by Edward J. Muller.

FIGURE 5.41   Examples of one-point perspectives.

FIGURE 5.42   Example of a railroad track that vanishes to one point.

a set of railroad tracks (see Figure 5.42). Outdoors, the view does not stop at the back wall but instead vanishes to a point. The trait of vanishing to one point defines this type of perspective.

Two-Point Perspectives

Two-point perspective works best when the object's focus is one corner. This two-point perspective relates more to an isometric, as the two sides head off in different directions. A two-point perspective uses two different vanishing points to generate depths (see Figure 5.43). Notice that as the sides head closer to their individual vanishing points, the vertical lines are drawn shorter, just like in the one-point perspective. The advantage to using two-point perspective is that it can give a more realistic view. For this reason, it is often used by interior designers to illustrate room designs.

Three-Point Perspectives

The three-point perspective incorporates a third vanishing point, which can be used in a variety of ways. A third point can be placed high in the sky to have the object's vertical lines taper in, or a light source, like the sun, can be placed in the drawing and a vanishing point can be projected down to the horizon. Using a light source and a third vanishing point helps plot out shadows on a drawing (see Figure 5.44).

Some drawings have many more vanishing points than three, but understanding how to use two points is a good starting place. Adding shades and shadows tends to bring out the artist in the drafter.

Vanishing Point Left   Vanishing Point Right

FIGURE 5.43   Two-point perspectives.

FIGURE 5.44　Three-per-spectives.

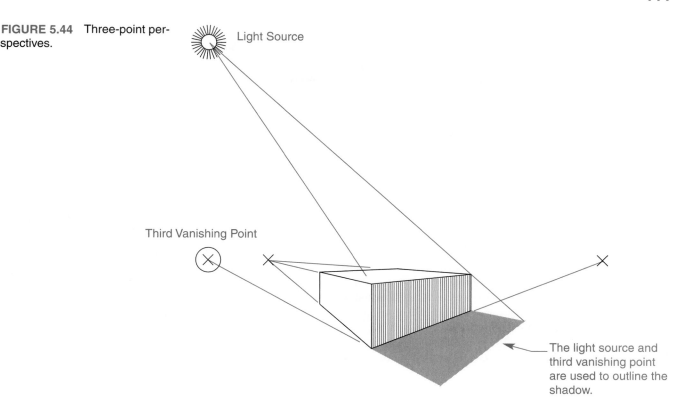

Light Source

Third Vanishing Point

The light source and third vanishing point are used to outline the shadow.

These examples of perspective drawing are very basic. The techniques allow for tremendous detail and complexity. Perspectives really test a drafter's love of drawing; however, the end result can be well worth it.

Computer-Aided 3D Drawings

Before the advent of CAD, pictorials were drawn and constructed on a two-dimensional surface. None of the pictorials were true three-dimensional ones because paper and polyester have no real depth to them. It was only an illusion created by the drafter. Now, with CAD, drawing in 3D is a reality. All the different types of pictorials can be drawn in AutoCAD; however, the fastest way to generate a pictorial is to use true 3D.

Two methods for drawing in true 3D are wireframe and solids. A 3D wireframe is a hollowed-out object (see Figure 5.45). It produces the effect of a glass box. A solid 3D, on the other hand, has solid mass just like an ice cube. The lines behind the solid features can be blocked out very easily (see Figure 5.46).

One problem with 3D drawing is that although the drafter can draw with true lengths, widths, and depths on the computer, when the drawing is printed or plotted it comes out on flat, 2D paper. The best way to view the drawing in 3D is on a computer screen or on a videotape (see Figure 5.47).

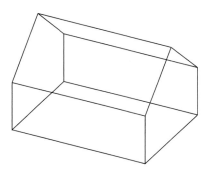

FIGURE 5.45　Example of a 3D wireframe.

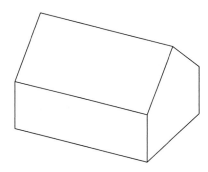

FIGURE 5.46　Example of a 3D solid drawing.

FIGURE 5.47   Rendered 3D solid. Courtesy of Jason Austin.

Presentation Drawings

So far we have discussed construction drawings and working drawings, which are used to make ideas a reality. One drawing area not discussed yet is presentation or marketing drawings. Presentation drawing incorporates all types of drawings in order to sell a design to a client.

Presentation drawings are not detailed like a set of working drawings. Often dimensions are omitted along with other items needed for construction that are not critical when trying to get funding for a project. Typically, a set of architectural presentation drawings includes perspectives, floor plans with basic dimensions, exterior and interior elevations, a very basic site plan, and building sections. See Figure 5.48 for presentation examples.

It is not unusual for a designer or drafter to ink, color, or even render/shade these drawings. These drawings are a designer's selling tool when competing for projects against other design groups. In today's

FLOOR PLAN
Scale: ⅛″=1′-0″ 2162 SF

FIGURE 5.48   Presentation drawings.

FIGURE 5.48 *continued*

FRONT ELEVATION
Scale: ⅛″=1′-0″

SIDE ELEVATION
Scale: ⅛″=1′-0″

world, with the help of computers and animation software, a designer can walk a client through a virtual building on a computer screen or on a video, producing the most real-life effect possible.

REVIEW QUESTIONS

1. List all the different types of technical drawings.
2. What are the characteristics of a technical drawing?
3. Explain how an auxiliary view is different from an orthographic view.
4. What are some typical sections found in architectural drawings?
5. Sketch an example of an oblique drawing.
6. What are the characteristics of an oblique drawing?
7. Sketch an isometric cube and label the interior angles.
8. Why would a dimetric or trimetric drawing be used instead of an isometric drawing?
9. List all the types of pictorial drawings.
10. What are some disadvantages when drawing dimetrics or trimetrics?
11. Sketch an example of a one-point perspective.
12. What is the purpose of the third vanishing point in perspective drawing?
13. What type of pictorial drawing is a true 3D drawing?
14. When is a pictorial drawing needed? What determines the need for a technical drawing?

EXERCISES

Elevation Identification

EXERCISE 5.1

For the elevations given in Figure 5.49, place the letter of the correct elevation in the proper blank to match the building shown.

EXERCISE 5.2

Sketch the roof plan for each example in exercise 5.1, using 8 × 8 gridded vellum.

EXERCISE 5.3

Sketch the shapes in Figure 5.50 three times each on 8 × 8 gridded vellum.

FIGURE 5.49　Exercise 5.1. Courtesy of *Reading Architectural Working Drawings,* Vol. I, by Edward J. Muller.

FIGURE 5.50 Exercise 5.3.
Courtesy of Mirella Lancaster.

EXERCISE 5.4

Sketch the shapes in Figure 5.51 in isometric form.

EXERCISE 5.5

Sketch figures A, B, D, E, and F from exercise 5.4 in oblique form.

FIGURE 5.51　Exercise 5.4.

Architectural Concepts

Drawn by Jason Austin

Introduction to Architectural and Interior Drawings

6.1 Overview

Unless you are currently building a house, you may take the structures that you encounter every day for granted. Take a moment to consider that these buildings started as an idea in the mind of an owner or an architect. Before that idea could become reality, it had to be put down on paper. Architectural drawings and specifications form a bridge between dreams and reality: Walls must be laid out. Plumbing fixtures must be located. The size and placement of windows and doors must be specified (see Figure 6.1). The list is endless. Architects such as Frank Lloyd Wright have even designed furniture to fit a specific project.

Architectural drawings can be broken down into presentation drawings and working drawings. The presentation drawings are useful in working out the general concepts of a project to ensure that the designer and owner are on the same wavelength. Presentation drawings are also useful sales tools that provide a picture of what the finished product is supposed to look like (see Figure 6.2).

Working drawings, the focus of this chapter, are the drawings used by the contractor to construct the building. In conjunction with the specifications, the working drawings must give the builder enough information to allow him or her to complete the entire building from the foundation to the last piece of finish carpentry. The size and complexity of the project will dictate the number and type of drawings included in a set of plans. A complex set of plans might include the following types of drawings (in addition to specifications):

- **Title Page and Index:** This page identifies the project and provides a list of the individual drawings included in the set. A perspective of the project is sometimes also placed on this page.
- **Site Plan:** The site plan can encompass several types of drawing, including a plot plan, a topographic map, and a profile drawing. The plot plan shows the placement of the structure on the piece of property where it will be built. A topographic map uses contours to chart the features of a piece of property using elevation changes. A profile drawing basically is a side-view slice of a topographic map.
- **Foundation Plan:** Details of the layout of the foundation are given on the foundation plan. Information about the design of the basement may also be found on this sheet.
- **Floor Plans:** The floor plans show the locations and dimensions of the walls of each floor in the building. The locations of doors, windows, plumbing fixtures, and appliances are also given.
- **Elevations:** Elevations provide outside views of each side of the house
- **Section Views:** A look at the "insides" of the structure is provided by the section view.
- **Detail Drawings:** Additional details are shown for any portion of the structure that cannot be adequately shown on the plan or elevation drawings. Details are usually drawn at a larger scale.
- **Schedules:** Information that is too detailed or cumbersome can be placed on a schedule. The most common schedules contain information about the size and type of doors and windows.

FIGURE 6.1 The progression from idea to reality. (a) Floor plan. (b) Elevation. (c) Picture.

(a)

(b)

FIGURE 6.1   *continued*

(c)

- **Roof and Floor Framing Plans:** These drawings provide information about the "bare bones" of the structure. For example, the direction and spacing of floor and ceiling joists is commonly shown.

- **Column and Beam Schedules:** Column and beam schedules seldom appear on residential plans. They are a specialized type of drawing generally reserved for more complex projects. Information contained on the schedule will include placement, length, description, and the number of columns or beams required.

- **Structural Details:** The supplier of the structural component, such as steel, often prepares specialized shop drawings. These drawings detail each element along with information about the length, weight per foot, and placement of holes for fasteners.

- **Electrical Plans:** The electrical plans detail the placement of electrical circuits and systems within the structure. If not too complicated, the electrical information may be placed on the floor plans. Otherwise, a separate drawing is produced. Likewise, the lighting plan may be included with the electrical plans or produced as a separate set of drawings.

- **Mechanical Plans:** Mechanical plans may include HVAC (Heating, Ventilation, and Air Conditioning) as well as piping and plumbing. In complex structures, these may be broken down into separate drawings.

Taken together, these drawings form a complete picture of the structure being built. There are components of art and science to producing meaningful blueprints. The drafter must decide which information needs to be included and how it should be displayed. Typically, the structures being detailed are too large to draw full scale (Imagine trying to handle a set of blueprints the size of your house!), so the drawings are drawn to scale. The most common scale for a residential plan is ¼″=1′-0″. Larger designs, such as most commercial plans, are usually drawn at a scale of ⅛″=1′-0″. Abbreviations and symbols are often used in order to fit all the desired information on the page without unnecessarily cluttering the drawing. This is where artistry comes into play. All the information needs to be placed on the page in a manner than is both pleasing to the eye and easily read. Dimensions must be provided so that there is no guesswork involved on the part of the contractor.

The rest of the chapter discusses in detail the various types of architectural and interior drawings. For purposes of illustration, the examples used refer to residential construction; however, the concepts are easily applied to commercial construction.

(a)

PROPOSED FIRST PLAN
Scale:1/8" = 1'-0"

PROPOSED SECOND PLAN
Scale:1/8" = 1'-0"

(b)

FIGURE 6.2 Example of presentation drawings.

PROPOSED FRONT ELEVATION
Scale: 1/8" = 1'-0"

PROPOSED SIDE ELEVATION
Scale: 1/8" = 1'-0"

(c)

(d) Site plan for a sports complex

FIGURE 6.2   *continued*

6.2 Elevation Views

The image of a dollhouse may be helpful for describing architectural drawings. The elevation views give you all the information you could get by looking at the outside of the dollhouse. Each side of the house is drawn as though you were standing in the yard looking at the side of the house directly in front of you. Elevation views are two dimensional and drawn to scale. A typical house has four elevation views. These are usually designated as Front, Rear, Right, and Left. Alternatively, the views may be labeled North, East, South, and West. The compass designations do not indicate an exact direction, just the general direction that the wall faces. The drafter must determine how many elevations are required. Some very simple buildings do not require four views, whereas some complex structures, such as a house built around a courtyard, may require many more than four elevations. The rule is to provide as many elevations as are needed to give a complete picture of the structure.

Information provided on the elevation views includes the following:

- Materials used on the exterior of the structure
- Finished floor–to–finished floor heights (finished floor–to–finished ceiling height for top story)
- Arrangement of doors and windows
- Indication of roof pitch or slope
- Height of the roof
- Depth of footings
- Chimneys and masonry walls

Hidden (dashed) lines are used to show any features below grade such as footings. The siding material is often simplified on the elevation views. For example, only a small portion of the elevation may be covered with the symbol for the siding material (see Figure 6.3). Brick may be shown as a few horizontal lines about 3″ (on scale) apart. In this case, any brick accents such as bricks laid on edge for windowsills or door heads should be detailed. Doors and windows are also often simplified. Sometimes one window will be drawn in detail, and the rest will simply be shown as rectangles. The dashed lines in Figure 6.4 indicate the location of hinges on the cabinet doors.

In a perfect world, the exterior of a house complements the interior. In general, if the interior is formal, the exterior should follow suit, often utilizing symmetry and balance. An informal interior allows the architect more play with the exterior. Unity, harmony, and balance must still be considered. The scale of the design will influence the way people interact with the structure.

Sometimes, elevation views are required for features on the inside of the building. These views are referred to as *interior elevations.* Interior elevations are useful in rooms with many cabinets and built-in fixtures. The two types of rooms most commonly described with interior elevations are the kitchen and the bathroom (see Figure 6.4). Fireplaces, staircases, and built-in bookshelves also are occasionally pictured with interior elevations.

FIGURE 6.3   Example of hidden lines.

FIGURE 6.4 An interior elevation.

KITCHEN ELEVATION
Scale: 1/2" = 1'-0"

6.3 Foundation and Floor Plans

Recall again the image of a dollhouse. Now, imagine lifting the lid off the house and peeking inside. Just looking at the outside of the house gives you some idea of what it is like, but seeing the inside tells you so much more. A floor plan drawing provides the same insight. Plan views are drawn as though someone cut the house open about 4 ft above the level of the floor being drawn. No drawings in the set provide more information. The floor plan provides the layout of the structure, the size of the rooms, the location of doors and windows, the placement of bathroom and kitchen fixtures, the position of fireplaces, and the orientation of stairways. Additional views such as sections and details are generally referenced to their location on the floor plan. The cutting plane may be considered as jogging up or down to include a relevant feature. The drafter may want to include a small window that is placed above the cutting plane (see Figure 6.5), or perhaps a low opening in the wall such as a fireplace.

Drafters need to develop a palette of abbreviations and symbols used on architectural drawings. Hidden or dashed lines may be used to show features that exist above or below the cutting plane, such as arched or cased openings, closet rods, hidden beams, and upper cabinets. Symbols are used to indicate the type of material being used. Figure 6.6 shows some of the most commonly used symbols for architectural materials. Different symbols are often used depending on whether the material is shown in plan view or elevation view.

Kitchen and bathroom fixtures are also indicated with symbols (see Figure 6.7). These are some of the easiest to read because they generally look like the piece of equipment being represented. Templates are readily available for fixtures drawn at either 1/4"=1'-0" or 1/8"=1'-0" scale.

Typical stairway symbols are illustrated in Figure 6.8. Notice that every step is not necessarily drawn. A complex set of stairs may call for a separate stair layout. Otherwise, the importance of the stair symbol on a floor plan is to indicate the location of the stairs and whether they are going up or going down.

The location of doors and windows is critical information given on the foundation and floor plan drawings. Figure 6.9 shows the symbols typically used to indicate the different types of doors and windows. Notice that on exterior doors the sill is shown on the outside of the house, whereas on interior doors no sill is shown. The actual size of a door or window is usually placed on a separate schedule to avoid crowding the drawing.

Fireplaces and wood stoves should also be located on floor plan drawings. Figure 6.10 shows some typical configurations.

FIGURE 6.5 Example of a horizontal cutting plane.

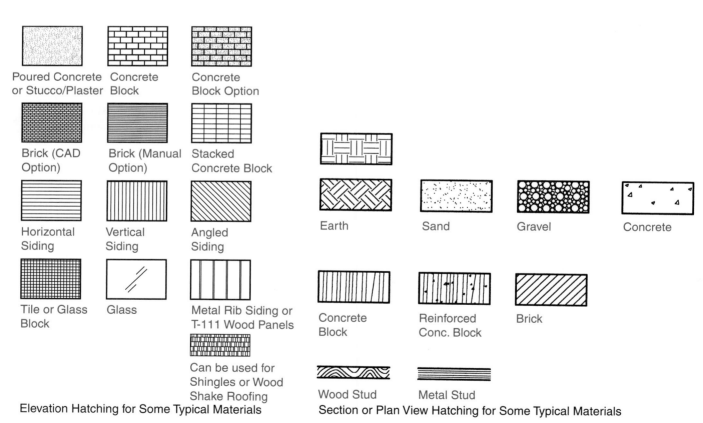

Poured Concrete or Stucco/Plaster

Concrete Block

Concrete Block Option

Brick (CAD Option)

Brick (Manual Option)

Stacked Concrete Block

Horizontal Siding

Vertical Siding

Angled Siding

Tile or Glass Block

Glass

Metal Rib Siding or T-111 Wood Panels

Can be used for Shingles or Wood Shake Roofing

Elevation Hatching for Some Typical Materials

Earth

Sand

Gravel

Concrete

Concrete Block

Reinforced Conc. Block

Brick

Wood Stud

Metal Stud

Section or Plan View Hatching for Some Typical Materials

FIGURE 6.6 Symbols for architectural materials.

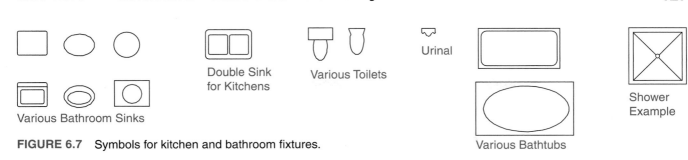

Various Bathroom Sinks

Double Sink for Kitchens

Various Toilets

Urinal

Various Bathtubs

Shower Example

FIGURE 6.7 Symbols for kitchen and bathroom fixtures.

FIGURE 6.8 Symbols for stairs.

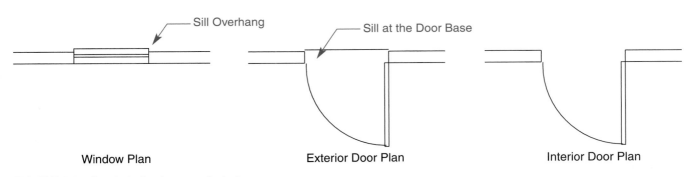

Stair Hand Rails

Directional Note on Stairs

DOWN

Breakline Indicating Stairs Going to the Next Floor Level

Plan View of Stairs

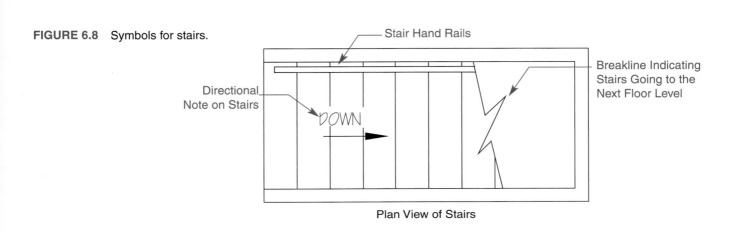

Sill Overhang

Sill at the Door Base

Window Plan

Exterior Door Plan

Interior Door Plan

FIGURE 6.9 Symbols for doors and windows.

FIGURE 6.10 Symbols for fire-places and wood stoves.

Fireplace Plan View

Wood Stove Plan View

Information that applies to the overall project may be placed in a section labeled General Notes. The General Notes should be located in an area off to the side of the main body of the drawing at least ½″ away from the border. They should not visually interfere with the rest of the information given. Remember that your aim is to produce a drawing that is uncluttered and easy to read. Even though the scale may apply to the entire drawing, this information is usually placed in the title block.

6.4 Schedules

Schedules play a vital role in keeping a set of drawings organized and readable. Information that would tend to clutter a drawing can be gathered together and organized into a table. For example, rather than trying to squeeze in the size and type of each window shown on the plan views, you can group the information together and place it on a window schedule (see Figure 6.11). Each time you want to specify a particular size and type of window, you can place a symbol on the plan view next to the location of that window. One column on the schedule will provide a key to the symbols, usually either a number or letter placed within a circle or triangle. The type of windows typically used in residential construction includes double hung, casement, awning, sliding, and fixed (see Figure 6.12). The windows are usually grouped within types from the largest to the smallest. Rough openings sizes should be called out on the schedule. In addition, the vendor and the item number may also be included.

FIGURE 6.11 Example of a window schedule.

WINDOW SCHEDULE

MARK	SIZE	TYPE	REMARKS
A	10″ x 6'-10″	SIDE LITE	WD. & BRICK JAMB
B	1'-10″ x 4'-9″	FIXED	WD. & BRICK JAMB
C	2'-6″ x 6'-6″	D.H.	WD. & BRICK JAMB
D	3'-6″ x 4'-9″	D.H.	PICTURE WINDOW IN BREAK. RM.
E	5'-1″ x 5'-6″	PICTURE	WD. & BRICK JAMB
F	2'-6″ x 2'-0″	HORIZON	WD. & BRICK JAMB
G	5'-1″ x 2'-6″	HORIZON	WD. & BRICK JAMB
H	1'-10″ x 2'-6″	D.H.	WD. & BRICK JAMB
I	3'-6″ x 2'-6″	HORIZON	WD. & BRICK JAMB
J	3'-6″ x 1'-6″	DECOR	W/ 3'-6″ x 3'-0″ FIXED GLASS BELOW

Double Hung   Casement   Awning   Sliding

Bay Window

FIGURE 6.12   Window types.

Information about the size and style of doors is also commonly placed on a schedule (see Figure 6.13). Door styles include hinged, pocket, French, sliding, and bifold and many more (see Figure 6.14). Additionally, doors may be painted or stained. Windows are usually specified with letters, so the doors should be specified using numbers to avoid confusion.

A schedule of interior finishes can add clarity to a job. This type of schedule is most often seen in commercial construction but is also used for residential design. Information on the schedule may include the treatment to be used on the floors, walls, and ceiling. The schedule may simply indicate that paint will be used, or it may specify the particular brand and color of paint to be used. Finishes such as wallpaper and moldings may be called for. On a simple plan, the interior finish schedule may refer to the rooms by name. On more complex designs, the rooms are generally assigned numbers.

Schedules may be placed anywhere within a set a drawings. Generally, the drafter looks for an empty space on the floor plans or elevations. The closer the information is to the reference drawings the better for everyone. Occasionally, the schedules are placed together on a separate sheet.

Although schedules are most commonly drawn in the form of tables, an alternative is to place the information on a series of pictures of the appropriate component. Thus, rather than calling for a 6′-8″ × 3′-0″ six-panel wooden door, the drafter can draw a picture of the door with dimensions and label it with the symbol to be used whenever that type of door is to be used.

DOOR SCHEDULE

DOOR NUMBER	DOOR SIZE	Door MATERIAL	Door TYPE	Door FINISH	FRAME MATERIAL	FRAME SIZE	FRAME TYPE	FRAME FINISH	ASSEMBLY RATING	HARDWARE FUNCTION	CLOSER	SIGNAGE	DETAILS HEAD	DETAILS JAMB	DETAILS SILL	REMARKS
1	3'-0"x7'-0"x1 3/4"	HM	C	PAINT	HM	8 3/4"	II	PAINT	3/4 HR C	PANIC	YES	TYPE A	1/A7.1	2/A7.1	-	
2	3'-0"x7'-0"x1 3/4"	HM	C	PAINT	HM	8 3/4"	II	PAINT	3/4 HR C	PANIC	YES	TYPE A	1/A7.1	2/A7.1	-	
3	3'-0"x7'-0"x1 3/4"	SC WOOD	B	STAIN	HM	8 3/4"	II	PAINT	NONE	LOCKSET	NO	TYPE A	1/A7.1	2/A7.1	-	
4	3'-0"x7'-0"x1 3/4"	SC WOOD	B	STAIN	HM	8 3/4"	II	PAINT	NONE	LOCKSET	NO	TYPE A	1/A7.1	2/A7.1	-	
5	3'-0"x7'-0"x1 3/4"	SC WOOD	B	STAIN	HM	8 3/4"	II	PAINT	3/4 HR C	LOCKSET	YES	TYPE A	1/A7.1	2/A7.1	-	
6	3'-0"x7'-0"x1 3/4"	SC WOOD	B	STAIN	HM	8 3/4"	II	PAINT	3/4 HR C	LOCKSET	YES	TYPE A	1/A7.1	2/A7.1	-	
7	3'-0"x7'-0"x1 3/4"	SC WOOD	A	STAIN	HM	6"	I	PAINT	NONE	LOCKSET	NO	TYPE A	3/A7.1	4/A7.1	-	
8	3'-0"x7'-0"x1 3/4"	SC WOOD	A	STAIN	HM	6"	I	PAINT	NONE	LOCKSET	NO	TYPE A	3/A7.1	4/A7.1	-	
9	3'-0"x7'-0"x1 3/4"	SC WOOD	A	STAIN	HM	6"	I	PAINT	NONE	LOCKSET	NO	TYPE A	3/A7.1	4/A7.1	-	
10	3'-0"x7'-0"x1 3/4"	SC WOOD	A	STAIN	HM	6"	I	PAINT	NONE	LOCKSET	NO	TYPE A	3/A7.1	4/A7.1	-	
11	3'-0"x7'-0"x1 3/4"	SC WOOD	A	STAIN	HM	6"	I	PAINT	3/4 HR C	LOCKSET	YES	TYPE B	3/A7.1	4/A7.1	-	
12	3'-0"x7'-0"x1 3/4"	SC WOOD	A	STAIN	HM	6"	I	PAINT	NONE	LOCKSET	NO	TYPE A	3/A7.1	4/A7.1	-	
13	3'-0"x7'-0"x1 3/4"	SC WOOD	A	STAIN	HM	8 3/4"	II	PAINT	3/4 HR C	LOCKSET	YES	TYPE B	1/A7.1	2/A7.1	-	
14	3'-0"x7'-0"x1 3/4"	SC WOOD	A	STAIN	HM	8 3/4"	II	PAINT	3/4 HR C	LOCKSET	YES	TYPE B	1/A7.1	2/A7.1	-	
15	3'-0"x7'-0"x1 3/4"	SC WOOD	B	STAIN	HM	8 3/4"	II	PAINT	NONE	LOCKSET	NO	TYPE A	1/A7.1	2/A7.1	-	
16	3'-0"x7'-0"x1 3/4"	SC WOOD	A	STAIN	HM	8 3/4"	II	PAINT	3/4 HR C	LOCKSET	YES	TYPE A	1/A7.1	2/A7.1	-	
17	3'-0"x7'-0"x1 3/4"	SC WOOD	A	STAIN	HM	8 3/4"	II	PAINT	3/4 HR C	LOCKSET	YES	TYPE A	1/A7.1	2/A7.1	-	
18	3'-0"x7'-0"x1 3/4"	SC WOOD	B	STAIN	HM	8 3/4"	II	PAINT	NONE	LOCKSET	NO	TYPE A	1/A7.1	2/A7.1	-	
19	3'-0"x7'-0"x1 3/4"	SC WOOD	A	STAIN	HM	6 3/4"	I	PAINT	3/4 HR C	LOCKSET	YES	TYPE A	1/A7.1	2/A7.1	-	
20	3'-0"x6'-8"x1 3/4"	SC WOOD	A	STAIN	HM	6 3/4"	I	PAINT	3/4 HR C	LOCKSET	YES	TYPE A	5/A7.1	6/A7.1	-	FIELD VERIFY FRAME DEPTH
21	3'-0"x7'-0"x1 3/4"	SC WOOD	A	STAIN	HM	8 3/4"	II	PAINT	3/4 HR C	LOCKSET	YES	TYPE B	1/A7.1	2/A7.1	-	
22	3'-0"x6'-8"	NONE	-	-	HM	6 3/4"	I	PAINT	NONE	-	-	-	7/A7.1	8/A7.1	-	FIELD VERIFY FRAME DEPTH – CASED OPENING
23	3'-0"x6'-8"x1 3/4"	SC WOOD	A	STAIN	HM	6 3/4"	I	PAINT	3/4 HR C	LATCHSET	YES	-	7/A7.1 SIM.	8/A7.1 SIM.	-	FIELD VERIFY FRAME DEPTH

FIGURE 6.13 Example of a door schedule.

Hinged Door   Pocket Door   Sliding Door   French Door

FIGURE 6.14   Door types.

6.5 Detail and Section Views

Looking at the floor plans and the elevation views can provide you with a good idea of what a structure will look like once it is complete, but this is usually not enough information to begin building. The contractor needs to know details of construction such as the type of wall system, amount of insulation, foundation details, and a host of other information that would be difficult to fit on the elevation and plan views. These details help ensure that the finished product is of the quality envisioned by the architect and the owner. Section views and detail drawings are useful vehicles for providing this necessary information.

Picture an imaginary cutting plane, like a knife, slicing through the structure (see Figure 6.15). Everything along the plane of that knife will be shown on the section view, much like opening up a dollhouse that is hinged to expose the rooms inside. As the cutting plane passes through walls, the inside of the wall as well as the structural systems will be shown. If the cutting plane passes through the entire building, the drawing is referred to as a structural or building section (see Figure 6.16). Structural sections are generally drawn at the same scale as the plan views, so the typical residential structural section will be drawn at $\frac{1}{4}''=1'-0''$. In addition to the method of construction, these sections may also provide information on the rigidity of the framing and the length of particular members.

If the cutting plane passes through only one wall, it produces a wall section. Wall sections are generally drawn at a larger scale to enhance detail and clarity. Scales of $\frac{3}{4}''=1'-0''$, $1'=1'-0''$, and $1\frac{1}{2}''=1'-0''$ are typical. The wall section will provide information on the construction of the wall, the type of material to be used, and the sizes of the various components (see Figure 6.17).

If the design of the structure calls for a special or unusual type of construction, a detail drawing should be provided (see Figure 6.18). The detail drawing will utilize a larger scale than the other drawings in the set. Some details are even drawn at full scale. Examples of features often shown in detail drawings include footing details, fireplace layouts, stairway information, and guttering.

FIGURE 6.15   Example of a vertical cutting plane.

Vertical Cutting Plane

FIGURE 6.16 A structural or building section.

BUILDING SECTION
Scale: 1/2" = 1'-0"

The following labels appear in the figure:

CONTINUOUS RIDGE VENT
ROOFING SHINGLES AS SELECTED BY OWNER
2 LAYERS OF 15# FELT
3/4" TONGUE AND GROOVE PLYWOOD ROOF DECKING
RB 47 CROWN MOULD
2 x 6 RAFTERS AT 16" O.C.
EXTEND EVERY OTHER RAFTER TO PROVIDE ROOF OVERHANG MATCH EXISTING CONDITIONS
METAL EAVE TRIM
PAINTED GALVANIZED METAL OGEE GUTTER
FOIL FACED POLYISOCYANURATE SHEATHING BOARD — PROVIDE PLYWOOD AT EXTERIOR AND INTERIOR CORNERS
TYVEK HOUSEWRAP OR AN APPROVED EQUAL
1 x 10 WOOD SIDING — MATCH EXISTING EXPOSURE
METAL FLASHING
ROOFING SHINGLES AS SELECTED BY OWNER
2 LAYERS OF 15# FELT
3/4" TONGUE AND GROOVE PLYWOOD ROOF DECKING
2 x 6 RAFTERS AT 16" O.C.
RB 28 RAKE MOULD
1 x — WOOD FASCIA
2 x 4 OUTLOOKERS AT 16" O.C. MAX.
3/4" TONGUE AND GROOVE PLYWOOD SOFFIT
RB 47 CROWN MOULD
EXTEND EXISTING WALLS UP WITH NEW 2 x 4 STUDS AT 16" O.C. TO PROVIDE NEW VAULTED CEILING IN BREAKFAST ROOM — PROVIDE PLASTER TO MATCH EXISTING
EXISTING CONSTRUCTION
BREAKFAST
ATTIC
2 x 4 DOUBLE TOP PLATE
2 x 4 WOOD STUDS AT 16" O.C. MAX.
2 x 4 SILL PLATE
WALL FINISH AS SELECTED BY OWNER
FLOOR FINISH AS SELECTED BY OWNER
CLOSET
ATTIC
2 x 8 CEILING JOISTS AT 16" O.C. MAX.
1/2" GWB
CEILING INSULATION R-30
BATT INSULATION R-18
BATT INSULATION R-11
MASTER
TRIPLE 2 x 12 JOISTS NAILED TOGETHER
NEW 3/4" UNDERLAYMENT
NEW 3/4" TONGUE AND GROOVE SUBFLOORING
NEW 2 x 12 FLOOR JOISTS AT EACH EXISTING CEILING JOIST
LOCATE NEW WALL OVER EXISTING WALL — PROVIDE SOLID BLOCKING TO STRUCTURE BELOW
FLITCH BEAM — 2 x 12 BOLTED TO EACH SIDE OF A CONTINUOUS STEEL PLATE 3/4" x 11" STAGGER 3/4" DIA. THRU BOLTS AT 12" O.C.
KITCHEN
EXISTING CONSTRUCTION
DINING
EXISTING CRAWL SPACE
TRIPLE 2 x 12 JOISTS NAILED TOGETHER
EXISTING CONSTRUCTION
NEW DORMER BEYOND
LIVING
8'-0"
±10'-0"
12
6
12
±8

ASPHALT SHINGLES

TWO LAYERS OF
15# ROOFING FELT

5/8" PLYWOOD
EXTERIOR GRADE
PLYWOOD

INSULATION STOP

METAL EAVE
TRIM

1 x 8 WOOD
FASCIA

2" CONT METAL
VENT STRIP

1 x 12 WOOD
SOFFIT

1 x 4 WOOD
TRIM - TYPICAL

2 x 12 STRINGER
CUT FROM A 2 x 6
AT EACH TRUSS

NOTE: CAULK ALL JOINTS IN
WOOD RUNNING TRIM

NEW 4" SPLIT FACE
CMU

EXISTING BRICK

PROVIDE SIMILAR
REINFORCING AT EXISTING
WALLS AS NEW WALLS
EXCEPT OMIT DOWELS
AT THE FOOTING.

GRADE

WOOD TRUSS AS DESIGNED
AND FABRICATED BY TRUSS
MFR

ANCHOR TRUSSES TO NAILERS
WITH HURRICANE TYPE CLIPS

2-2x8 WOOD PRESSURE TREATED

R30 INSULATION

EXTERIOR GYPSUM
SOFFIT BOARD

RB623 WOOD
BASE MOULDING
INVERTED AND
QUARTER ROUND
MOULDING

5/8" DIA x 10"
LONG ANCHOR
BOLTS AT 2'-0"
O.C MAX.

NEW CONCRETE BOND
BEAM REINFORCED
WITH 1 # 5 BAR
TOP AND BOTTOM
AND FILLED WITH
CONCRETE

NEW 8" CMU

PROVIDE INSPECTION HOLE
AT MID-HEIGHT OF WALL
AND BOTTOM TO ASSURE
THAT CONCRETE FLOWS
TO BOTTOM OF WALL

EXISTING 8" CMU

BASE FINISH AS
SCHEDULED

FLOOR FINISH AS
SCHEDULED

EXISTING
CONCRETE SLAB

FIN.
FLR.

CONCRETE FOOTING

WALL SECTION
3/4" = 1'-0"

3 1/2"

3'-0"

1'-7"

8'-0"

9'-7"

3"

1'-0"

3" CLR.

3" CLR.

2'-0"

FIGURE 6.17   A wall section.

FIGURE 6.18 A detail drawing.

ASPHALT SHINGLES

TWO LAYERS OF
15# ROOFING FELT

5/8" PLYWOOD
EXTERIOR GRADE
PLYWOOD

WOOD TRUSS AS DESIGNED
AND FABRICATED BY TRUSS
MFR.

METAL EAVE
TRIM

ANCHOR TRUSSES TO NAILERS
WITH HURRICANE TYPE CLIPS

1 x 8 WOOD
FASCIA

2–2x6 WOOD PRESSURE TREATED

PRESSURE TREATED
2 x 4

EQ. EQ. EQ.

2" CONT. METAL
VENT STRIP

1 x 12 WOOD
SOFFIT

1/2" EXTERIOR GRADE
MDO PLYWOOD—PROVIDE
SOLID WOOD LATTICE
STRIPS OVER JOINTS—REFER
TO THE REFLECTED
CEILING PLAN

1 x 4 WOOD
TRIM – TYPICAL

3 1/2"   1'–11"   3 1/2"

2 x 12 STRINGER
CUT FROM A 2 x 6
AT EACH TRUSS

PRESSURE–TREATED
2 x 6

8'–0" A.F.F.   1'–7"

NOTE: CAULK ALL JOINTS IN
WOOD RUNNING TRIM

2x4 WOOD FRAMING
AT EACH STRINGER

EAVES DETAIL
Scale: 3/4" = 1'–0"

6.6 Framing Plans

A complete set of architectural drawings may include framing plans for the roof and the flooring. These plans detail the type of support system that will be used for the structure. Included in the framing plans are the size of material, the spacing between beams and joists, and the direction in which each member will be laid (see Figure 6.19). In commercial construction, a structural engineer will usually generate the framing plan. In residential construction, the wood manufacturer will often provide the framing plan as a part of its service. Figure 6.20 illustrates several roofing styles commonly used in residential construction.

Note: Black lines indicate
the roof framing.

EXISTING 2 x 6 RAFTERS
AT 16" O.C.

EXISTING 2 x 6 RAFTERS
AT 16" O.C.

EXISTING 2 x 6 RAFTERS
AT 16" O.C.

EXISTING 2 x 6 RAFTERS
AT 16" O.C.

EXISTING 2 x 6 RAFTERS
AT 16" O.C.

EXISTING 2 x 6 RAFTERS
AT 16" O.C.

EXISTING 2 x 6 RAFTERS
AT 16" O.C.

EXISTING 2 x 6 RAFTERS
AT 16" O.C.

EXISTING 2 x 6 RAFTERS
AT 16" O.C.

EXISTING 2 x 6 RAFTERS
AT 16" O.C.

EXISTING ROOF FRAMING PLAN
Scale: 1/4" = 1'–0"

FIGURE 6.19 A framing drawing.

FIGURE 6.20   Roof styles.

Gable Roof

Hip Roof

Flat Roof

Shed Roof

Mansard Roof

Gambrel Roof

6.7 Dimensioning Architectural Drawings

Dimensioning is critical to architectural drawings. Without dimensions, the drawing is just a concept. If the dimensions are not applied properly, the drawing looks cluttered and can be difficult to read. You, as a drafter, must learn to place your dimensions in the best locations. Mentally walk yourself through the building process to make sure you have not left off any dimensions needed for construction. Any dimension that a builder might require is worth putting on the drawing. A well-crafted drawing does not require additions or deletions to be performed on site. Obvious dimensions such as a door that is located at the corner of a room or centered at the end of a hallway are sometimes omitted in the interests of a more readable drawing.

On floor plans, you will often find three lines of dimensions around the outside of the structure (see Figure 6.21). The outside line of dimensions usually details the overall length of the building. The next set of dimensions locates the walls within the structure. The third set of dimensions places the doors and windows. Additional dimensions may be needed to locate features within the interior of the structure. In this case, you should try to locate the dimensions in an area close to the element being detailed without making the drawing difficult to read. This is one of the places that art comes into play.

Note: More information about dimensioning styles using AutoCAD is provided in Chapter 17.

As discussed in Chapter 3, a set of dimensions includes dimension and extension lines along with a number indicating the length being described. The dimension and extension lines should be thin and dark yet secondary to the main object lines. The dimension line may intersect the extension lines with an arrow, a dot, or a slash (see Figure 6.22). The extension lines should not touch the object lines, and there should be approximately 1/16″ between the structure lines and the extension lines. Each dimension line should be spaced at least 3/8″ from the main object and from other dimensions to provide for easy reading. If space is available, you may want to space the lines even farther apart at 1/2″ or even 3/4″. The extension lines should extend slightly beyond the dimension lines, about 1/8″ (see Figure 6.23). The information provided for the dimensions is usually centered on the dimension line and can be placed either within a break in the line or on top of the line (see Figure 6.23). The numbers should always be aligned so they can be read from either the bottom or the side. You do not want to force your client to turn the drawing around in four directions in order to read the dimensions. Typical lettering size for a residential plan is 1/8″ letters. For architectural drawings, any dimension over 12″ is given in feet and inches with an accuracy to the nearest 1/16″. Symbols are used to indicate feet (′) and inches (″). If the measurement is less than a foot (12″), a zero is *not* used in front of the given inches.

Because walls have a certain thickness a decision must be made whether to dimension to the centerline of the wall, to one side of the wall, or to each side of the wall. Unfortunately, there is no hard and fast rule about this. It may depend on the preference of the architect, builder, or designer with whom you are working. These differences come into play mainly with frame construction. For masonry construction, each wall and each opening is dimensioned to the face of each component (see Figure 6.24). The width of the opening for every window and door is dimensioned. The overall dimensions are given to the outside of the masonry wall. The thickness of the partitions will be given on the plan view of a masonry building.

FIGURE 6.21 Floor plan with three lines of dimensions. Courtesy of Edward J. Muller, *Architectural Drawing and Light Construction.*

FIGURE 6.22

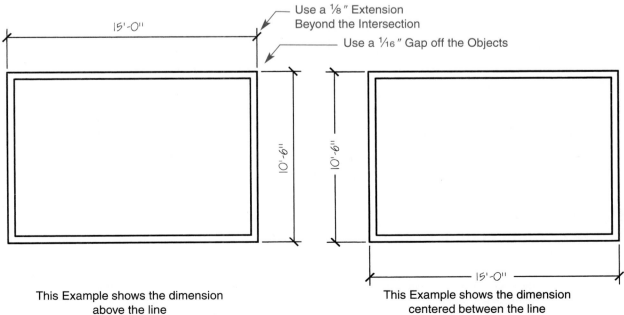

This Example shows the dimension
above the line

This Example shows the dimension
centered between the line

FIGURE 6.23　Dimensioning examples.

FIGURE 6. 24 Dimensioning masonry construction.

FIGURE 6.25 Dimensioning wood frame construction.

The overall dimension of a frame building is given to the outside of the frame or stud wall, not to the outside of any siding or brick. The most common practice is to dimension to the centerline of wall partitions (see Figure 6.25). Doors and windows are also located with a centerline dimension. The thickness of the wall is usually provided on a detail drawing. Structures with masonry veneer are generally dimensioned using the same system as frame construction.

6.8 Plot Plans, Topographic Maps, and Landscape Architectural Drawings

The drawings we discussed in the previous sections were concerned with structures. Additional drawings are required to provide information about the land on which the structure will be built. Landscape plans, topographic maps, plot plans, grading plans, site analysis plans, erosion control plans, and subdivision layouts are all examples of drawings focusing on land and land development. These plans are drawn using an engineer's scale as opposed to an architect's scale.

In some ways a topographic (topo) map is the most basic of these types of plans, but that is not to say it is the simplest. A topographic map uses contour lines to physically describe the changes in elevation on a plot of land (see Figure 6.26). All the points on a particular contour line are at the same elevation. Once you gain experience reading this type of drawing, you will quickly be able to form a mental picture of the property being portrayed. The areas where the contour lines are closest together will be the steepest sections of the site. The elevations of each contour line will be given either with reference to sea level or to a defined datum point. Spot elevations may be given at places such as the corners of the buildings, the corners of the plot, the high point of a hill, or the low point of a depression. The finished floor elevation is usually provided for structures shown on a topo. A scale of 1″=20′ is common for residential topographic plans, but other scales are used depending on the size of the plot of land being depicted. AutoCAD has become a valuable tool for mapping topographic information. Before the advent of computers, drafters spent countless hours transferring data collected in the field by surveyors onto maps.

A developer may initially use a topographic map in deciding whether to develop a site. From then on the topo provides a foundation for several other types of drawings generally known as *plot plans*. A plot plan maps a specific tract of land (see Figure 6.27). All the topographic information may be shown, or the plan may include only certain relevant elevations. Most people think of a plot plan as showing the construction plans for a specific site, but drawings such as grading plans and erosion control plans can also be considered plot plans. The grading plan for the site will provide existing and proposed contours to indicate cut-and-fill requirements for the site. Erosion control and site analysis drawings may also contain topographic information. The plot or site plan may be for a specific lot or it may cover an entire subdivision.

Information provided by a plot plan might include the following items:

- **Legal Description:** This description of the tract will be based on survey information, including items such as the lot and block number of the lot.

- **Property Lines:** The length and bearing of each property line will be given. The bearing defines the compass direction of the line with respect to a given meridian or reference line. The length of each boundary line of the property should be given to the nearest hundredth of a foot. The property lines define the shape of the lot.

- **North Arrow:** The north arrow may be referenced to true or magnetic north. The arrow may also simply be referenced to a site north.

FIGURE 6.26   A topographic map.

Existing Contour for the
Vertical Distance (Height Above Sea Level)

New Contour (A Change from the Existing Contour) for the
New Vertical Distance (Height Above Sea Level)

FIGURE 6.27 A plot plan drawing.

LINE AND CURVE NUMBER	BEARING	DISTANCE	ARC	RADIUS
1	S 48 17' 12" E	28.68'	28.68'	1153.00'
2	S 13 09' 54" W	8.63'		
3	S 03 18' 34" E	52.05'		
4	S 40 29' 52" E	49.75'		
5	S 53 15' 03" E	51.90'		
6	S 00 43' 56" E	52.68'		
7	S 29 30' 37" W	8.20'		
8	S 14 00' 28" W	56.39'		
9	S 31 55' 46" E	53.47'		
10	S 35 25' 37" W	45.24'		
11	S 27 53' 20" E	33.72'		

- **Scale:** Plot plans are drawn using engineer's scales such as 1″=10′ or 1″=20′.
- **Building Locations:** Any existing or proposed buildings on the property should be located. Decks, sidewalks, and driveways should also be shown.
- **Roads and Easements:** The width, name, and direction of any roads adjacent to the property should be provided. Any easements (or rights of way) should be noted. Setbacks should also be dimensioned.
- **Utilities:** The location of any existing or proposed utilities such as water, sewer, electric, gas, and telephone lines should be shown. Manholes and the elevation of the bottom inside of the sewer line (referred to as the INVERT EL.) will be noted on the plan. Fire hydrants should also be shown.
- **Landscape Information:** The location of existing and proposed trees may be required. A landscape plan will also include the locations for additional plantings such as shrubs, bedding plants, and lawn areas.
- **Topographic Information:** The topographic information may or may not be included depending on the requirements of the drawing.

6.9 Constructing a Floor Plan

Now that you are familiar with the symbols and abbreviations used on floor plans, it is time to begin drawing. As you construct your plan try to imagine walking through the building. Is the entryway welcoming? Does the traffic flow make sense for this design? Think about the location of the fixtures in the bath and kitchen. Walk yourself through cooking a meal. Envision getting ready for work. Will the bathroom be convenient for the people who will occupy this house? Give some thought to the door swings. Do the doors bang against each other? Do they block a critical area? Imagine possible furniture layouts. Could you make a room more livable by relocating a door or window? You do not have to consider these questions to draw a floor plan, but they can lead you to a more desirable end result.

Layout Procedure for Floor Plans

1. *Determine the size of the drafting medium.* Before you begin drawing you will need to determine the sheet size that you will be using. A number of factors come into play here. First, your firm or school may require you to use a particular size of paper. The size of the project being drawn and the scale you wish to use will also impact your decision. Because the most common scale for residential design is ¼″=1′-0″ we will use that scale for our example (see Figure 6.28).

FIGURE 6.28 Sketch of a floor plan.

KITCHEN

9'-6" x 11'-3"

BEDROOM #1

13'-0" x 15'-0"

DINING

11'-8" x 15'-4"

BATH #1

5'-4" x 5'-6"

BATH #2

5'-4" x 5'-6"

FAMILY ROOM

15'-4" x 15'-4"

BEDROOM #2

13'-0" x 15'-0"

Single-Line Layout for Two-Bedroom Apartment

- For our example we will be drawing a house with overall dimensions of 31'-6" × 38'-4". Our first step is to figure out how much room this house will take up when drawn to scale. A scale of ¼" = 1'-0" means that every foot of the full-size completed house will take up ¼" on the sheet of drawing paper. To find out how many inches the drawing will require, divide 31'-6" × ¼"/1'. The result is 7.875". The other dimension, 38'-4", divided by 4" per foot yields a result of 9.583", so the drawing of the house will require a space of 7.875" × 9.583" (7⅞" × 9⁹⁄₁₆"). But this number does not include room for dimensions. As a rule of thumb, allow at least 2" on each side of your structure for dimensions. So the final size required for this drawing will be (7⅞" + 2" + 2") × (9⁹⁄₁₆" + 2" + 2") = 11⅞" × 13⁹⁄₁₆".

- Now, choose a paper size based on the required size for the drawing, the amount of expected detail, the space needed for notes, and the standards of your firm or school. For this illustration, we will use 18" × 24" vellum. Using a top, bottom, and right border of ½" and a left border of 1½" leaves a working area on the sheet of (18" − ½" − ½") × (24" − ½" − 1½") = 17" × 22". This should leave us plenty of room for notes or details. If the working area of a sheet does not allow generous room around the drawing and dimensions, the result may be a drawing that looks crowded.

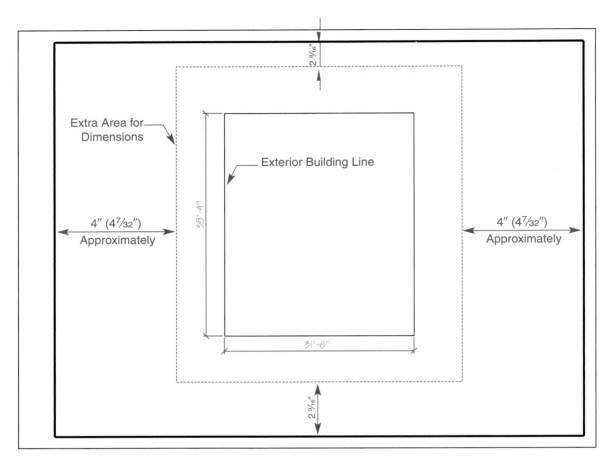

FIGURE 6.29   Layout of drawing size with borders.

2. *Center the drawing (Figure 6.29).* Unless you decide to offset the plan view to leave room for notes or other details, the next step in beginning your floor plan is to center your drawing within the working area. We have already determined that the height of the working area is 17″. The maximum height of the drawing will be 11½″. The difference between these two numbers (17′ − 11⅞″) is equal to 5⅛″ or 5.125″. Because you want to leave the same amount of space above and below your drawing, divide this number in half: 5.125″ ÷ 2 = 2.562″. Thus, the space above and below your floor plan will be 2.562″ or 2⁹⁄₁₆″. To determine the space on either side of your drawing, follow the same basic steps. The length available for drawing is 22″. The space required for the length of this floor plan is 13⁹⁄₁₆″, so the space on either side of your drawing will be (22″ − 13⁹⁄₁₆″) ÷ 2 = 4.219″ or 4⁷⁄₃₂″. When you attempt your first floor plans, you may wish to lightly draw in construction lines outlining the maximum area of your drawing. Experienced drafters will use these calculations as a guide. It is not critical that the drawing be precisely centered on the page, only that it be pleasing to the eye.

3. *Lay out exterior walls (Figure 6.30).* You are now ready to begin drawing. Using construction lines, lay out all the exterior walls. Assume a wall thickness of 6″. Using construction lines allows you to easily erase if you make a mistake. Use your architect's scale to determine the length of the lines.

Note: The space required for dimensioning was not included in this calculation.

Note: Once you begin this stage of the drawing, you can forget about actual inches and simply "live" within the world dictated by the ¼″=1′-0″ scale.

FIGURE 6.30 Layout of exterior walls.

38'-4"

31'-6"

Thicken Exterior Walls

4. *Lay out interior walls (Figure 6.31).* Continuing to use construction lines, lay out the interior walls. Assume a wall thickness of 5″.

5. *Doors and Windows (Figure 6.32).* Block out the locations for the doors and windows of your structure. This is a good time to begin considering traffic flow and furniture arrangement.

6. *Plumbing Fixtures (Figure 6.33).* Draw all plumbing fixtures such as sinks, toilets, and tubs. Your residential template will come in handy for this step.

7. *Fireplaces and Hearths.* Using construction lines, locate any fireplace openings and hearths. The house used in our example does not have a fireplace; however, typical measurements are 5′-wide single-face fireplace with a 36″ opening. The hearth is adjacent to the fireplace and extends the length of the room at a depth of 1′-8″. Add a 4″ stone veneer to the wall. Figure 6.10 shows some fireplace symbols.

FIGURE 6.31   Layout of interior walls.

Thicken Interior Walls

FIGURE 6.32   Layout of doors and windows, cabinets, and appliances.

FIGURE 6.33 Plumbing fixtures.

8. *Stairs.* Continuing to use construction lines, lay out any stairs. Draw in several 12″ treads up to a long break line. Remember to show handrails and guardrails. Since the house in example does not have a second story or a basement, no stairs are shown. See Figure 6.8 for stair plan view example.

9. *Cabinets (Figure 6.32).* Draw in any cabinets, still using construction lines. Typically, cabinets are located in the kitchen and bath, but this does not mean they cannot be located elsewhere. Standard base cabinets in a kitchen are 24″ deep, with the upper cabinets being 12″ deep. Bathroom vanities are typically 22″ deep.

10. *Appliances and Utilities (Figure 6.32).* Using construction lines, draw in any appliances and utilities. A template of residential fixtures can be used to speed up this step. Typical sizes for appliances are given in Appendix C. A more complete list can be found in *Architectural Graphic Standards.*

11. *Check layout and darken lines (Figure 6.34).* Double-check your drawing for accuracy. If you are pleased with the layout, darken in the lines. Draw in the doors and windows using the appropriate symbols for floor plans.

12. *Dimensioning (Figure 6.34).* Lay out your dimension lines around the exterior of the structure. Typically, you will use three lines of dimensions on each side. The first (or outside) line of dimensions gives the overall dimensions of the structure. The middle string of dimensions locates the interior wall. The final (or inside) string of dimensions locates the placement of doors and windows. Dimension to the exterior face of any walls between the garage and the house because of the change in foundation materials. Any dimensions that cannot be detailed along the exterior of the structure may be placed in the interior of the drawing. Use ⅛″ guidelines approximately 1⁄16″ away from the dimension lines for placing the numerals.

13. *Window and Door Sizes.* You may place window and door sizes on the drawing at this time. An alternative to this is to place symbols referencing door and window schedules (see Section 6.4).

14. *Notes.* Use guidelines to letter in any notes.

15. *Titles.* Label all rooms using 3⁄16″ spaced guidelines. The title for the drawing may either be centered beneath the drawing or placed in the title block. If the title is positioned beneath the drawing, it is usually 3⁄16″ to ¼″ high and double underlined. Complete the title block.

FIGURE 6.34 The finished floor plan.

16. *Symbols.* At this time you may add any material symbols such as brick or stone to the drawing. Some drafters prefer to shade in walls. If you chose this method, shade on the backside of the drawing to avoid smudging. Place a sheet of paper between the drawing and the board to avoid getting lead on your drafting table. See Figure 6.6 for hatching.

Second-Floor Plans

Additional floor plans are laid out in a fashion similar to that of the first-floor layout. Once you have laid out the first floor, you may be able to use that layout to begin drawing. Tape the First-Floor Plan (or a copy of the plan) to your board. Attach the new sheet on top and trace the walls that the two floors have in common.

Basement Plans may be laid out in a similar manner, or they may be included in the Foundation Plan. Be sure to take into account any differences in the thickness of the exterior walls between the basement and the main floors.

6.10 Constructing Elevation Views

Elevation views offer a glimpse into the personality of a house. Small changes can sometimes make a huge impact on a design. The next time you are in a residential neighborhood notice the fronts of the homes from a design viewpoint. Is the exterior formal or informal? Are the windows and doors placed symmetrically? Would the house have been more pleasing with larger or different windows? Do the porches and decks enhance the design? What type of material and trim was used? Years ago, builders learned that they could make a house seem completely different by changing the facade while leaving the floor plan the same. Today, there is a trend toward remodeling older homes. Updating the exterior and interior of a home can take a house from ordinary to extraordinary. Properly drawn elevation and plan views allow the client to preview any changes before construction begins.

Before you begin drawing an elevation, take a moment to visualize the overall process. Your first general step will be to lay out the basic shape of the structure. Start with the body of the building and then move on to the roof. Once the shape of the building in intact, you can begin adding in any openings such as doors and windows. Trim and siding will usually complete the picture. Add any necessary lettering to complete your drawing.

Layout Procedure for Elevation Views

1. *Determine the size of the drafting medium.* If you have already completed the plan drawings, use the same size paper for the elevation views. Otherwise, use basically the same procedure outlined in steps 1 and 2 on the floor plan instructions (see pp. 140–142). On the elevation drawings, the height and width of each elevation will determine the overall size required for your drawing.

2. *Procure the necessary information.* To begin your drawing, you will need a copy of the floor plans, foundation plans, and roof plans. If a separate roof plan has not been drawn, you will need to obtain the necessary information. Using the floor plan (Figure 6.34) as a guide, outline the outer edge of the roof. The type of roof as well as the ridges and valleys will need to be determined. For our example, we will assume a roof overhang of 24″ and a gable end wall overhang of 12″ (see Figure 6.35).

3. *Lay out the overall width of the elevation using the floor plan of the structure (Figure 6.36).* Use construction lines for this phase of the project. Partial floor plan is placed above the elevation.

- Draw a horizontal line to represent the baseline of the elevation view. This line will be at the finished grade of the structure.

- Draw lines to represent the outside edges of the building. These lines may be determined by projecting the dimension off the plan views or by measuring.

- Draw a line establishing the location of the finished floor. The type of construction being used will dictate the height of the finished floor above the finished grade.

- Draw a line representing the ceiling height above the finished floor. A ceiling height of 8′ has been typical for residential construction; however, many homes are now specifying higher ceilings, so check on this number.

- Determine the depth of the floor joists. If the depth has not been established, assume a minimum of 8″ for the purposes of drawing the elevation. The finished floor height of the second floor will be measured at the distance of the floor joists above the first-floor ceiling.

- Continue this process until you have laid out all the floors in your structure.

FIGURE 6.35 Roof plan.

FIGURE 6.36   Initial layout of building shape.

PARTIAL FLOOR PLAN

Transfer widths from the floor plan to the elevation below.

Eave Height

Ground Line

4. *Lay out the roof (Figure 6.37).* Continue to use construction lines for this phase of your layout.

- Sketch in lines showing the extent of any overhangs. For this example, the gable end wall overhang will be 12″. The overhang for the side projections will be 2′-0″ (24″).
- Now, draw in a line to represent the location of the ridge of the roof. In our example, the ridge is centered over the house.
- Your next step is to determine the height of the roof. The slope of the roof is referred to as the pitch. The height of the roof is based on the width of the structure and the pitch of the roof. Occasionally, the roof pitch will be dictated by documents such as subdivision covenants. Otherwise, the designer chooses the pitch based on aesthetics as well as structural considerations such as snow and wind loads. To draw in the first roof line, locate the intersection of the outside wall and the upper ceiling lines. Draw a line through this intersection at the angle of the roof until you reach the location of the roof ridge. This line will represent the bottom of the roof truss or rafter. Do not forget to continue the line past the outer edge of the building to the extent of the overhang.
- Draw a parallel line 6″ away from the line drawn in the previous step. This new line will represent the top of the roof truss or rafter. Unlike on section view, it is not critical that the precise depth of the roof rafter be used on the elevation view. As with the line drawn in the previous step, stop the line at the ridge of the roof and the edge of the overhang.

Note: See Figure 6.39 for an example of a callout for a roof pitch on an elevation drawing. The pitch shown is 8:12, which means that for every 12″ of horizontal run you have 8″ of vertical rise. The pitch is always given based on 12″ of horizontal run.

5. *Lay out openings in the elevation view (Figure 6.38).* Locate the line representing the finished floor height.

- Draw a construction line indicating the height of the top of your doors and windows above the finished floor. For our example, we have used a height of 6′-8″, which is common for residential construction. If you have garage doors in your house, remember that the height of a garage door is measured from the ground or grade rather than the finished floor.
- Use the floor plans and schedules to sketch in the width of any doors, windows, and skylights.
- Use the window schedule or floor plan to determine the depth of your windows. Lightly draw a line across the bottom of you window opening.
- Skylights provide a different challenge. Their height will be provided in the window schedule; however, they are usually installed in the slope of the roof. To illustrate them properly you must figure out how this height will project onto the horizontal. See Figure 6.38 for an illustration of this procedure.

6. At this point you have reached a milestone in your construction: You have blocked out the basic overall shape of one side of your structure. Your next phase will be to follow this same procedure for the other sides of the building. The information that you gathered in preparing your first elevation view will make drawing the rest of the elevations easier.

FIGURE 6.37 Developing the eaves and roof line.

FIGURE 6.38 Layout of openings in structure with sketch of skylight.

FIGURE 6.39 Finished elevation.

7. *Draw in finish-quality lines (Figure 6.39).* So far, you have used construction lines on all your linework. Once you have laid out the outline of the structure, the roof, and any openings you are ready to darken in these lines to a finish quality. Remember to follow the instructions given in Chapter 3 about working from the top to the bottom of your drawing.

8. *Draw in any trim or siding that is to be shown (Figure 6.39).*

9. *Draw in any deck, porches, or posts that should be shown.*

10. *Draw in roofing material symbols.*

11. *Letter any information that is required on the elevation view (Figure 6.39).* Typically, information such as roof pitch, siding and roofing material, flashing, and eave, window, and door heights as well as an overall view of the exterior is provided on the elevation views.

12. *Repeat steps 7 through 11 for each elevation that needs to be drawn.*

6.11 Drawing Interior Elevations

Interior elevations are drawn using a procedure similar to that used for exterior elevation views. Of course, with interior elevations you are concerned with ceiling heights but not the roof lines. The following example uses a kitchen elevation, since that is one of the most common types of interior elevations. The cutting plane for each elevation will be shown with symbols on the plan view. Imagine that you are standing in front of the wall looking in the direction indicated by the arrows on the plan view.

Depending on the degree of detail required, you may draw the interior elevation at the same scale as the floor plans or at a larger scale such as ⅜″ = 1′-0″ or ½″ = 1′-0″. Based on the scale chosen, determine the amount of space that will be required for your interior elevation view. Interior elevations are often placed with other types of drawings such as details or plan views.

Layout Procedure for Interior Elevations

1. Use the information provided on the floor plan to determine the dimensions of your view. Use construction lines to outline the length of the wall you are drawing. If the scale is the same for both the interior elevation and the plan view, you may transfer the dimensions directly from one drawing to the other (see Figure 6.40).

2. Determine the height of the wall from the finished floor to the ceiling. Using construction lines, draw two horizontal lines to represent the ceiling and the floor. For example, if the ceiling height is 8′, draw the two lines 8′ apart (using the appropriate scale) (see Figure 6.41).

FIGURE 6.40 The plan view relating to interior elevations.

Partial Kitchen Floor Plan

Imaginary Vertical Cutting Plane

Project lines down from the plan view to generate widths.

Choose a finished floor line

KITCHEN ELEVATION

FIGURE 6.41 Initial layout of interior elevation.

Cutting Plane

9′ Ceiling Ht. Option

8′ Ceiling Ht.

Top of Cabinet.

54″ Cabinet Bottom Ht.

36″ Cabinet Ht.

Floor Line

KITCHEN ELEVATION

3. The cutting plane of your elevation comes into play at this point. In our example, the cutting plane runs across the width of the kitchen. Imagine that you have sliced open the kitchen at this point (see Figure 6.40). The cabinets, shown in the plan view, continue around the corner. That means that in "cutting" open the kitchen you would expose the inside of a portion of the cabinet. Hatch this portion of the cabinet in the interior elevation to indicate a cut surface. Another way to look at this is to think about standing in the middle of the kitchen. As you look at the wall in front of you what do you see? Along most of the wall you see the fronts of cabinets and drawers, but at the corner, the cabinetry turns the corner and you can see only the cabinets coming toward you.

4. Using construction lines, lay out the features of the cabinets such as doors, drawers, and appliances. Also draw in features such as windows, backsplashes, and doors that would be seen from the vantage point of the cutting plane (see Figure 6.42).

5. Once you have laid out all the features of the interior elevation, darken the cabinet lines. Hidden items such as sinks and shelves can be indicated with a dashed line (see Figure 6.42).

6. Add any dimensions and notes to your drawing. (see Figure 6.43). The amount and quantity of information provided on the interior elevation will vary with the purpose of the drawing. The heights and widths of each cabinet and component may be shown. In some offices, cabinets are dimensioned with inches or millimeters only. Occasionally an interior elevation is drawn simply to provide a feel for the look of a room or element. In this case, only minimal dimensions are provided.

Follow this same procedure for any additional interior elevations. Figure 6.43 shows a completed elevation for the kitchen shown in the plan view in Figure 6.40. Figure 6.44 illustrates an interior elevation for a bathroom area. The basic procedure will work for all interior elevations whether they are of a kitchen, a bath, millwork such as built-in bookshelves, or other areas of a structure (see Figure 6.45) in Exercise 6.1.

PARTIAL KITCHEN PLAN

KITCHEN ELEVATION

FIGURE 6.42   Layout of cabinet features.

KITCHEN ELEVATION

FIGURE 6.43   Finished interior elevations.

FIGURE 6.44 Bathroom elevations and plan view.

QUESTIONS

1. Describe the difference between presentation and working drawings.
2. List the types of drawings that are typically found in a complex set of plans.
3. What is the most common scale used for residential drawings?
4. Define the term *elevation view*.
5. How many elevation views would a typical house have? Is this number of views always provided? Why?
6. List seven types of information typically found on an elevation view.
7. What type of line should be used to show features that are below grade?
8. Why would an interior elevation be used with a set of drawings? Name the two rooms most often shown with an interior elevation.
9. Define the term *plan view*.
10. List five types of information typically found on a plan view.
11. What is the purpose of General Notes?
12. What is a schedule? What type of information might be included on a schedule?
13. Name three types of schedules often found in a set of drawings.
14. What is the difference between a detail drawing and a section drawing? Include a definition of each type of drawing in your answer.
15. What is a framing plan? What information is typically provided on a framing plan?
16. Sketch three ways to show the intersection between dimension and extension lines.
17. In typical frame construction, should you dimension to the outside edge of the stud wall or to the outside edge of the siding?
18. Is an engineer's scale or an architect's scale more commonly used on plot plans, landscape plans, and topographic maps?
19. What do the contour lines on a topographic map show?
20. List nine types of information typically found on plot plans.

EXERCISES

EXERCISE 6.1
Draw the cabinet sketches in Figures 6.45a and b at a $\frac{3}{8}'' = 1' - 0''$ scale.

EXERCISE 6.2
Draw a plan view and elevation of the furniture in Figure 6.46 at a $\frac{3}{8}'' = 1' - 0''$ scale.

FIGURE 6.45   Exercise 6.1.

ELEVATION A

(a)

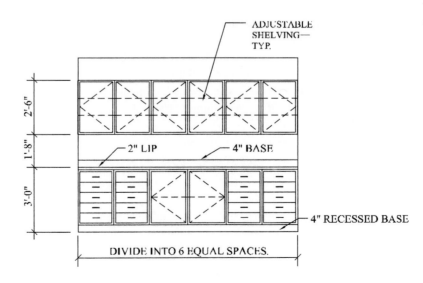

ELEVATION B

Scale: 1/4" = 1'-0"

NOTE: PROVIDE PLASTIC LAMINATE
ON ALL EXPOSED WOOD SURFACES.

PROVIDE LOCKS ON ALL DOORS AND DRAWERS.

(b)

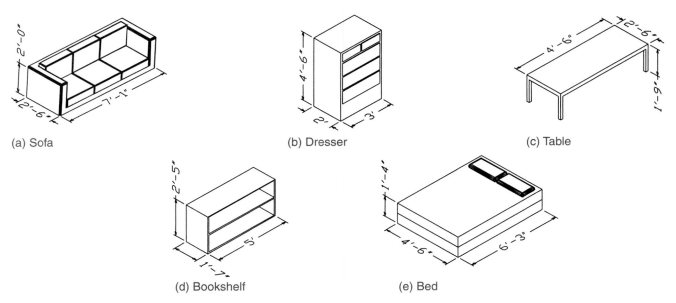

(a) Sofa

(b) Dresser

(c) Table

(d) Bookshelf

(e) Bed

FIGURE 6.46 Exercise 6.2.

DRAWING ASSIGNMENTS

1. Draw the elevations in Figure 6.47 using the scale shown.

2. Draw the plan views in Figure 6.48 using the scale shown.

3. Draw the two-bedroom apartment floor plan from the single-line layout in Figure 6.49. Use ¼ ″ = 1′-0″ scale and dimension the plans. Approximate room sizes are given. Use 4″ thickness for the walls and use 31′-6″ × 3′-0″ for the outside dimensions.

4. Draw the kitchen plan and interior elevation A in Figure 6.50. Use ½″ = 1′-0″ scale and place it on a 24″ × 36″ sheet. After completing elevation A, draw elevation B on your own. Match the existing style.

5. Draw the given master bathroom plan and interior elevation A in Figure 6.51. Use ½″ = 1′-0″ scale and place it on a 24″ × 36″ sheet. After completing elevation A, to draw elevation B on your own.

6. Use your finished floor plan from assignment 3 and construct a front elevation of what the apartment would look like if it was a duplex. Use a 3′-0″ × 6′-8″ door and 2′-8″ × 5′-0″ windows. Lay out an eave height of 8′–6″.

7. Using bathroom plan A from assignment 2, draw an interior elevation looking at the counter.

FIGURE 6.47   Drawing Assignment 1.
continued on next page

ELEVATION A

Scale: 1/ 4" = 1'-0"

ELEVATION B

Scale: 3/ 16" = 1'-0"

ELEVATION C

Scale: 3/16" = 1'-0"

ELEVATION D

Scale: 3/16" = 1'-0"

FIGURE 6.47 *continued*

PLAN A

Scale: 1/4" = 1'-0"

TOILET
BATHROOM
SINK
TUB
12" SEAT
3'-6"
SHOWER
SINK

Use a 4" thickness for your walls. Research the dimensions that are not given. Look in the *Architectural Graphic Standards* or a manufacturer's catalog.

PLAN B

Scale: 1/4" = 1'-0"

WALK-IN CLOSET
WALK-IN CLOSET
MASTER BATH

KITCH.
FAMILY ROOM
BEDROOM 1
CLOSET
CLOSET
BEDROOM 2
BATH

VACATION SUITE PLAN C

Scale: 1/4" = 1'-0"

FIGURE 6.48 Drawing Assignment 2.

TWO-BEDROOM APARTMENT

FIGURE 6.49 Drawing Assignment 3.

KITCHEN PLAN
Scale: 1/2" = 1'-0"

KITCHEN ELEVATION
Scale: 1/2" = 1'-0"

FIGURE 6.50   Drawing Assignment 4.

<u>MASTER BATH PLAN</u>
Scale: 1/2" = 1'-0"

<u>MASTER BATH ELEVATION</u>
Scale: 1/2" = 1'-0"

FIGURE 6.51   Drawing Assignment 5.

○ ○

Pictorial Drawing and Sketching

Learning how to draw and sketch pictorials is one of the most fun parts of drafting. It can be quite rewarding visually to draw something that looks three dimensional (3-D). Time and practice are required to be proficient at pictorial drawings. If you struggle somewhat in the beginning and your instructor comes over and makes it look easy, take a deep breath and remember that your instructor has done these drawings a few hundred times. The power of practice and knowing the concepts of the drawing will empower you one day.

7.1 Axonometric Drawing

The three types of axonometric drawings were explained in Chapter 5. An isometric drawing has three equal isometric axes. A dimetric drawing has two equal axes, and a trimetric drawing has three different angles (see Figure 7.1).

Isometric drawing is one of the most popular pictorials used in drafting. It becomes fairly natural to most people after a short time. Recall the isometric example from Chapter 5.

Steps for Drawing Isometrics

Step 1. When drawing an isometric object, you need a scaled orthographic drawing from which to take measurements (see Figure 7.2).

Step 2. Draw the vertical line located where the three isoaxes intersect (see Figure 7.3 and the isometric example in Figure 7.1). This is needed to view your object looking at the top or bottom.

Step 3. Using a 30°-60°-90° triangle go the bottom of the vertical line and draw your length along the right side at a 30° angle (see Figure 7.4). Then go back to the bottom of the vertical line and draw the width along the left side at a 150° angle (see Figure 7.5).

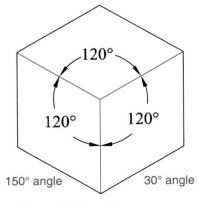

Isometric Example

Iso interior angles are true to scale and highlighted in blue.

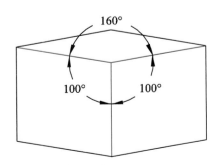

Dimetric Example

Any two angles can be equal to form a dimetric. Scale along axes can be adjusted.

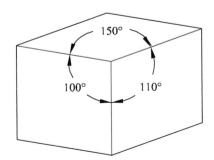

Trimetric Example

All three interior angles must be different to form a trimetric. Scale along axes can be adjusted.

FIGURE 7.1 Isometric, dimetric, and trimetric examples.

FIGURE 7.2

41'-0"

20'-0"

Plan View

8'-0"

10'-0"

Front Elevation

FIGURE 7.3 Orthographic drawing of a building.

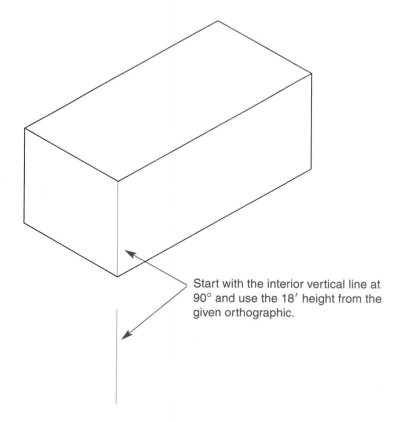

Start with the interior vertical line at 90° and use the 18' height from the given orthographic.

FIGURE 7.4 Isometric construction.

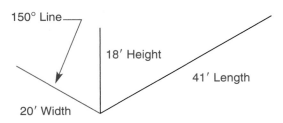

FIGURE 7.5 Isometric construction.

Step 4. Go to the end of the 30° angled line and draw an 18'-tall vertical line on the far right end (see Figure 7.6). Then go to the end of the 150° width line and draw another 18'-vertical line on the far left end (see Figure 7.7).

Step 5. Go to your interior vertical line and connect from its endpoint a 30° line along the right-hand side going to the end of the vertical line on the right-hand side (see Figure 7.8). Now, go back to the interior vertical line and do the same thing going to the left (see Figure 7.9). At this point you see the walls or sides being established.

Step 6. Starting at the top of the right-hand vertical line draw a line using a 150° angle back to the left (see Figure 7.10). Now, go to the top of the left-hand vertical line and draw a line at 30° going back to the right, finishing off the top vertical surface (see Figure 7.11). When drawing or sketching isometrics always lay out the overall box to be constructed and draw within it.

FIGURE 7.6 Isometric construction.

FIGURE 7.7 Isometric construction.

FIGURE 7.8 Isometric construction.

FIGURE 7.9 Isometric construction.

FIGURE 7.10   Isometric construction.

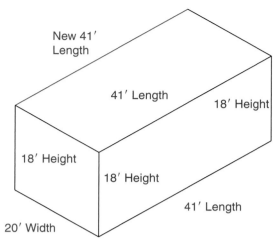

FIGURE 7.11   Completed iso box. The iso box is constructed with the overall length, width, and height. All angles are formed with angles of 30°, 90°, and 150°.

Step 7.   Once the overall box is finished, it is time to start measuring within the box using the iso box lines (see Figure 7.12). Start from the bottom and work your way up going from side to side. Then go to the vertical lines and measure across the 150° line and get the width dimensions (see Figure 7.13). *The key is always to measure along the iso lines for your width and lengths (see Figure 7.14). Always measure heights along the vertical lines (see Figure 7.15).*

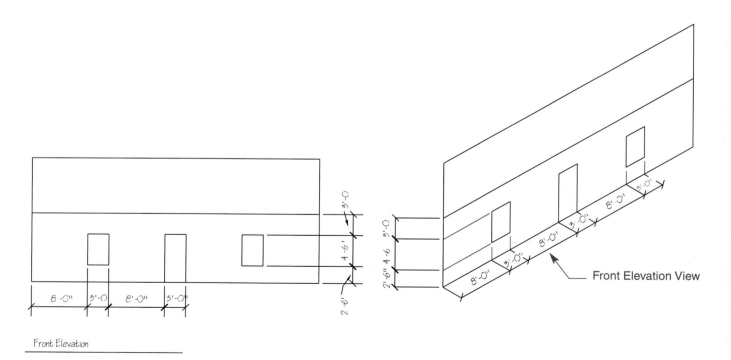

FIGURE 7.12   Iso house I. Laying out the front elevation on the iso drawing. Note that all measurements are taken along the iso axes when transferred from the orthographic.

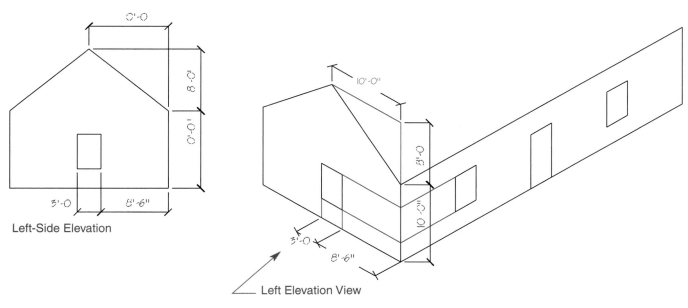

Left-Side Elevation

Left Elevation View

FIGURE 7.13 Iso house II. Laying out the left side elevation on the iso drawing.

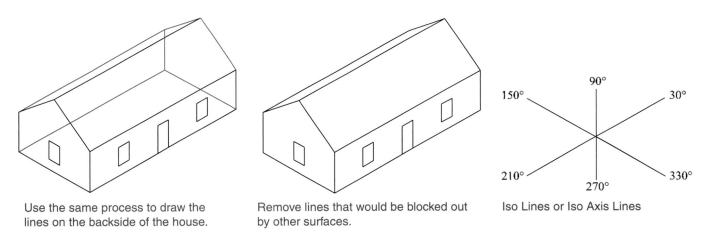

Use the same process to draw the lines on the backside of the house.

Remove lines that would be blocked out by other surfaces.

Iso Lines or Iso Axis Lines

FIGURE 7.14 Finished iso house.

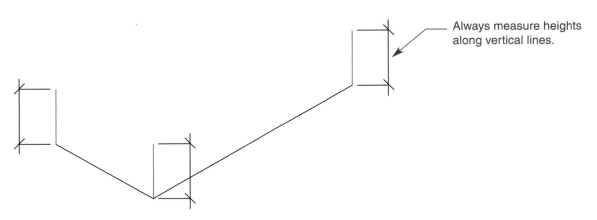

Always measure heights along vertical lines.

FIGURE 7.15 Iso vertical line.

Nonisometric Lines

In an isometric some lines will not fall on or be parallel with the isometric lines. When this happens you must plot out the nonisometric line, finding its endpoints based off the isometric lines (see Figure 7.16). In the previous example the roof had to be done this way.

Figure 7.16 shows how nonisometric lines are drawn. It is a matter of plotting out the endpoints and connecting the points with lines (see Figure 7.17).

Now, let's look at an example of a hip roof that also requires an additional point to plot (see Figure 7.18). Using the same technique as shown on the earlier example, plot the left side (see Figure 7.19).

In general, pictorial drawings do not show any centerlines or hidden or construction lines in the final drawings. Sometimes it is necessary to draw them in during the construction of visible lines.

One thing that tends to give students a problem in pictorials is changing directions around corners. The next drawing will use corner 2 as the starting point to start the construction of the isometric.

An Example of Plotting out Corners on an Isometric Drawing (see Figure 7.20)

Step 1.   Draw a vertical line for corner 2 first using the height measured from the front or side view (see Figure 7.21). This will be our starting reference line.

Step 2.   Draw a 30° and 150° line off the bottom endpoint of corner 2 (see Figure 7.22).

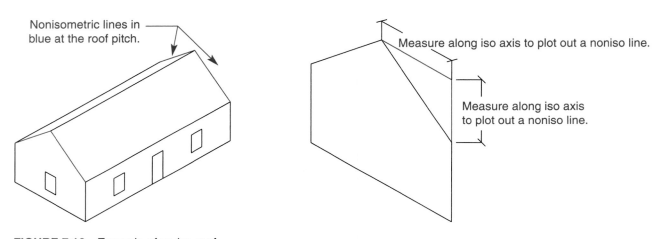

FIGURE 7.16   Example of an iso roof.

FIGURE 7.17   Iso roof plot.

Get this distance to plot it on the isometric view.

Hip example has two new points that need to be plotted out.

Plan View of Roof

Side Elevation

Front Elevation

Hip roof noniso lines need to be plotted out.

FIGURE 7.18   Hip roof in isometric form.

Extra Step for a Hip Roof Iso Layout

A new measurement will be taken along the other iso axis to generate the slope of the hip roof. Get the measurements or dimensions from the given orthographic views.

Measure along iso axis.

Measure along iso axis.

Construct the same way as in the previous example.

Connect the corners to the new additional points.

FIGURE 7.19   Hip roof iso plotting method.

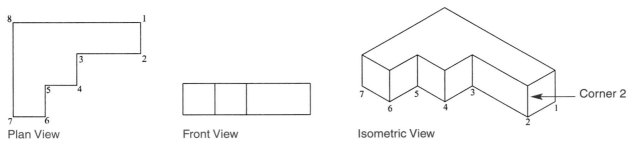

Plan View

Front View

Isometric View

Corner 2

FIGURE 7.20   Iso corner ortho.

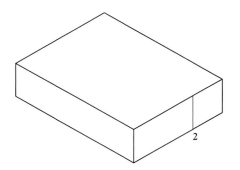

FIGURE 7.21   Take the overall dimensions and construct an iso box.

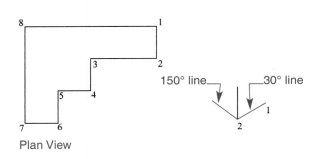

FIGURE 7.22

Plan View

Step 3.   Measure where corner 1 will be drawn along the 30° line going toward the right side, then take a 150° line from the bottom of corner 2 and draw it back to the left, stopping at the measured distance from the top view (see Figure 7.23).

Step 4.   Now, draw a line going 210° from corner 3 heading to the left. Stop at the distance measured from the orthographic for corner 4 taken from the plan view (see Figure 7.24). Continue on to corner 5 by drawing a 150° line from corner 4. The base is being laid out first, which is the best way to learn (see Figure 7.25). Going to corner 6 is just a matter of starting from corner 5 and drawing a 210° angled line back down toward the left (see Figure 7.26). Find-

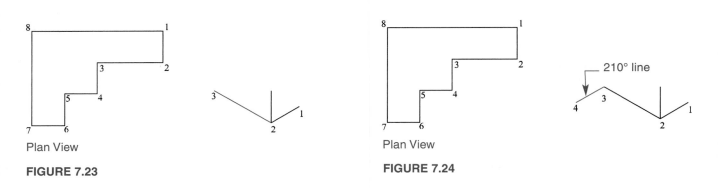

Plan View

FIGURE 7.23

Plan View

FIGURE 7.24

FIGURE 7.25

Plan View

FIGURE 7.26

Plan View

FIGURE 7.27

FIGURE 7.28

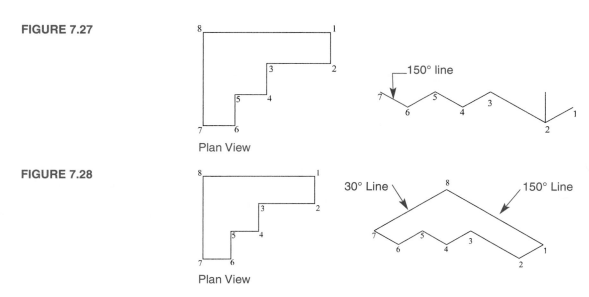

ing where corner 7 will be is just a matter of drawing a 150° line upward toward the left using the distance measured off the plan view (see Figure 7.27). The final corner, 8, can be found by drawing a 30° line from corner 7 and a 150° line from corner 1 and intersecting the two lines to complete the base (see Figure 7.28).

Step 5. With the base completed, go to each corner and draw the vertical lines at 90°. Use the height from the front orthographic view for the correct distance (see Figure 7.29).

Step 6. The top position is left to complete. It is easy to go to each top corner and simply connect the top ends with lines parallel to the base (see Figure 7.30). After the top lines are drawn, go back and erase the baselines on the back side (see Figure 7.31).

FIGURE 7.29   **FIGURE 7.30**

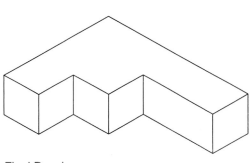

Final Drawing

FIGURE 7.31   Completed iso example.

Distortion does occur in isometrics. Do not be fooled just because your dimensions along the axis are true to scale. The iso lines sloped at 120° each create a 3-D look but also cause distortion. Circles are distorted into ellipses and require special techniques to be drawn. This topic will be covered later for all pictorials. The same principles can be applied to each one.

Dimetric Drawing

In dimetric drawing, the central angles are set up so that two of them are equal (as explained in Chapter 5). Any two can be equal, but the three added together must sum to 360° (see Figure 7.32).

The philosophy behind using a dimetric instead of an isometric is that changing the angle measurements allows the drafter to emphasize a certain side with the unequal angle and can reduce some of the distortion on that surface. Full or the true scale may be used and applied to the desired surface. The other surfaces with the sharper angles are drawn at reduced scales. Different drafters use a variety of scales such as ½, ⅝, or even ¾. It is not an exact science; sometimes trial and error is the only way to find the scale that looks the best (see Figure 7.33). Except for setting up the new angles and scales, you repeat all the steps and principles used in isometric drawing for dimetric drawing.

Trimetric Drawing

The final axonometric, known as a trimetric, uses three unequal central angles and allows the drafter to choose the scales along the angled lines (see Figure 7.34). Thus, trimetric puts a lot of control in the drafter's hands to find a good view. As with the dimetric, the versatility found in the trimetric is designed to reduce distortion and give a more realistic view. Once the angles and scales are set, the drawing principles of a trimetric copy that of the isometric and dimetric.

Considering the distortion created with an isometric view, you may wonder why the isometric is very popular and why the other two axonometrics are seldom used. The answer lies in the drafter's tools and equipment. The isometric has all the tool benefits over the other two. The 30°-60°-90° triangle draws all the iso lines for quick iso drawing (see Figure 7.35). Even the drafting arms and machines are set up to lock

FIGURE 7.32   Dimetric example.

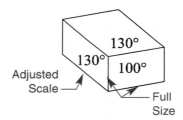

FIGURE 7.33   Dimetric example adjusted scale.

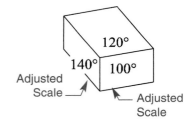

FIGURE 7.34   Trimetric example.

FIGURE 7.35   Isometric triangle example.

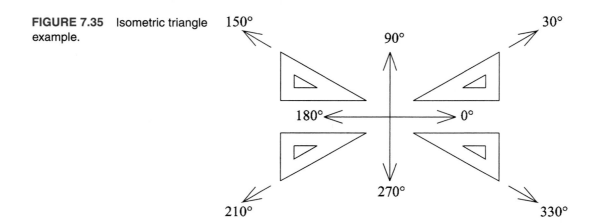

every 15°, which works well with iso drawing. The AutoCAD program also favors isometric lines. An Auto-CAD operator can turn on an isogrid, which sets up an automatic iso environment for easy drawing.

Another advantage of isometrics is the isometric templates used for drawing elliptical circles in iso form. The templates are the fastest way to draw iso ellipses on the drawing board, and they come in a wide range of sizes. AutoCAD can draw iso circles or ellipses quickly and easily if the isogrid is turned on. It can even change from a horizontal ellipse to left vertical to right vertical with the touch of a key on the keyboard (see Figure 7.36).

Axonometrics can be drawn in a variety of forms. They can be exploded or assembled (see Figure 7.37). Sections can be cut through them (see Figure 7.38). The viewing positions can be shifted to many ori-

FIGURE 7.36 Isometric cube with ellipses.

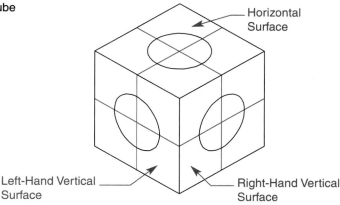

Horizontal Surface

Left-Hand Vertical Surface

Right-Hand Vertical Surface

FIGURE 7.37 Isometric exploded and assembled.

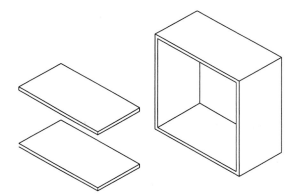

Assembled Isometric of a Bookshelf

Partial Exploded Isometric of a Bookshelf with the Shelves Out

FIGURE 7.38 Isometric section at a footing.

Looking Down on
the Top Surface

Looking Up at the
Bottom Surface

Looking at the Right
Surface

Looking at the Left
Surface

FIGURE 7.39   Isometric views of a cube.

entations (see Figure 7.39). Given the different options of viewing, most people still tend to visualize better looking down on objects.

7.2 Oblique Drawing

As discussed in Chapter 5, oblique drawing combines a true flat 2-D surface with an angled distorted surface (see Figure 7.40). Just as with the axonometric, there is flexibility in adjusting the scales on the distorted or stretched surface. As seen in Figure 7.41, there are three types of obliques:

1. Cavalier style uses true scale for the depth.
2. Cabinet style uses half the true scale for the depth.
3. General style allows the drafter to adjust the depth scale as needed to reduce distortion.

Drawing an oblique begins with deciding which surface will be drawn true and which one will be distorted. The obvious answer to this question is to take the most complex side and put it on the true surface or shape and to place the simpler side on the angled surface. This approach works fairly well except with some rare exceptions when the appearance of the depth is too distorted (see Figure 7.42). Then a good drafter or designer tries to adjust the depth scale to make the drawing more realistic. Other options the drafter has are to change the angle of the sloped side The angles used for oblique drawing as a rule are between 30° and 60°. The three commonly used angles are 30°, 45°, and 60°. Once again the drafting equipment is geared toward making these angles easily with the 30°-60°-90° triangle, 45°-45°-90° triangle, and the ability of the drafting

FIGURE 7.40   Oblique example.

Front and rear surfaces
are true shapes.

Distortion occurs along
the angled surface.

Full Depth

Cavalier Oblique

Half Depth

Cabinet Oblique

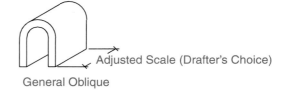

Adjusted Scale (Drafter's Choice)

General Oblique

FIGURE 7.41   The three types of obliques.

FIGURE 7.42   House oblique.

Oblique with a good
proportion at the depth

Oblique with a lot of
distortion at the depth

FIGURE 7.43

Oblique with
a 30° angle

Oblique with
a 45° angle

Oblique with
a 60° angle

arms/machines to lock every 15°. In AutoCAD, using a 30° angle will give the drafter a little bit of an edge. An iso setting will allow an AutoCAD operator to draw 30° lines quickly with this iso mode turned on (see Figure 7.43).

The following are some steps and strategies to use when learning to draw an oblique.

Step 1.   Get two scaled orthographic views or elevations and select the view to be drawn on the flat surface and the one to be placed on the angled surface. Construct an oblique box using the overall dimensions from your orthographic views. Most drafters start off trying a 30° angle for the sloped surface along with using the cavalier style oblique in order to use the same scale for all surfaces (see Figure 7.44). If the drawing is not looking quite right, you may want to construct a box using a cabinet or general style.

FIGURE 7.44   House orthographic with oblique setup.

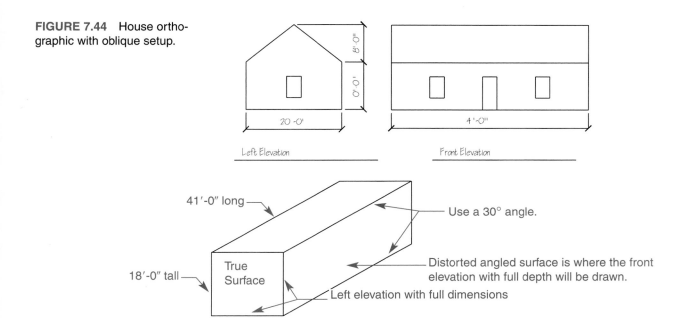

8'-0"

0'-0"

20 -0'

4 '-0"

Left Elevation

Front Elevation

41'-0" long

Use a 30° angle.

True
Surface

Distorted angled surface is where the front
elevation with full depth will be drawn.

18'-0" tall

Left elevation with full dimensions

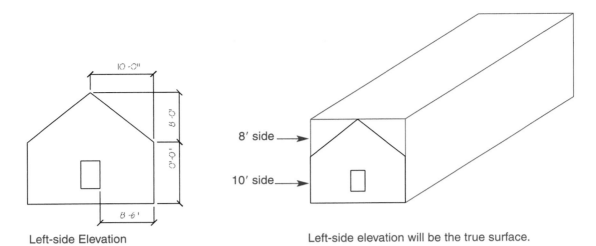

FIGURE 7.45   Oblique showing true surface.

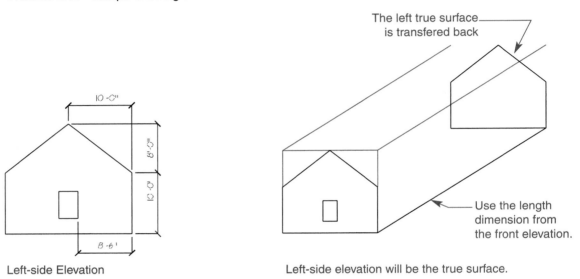

FIGURE 7.46   Oblique transferring back surface.

Step 2. Once the overall box is laid out with construction guidelines start drawing the true view inside the box (see Figure 7.45). If there are other true surfaces parallel to the front, drop back along the angled base line for the depth setback, then draw the true surface at its new position (see Figure 7.46).

Step 3. Now that the 2D surfaces are laid out, go to the angled surface and connect endpoints between the true surfaces (see Figure 7.47). Erase lines as you need to. As you develop the drawing you will want the drawing to appear solid, so eliminate lines that make the view look hollowed out (see Figure 7.48).

Step 4. Take your orthographic view and measure the lengths needed for plotting out the lines on the angled surface (see Figure 7.49). Then measure on the vertical edge to get the height set correctly. Use lines parallel to the angle on the bottom and draw them angling across the sloped surface (see Figure 7.50).

This technique is the same one used in axonometrics found earlier in the chapter. To get the best looking drawing possible, do not darken the visible lines until everything is laid out and correct. This will help keep you from smearing and having to erase mistakes that were darkened prematurely. Some drafters will erase their construction lines on a pictorial to make the drawing look as much like a real picture as possible.

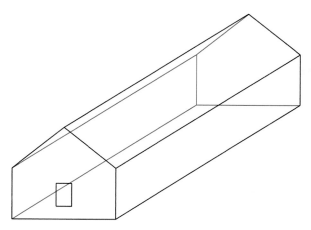

FIGURE 7.47 Oblique transferring distorted surface.

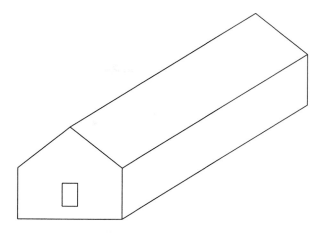

FIGURE 7.48 Oblique with wireframe line removed.

Front Elevation

FIGURE 7.49 Oblique laying out windows.

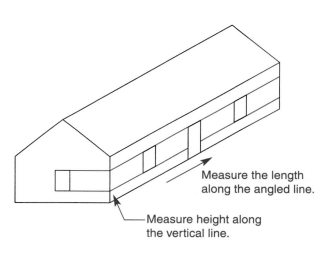

Measure the length along the angled line.

Measure height along the vertical line.

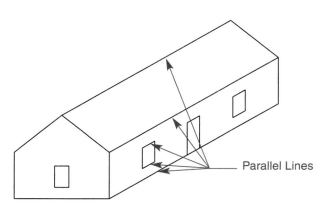

Parallel Lines

FIGURE 7.50 Oblique showing parallel lines.

FIGURE 7.51　Oblique show-ing hip roof layout.

Plan View

Hip points must be measured from here and then plotted out on the oblique drawing.

Front Elevation

Plotting Out the Hip
Measure along the angle line to find the hip point.

Connect points to draw the hip roof.

Looking down at the top with the angle going up to the left

Looking down at the top with the angle going up to the right.

Looking up at the top with the angle going down to the left

Looking up at the top with the angle going up to the right

FIGURE 7.52　Oblique views of box.

　　　Lines that are not parallel to the oblique box must be measured and plotted out just like the noniso lines in an isometric drawing. Measure the height needed on the true view and then the depth along the slope surface (see Figure 7.51). The possible viewing layouts for an oblique drawing are shown in Figure 7.52.

Circles in Pictorial Drawing

The only true circles in pictorial form exist on the 2-D surface of an oblique or in a 3-D computer-generated drawing. Due to the angles generated in pictorial drawing, circles are transformed into ellipses (see Figure 7.53). Isometric ellipses are drawn in two forms: isometric drawing and isometric projection. In true isometric drawing the ellipse diameter is measured along the isometric axis (see Figure 7.54). This is the easiest and most common one used in drafting because measuring with the iso axis keeps the scale uniform throughout the drawing. Isometric projection is not used as often. This technique allows you to measure the diameter along the horizontal line (see Figure 7.55). This alters the drawing scale along the iso axis by approximately 20%.

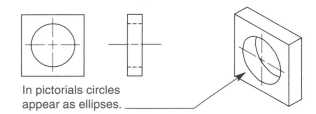

In pictorials circles appear as ellipses.

FIGURE 7.53　Circle in orthographic and isometric forms.

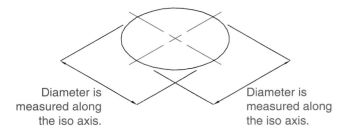

Diameter is measured along the iso axis.

Diameter is measured along the iso axis.

FIGURE 7.54　Ellipse in Isometric Drawing form.

Diameter is measured
along here.

FIGURE 7.55 Example of isometric projection. Notice that the ellipse is reduced by 20% when the projection method is used.

FIGURE 7.56 Isometric templates.

Ellipses can be drawn either way by using one of the following four methods.

1. *Templates.* Templates for isometric drawing or projection can be used for drawing ellipses (see Figure 7.56). Using templates is the preferred method because of the speed and accuracy. Just make sure you are using the correct template for drawing versus projection. Look at the template and see if it reads "dimensions refer to isometric axes." If it does, it is an isometric drawing template.

2. *Four-Center Method.* The four-center method requires a compass.

Step 1. Use a 30°-60°-90° triangle to construct the isometric box. All four sides are as long as the ellipse's diameter. Place tick marks at the midpoints (see Figure 7.57).

Step 2. Draw some construction lines from the midpoints to the vertex of the wide angles (see Figure 7.58).

Step 3. Where the lines cross will give two of the four centers required. Use these intersections as centers to draw the first two arcs using the compass. Stop when you hit the midpoints (see Figure 7.59).

Step 4. Draw the final two arcs from the big angles. Insert the compass needle at the intersection of the big angle and open the compass until it tangents the two arcs on the other side. The method is not that accurate; the ellipse is shorter (see Figure 7.60).

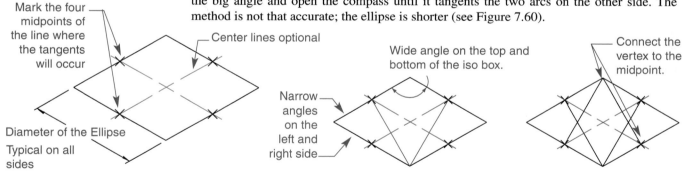

Mark the four midpoints of the line where the tangents will occur

Center lines optional

Diameter of the Ellipse
Typical on all sides

FIGURE 7.57 Isometric projection.

Wide angle on the top and bottom of the iso box.

Narrow angles on the left and right side

Connect the vertex to the midpoint.

FIGURE 7.58 Isometric projection.

FIGURE 7.59 Isometric projection.

FIGURE 7.60 Isometric projection.

Two center points as marked

Using the two centers, draw an arc until it hits the tangent point or midpoint of the line.

Use the corners of the 120° angles as the centers to complete the ellipse. Draw the arc from tangent to tangent.

179

3. *Plotting from the Orthographic Using X and Y Coordinates.* Plotting out the ellipse will require a scaled drawing in orthographic form, a French curve, and drafting triangles.

Step 1. First, take the orthographic and divide the circle into 15° segments. (The more you divide it, the more accurate the plot will be.) Also label the horizontal axis X and the vertical axis Y (see Figure 7.61).

Step 2. Lay out the X and Y iso axes on the iso box. Measure the radius distance on all four axis lines (see Figure 7.62a). Get the measurements from the orthographic drawing and plot them along the iso X and Y axes. Follow the arrows.

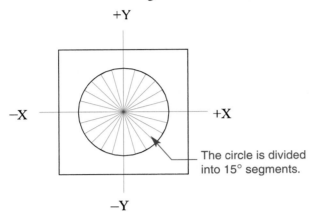

The circle is divided into 15° segments.

FIGURE 7.61

Ortho Layout

Iso Layout

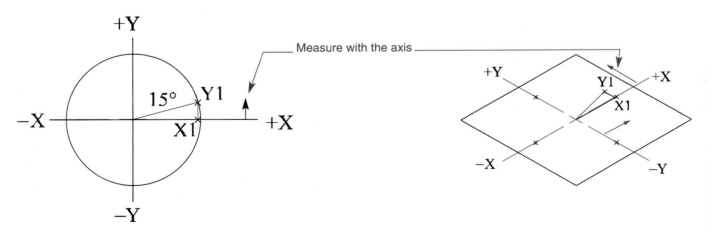

(b)

FIGURE 7.62 Isometric ellipse plotting.
continued on next page

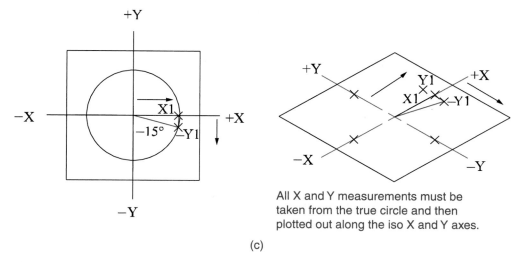

All X and Y measurements must be
taken from the true circle and then
plotted out along the iso X and Y axes.

(c)

FIGURE 7.62   *continued*

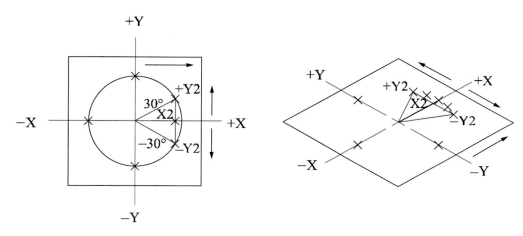

FIGURE 7.63   Circle and isometric plotting points.

Step 3.   Go to the orthographic and draw a line from the intersection point where the 15° angled line
meets the circle down to the X axis. Once you have the X1 and Y1 measurements, go to the iso
box and plot the 15° intersection measurement along the iso X and Y axes (see Figure 7.62b).

To save time go ahead and measure the Y1 in the negative direction (see Figure 7.62c).

Step 4.   Repeat Step 3 for the 30 ° intersection point (see Figure 7.63).

You need to plot out every increment to give you enough points to use a French curve to connect the ellipse (see Figure 7.64). To make a smooth ellipse takes a good set of plotted points and running your French
curve through as many points as possible to get a continuous smooth arc.

4. *Grid Method for Plotting Ellipses.* The grid method is very similar to the X and Y coordinate plotting method. It requires an orthographic drawing from which to measure. A grid is laid out on the
orthographic drawing and then the same grid is drawn in isometric form on the pictorial (see Figure 7.65). Basically, you transfer the points where the circle intersects the grid boxes on the orthographic drawing, then reproduce the same grid in isometric form locating the intersection points
on the boxes by measuring or visually approximating the distances.

Step 1.   Draw the circle in orthographic form. Choose the size the little grid boxes should be. The
smaller the circle, the smaller the grid boxes should be. (Just as in the previous method, the

FIGURE 7.64 Plotted points form an ellipse pattern.

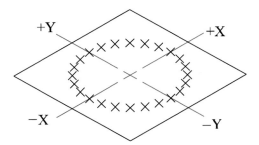

FIGURE 7.65 Isometric grid method part 1.

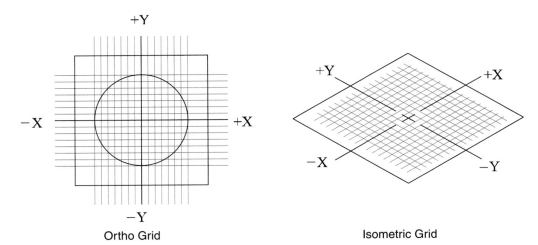

Ortho Grid

Isometric Grid

FIGURE 7.66 Isometric grid method part 2. Locating the quadrants on the X and Y axes.

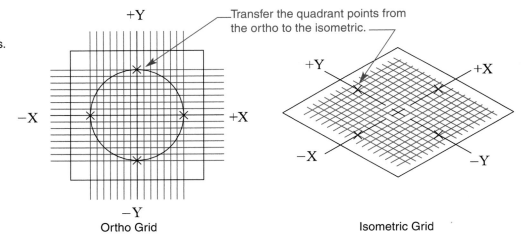

Transfer the quadrant points from the ortho to the isometric.

Ortho Grid

Isometric Grid

more points you have to construct the ellipse with the more accurate the ellipse will be.) (See Figure 7.66.) Lay out the isometric axes, X and Y, and divide the boxes using the same distances found and the orthographic.

Step 2. Start out on the end of the X axis and mark a point on the grid box where the circle intersects it, then move to the isometric drawing and count out the same number of boxes used on the orthographic and place a mark at the corresponding grid box (see Figure 7.67).

Step 3. Move up or down to the next row of boxes and measure from the orthographic the next intersection points. Go to the isometric drawing and measure where the intersection points would occur on the isometric grid (see Figure 7.68). Once this row is complete, continue on to the next rows, repeating this sequence for every row until all the intersecting points have been plotted out (see Figure 7.69).

The grid method can be used to plot out any shape. It is not normally used on regular ellipses because templates are much faster to use on predictable shapes. Irregular shapes on flat surfaces and irregular shapes

FIGURE 7.67 Isometric grid method part 3. Placing points where the circle intersects the grid.

Ortho Grid

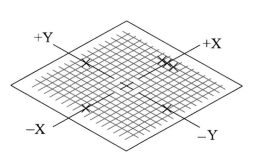

Isometric Grid

FIGURE 7.68 Isometric grid method part 4. Points completed.

Ortho Grid

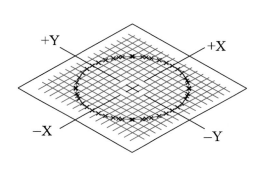

Isometric Grid

FIGURE 7.69 Completed ellipse. Connect the points to form the ellipse.

Ortho Grid

Isometric Grid

Ortho Grid   Isometric Grid

FIGURE 7.70   Plotting isometric curves from an orthographic.

on irregular surfaces can be drawn fairly easy using the grid method or even the X and Y plotting technique (see Figure 7.70). Using grids is not limited to isometric drawing but can be used in all the pictorials, especially the ones that do not have time-saving templates.

7.3 Perspective Drawing Basics

Structured perspective drawing began two thousand years ago and was initially based on some of Euclid's geometric principles. The evolution of perspective drawing has spawned different techniques. If you watch several skilled designers draw a perspective of an object it is quite possible that each one will use a different method. This book demonstrates the technique called the *plan method*. It is a technique that is fairly easy to understand after a few tries.

The plan method can be used for one-point, two-point, and three-point perspectives. Each one of these perspectives will be demonstrated using a basic setup to help build a foundation and understanding for a beginner.

Perspective Drawing Setup and Definitions

Phase I: Setting Up a Plan View with the Picture Plane

Step 1.   First, on a small sheet of paper at the scale of your choice, draw a plan view (top view) of the object to be drawn in perspective form. Next, on a large sheet of paper draw a horizontal line near the top representing what we will label as the picture-plane line (see Figure 7.71).

Step 2.   Pick a point on the picture-plane line and draw a line at a 30° angle. Lay a front corner from your plan view on the corner where the 30° line touches the picture plane line. Put the

FIGURE 7.71   Start of perspective drawing.

FIGURE 7.72   Alignment for two- and three-point perspectives.

FIGURE 7.73   Alignment for one-point perspectives.

FIGURE 7.74   (a) Example of a two- and three-point perspective. (b) Example of a one-point perspective.

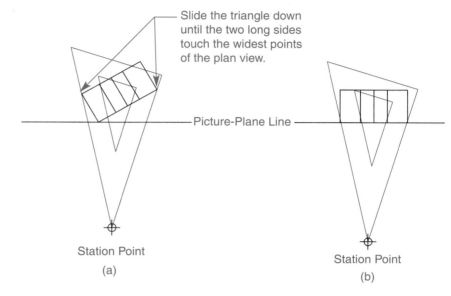

Slide the triangle down until the two long sides touch the widest points of the plan view.

Picture-Plane Line

Station Point
(a)

Station Point
(b)

longest side of the plan view (or the side you want to emphasize) along the 30° line and tape it down (see Figure 7.72). If a one-point perspective was desired, then the plan view side would be placed on top of the picture plan line (see Figure 7.73).

Step 3.   Choose a station point (the distance the viewer is standing away from the object) (see Figure 7.74). To cut down on distortion, most instructors will have beginning students use a 30°-60°-90° triangle to set the station point location.

Timeout for Definitions and Analysis

Definitions:
  A. The plan view is the top view of your object.
  B. The picture plane is similar to a viewing window or the film in a camera. It defines the surface where it will be seen by the viewer. The objects tend to taper to a smaller size (see Figure 7.75).

Analysis: The plan view can be located in a variety of positions on the picture plane (see Figure 7.76). For a beginner, it is much easier to put the front corner for a two-point or for a three-point perspective on the picture plane. For one-point perspective, it is easier to put the front of the object on the picture-plane line. Your instructor can change this setup when you are ready for advanced work.

Note   The actual distance from the picture plane line to the ground line has no scale to it and is not important to the perspectives. It is important that you have a long triangle or drafting machine that can draw vertically from the picture plane to the ground line.

Phase II: Setting Up Ground and Horizon Lines
  Step 1.   Drop down below the picture plane line toward the bottom of the large sheet. Draw a horizontal line across the sheet that is parallel to the picture-plane line. This will be your ground line (see Figure 7.77).

  Step 2.   You have the following three choices or options when drawing the next line, which will represent the horizon line. This horizon line will be parallel to the ground line, and the distance for the ground line will be a scaled measurement.

FIGURE 7.75   Example of a picture plane.

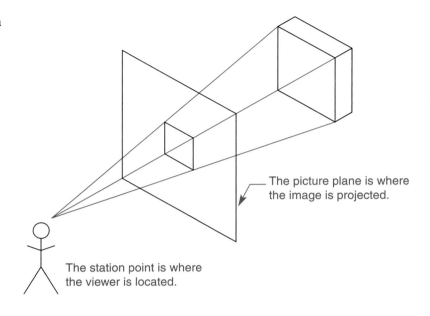

The picture plane is where the image is projected.

The station point is where the viewer is located.

Picture-Plane Line

Back corner touching

Plan view floating off the picture-plane line

Picture-Plane Line

FIGURE 7.76   Object and picture-plane locations.

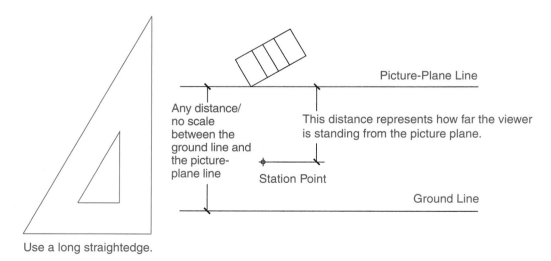

Picture-Plane Line

Any distance/ no scale between the ground line and the picture-plane line

This distance represents how far the viewer is standing from the picture plane.

Station Point

Ground Line

Use a long straightedge.

FIGURE 7.77   Perspective with picture-plane line and ground line.

FIGURE 7.78 Perspective with bird's-eye view.

FIGURE 7.79 Perspective with person's-eye view.

1. *A bird's-eye view* is obtained by placing the horizon line high above the ground line. Measure the height desired, 30' or higher works well (see Figure 7.78).
2. *A person's-eye view* is obtained by placing the horizon line around 5' to 6' above the ground line. This height is supposed to give a view that an average person would see standing on the ground (see Figure 7.79).
3. *A worm's-eye view* is obtained by placing the horizon line well below the ground line. The purpose of a worm's-eye view is to see the bottom of the object. The farther down the horizon line is placed the more of the base will be seen by the viewer (see Figure 7.80).

Step 3. Draw a front or side elevation (at the same scale as the plan view) of the object on a small sheet and tape it down on top of the ground line, aligning the bottom with the ground line (see Figure 7.81).

At this point the setups will look similar to Figure 7.82.

FIGURE 7.80 Perspective with worm's-eye view.

FIGURE 7.81 Perspective with elevation.

Example of a One-Point Perspective at the End of Phase I

Example of a Two-Point Perspective at the End of Phase I

FIGURE 7.82 Perspective, phase I.

Phase III: Getting the Vanishing Points and the True-Height Line

Step 1. The true height is determined when the plan view touches the picture-plane line. Draw a line straight down from this point and stop when it intersects the ground line (see Figure 7.83).

Step 2. (Go to step 3 if you are setting up a two-point layout.) When placing the vanishing point in a one-point perspective, draw a line through the station point and stop when it intersects the horizon line (see Figure 7.84). This is where your vanishing point is located, and it is always on the horizon line. This is the basic layout for a one-point perspective. Step 3 will show you the complete two-point layout.

Step 3. In a two-point perspective the vanishing points require a little more work. Transfer the 90° angle on the plan view down to the station point, and extend the lines to the picture-plane line, shown in Figure 7.85 as points A and B.

Step 4. Draw vertical lines straight down from points A and B until they touch the horizon line. These new points represent the left and right vanishing points on a two- and three-point perspective. Adding a third vanishing point will be shown when the three-point method is demonstrated later.

Figure 7.86 shows the completed setup needed to start drawing a perspective. Use this format for your perspective drawing. One-point perspectives work well for a lot of interior drawing or when you desire to converge the elements of the drawing to a single vanishing point. (This tends to give an oblique effect.) The two- and three-point perspectives work well for more of a realistic effect.

Example of a One-Point Perspective
Showing the True Height Line

Example of a Two-Point Perspective
Showig the True Height Line

FIGURE 7.83   Perspectives with true-height line.

FIGURE 7.84   Perspectives finding one vanishing point.

FIGURE 7.85 Perspectives finding two vanishing points.

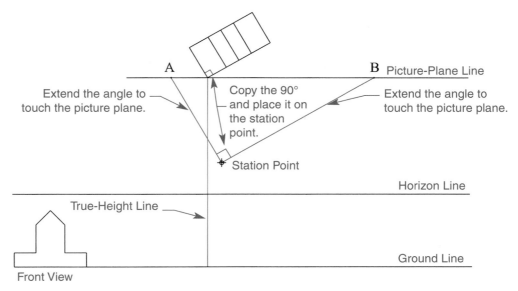

FIGURE 7.86 Completed two-point perspective layout.

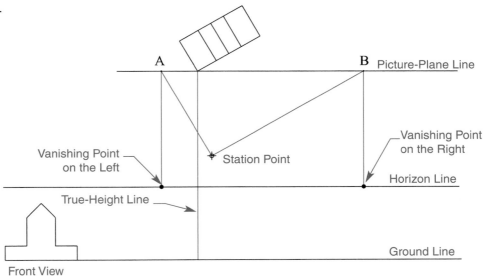

The following examples will use these abbreviations:

GL—ground line

PP—picture-plane line

HL—horizon line

VP—vanishing point

SP—station point

TH—true-height line

One-Point Perspective Example (see Figure 7.87)

Step 1. Draw a plan view and elevation on separate 8½″ × by 11″ sheets. Get a big sheet (17″ × 22″) and lay out the picture-plane line, ground line, and horizon line. Use a scale of ⅛″ = 1′-0″ as a minimum choice (see Figure 7.88). Tape the plan view sheet down on a picture-plan line. Next, tape the elevation down on the ground line (see Figure 7.89).

FIGURE 7.87   Isometric of floor plan.

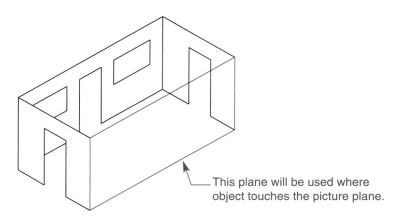

This plane will be used where object touches the picture plane.

FIGURE 7.88

All windows are 3′ × 5′.

All openings are 3′ × 7′.

Floor Grid

Plan view

All windows are 3′ × 5′.

Front Elevation

PP

Use a 5′-0″ distance here for a person's-eye view.

HL

GL

FIGURE 7.89   One-point perspective setup.

Tape down your plan view and elevation here.

PP

HL

GL

FIGURE 7.90 One-point perspective finding the station point.

Step 2. Locate the station point. This example will put the viewer 8′ away from the picture-plane line and slightly to the left of the building's center (see Figure 7.90).

Step 3. Next, locate the true-height lines by passing a line through the front corners that touch the picture plane straight down until it intersects the ground line. Note that heights can be measured only off the true-height line (see Figure 7.91).

Step 4. Find the vanishing point by drawing a vertical line through the station point and intersecting the horizon line (see Figure 7.92).

Step 5. The setup is complete, and it is now time to start drawing the perspective. It works well to start at the bottom and work your way up, laying out the walls first. Go to where the ground line and the true-height line intersect. These are your two outside corners (see Figure 7.93).

FIGURE 7.91 One-point perspective finding true heights.

FIGURE 7.92 One-point perspective finding vanishing point.

FIGURE 7.93 One-point perspective finding base of wall.

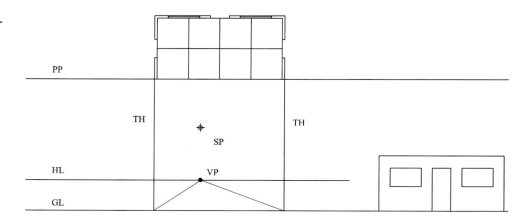

FIGURE 7.94 One-point perspective finding ceiling line.

Step 6. From the ground line draw lines from points 1 and 2 back to the vanishing point. Now go to the elevation and project a horizontal line from the top of the wall over to the true-height lines (see Figure 7.94).

Step 7. Starting at the top points on the true-height, draw lines back to the vanishing point (see Figure 7.95).

Step 8. To find the back wall go to the plan view's back corners labeled 3 and 4, and draw a line from the station point to these corners crossing the picture-plane line. From these intersections, labeled A and B, draw vertical lines straight down, crossing the tapering lines (see Figure 7.96).

FIGURE 7.95 Taking walls to the vanishing point.

FIGURE 7.96 Locating back corners.

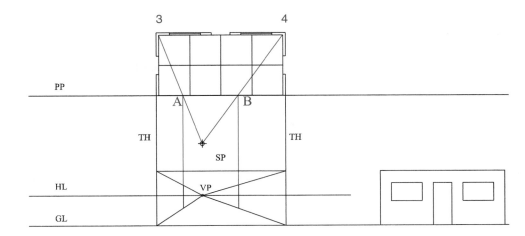

FIGURE 7.97 Locating back wall.

Step 9. These two lines represent the back corners on the one-point perspective. To finish up the back floor and ceiling lines connect the bottom points as well as the top points with a straight line (see Figure 7.97). Now, erase the inside lines that should disappear behind the back wall (see Figure 7.98).

Step 10. To draw the big tile floor follow the same pattern. Go to the plan view and draw the vertical lines straight down from the picture-plane line to the ground line (see Figure 7.99).

Step 11. The vertical lines mark where the grid will start on the ground line. Simply draw from these intersections back to the vanishing point (see Figure 7.100). (Remember to erase the lines that disappear behind the back wall.)

Step 12. To get the horizontal grid line go to the plan view, locate the intersection with the left wall, and draw a line from this point back to the station point. Where it crosses the picture-plane line draw a vertical line down to the bottom left wall in the perspective drawing (see Figure 7.101). Connect the bottom points with a straight line to complete the floor grid.

Step 13. Next, you are going to lay out the heights for the doors and windows on the true-height lines. Draw horizontal lines from the elevation that shows the height of the doors and windows (see Figure 7.102).

FIGURE 7.98 Darkening back wall.

The overall room size is now outlined.

FIGURE 7.99 Floor grid part I.
Transferring grid from the picture
plane to the ground line.

Transfer the floor lines
down to the ground line.

FIGURE 7.100 Floor grid part II.
Drawing the grid from the ground
line to the vanishing point.

Draw the line from the ground
line back to the vanishing point.

Trim out where the floor
hits the wall.

FIGURE 7.101 Drawing the
horizontal grid line.

Connect the points
with a line.

FIGURE 7.102 Getting door and window height #1. (Height on the side walls.)

Transfer window and door height to true-height lines.

Transfer window and door height to true-height lines.

Draw from the true-height line intersections to the vanishing point.

FIGURE 7.103 Getting door and window height #2. (Height on the back wall.)

When the lines hit the back corners the lines will go horizontal along the back wall.

Once the heights are established on the true-height line, draw lines from those intersections to the vanishing point (see Figure 7.103).

Step 14. By now you may have realized that the plan view is needed to find the vertical lines that belong with the perspective shown in Figure 7.105. Using the plan view, go to each corner on the doors and windows and draw a line from there to the station point, passing the lines through the picture plane (see Figure 7.104).

Step 15. The intersection points along the picture-plane line can be projected down with a vertical line to form the openings on the door and windows (see Figure 7.105).

Erasing lines when they are no longer needed can make it easier to see the perspective. Perspectives are not complicated once you have mastered the system because so much is repetition that can be picked up quickly.

Two-Point Perspective Example (see Figure 7.106)
If you use the two-point setup method shown earlier in this chapter, a basic setup should look like Figure 7.107.

Step 1. Lay out the bottom of the object first. Find the outside corners in the plan view and draw a line from the corners to the station point, passing the lines through the picture-plane line

FIGURE 7.104 Locating corners of door and window #1. (Drawing from the corners through the station point.)

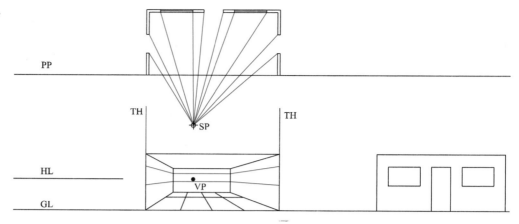

FIGURE 7.105 Locating corners of door and window #2. (Transferring the corners from the picture plane to the floor line.)

Erase the extra lines so that the doors and windows are clearly defined.

Final Drawing

FIGURE 7.106 Plan and elevation for two-point perspective.

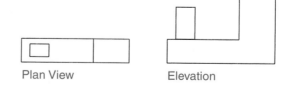

Plan View　　　Elevation

FIGURE 7.107 Two-point perspective layout.

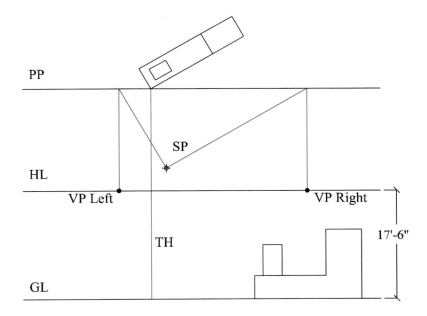

FIGURE 7.108 Drawing a line from the station point to the corners.

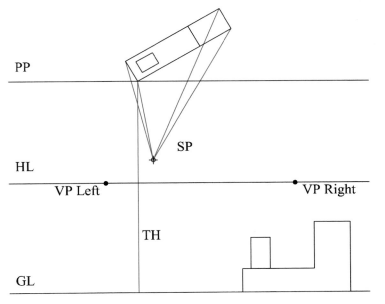

(see Figure 7.108). Project these intersection points on the picture-plane down with vertical lines to the ground line (see Figure 7.109).

Step 2. The corner that touches the picture-plane line in the top view is also where the corner touches the ground line in the perspective part of the drawing. Use this intersection on the ground line to start boxing out the base by drawing lines back to the vanishing points (see Figure 7.110).

Step 3. Go to the plan view and locate the box shape with the little rectangle inside it. Draw lines from the corners back to the station point, passing through the picture plane. Use these intersections to draw vertical lines down to locate the corners in the perspective (see Figure 7.111).

Step 4. On the elevation drawing, transfer the height of the box across to the true-height line. Take the point where it intersects the true-height line, and vanish it to the left vanishing point and then to the right vanishing point (see Figure 7.112).

FIGURE 7.109   Transferring vertical lines.

FIGURE 7.110   Finding the base.

FIGURE 7.111 Darkening the base.

These vertical lines projected down will form the corners when they cross the lines that vanish.

Start here where the true-height line touches the ground line. Vanish to the left point, then repeat to the right vanishing point.

FIGURE 7.112 Drawing level 2 height.

These vertical lines projected down will form the corners when they cross the lines that vanish.

Start here, where the true-height line touches the height from the elevation.

FIGURE 7.113 Showing changing direction at corner. (Vanishing to the left.)

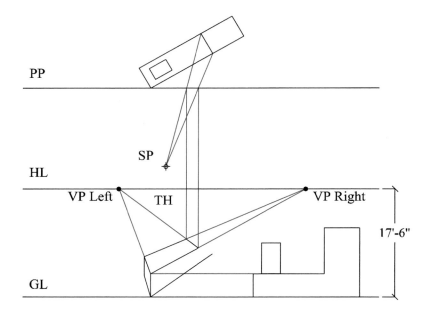

When the vertical lines are intersected, you must vanish back to the other vanishing point to make the change of direction (see Figure 7.113). (This is very similar to changing directions in isometric drawing but instead of going from a 30° line to a 150° line where a corner stops, you go from the left vanishing point to the right vanishing point.)

Note: The most common error made is transferring the height from the true-height line along the lines that follow the vanishing points. Sometimes you must do a little work to find the right height at the right location. A good example appears in the final part of our drawing.

Step 5. Repeat steps 3 and 4 for the highest box on the object (see Figure 7.114).

Step 6. The final part of drawing is the minitower coming out of the middle part of the object. The best way to find the correct location is to use a grid on the plan view (see Figure 7.115). This grid needs to be redrawn on the perspective part of the drawing, but it must be transferred down just like every other point. This requires repeating the steps of going to the plan view and drawing lines from the corners back to the station point and crossing the picture-plane line (see Figure 7.116). Once you have done this, use vertical lines to transfer down the locations of the corners. When you have brought the four points down, vanish them back to the correct vanishing points to form the grid (see Figure 7.117).

FIGURE 7.114 Showing top level.

FIGURE 7.115 Grid minitower plan view. (Extend lines to intersect the outside edge.)

FIGURE 7.116 Transferring points to station point.

FIGURE 7.117 Grid on perspective.

Note: In the beginning, some students have a problem knowing which vanishing points to use. It is helpful to look at the line in the plan view. If it is angling to the right side, then it goes to the right vanishing point; if it angles to the left, then it will vanish to the left point (see Figure 7.118).

Step 7. Now that the base of the minitower is complete, it is time to find the top grid. Go to the elevation and transfer the height of the minitower to the true-height line. Once you have done this, vanish this intersection to the left and right vanishing points, crossing the vertical lines to locate the grid placement (see Figure 7.119). Vanish the four points where vertical lines intersect at the top level to form your grid. Connect the bottom corners to the top corners of the grid with vertical lines. Your minitower as well as your two-point perspective is complete (see Figure 7.120).

FIGURE 7.118   Comparing plan with perspective.

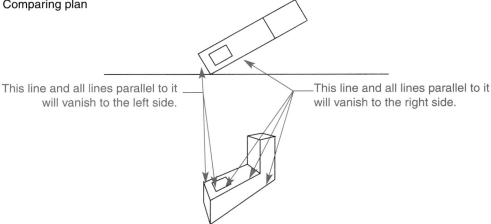

This line and all lines parallel to it will vanish to the left side.

This line and all lines parallel to it will vanish to the right side.

FIGURE 7.119   Grid top of tower.

PP

HL

SP

VP Left

VP Right

TH

GL

FIGURE 7.120   Complete two-point perspective.

Three-Point Perspective Example

The steps used to draw a three-point perspective are the same as in the two-point example except once the object is drawn, a third vanishing point is added so some shade and shadow lines can be drawn to give the perspective drawing a little more life.

Figure 7.121 is a typical completed two-point perspective drawing with the standard setup. Making the third vanishing point is a matter of positioning where you want the sun (or a light source) to cast shadows on your drawing. In this example, we will place it in the left-hand sky (see Figure 7.122). Now, using the sun's location draw a vertical line straight down, intersecting the horizon line. This will be the third vanishing point (see Figure 7.123).

Remember that all the vanishing points will fall on the horizon line. The third vanishing point will be used in combination with the sun location to generate the shadow outline, using the following steps.

FIGURE 7.121 Three-point perspective setup.

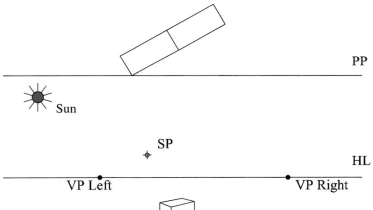

FIGURE 7.122 Three-point perspective showing sun.

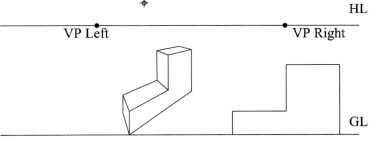

FIGURE 7.123   Finding the
third vanishing point.

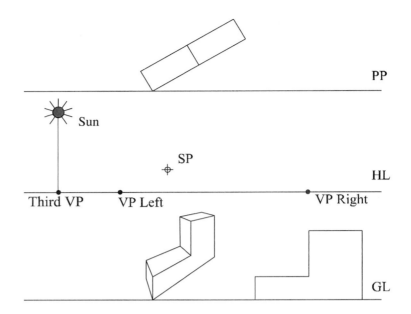

Step 1.   The backside corners have been labeled to help you follow this example (see Figure 7.124).
First, draw a line from the third vanishing point through point A (see Figure 7.125).

Step 2.   Draw a straight line from the sun through point B, intersecting the last line you drew (see
Figure 7.126).

Step 3.   Draw a line from this intersection to the right vanishing point (see Figure 7.127).

Step 4.   Go back to the sun and draw a line from it through point C. At this intersection go to the
third vanishing point and project the line forward (see Figure 7.128).

Step 5.   Draw a line from the sun through point D, intersecting the previous line (see Figure 7.129).

Step 6.   Draw a line from this intersection to the right vanishing point (see Figure 7.130).

Step 7.   Draw a straight line from the third vanishing point through point F, intersecting the last line
drawn (see Figure 7.131).

This completes the shadow's outline for the object. Most drafters hatch the inside with lines that are
parallel to the lines drawn with the third vanishing point (see Figure 7.132). The shadow is the shape caused
by the object when the light source shines on it. The shadow is cast on the ground or some other object. The
shade falls on the object itself, so light is blocked out on that side. Simply draw lines parallel to the vertical
ones shown on the object to hatch the shade.

FIGURE 7.124   Adding letters
to corners.

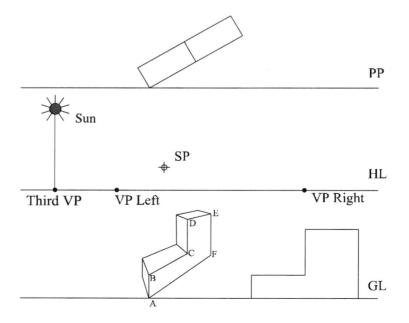

FIGURE 7.125 Drawing a line from the third point to point A.

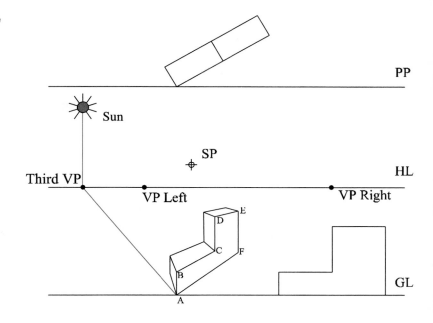

FIGURE 7.126 Drawing a line from the sun to point B.

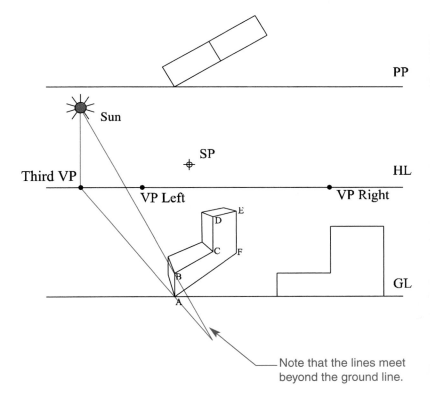

Note that the lines meet beyond the ground line.

FIGURE 7.127   Taking the intersection to the right vanishing
point.

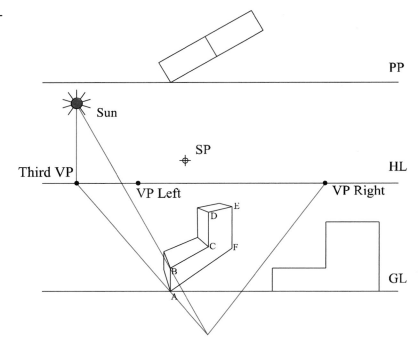

FIGURE 7.128   Drawing a line
to the sun through point C and
third point through C.

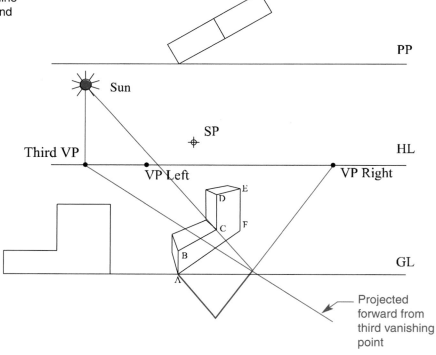

FIGURE 7.129 Drawing a line to the sun through point D.

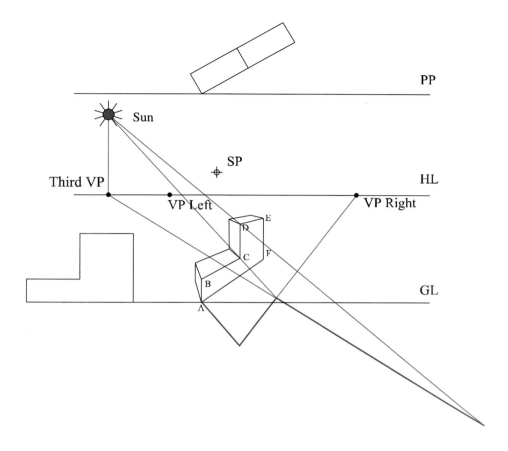

FIGURE 7.130 Taking the intersection point to the third vanishing point.

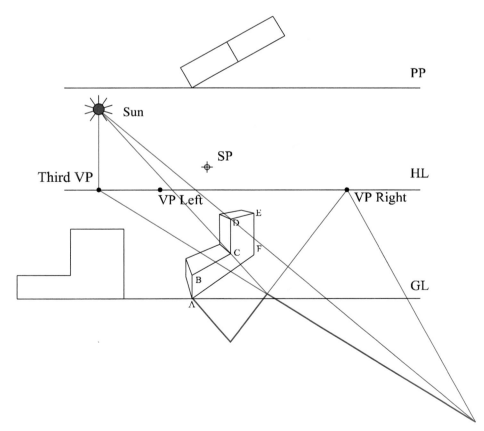

FIGURE 7.131 Completed three-point perspective.

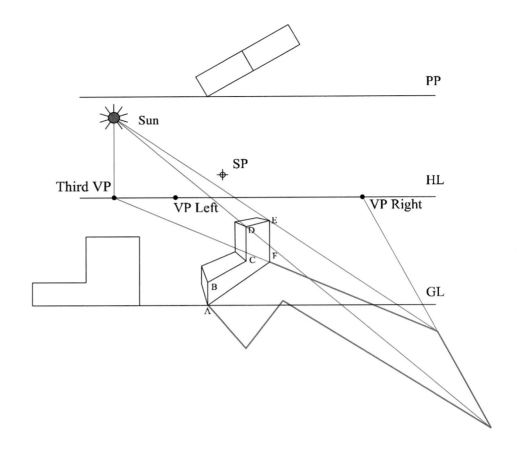

FIGURE 7.132 Drawing shade and shadow.

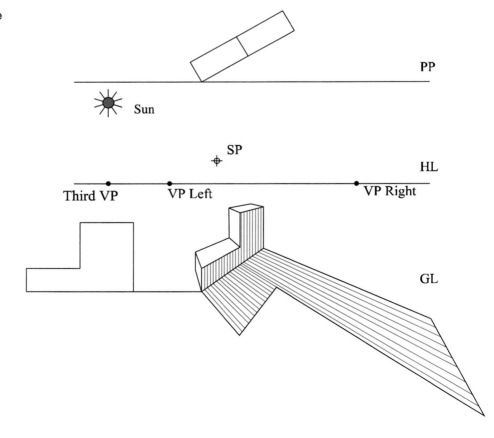

FIGURE 7.133 Circle divided into 15′ segments.

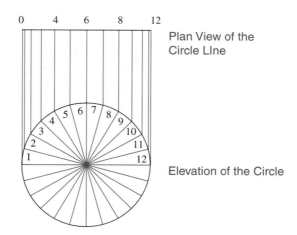

Plan View of the Circle LIne

Elevation of the Circle

Circles in Perspectives

There is no magical template for drawing circles or ellipses for perspectives. Positioning perspectives can vary so much that there is no easy out when drawing circles in perspective form. In perspective drawing, circles take the form of ellipses just like in axonometrics. In this case, two methods are very similar for constructing the elliptical shapes.

The first method involves drawing the circles in the elevation view and the plan view. Once the circles are drawn, divide the circle into 15° segments in the elevation view, then transfer the intersection points onto the plan view (see Figure 7.133).

At this point insert the views into the standard perspective setup at the location required in the plan view and elevation. The procedure at this point is the same for any perspective. Plot the points needed from the plan view and elevation, forming the outline in perspective form (see Figure 7.134). When you have plotted out enough points, use a French curve to connect the points to form the ellipse.

The other method is the grid method. It is done in the exact same order as the previous method and uses a similar technique. The difference is that the grid spacing determines the points to be plotted (see Figure 7.135).

FIGURE 7.134 Perspective plotting of circle.

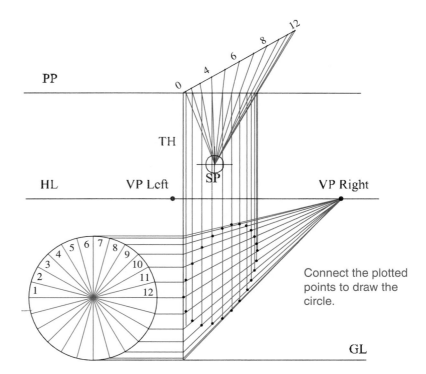

Connect the plotted points to draw the circle.

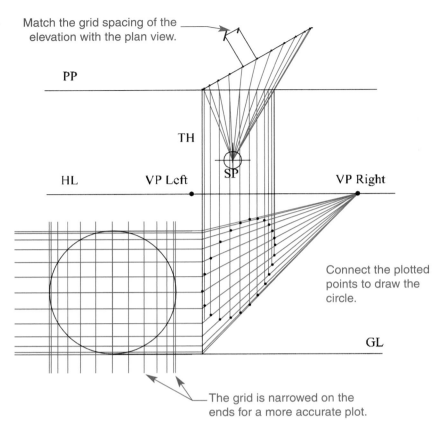

FIGURE 7.135   Perspective of gridded circle.

Match the grid spacing of the elevation with the plan view.

Connect the plotted points to draw the circle.

The grid is narrowed on the ends for a more accurate plot.

Sketching Pictorials

The techniques for sketching pictorials follow the same general guidelines used in technical drawing as discussed in Chapter 4.

As a drafter, the temptation to sketch like an artist becomes greater when it comes to pictorials. The pictorials are artistic, but do not allow yourself to get trapped into sketching like an artist unless you are one. A pictorial can be treated exactly like other sketches as a way to communicate and explain ideas.

Here is a review of sketching guidelines:

1. Draw visible lines with continuous strokes.
2. Do not use templates.
3. Use blue lead for plotting points, construction layout, and boxing out shapes.
4. Use grided vellum pads if needed.

Special isometric grid paper is available for sketching. The blue guidelines are set to 30°, 150°, and 90° angles. The iso boxes that are on the gird are not proportional vertically to the other directions. You cannot count boxes when trying to stay in scale vertically because of this discrepancy, so avoid this pitfall. Recall that one advantage of sketching is that no scale is required. (NTS means not to scale.) Just be proportional.

Grids are also used when plotting out ellipses. First, choose the correct isometric surface in which to place the ellipse (see Figure 7.136). Remember to turn or place the narrow or smaller ends of the ellipse into the small or acute angles (see Figure 7.137). Lay out the box for the surface and also the axis lines lightly or in blue lead (see Figure 7.138). Place points at the intersection of the axis and construction box (see Figure 7.139). Next, layout some small iso boxes inside the big box (see Figure 7.140). Once the grid is in place put some points at the far ends of the ellipse (see Figure 7.141).

At this stage there are eight points in place to help you sketch out the ellipse. Add a few more points if desired to lay out the ellipse, then keeping as steady as possible, sketch in the ellipse a quarter piece at a time.

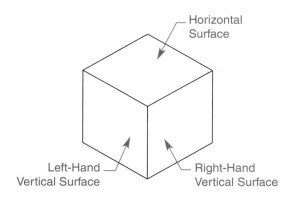

FIGURE 7.136   Identify the iso surface.

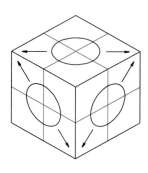

FIGURE 7.137   Ellipses on an iso cube.

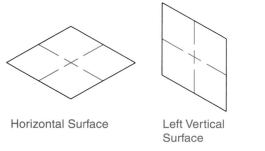

Horizontal Surface   Left Vertical
Surface

Right Vertical
Surface

FIGURE 7.138   Axis on iso ellipse.

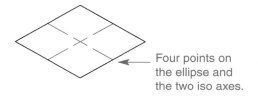

Four points on
the ellipse and
the two iso axes.

FIGURE 7.139   Finding points
on the iso axes.

FIGURE 7.140   Grid of the iso
surface.

FIGURE 7.141   Using the grid to lay out points.

If a really smooth curve is desired, add more points to develop a better quality sketch (see Figure 7.142). Using this approach will give you smoother, nicer looking ellipses.

You can sketch an oblique on normal grid paper for the flat views, then use 45° for the angled depth. The iso grid paper works well when you are using a 30° angle for your depth.

Trying to sketch perspectives is a bit more challenging than other pictorials, but it is occasionally done. Set up a perspective sketch just like a drawing. Buy or make a perspective grid if you prefer using it. Handle the sketch just like a drawing. A sketch requires few tools; however, this does not mean the drawing should be sloppy or messy. As a drafter gets better, grids and pencils become a thing of the past; experienced professionals use transparent sketch paper rolls and felt markers. Look at sketching as a fast way to communicate ideas to others and not as something to be hung in an art gallery.

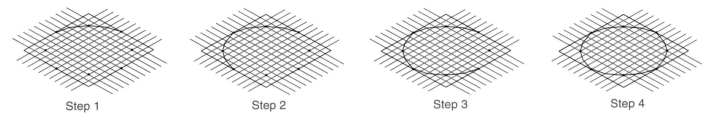

Step 1   Step 2   Step 3   Step 4

Sketch a quarter section at a time.

FIGURE 7.142   Sketching the ellipse.

REVIEW QUESTIONS

1. Sketch an example of a cube in isometric, dimetric, and trimetric form. Label the interior angles and the characteristics.
2. Why are depth scales adjusted on dimetric and trimetric drawings?
3. Explain the difference between ellipses drawn in isometric projection form versus isometric drawing.
4. List the different methods used to draw an ellipse in isometric form.
5. Draw an ellipse with a 1½″ radius using the four-center method. Put it on a right-hand vertical surface.
6. List the three different types of obliques and explain how they differ from one another.
7. Is it possible to have a circle and an ellipse in oblique forms on the same drawing?
8. Sketch an isometric and an oblique cube looking at the bottom horizontal surface.
9. Make a list of the major components used in a perspective setup.
10. How would a perspective be set (where would the horizon line be placed) to draw the following perspective views:
    a. Worm's-eye view
    b. Bird's-eye view
    c. Person's-eye view
11. From where is a true-height line generated on a perspective drawing?
12. In a perspective, what does the station point represent?
13. Explain how to find the vanishing points on a two-point perspective.

EXERCISES

EXERCISE 7.1

Using the isometric drawings in Figure 7.143, sketch the front elevation, side elevations, and the roof plan on 8 × 8 grided vellum.

EXERCISE 7.2

Sketch the figures in exercise 7.1 in oblique form using a 30° angle for the depth.

EXERCISE 7.3

Using the given front elevations, right side elevations and plan views, sketch the isometric figures in Figure 7.144.

FIGURE 7.143 Exercise 7.1.

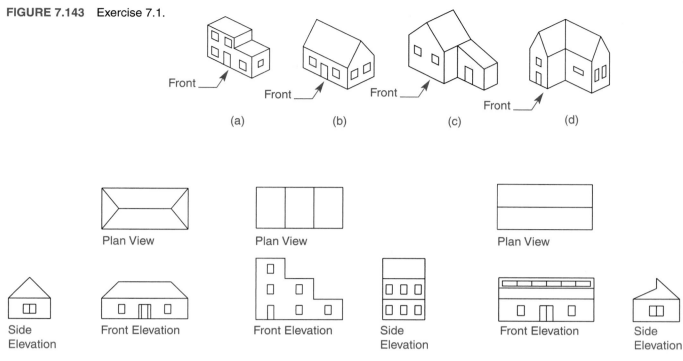

Front ___→ (a)   Front ___→ (b)   Front ___→ (c)   Front ___→ (d)

Plan View

Plan View

Plan View

Side Elevation   Front Elevation

Front Elevation   Side Elevation

Front Elevation   Side Elevation

FIGURE 7.144 Exercise 7.3.

EXERCISE 7.4

Lay out the given one-point perspective setup in Figure 7.145 on an 11″ × 17″ sheet at a ¼″ = 1′-0″ scale. Construct a one-point perspective using the given setup showing all construction lines.

EXERCISE 7.5

Lay out the one-point perspective setup in Figure 7.146 on an 11″ × 17″ sheet at a ¼″ = 1′-0″ scale. Construct a one-point perspective using the given setup showing all construction lines. After completing the ceiling tile, add a 2′ × 2′ floor tile grid to your one point perspective.

FIGURE 7.145 Exercise 7.4.

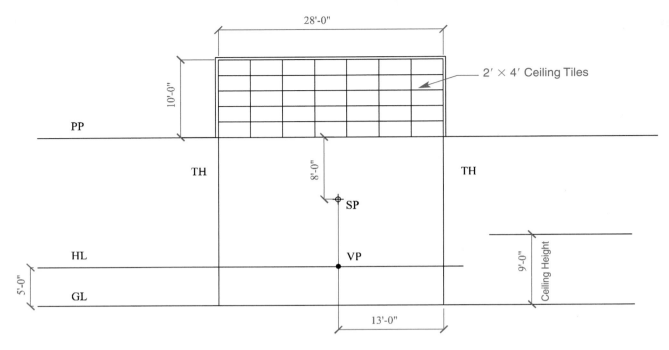

FIGURE 7.146   Exercise 7.5.

EXERCISE 7.6

Redraw the two-point perspective layouts in Figure 7.147 on an 11″ × 17″ sheet of vellum. Construct the two- point perspective showing all construction lines.

EXERCISE 7.7

Using Figure 7.148, add the shadows using a light source and a third vanishing point. See Figures 7.151 and 7.152 for approximate light source positions.

FIGURE 7.147   Exercise 7.6.
continued on next page

(a)

FIGURE 7.147 *continued*

(b)

(c)

FIGURE 7.148   Exercise 7.7

(a)

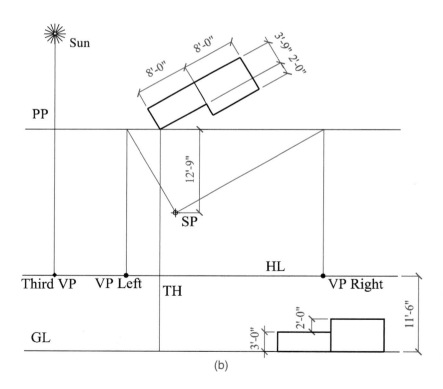

(b)

DRAWING ASSIGNMENTS

Use the plans and elevations given in Figure 7.149 to construct various pictorial drawings specified below.

1. Using architectural scales of your choice (⅜″ = 1′-0″ or ½″ = 1′-0″), construct isometric drawings of Figures a-h. Place the drawings on an 8½″ × 11″ sheet of vellum.
2. Using architectural scales of your choice (⅜″ = 1′-0″ or ½″ = 1′-0″), construct the following types of oblique drawings. Place the drawings on an 8½″ × 11″ sheet of vellum.
   a. Cabinet drawings for Figures a, b, c, d, g, and h.
   b. Cavalier drawing for Figures e and f.
3. Using an architectural scale and layout of your choice, construct a one-point perspective of Figures a, b, c, d, e, and h. Put each drawing on a separate 17″ × 22″ or 18″ × 24″ vellum sheet.
4. Using an architectural scale and layout of your choice, construct a two-point perspective of Figures a, b, c, e, f, g, and h. Put each drawing on a separate vellum sheet of 17″ × 22″ or 18″ × 24″.
5. Take your two-point perspective drawings of Figures a, e, and g and add a light source and third vanishing point to the drawings, and lay out the shadow of the figures.
6. Take the pictorials given in Figure 7.150 and draw the plan view, front view, and side view.

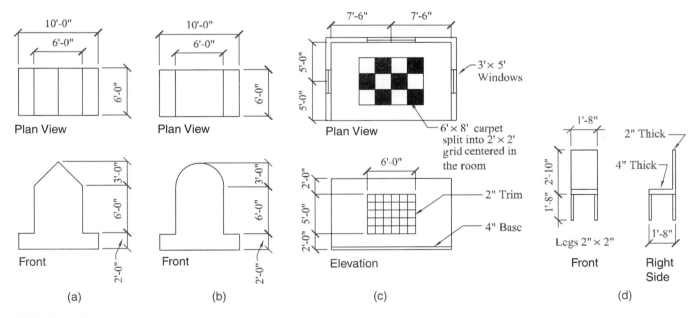

FIGURE 7.149 Drawing Assignment 1.
continued on next page

FIGURE 7.149 *continued*

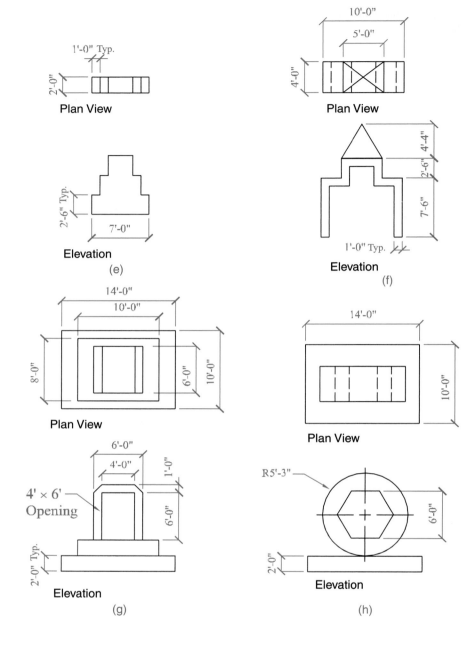

FIGURE 7.150 Drawing Assignment 6.

NOTES:
1. WINDOW SIZE 3'X 4'. ALL WINDOWS ARE CENTERED ON EACH WALL.
2. ALL DOORS ARE 3' X 7'. THE TOP OF THE DOORS AND WINDOWS LINE UP.

House Pictorial

NOTES:
1. TABLE LEGS ARE 3" X 3" SQUARE
2. TABLE TOP 2'-6" X 5'-O". GLASS CENTER 22" X 52".

Table Pictorial

AutoCAD for Beginners

CHAPTER 8

○ ○

Introduction to Computer Basics

The computer age arrived and took many people by surprise. Even today there are individuals in the drafting fields who have never touched a computer, and some brag that they never intend to do so. This is not something in which to take pride or live in ignorance of. Too many people lost their jobs in the 1990s because of insufficient computer and CAD skills. Today, people must learn new skills and update old ones to stay current with industry.

At some point those who are willing to learn about computers and CAD need a comfortable entry point, one that assumes no previous knowledge and, to use a common term, is user friendly. The following chapters are designed to ease a beginner into the computer and AutoCAD world.

8.1 The Computer/CAD Station

In this section the three elements that make drawing on a computer successful will be discussed and analyzed. These three elements are the CAD operator/drafter, the hardware (computer equipment), and the software (programs). Each of these elements is equally important, but starting with the human side will help you understand that people can draw some amazing things using this technology. Remember that hardware and software are tools for the drafter, they are controlled and managed by a human and not the other way around. Of course, sometimes it may not feel that way.

CAD Operator/Drafter

There are some people who believe that drawing on a computer eliminates the need to learn basic drafting skills. They believe they can simply jump right in and learn the software and become productive drafters instantly. A high percentage of these people are greatly disappointed. Can you imagine teaching someone to type who cannot read, spell, or punctuate yet can copy what he or she sees in front of him or her? Drafters in any discipline must understand what they are drawing in order to get promoted and better themselves. Make sure to learn the fundamentals of drafting first. It does not matter if they are taught to you on a drawing board or a computer. One good thing about drafting basics is that they do not change as rapidly as do computer software and hardware.

Interacting with Computers.

Learning how to use a computer is sometimes frustrating in the beginning, so make sure you are in a comfortable environment. Check your equipment; the chair should be set to the right height for you and should support your back correctly. The keyboard and mouse also should be set to comfortable positions. If you have never seen a mouse or keyboard see Figure 8.1. Keyboard pads can be used for wrist support.

The room lighting and monitor angle are also important to your viewing comfort. Most monitors have adjustable settings that allow the viewer to tilt the screen parallel to eye level. Having a lot of light may be desirable around a drawing board but not around a monitor screen. The glare becomes a problem for the eyes, so generally a dull or soft light setting works better.

These measures are designed to prevent physical problems that have been known to develop over a period of time. Carpal tunnel syndrome is a repetitive wrist motion problem that affects some individuals, and

FIGURE 8.1   Student CAD station.

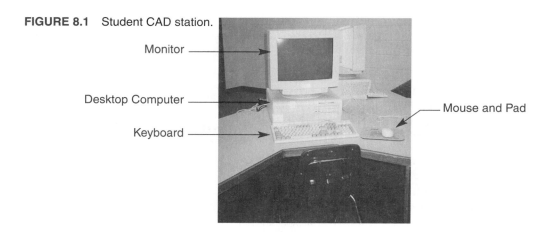

back problems can occur when chairs are not aligned properly. Studies in the United States and Sweden have been inconclusive in trying to link health problems to daily exposure to electromagnetic radiation from the computer's monitor. Proper lighting is essential for alleviating eyestrain. Remember to periodically look away from the screen. A basic student station looks similar to Figure 8.1.

Once you have established a good environment, it is time to become familiar with your computer equipment. Turning a computer station on and off is generally a matter of finding the correct switches. In a standard setup the computer, monitor, and printer must be turned on separately. Newer computers have a standby mode that is activated when the operator stops using it for a period of time. Pushing the on switch, moving the mouse, or pressing a key on the keyboard returns the computer to normal mode. There are normally two switches at the front of the computer: one turns the computer on and off, and the other resets or reboots the computer when it locks up or freezes during normal usage.

The monitor has its own on/off switch along with other switches for fine-tuning the brightness and adjusting the screen. If the screen needs changing, read the monitor's users guide or ask your instructor for help. These adjustments are easy to make to get the best quality viewing.

Another piece of equipment that commonly needs turning on and off is the printer. Printers will have any number of buttons depending on the complexity of the system. The buttons found most universally are the on/off, jam/form feed, and the test page. On some printers now the on/off switch has been phased out, and the printers programmed to come on automatically when the computer starts communicating with them.

The sooner you learn the basic setup, the more confident, comfortable, and relaxed an operator you can be. Look for small green indicator lights to come on when your equipment is turned on and running properly.

Computer Hardware

Hardware is the physical equipment or parts that make up the computer station. The following items are considered computer hardware:

- **Input Devices:** keyboard, mouse, trackball, microphone, and digitizer tablet/puck.
- **CPU (central processing unit) Components:** computer case/tower/desktop, processor, hard drive, motherboard, cache, RAM, power supply, floppy drive, video/graphics card, sound card, network card, CD-ROM/DVD, tape backup drive, zip drive, modem card
- **Output Devices, External Hardware, and Peripheral Equipment:** monitor/printer/plotter/scanner, speakers, network server, fax machine, camera.

As you can see, many components work together to run a computer smoothly.

Input Devices

An *input device* is the means by which the operator transmits instructions to the computer. Some people say this is how the operator interacts with the computer. The operator gives an instruction or command, and the computer performs the request. That is the way it is supposed to work, but problems do occur. A malfunction in the hardware or glitch in the software occasionally happens, but the primary cause of problems is that the operator does not look at the screen for the feedback that the computer gives after receiving a command. Sometimes the operator is two commands ahead of the software before realizing that the software is hung up in a command that never got finished. The lesson here is always to read your monitor's screen for feedback. You must interact with your computer to avoid frustrating miscommunication.

Keyboard.   This input device is the most recognized and the most feared (see Figure 8.2). It has some keys that resemble a typewriter's alignment, and if the CAD operator knows how to type, it is a definite plus. Fear not, though, the keyboard and most software have built-in shortcuts that require using only one or two keys to generate a lot of commands. Computer and software manufacturers have realized that most people do not type at high rates of speed and have learned to cater to them.

Mouse.   The mouse is a fast-working input device that allows the user to move all over the screen and select menu options (see Figure 8.3). To a CAD operator, the mouse is a tremendous aid in speeding up drawing. A two-button mouse is standard on most computer systems. The left-hand button is used to pick or select items from the screen menus. Some options require the user to press the left button two times quickly (double-click) to select an option. It takes a little time to get the feel or learn the touch, so practice.

In AutoCAD the right-hand button performs a return function like the Enter key on the keyboard. and can also exit a command or bring back the last command if used two times in a row. It will even access other commands in some cases. If you are left-handed, it may be more comfortable to make the right-hand button the pick option and the left one the return button. It is easy enough to do this, so ask your instructor to make the adjustment. Curved and contoured mice are available to give users as comfortable a feel as possible.

A three-button mouse became popular among AutoCAD users in the mid 1990s. The middle button allows a few more shortcuts or functions. Microsoft's IntelliMouse incorporates a wheel as the middle button. It can be pressed to function as a button and may be turned to perform other options. AutoDesk recommends using the IntelliMouse.

A digitizer with a puck is not an uncommon sight at a CAD station (see Figure 8.4). A digitizer tablet can incorporate a variety of menus to help speed up selection of commands. The puck has buttons like a mouse, but they are much smaller. This allows more buttons to be placed on the puck so that more options can be provided in the setup of the device. At one time this was a very popular input device, but as the Windows programs developed using on-screen icons/buttons the mouse became more effective.

A trackball is another input device that works similarly to a mouse. A mouse needs to be rolled around to move an arrow or a cursor to different locations on the screen. The trackball has a ball mounted on top that spins and moves the arrow around the screen. It also has buttons that can be used just like those on a mouse. People with limited hand mobility tend to favor a trackball.

A microphone is one of the newer input devices. It can be used to activate commands by voice signals. Improvements in technology have made the voice-activated system better with time, but bugs tend to be more prominent with a microphone. This device must also be trained to an individual's normal voice and requires special software to work with computer programs. Individuals who have limited use of their hands may find a microphone to be the key to being a successful CAD operator.

FIGURE 8.2   The parts of a keyboard.

FIGURE 8.3   A mouse.

FIGURE 8.4   Digitizer and puck.

Digitizer ———

Template ———

Puck ———

Computer or Central Processing Unit and Components

The heart and soul of your computer is contained within the computer case, which can be either a tower or desktop style. The case protects the motherboard as well as other components such as the various disk drives. The motherboard can be thought of as the spinal cord for your computer because everything eventually connects into it. In addition to containing the memory and the microprocessor, the motherboard has slots for accessories such as video, network, modem, and sound cards.

Note: the term *random access* distinguishes RAM from other memory devices that are accessed sequentially. The hard disk, CD, and floppy disk are all sequential devices.

The CPU (central processing unit) is the brains of the computer. It has several vital parts. Let's start with the microprocessor. This is the "chip" that is so important when selecting a computer. It performs millions of computations per second. This value is sometimes quoted in MIPS—millions of instructions per second. The clock rate of the CPU chip is expressed in MHz or megahertz (millions of clock cycles per second). The microprocessor is fed a steady stream of instructions and data that come from memory devices. The primary source of the data stream is the main memory or RAM (Random Access Memory).

RAM is composed of chips as well and comes in several varieties: DRAM, SRAM, SDRAM. All RAM chips have one serious shortcoming; they are volatile, that is, they lose all their data when the power is turned off. (You may have experienced this situation!) The hard disk is used to store data on a "nonvolatile" medium—a magnetic disk. This is referred to as ROM or Read-Only Memory. Why can't the microprocessor just get its information from the disk? RAM is much faster (about 10 times faster), but it is also more expensive per unit of storage capacity (the megabyte), so most computers have 10 to 50 times more hard disk storage available than RAM.

Even though RAM chips are faster than the hard disk, the microprocessor could perform more operations (MIPS) if it could get the data faster still. Most current computers have a smaller amount of very fast RAM (which is also more expensive) called *cache*. Normally the entire program that you are running will be loaded from the hard drive into RAM along with all your data, which can occupy a lot of RAM. But at any given instant, the microprocessor is concerned with only a small subset of this information. The cache controller tries to anticipate what the microprocessor is going to need next and moves it from the main RAM into the cache RAM. Software is written so that in most cases the next instruction is nearby; thus, a small amount of cache can make the computer run much faster. Wouldn't it be great if the cache were on the microprocessor chip itself? In fact, the most powerful microprocessors do have some amount of built-in cache, which is faster still. There can also be cache on the motherboard.

Computer Memory

Memory is measured in *bytes*. For instance, a 3½″ floppy disk can hold approximately 1.44 megabytes (MB) of information. The byte unit can be broken down even further into smaller units called *bits*.

1 byte = 8 bits

A bit is a single digit of binary information (number system base 2). It has two possible values: 1 or 0. A single bit can represent one of two choices, on or off, high or low, left or right, and so on. Because a byte is a collection of 8 bits, a byte can represent up to 256 choices. A byte can represent all the possible colors to be displayed, for example. Think of your area code and phone number. It is just a collection of 10 decimal digits. Your phone number has been assigned to represent your phone's address. With 10 decimal digits there are 10,000,000,000 (10 billion) possible choices.

8 bits = 1 byte
1 megabyte (MB) = approximately 1 million bytes (1,048,576 bytes)
1 gigabyte (GB) = approximately 1 billion bytes (1,073,741,824 bytes)

- 1 floppy disk holds 1.44 megabytes
- RAM is commonly measured in megabytes
- Hard drives are commonly measured in gigabytes
- AutoCAD 2000 fully loaded takes up approximately 169 megabytes.

Note that when you are buying a computer, "128 MB of memory" refers to the amount of main RAM, and "9.0 GB disk" refers to the amount of hard drive storage (GB is a gigabyte, or about a billion bytes, or about a thousand MB).

The memory system of a computer is a multilevel conglomeration of different devices. On one end of the spectrum is very fast, very expensive, very limited capacity. On the other end is slower, cheaper, huge capacity, and, very importantly, nonvolatility.

Another component that is plugged into the motherboard is a video card, which enhances the graphic images on the monitor. The cards with the most video RAM will produce sharper images at a faster rate of speed. Network cards can also be found plugged into the motherboard. These cards support linked computers so they can communicate with one another and exchange data or information. A modem card is another common accessory, which can give a computer Internet access throughout the world by plugging into a telephone line. Documents can also be transferred by fax with this card. Sound cards are used in CPUs for any audio interaction, whether receiving or sending sounds.

Some of the more familiar devices are seen on the front of the computer. A floppy disk drive is used to save drawings and other computer work on a 3½″ inch disk, a common storage device. Another standard device that is well known is the CD-ROM (Compact Disk Read-Only Memory) drive. Most of today's software programs come on CDs and are installed onto the hard drive through the CD-ROM drive. Some software, however, must have the CD in the CD-ROM drive to operate. Software can also be installed through the floppy disk drive.

A DVD-ROM (Digital Video Disk Read-Only Memory) is becoming increasingly popular. The DVD drive is more versatile in that it will run a DVD or a CD. A CD-ROM drive will not run a DVD, so check the disks and drives to become familiar with your CAD station and the disks it will access.

Tape backup drives and zip disk drives are additional devices on a computer but are not necessarily standard yet. These hardware components are used to back up or save large chunks of information or files. A hard drive can be backed up using a tape drive. Remember that if information is irreplaceable, it needs to be backed up. Floppy disks and Zip disks look similar, but a 3½″ floppy will hold about 1.44 MB of data, whereas a Zip disk will hold up to 250 MB. A floppy disk can be write-protected by moving a plastic tab on it to prevent accidental overwriting.

Output Devices, External Hardware, and Peripheral Equipment (see Figure 8.5)

Basically, an *output device* transmits images or sounds. For example, a monitor is used to display images on a screen for the operator to see and interact with the software. A printer is used to print images on paper. There are a wide variety of options when it comes to selecting a printer for CAD. Many firms have two types of printers: a small laser printer and a large ink-jet printer.

A laser printer gives superior image quality and is a fairly inexpensive device for printing 8½″ × 11″ size sheets. Large drawings can be scaled down to an 8½″ × 11″ size on a laser printer and have great readability for checking in-house drawings. Ink-jet printers are commonly used to print out a variety of large sheets (24 ″ × 36″) that are big enough to read clearly and can be given to contractors for construction. Large electrostatic plotters are also available but cost a good deal more than the ink-jet. These printers are replacing ink-pen plotters that were used in CAD's earlier days. Pen plotters draw with single lines and are too slow to compete with the other plotters on complex drawings with many lines.

Fax machines and scanners can be used with a computer to transfer images. Scanners capture images that can then be attached to a variety of files, E-mails and Web sites. Faxes are generally used to transmit black-line images to other machines at different locations. The quality of faxes is fair at best, and sheet sizes are limited to 8½″ × 11″ and legal-size (8½″ × 14″) sheets.

A network server has become a very valuable tool in the office environment (see Figure 8.6). Think of a server as a big storage bank or a detached hard drive that can be linked to other individual computers. The server can share information, software, or data with the other computers simultaneously. It also helps reduce the size of the storage memory on the smaller computer hard drives.

(a) Computer Speakers

(b) Network Server

(c) Small Printer (Desktop)

(d) Large Printer (Upright)

(e) Scanner and Fax

(f) Digital Camera

(g) Monitor

FIGURE 8.5   Computer peripherals.

FIGURE 8.6   A network setup.

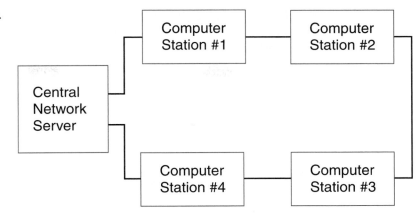

The downside to having a server is that when it goes down, it can suddenly bring work to a halt or to a snail's pace. Work can be done offline, but having limited access to outside information can be frustrating.

Digital cameras that interface with computers are one of the latest hardware additions to the world of technology. A picture taken with a digital camera can easily be put into a memory chip for sending with E-mail or displaying on Web pages.

Software and Basic Terminology

By definition, software programs are routines that perform some function or operation. Software provides the instructions that make the hardware work. A program normally comes on a CD or a 3½″ floppy disk, but some can be obtained electronically over the Internet using a process called *downloading* (see Figure 8.7). Software programs are written to do literally almost anything the human mind can conceive. It seems that if there is a need, some programmer will write a program to make it happen. That is how CAD has evolved.

The AutoCAD software is installed onto the hard drive for permanent storage. To be used, the software must be loaded from the hard drive to the RAM or working memory. The RAM does not transfer the whole program at once but instead processes what it needs as the CAD operator chooses various commands. This can take some time when using graphics software, which is why a fast CAD station needs a powerful micro-processor and up-to-date cache. Also, having a lot of RAM gives the computer more working memory, so it does not constantly have to tap into the hard drive to retrieve more information.

It is time to stop reading about computers and jump in and learn some fundamentals about operating them. Locate the on/off switches on the computer and monitor (*Hint*: Look in the lower right-hand corners. They are normally the largest buttons to be found.) and push them in and wait for the system to boot up. While you are waiting, look at the other buttons on the front face of the computer. One will open the CD-ROM drive, and another will eject a floppy disk if one has been previously loaded. A reset or reboot button can also be found on the front CPU face. It is used in case the software locks up the system. The monitor also has some buttons, but read the manual first before trying to adjust the screen. Several things can cause errors during the booting process: having a floppy disk inserted into the A: drive, pressing keys on the keyboard, or not having all the components (mouse/keyboard/monitor) plugged in correctly.

FIGURE 8.7   Floppy disks and a CD.

8.2 Using Windows with AutoCAD

A computer must have an operating system software to run programs. For years most computers used an operating system called DOS (Disk Operating System). It required a person to have a good memory and a lot of good typing skills to use it effectively. Fortunately, a more user-friendly operating system was developed called *Windows* (see Figure 8.8). This system uses pictures/icons for the user to select options to move through software operations rapidly. A lot of power was placed in the mouse to pick desired programs, commands, and subcommands on the screen. This made operating a computer system much easier for the average person, so Windows is a very popular operating system.

Learning how to handle the mouse will take a short period of time if you have never used one before. The terms *picking* and *clicking* are used interchangeably. They both mean the same thing: pressing the buttons on the mouse (see Figure 8.9).

The left pick button can be used when the mouse arrow is on an icon. Picking once highlights the icon/program. Watch the My Computer icon image change when you try this. If you choose the icon again, the font caption below it will be highlighted and will blink (see Figure 8.10). When the caption is highlighted, it can be edited, but if you are just learning, it is better to stay away from editing things you did not create or do not understand.

To start or launch a program place the mouse arrow over the icon and double-click the left pick button (press it twice very quickly). This should bring the program up into the RAM and allow you to use the opened software program.

Closing down a program or software package is quite easy. Look in the upper right-hand corner of the screen, and notice the three boxes side by side (see Figure 8.11). Simply place the mouse arrow on top of the box with the X and pick once with the left mouse button (left-click). As soon as you click on the X, the software program closes down and brings the desktop screen back so a new selection can be made.

FIGURE 8.8 Windows Desktop.

FIGURE 8.9 Mouse styles.

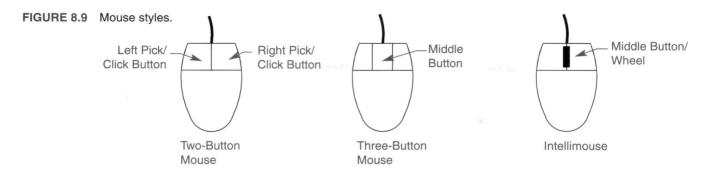

Left Pick/ Click Button — Right Pick/ Click Button

Two-Button Mouse

Middle Button

Three-Button Mouse

Middle Button/ Wheel

Intellimouse

Icon Darkens/Highlights When Selected

FIGURE 8.10 Icon with highlighted caption.

Found in the Upper RIght Corner of the Screen

FIGURE 8.11 Minimize, Restore, Close buttons.

Restore/Reduce Screen Size

Minimizes Program — — Close Program

FIGURE 8.12 Minimize, Restore, Close buttons.

Resizes the Screen to Maximum Size

Minimizes —

FIGURE 8.13 Minimize/maximize buttons.

The middle box is used to adjust the program's screen area (see Figure 8.12). It is used to fill up the screen completely or to reduce the size depending on your needs. It performs a restore or a maximize (see Figures 8.13 and 8.14 for the variations).

The left box with the dash is the minimize button. Clicking the left mouse button here minimizes the program or file to a small box at the base of the screen. The program remains loaded in RAM. The Windows operating system does not shut the program down; it just reduces it to the small rectangle box or button. To bring it back, place the mouse arrow on the reduced rectangle at the base of the screen (see Figure 8.14) and click with the left mouse button.

The right pick button can be used when the arrow is over an icon or off by itself. If the mouse arrow is over an icon when the right-hand pick (a right click)is selected, a menu of options pops up that allows you to view and edit program information (see Figure 8.15). One of the selections is Open, and if you move the mouse arrow on top of it and pick once with the left mouse button (left-click) it will open the software linked to that icon.

FIGURE 8.14 Minimized icons on the task bar.

Task Bar

Minimized Program Displays at the Bottom on the Task Bar

FIGURE 8.15 Pop-up menu.

FIGURE 8.16 Arrange Icons suboptions menu.

If the mouse arrow is off to the side of an icon when you select (right-click) the right-hand mouse button, it opens a list of options for editing the desktop screen (see Figure 8.16). (The desktop is the screen that appears after the boot sequence is complete.) One of the options with which you can experiment without doing any harm is the Arrange Icons choice. Pick any of these suboptions and watch the icons get rearranged.

In the lower left corner of the Window's Desktop is the Start button. If you move the mouse arrow on top of it and left-click, a long list of options appears (see Figure 8.17).

The Shut Down option will become very familiar to you. It is used to shut the computer down safely when you are done using it. Make sure to shut down Windows before turning off the computer. If you choose the Shut Down option, three additional selections appear in the Shut Down Windows dialog box (see Figure 8.18): Restart, which will reboot the computer; Restart in MS-DOS mode; and Stand by, which will leave the operating system on. To display the Windows screen again, just push the CPU's ON button, and the Window's Desktop will return quickly.

Another suboption to the Start button is the Run option, which you use when you want to install new software on the hard drive. Many software programs today will go into an autorun mode when you insert the software's CD into the CD-ROM drive. If you need instructions, most software packages are set up to walk you through the installation process.

The Help option guides you through solving problems in Windows. On-line help is available over the Internet, and CDs can be purchased that are excellent for training someone new to the Windows environment. If you require hands-on, personal assistance, take a Windows Basics class.

A Programs option is also found in the Start button menu. This option lists all the programs loaded on the computer. Go to any program with the mouse arrow and pick the desired software, and it will open up. You will notice that cascading menus will pop up to the right (see Figure 8.19). Just be persistent and you will find the program you want.

FIGURE 8.17 Shut Down…
option of the Start pop-up menu.

FIGURE 8.18 Shut Down Windows dialog box.

FIGURE 8.19 Cascade menu for Programs option of the Start pop-up menu.

The arrow indicates that there is a cascading menu to the right.

Indicates another cascading menu

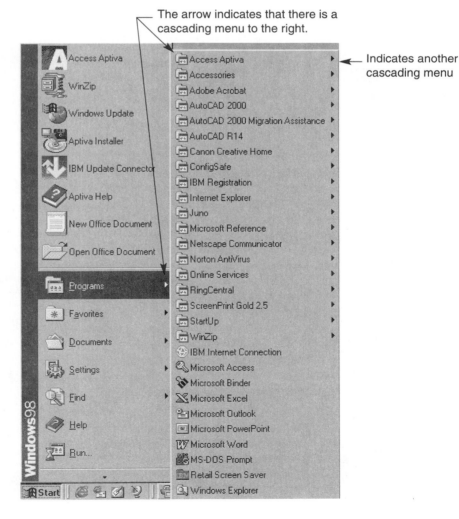

My Computer Icon

Becoming familiar with the power of the My Computer Windows Desktop icon is very important. Much can be gained by learning a few basic functions in this icon. The Explore option can be found by placing the mouse arrow on the My Computer icon and right-clicking (see Figure 8.20). Move down to the Explore option with the mouse arrow and left-click. Instantly you will see options that are critical to your success in operating the computer (see Figure 8.21).

The 3½ Floppy (A:) can be selected by double-clicking this option with the left-hand button. If a floppy disk is in the A: floppy drive, then it is possible to access information from A: using this route. Other options include the hard drive's root directory (C:), the CD-ROM drive, printer options, and control panel settings.

When you make a selection such as picking the 3½ floppy (A:), then it is possible to use the pull-down menus that are located across the top of the screen (see Figure 8.22). Left-clicking on the File pull-down menu displays many options below it (see Figure 8.23). The Open option displays all the files on the floppy disk. If you select a file with the mouse arrow and perform a left-double-click, the file will open if the soft-

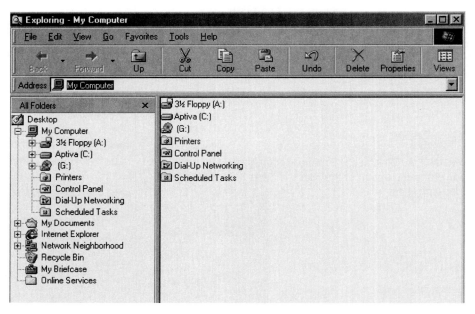

FIGURE 8.21   Explore option of the My Computer icon.

FIGURE 8.20   Windows explorer.

FIGURE 8.22   Pull-down file options for the A: floppy drive.

FIGURE 8.23   The File pull-down menu.

FIGURE 8.24 Menu options under 3½ Floppy (A:).

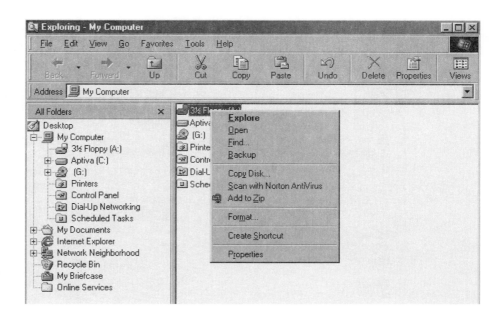

ware with which it was created can be found and accessed. A right-pick on 3½ Floppy (A:) will open some very useful commands (see Figure 8.24). Explore and Find are commonly used to do searches to locate files and other information.

The Backup option lets you make backup copies of large chunks of information such as the entire hard drive (C:) or separate programs. Backup hardware such as a tape is needed to do this.

The Copy Disk option lets you copy from one floppy disk to another. Just pick the copy from A: with the original floppy in the A: drive and the computer will temporarily store the information in RAM. When you are prompted to insert a new floppy, put it in and select the OK button. The information is copied from RAM to the new floppy disk.

The Format option wipes out all information on the disk and then prepares the disk for use in regular saving and retrieving functions.

Warning: Never format a disk unless you are prepared to lose all the information—programs, files, and everything. People have been known to wipe clean the entire hard drive, so be careful here.

Opening My Computer

Double-clicking with the left mouse button with the arrow on top of the icon opens the My Computer function. It has a somewhat different look than that under the Explorer option. Notice that folders are displayed in a larger icon or picture form, which is much easier on the eyes. The downside to this screen is that the All Folders sublist is not displayed, so navigating takes a little longer because in order to return to the previous screens the Back screen button must be clicked until the desired screen is reached. In the Explorer option, changing drives or directories is as easy as going to the All Folders display and picking where you want to go directly (See Figure 8.25).

Creating New Folders and Transferring Files (Check with your instructor before adding folders to the hard drive.)

There are two more topics to cover on our tour of survival skills for Windows. Making folders in which to store AutoCAD drawing files is a necessity. Folders help you stay organized with your drawing management.

Start by double-clicking on the My Computer icon to open it, then double-click on (C:). All the current folders are displayed. To add a folder for drawing files, left-click on the File pull-down menu (see Figure 8.26). Drop down to the New option and left-click on it, then go to the Folder option to the right and left-click on it. A new folder appears that must be named. Type in your name and hit the Return key. The folder has been created. Double-click on its icon to create folders inside the folder with your name (see Figure 8.27). Set up new folders in here for each drawing class for this semester or quarter. See the example in Figure 8.27, where two folders were created named Basic Design1 and Basic Drawing1. If you look at the address, you will see these folders are located in C:\Your Name.

If you want to delete these folders after the semester is over, just click on the folder and highlight it. Then press the Delete key on the keyboard, and the folder is sent to the Recycle Bin on the desktop (see Fig-

FIGURE 8.25   All Folders display in Explore.

FIGURE 8.26   New, Folder selected on the File pull-down menu.

FIGURE 8.27   Two new folders created.

FIGURE 8.28   Recycle Bin icon.

ure 8.28). To permanently remove the files and folders from the computer, go back to the desktop and double-click on the Recycle Bin icon, then go to the File pull-down menu and select the Empty Recycle Bin. Do not do this unless you are sure you are not going to need these files any more.

Drawings can be transferred using the My Computer Explore option. Right-click on the My Computer icon and then drop down and left-click on Explore. Repeat the same sequence again so that two sessions of Explore are open. They will overlap each other somewhat and will need to be moved a little so you can see into both of them. Go to the top of the explorer display with your mouse arrow where you see Exploring – My Computer in blue or gray and pick with the left mouse button and hold it down. While holding down the button, drag or roll your mouse and watch the current Exploring session move across the screen (see Figure 8.29). Do the same thing to the other Exploring session, separating them just enough to see into the My Computer area of each one (see Figure 8.30).

Now, go to one of the sessions and double-click on 3½ Floppy (A:) to list the files on A:. Move to the other session and double-click on (C:) to list all the folders in that session. With this setup it is easy to move files around. Go to the session showing the files in A: and pick a file and hold the left mouse button down. Now, drag or roll the mouse arrow toward the screen of the other session. Notice as you cross over to the other session that the mouse arrow reappears there. At this point, pick the folder into which to drop the file from the other session. When the arrow is over the folder icon just let go of the left mouse button. The file you grabbed in the A: drive

Note: Saving drawings in a folder on the hard drive (C:) will give you one copy of the work. It is good practice to save to the hard drive first, then copy to a floppy later. If you save directly to floppy drive A:, AutoCAD starts using that drive to work on and will destroy the floppy disks over time.

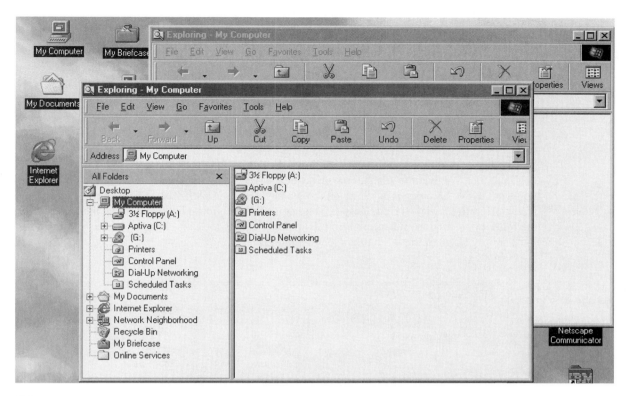

FIGURE 8.29 Opening double Explore sessions.

FIGURE 8.30 Moving double Explore sessions.

is instantly transferred into the folder on the C: drive. This operation can also be performed between directories and folders in C:. If you wish to keep a copy of a file in its original location, hold down the Ctrl key while dragging and dropping. Opening multiple sessions in Windows to copy or transfer data is a snap.

Tips for Copying Multiple Files
If you need to copy more than one file, here are two ways to do it.

1. While selecting files to be moved hold down the Ctrl key on the keyboard when picking the files you want to move with the left mouse button. When you have selected all the files to be moved, hold the left mouse button down on the last file chosen and drag over to the next session. All the selected files will move at the same time (see Figure 8.31).

2. If all the files you want to transfer are in sequence, go to the top or bottom and pick the first file you want. Next, hold down the Shift key on the keyboard and pick the last file desired. Notice that the whole string is highlighted. Keep holding down the left mouse button and drag the files over to the other open session. When the arrow is over the folder icon into which you wish to drop the files, simply let go of the left button (see Figure 8.32)

FIGURE 8.31 Using the Ctrl key to select files one at a time.

FIGURE 8.32 Using the Shift key to select whole columns of files.

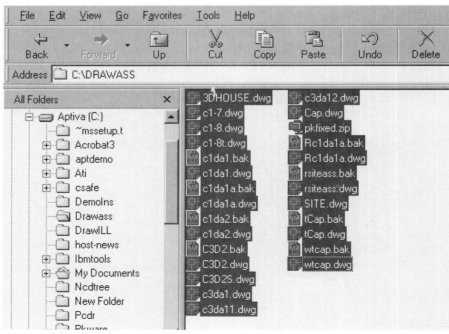

FIGURE 8.33   Closing a program.

└── Close Program

Tip for Tiling Multiple Sessions

Note: If a right click does not work in the toolbar area, move the cursor to a new location on the toolbar. Keep off the minimized icons.

After opening two sessions of Explore in Windows, move the cursor arrow down to the task bar at the bottom of the desktop, shown back in Figure 8.14. Right-click and select either Tile Windows Horizontal or Tile Windows Vertical. The screen will split up and make it easy to see each session clearly on the same screen.

If this is your first exposure to using the Windows operating system, it may take some time to get used to it along with the mouse picking and clicking operations. As long as you do not delete items that exist on the computer you are fairly safe in exploring and moving around in Windows. Remember to shut down programs when you are done using them (see Figure 8.33).

If you are shutting down the computer, go to the Start button in the bottom left corner and left-click on the icon. Then select the Shut down option and pick OK. The computer will then tell you when it is safe to turn it Off.

REVIEW QUESTIONS

1. List some of the physical problems that CAD operators have been known to develop over time.
2. Explain the difference between hardware and software.
3. What is the purpose of an input device?
4. How many buttons can a mouse have?
5. Make a list of all possible input devices to be found on a CAD station.
6. On what devices can information be stored?
7. What do the following abbreviations stand for?
   a. CPU
   b. RAM
   c. ROM
8. Explain some of the differences between RAM and ROM.
9. Make a list of external hardware and peripheral equipment.
10. List some of the advantages and disadvantages of being on a network server.
11. Define *software*.
12. How much memory can a floppy disk hold?
13. In what units is RAM commonly measured?
14. How do you start a program in Windows?
15. How do you minimize a program in Windows?
16. What are some of the important options found under the My Computer icon?
17. Why should you use caution when formatting disks?
18. How can the Explore option of My Computer be opened?
19. What is the purpose of the Recycle Bin?
20. What option is used to install software on a computer's hard drive?
21. How are files copied within the Windows environment?
22. Research DVDs, CDs, and their drives. Compare their quality, performance, and cost.

ASSIGNMENTS TO RESEARCH

1. Put together a checklist of computer requirements for a CAD station to run AutoCAD 2000.

2. Research AutoCAD LT and AutoCAD 2000 and compare them.

3. Call five architectural or interior design firms and ask them the following questions.

   a. How many different CAD software packages does your firm use?

   b. What operating systems are you using and why?

   c. How much CAD drawing versus board drawing is done in your office?

   d. What are some of the positive and negatives in CAD work?

4. Research the following software products made by AutoDesk.

   a. Architectural DeskTop

   b. 3D Studio

   c. Compare a and b with AutoCAD 2000.

CHAPTER 9

○ ○

Introduction to AutoCAD

9.1 Starting Up the AutoCAD 2000 Program

Once AutoCAD has been loaded onto your computer, it is accessed much like any other program by double-clicking on the AutoCAD 2000 icon (see Figure 9.1). You can also begin by clicking on the Start button at the bottom on your screen and then choosing Programs, AutoCAD 2000, AutoCAD 2000 in sequence (see Figure 9.2).

FIGURE 9.1   AutoCAD 2000 icon.

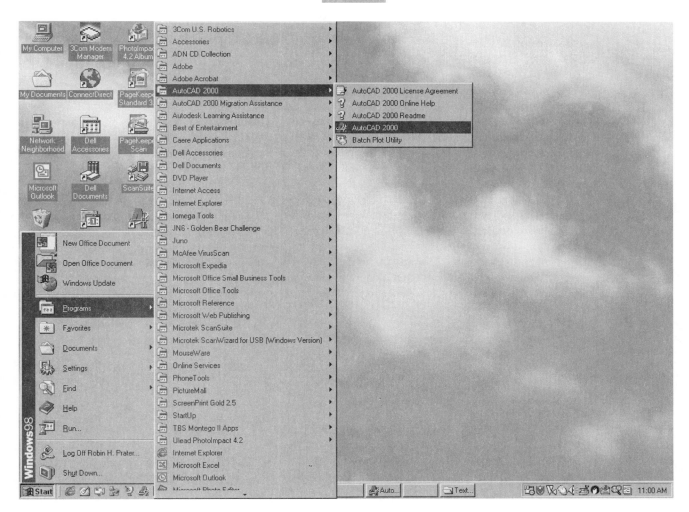

FIGURE 9.2   AutoCAD 2000 options in the Program menu.

FIGURE 9.3   Startup dialog box.

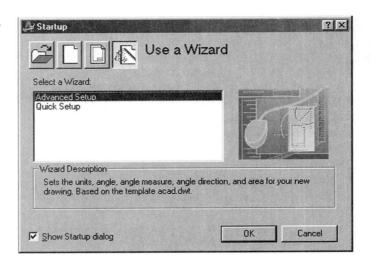

On startup, AutoCAD displays its standard screen with a Startup dialog box at its center (see Figure 9.3). **Dialog boxes** are one of the many ways that AutoCAD has to communicate with users. Basically, a dialog box walks you through a series of questions. We will go into more detail about dialogue boxes later in the chapter, but for now, close the Startup dialog box by left-clicking on the X button at the top right of the dialog box (See Figure 9.3). This will allow you to experiment with the program as we introduce some basic concepts.

9.2 Becoming Familiar with the AutoCAD Graphics and Text Screens

Take a moment to look over the AutoCAD screen (see Figure 9.4). If you have used other programs in the Windows environment, the screen may look somewhat familiar. The bar along the top tells you that you are working in AutoCAD 2000. Notice what happens if you move your mouse around. A set of crosshairs moves around the screen. The area in which the crosshairs move around is called the **graphics screen**. This is where your drawings will be displayed. Notice that a pair of numbers is displayed at the bottom of the screen. This area is called the **status bar**. The numbers are a coordinate display of the location of your cursor and will change as you move your cursor around the screen.

If you move your mouse outside the graphics screen, an arrow appears that allows you to pick from the buttons and pull-down menus. The pull-down menus are at the top of your screen. They include the File, Edit, View, Insert, Format, Draw, Dimension, Modify, Express, Window, and Help menus. Left-clicking on these buttons pulls down a menu of options. Try this now with the Draw pull-down menu.

Note: If you accidentally click on a command that you do not wish to execute, press the ESC button on your keyboard. This will take you out of the command.

Notice that some of the words in the menu have an arrowhead beside them. If you highlight one of these with your mouse, an additional menu will cascade out to the side. Try this now with the Circle command, found under the Draw menu (see Figure 9.5).

If there are three dots next to a word on the pull-down menu, that means a dialog box will appear if you click on that option. Try clicking on the Hatch command found under the Draw pull-down menu. If you open up a dialog box that you do not want to use, simply click on the Cancel button in the dialog box. You can also click on the close or X button at the top right corner of the dialog box.

The command line at the bottom of your screen is one of the key ways in which the AutoCAD 2000 program communicates with you. If you get in the habit of checking the command line, you will always know what the computer thinks you are trying to do. If the line says Command, the computer is waiting for you to begin a new set of instructions. Otherwise, it displays the command that is currently being executed. In addition, this is where questions that the program needs you to answer will be displayed.

For example, click on the Draw pull-down menu, then click on Line. The command line should now display Command: _line Specify first point:. It is waiting for you to tell it the first point of a line. There are many ways to do this, but if you wish to play a little, try left-clicking a few points on the graphics screen. When you have drawn enough lines, press Enter on your keyboard. This will take you out of the Line command. Notice that the command line now displays only Command:.

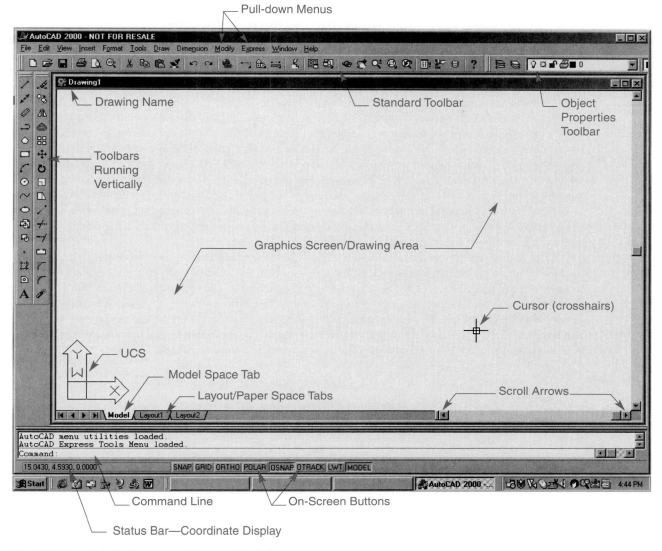

FIGURE 9.4   AutoCAD screen with parts labeled.

FIGURE 9.5   Cascade menu of the Circle command.

The two typewritten lines above the command line list the previous two commands issued. AutoCAD keeps a running history of the current session. The scroll bars on the side of these lines allow you to move up or down the list of commands that you have previously entered. If you press F2 on your keyboard, a list of all the commands you have given AutoCAD since you began the current session will be displayed in a larger window. If all the commands do not fit on the screen, you can scroll up or down to display them. When you have seen enough, press F2 again to close the window.

But what about all the other buttons around the graphics screen? If you move your cursor so that the arrow rests over one of the buttons, AutoCAD will display a tooltip or label that tells you what that button does. Notice that in addition to the tooltip, a description of the tool appears below the command line on the status bar. If a button has an arrow in the lower right hand corner of the image, clicking and holding down your left mouse button will cause a flyout menu to be displayed (see Figure 9.6). Keep the mouse button pushed down while you move the cursor down to the command you wish to execute. Releasing the mouse button will activate that command. It will also move that command to the top of the flyout menu so that this icon will now be displayed on the toolbar. Try this with the Zoom command by finding the icon that matches the one shown in Figure 9.6. Remember to check your command line to see what the program thinks is happening. Press Esc when you want to exit the command.

The buttons are grouped together on toolbars. The toolbars that are shown by default when you first load the program are the Standard Toolbar, the Draw toolbar, the Modify toolbar, and the Object Properties toolbar. You can find a list of additional toolbars by right-clicking on the toolbox (see Figure 9.7). The checks displayed next to each toolbar title tell you which toolbars are currently being displayed. To turn a new toolbar on, highlight the title with your cursor and left-click. To turn a toolbar off, repeat the process with a title that has a check mark beside it. Highlighting and clicking on the Customize feature at the bottom of the menu will allow you to customize the properties and icons displayed on your toolbars.

FIGURE 9.6 Zoom flyout menu.   **FIGURE 9.7** Toolbar menu.

Left-clicking along the border around the toolbars or on the raised bars at the end of the toolbars will allow you to move your toolbar to another part of the screen. You can even place a toolbar in the middle of the graphics screen for quick access. Take a minute to experiment with moving one of your toolbars to a new location. Don't worry if the toolbar does not go exactly where you want it to the first time; you can always move it again. AutoCAD considers the toolbar to be "docked" when it is back along the borders of the graphics screen.

9.3 Communicating with AutoCAD

If you have read through the previous section, you have already seen several ways in which AutoCAD communicates with the program user. One of the great things about AutoCAD is that there are usually several different ways to input any given command. You have the flexibility of finding which way suits you best.

Using your keyboard to simply type in the name of the command will access all commands in AutoCAD. Most commands also have a keyboard shortcut that is often, but not always, the first letter of the word. Sometimes the letter must be combined with the Alt or Ctrl key. The shortcut letter is underlined whenever the word appears on the screen. The function keys across the top of the keyboard also access certain basic commands (see Figure 9.8). Each pull-down menu also contains a list of commands, grouped according to function. Another way to access commands is to left-click on the appropriate icon displayed on the toolbars. The icons are designed to provide visual clues to their purpose. In addition, a tooltip or label pops up when you place the cursor over a button, and a description of the function of the button appears at the bottom of the screen in the status window.

If you become a frequent user of AutoCAD, you will probably find yourself memorizing some of the shortcuts. If you use the program only occasionally, just try to find the method that is easiest for you to remember. Everyone has his/her own learning/working styles, and even frequent users will differ on which method holds the most appeal. Remember always to check the command line to ensure that AutoCAD is executing the correct command.

Example

Let's use the Line command as an example once again. To access the command, you have several options, all of which allow you to draw a line. The most obvious is to use your keyboard to type in the name of the command, **Line** or **(line)**. In the case of the Line Command, the letter **L** (or **l**) provides a shortcut. If you become a frequent user of the program, you will probably find yourself memorizing these shortcuts. Otherwise, it takes very little time to type in the full word.

Left-clicking on the Draw pull-down menu and then choosing Line will also access the Line command (See Figure 9.9).

Look at the Draw toolbar. The default position is to the left of the graphics screen, but it may be located elsewhere on your display. The icon you are looking for looks like a diagonal line with red endpoints on each end. A left click on this icon accesses the Line command.

Try accessing the Line command using each of these methods. Which one did you find the easiest to use? Do not decide right away always to use only this technique. Experiment with the different methods of entry; your favorite may change after of few weeks of practice.

Line Icon

FIGURE 9.8 AutoCAD function keys.

F1	Help
F2	Text Window
F3	Osnap On/Off
F4	Tablet On/Off
F5	Isoplane
F6	Coordinates On/Off
F7	Grid On/Off
F8	Ortho On/Off
F9	Snap On/Off
F10	Polar On/Off
F11	Object Snap Tracking On/Off

FIGURE 9.9 Selecting the Line command in the Draw pull-down menu.

9.4 Crisis Control

One of the most comforting things to know about a computer program is what to do when things do not go exactly the way you expect them to go. The purpose of this section is to provide you with some valuable tools for just such a situation and to give you a feeling of being in control.

Canceling Commands in Progress

What happens when you realize that you have picked the wrong command, or maybe you just changed your mind? Are you stuck? No! AutoCAD allows you the flexibility of pressing the Esc key to cancel a command while it is running. Always check your command line to make sure it has returned to Command:. You may have to press the Esc key more than one time.

In addition, most dialog boxes have Cancel buttons as well as the X or close button in the upper right-hand corner. Picking the Cancel or Close button will close the current dialog box with no action taken, even if you have started picking options.

Help Command

AutoCAD provides you with lots of on-line help. Find Help at the top of your screen. The associated pull-down menu (See Figure 9.10) provides options including AutoCAD Help, Fast Track to Plotting, What's New, and Learning Assistance. AutoCAD Help allows you three ways of searching for information. Clicking on the Contents tab will show you a list of "chapters" dealing with various aspects of the program such as a Command Reference and a User's Guide. The Index tab functions much like a dictionary, allowing you to look up a word alphabetically. The Find tab gives you a search vehicle for locating the topic or command for which you need information. AutoCAD Help can also be located by typing **Help**, Alt + H, or pressing the F1 function key. Additionally, the question mark button on the Standard Toolbar will bring up the AutoCAD Help menu.

If you click on the question mark button located in the upper right-hand corner of a dialog box, you receive a slightly different kind of help. A shadowed question mark appears next to your cursor. Click on the area of the dialog box about which you have a question, and a short description will appear. This should provide enough information to get you going again.

FIGURE 9.10   Help menu.

U and REDO

Undo   Redo
Icon   Icon

If you have used a word processing program in the Windows environment, many of the buttons on the Standard Toolbar will be familiar to you. The two buttons showing curved lines with arrows access the **U** (Undo) and **Redo** commands. You can also access these commands by typing in **U** or **UNDO** and **REDO**. The Undo command allows you to take back the previous command. It can be used repeatedly so you can back up step-by-step canceling previously issued instructions. The Redo command allows you to reinstate a command that was undone by mistake. Redo can be used only once and must immediately follow an Undo. It works only for one command. So, for example, if you have used Undo to cancel five commands and then use Redo, only the last of the five commands will be reinstated. If you enter Redo again, you will get a message saying "REDO must immediately follow the U or Undo command," so choose your Undo and Redo commands carefully.

In addition to the curved arrow icon on the toolbar, Undo can also be accessed through the Edit pull-down menu, by pressing Ctrl + Z, by typing U at the command line, or by right-clicking to display the cursor menu, which contains Undo. Redo can be accessed by using the Edit pull-down menu, by pressing Ctrl + Y, by typing **REDO** at the command line, or by right-clicking to display the cursor menu.

The Save Time Command

Type **SAVE TIME** at the command prompt and then press Enter↵. The function of Save Time is to perform an automatic save while AutoCAD is running. Once Save Time has been activated, type in the time in minutes to set the automatic save interval. About 20 minutes is what most professionals recommend. Another option is to set the time according to what you are willing to redraw. If you are drawing something really complicated, do not wait for a Save Time to kick in. Perform a save yourself.

The Save Time command saves the drawing to the Windows/Temp subdirectory. The file extension will not be .dwg but instead will be .SV$. If an automatic save is performed before the drawing is given a name, the file name will look similar to the following:

> Drawing 1_1_1_6500.SV$

Giving the drawing a name such as Project prior to the automatic save would generate a save time file that looks similar to this:

> Project_1_1_5724.SV$

The numbers shown are randomly assigned by AutoCAD, so when you are hunting down this file, look for the drawing name and the SV$ extension. The file must be renamed with a .dwg extension before it can be opened in AutoCAD.

9.5 File Management

Beginning a New Drawing: Drawing Setup

When you begin a new session of AutoCAD, the program automatically provides a Startup dialog box to walk you through opening up a new drawing. If you have already done some work in AutoCAD before you decide to start a new drawing, there are several ways to access the Create New Drawing dialog box. You may select File from the pull-down menu and then click on New. You may also simply type in the word **NEW**. The keyboard shortcut for opening a new file is to press Ctrl + N. Whether you open a new drawing with the Startup dialog box (see Figure 9.3) or the Create New Drawing dialog box (See Figure 9.11), the procedure is virtually the same; only the title in the blue band across the top differs.

FIGURE 9.11   Create New
Drawing dialog box.

Four large buttons are located just below the blue bar. Each button provides you with a different option for starting an AutoCAD drawing. The far left button opens an existing drawing. You are allowed to choose this button only in the Startup dialog box. Once you are working in the program, you most open an *existing* file using a different set of instructions, which are covered in the next section of this text.

The next three buttons help you start a new drawing. You have the option of starting completely from scratch, using a template, or using what AutoCAD calls a **Wizard**.

Using Wizard

The far right button, the Wizard button, is picked by default. This is why the button looks like it has been pressed down, and the words "Use a Wizard" appear next to the buttons. If this is not the case, use your left mouse button to pick the Wizard button.

Once you decide to utilize a Wizard, your next choice is to use the Advanced Setup or the Quick Setup. The difference in these options is in the number of choices you are given. The Quick Setup asks you to make two choices, whereas the Advanced Setup asks you to make the same two choices plus three others. The common choices are units and area. Now you're probably hoping for a little more explanation than that, so here goes.

Units

The Units option refers to the type of units with which you would prefer to draw. The options include decimal, engineering, architectural, fractional, and scientific. You should make this choice based on the type of drawing that you wish to produce. Unless you work in several disciplines, most of your drawings will end up being in one particular system of units.

The default option is to use decimal units (see Figure 9.12). Decimal units can be used with either inches (English) or millimeters (Metric). This system of units is most often used for mechanical drawings, but it should work fine for initially exploring AutoCAD.

Engineering units contain feet and inches (see Figure 9.13). This type of unit is most often found on maps and civil engineering drawings. Civil drafting covers a wide range of projects ranging from plot plans and topography maps to bridge and dam design. Many landscape drawings will utilize engineering units.

You will no doubt have guessed that architects typically use architectural units. They contain feet, inches, and fractions of inches (see Figure 9.14). This system of units is typically found on drawings such as floor plans, elevation views, section views, and detail drawings. Most interior design drawings use architectural units.

The fractional system of units is helpful for drawings that consist of fractional parts rather than feet or meters (see Figure 9.15).

Scientific units are useful when the measurements in the drawing are either extremely large or extremely small. The letter *E* in the unit indicates that the first part of the number (such as 1.5500 in the example in Figure 9.16) is to be multiplied by an exponent of 10 given in the last part of the number (+01, or 10 to the first power, in the example shown in Figure 9.16). Another way to look at exponents of 10 is to think of the expo-

FIGURE 9.12 Units options with <u>D</u>ecimal units displayed.

FIGURE 9.13 Units options with <u>E</u>ngineering units displayed.

FIGURE 9.14 Units options with <u>A</u>rchitectural units displayed.

FIGURE 9.15 Units options
with Frac̱tional units displayed.

FIGURE 9.16 Units options
with S̲cientific units displayed.

Note: If you are
doing the Advanced
Setup, you can
choose the amount of
precision you need
for your project. For
example, in decimal
units you can round
to the nearest whole
number, or take your
calculations out to the
eighth decimal place.
Architectural units
may be rounded to
the nearest inch or
carried out to the
nearest $\frac{1}{64}''$.

nent as indicating how many zeros will follow the 1, so 10^1 equals 10 and 10^2 equals 100. A negative exponent indicates the number of places the decimal point moves to the left. So 10^{-1} equals 0.1 and 10^{-2} equals 0.01. The number written as 1.5500E+01 equals $1.5500 \times 101 = 1.5500 \times 10 = 15.5$. That seems like a lot of work for such a small number, but imagine if the number you were dealing with involved 10 or 20 zeros.

Decide which system of units suits you the best, then use your left mouse button to choose that option. The circles next to the list of units are called **radio buttons**. If a black dot appears in the center of the circle, that choice is activated. If the circle is blank, that choice has not been selected.

Area.   Once you have sorted out the type of units you will be using, the next step in the Quick Setup is to select the Area option for your drawing (see Figure 9.17). Select the size area that you will need to draw the object at full scale. For example, if your drawing would fit in an area 50′ by 75′ these are the numbers you input for the size of your drawing. You input dimensions at full scale. If a wall is 10′ long in "real life," you input the value into AutoCAD as 10′. You do not have to scale your input; AutoCAD will take care of that when it comes time to print. Now, obviously, your computer screen does not expand and contract depending on the size of your drawing. Nor would you want a 50′ by 75′ computer screen on your desk! The monitor works just like a television screen to display full-size elements in a small screen space. We will discuss scale and plotting in a later chapter.

Once you have chosen the units and area for your drawing, you are ready to click on the dialog box of the menu to complete the Quick Setup.

FIGURE 9.17 Area options.

Angle. The Advanced Setup allows you to choose the way you want angles to be displayed on your drawing. You can choose among decimal degrees, degrees/minutes/seconds, grads, radians, or surveyor units. In addition, you can select the amount of precision necessary for your project.

Reminder: There are 360° (degrees) in a complete circle, 60′ (minutes) in a degree, and 60″ (seconds) in a minute.

- Decimal Degrees (see Figure 9.18) is the default option and is often used in mechanical drafting.
- Deg/Min/Sec (See Figure 9.19) displays the angle values in degrees, minutes, and seconds depending on the amount of precision desired. This option is used in some mechanical drawings as well as in some architectural and civil work.
- Grads (see Figure 9.20) is an abbreviation for gradients. Notice that the angle measure is followed by a lowercase *g*. In the gradient system, a complete circle is made up of 400 grads, so a 90° angle is equal to 100 g.
- Radians (Figure 9.21) is a way to measure an angle based on rotation using π, the ratio between the circumference of a circle and its diameter. A radian is the angle between two radii of a circle such that the length of the arc between them is equal to the radii. Using radian notation, π radians equal 180°. One radian is equal to approximately 57.2958°. Try choosing the radian option on the angle dialog box. Notice how the display changes as you increase the precision of the angle. With a precision of 0g, a 90° angle reads as 2r, but if the precision is increased to 0.00g, the same angle reads as 1.57r.

FIGURE 9.18 Area options with Decimal Degrees displayed.

FIGURE 9.19   Area options
with Deg/Min/Sec displayed.

FIGURE 9.20   Area options
with Grads displayed.

FIGURE 9.21   Area options
with Radians displayed.

FIGURE 9.22 Area options with Surveyor units displayed.

FIGURE 9.22 Area options with Surveyor units displayed.

■ Surveyor (see Figure 9.22). Surveyors measure angles using bearings. Bearings are expressed in degrees, minutes, and seconds but differ from other angle expressions by having compass directions associated with them. The first part of the bearing gives the starting compass direction. The last part of the bearing gives the direction toward which the angle goes. So a compass bearing of N 45d E starts at north on the compass and measures 45° toward the east. Bearings are found on land surveys and plot plans.

Angle Measure. The Angle Measure option allows you to select the orientation for measuring angles. Normally, AutoCAD places 0° at due east on a compass. You can use this feature to begin measuring your angles at East, North, West, South, or any Other compass reading (see Figure 9.23).

Angle Direction. The default in AutoCAD is to measure angles in a counterclockwise direction (see Figure 9.24). You can use this feature to choose between counterclockwise and clockwise rotation.

Once you have worked your way through the five choices provided in the Advanced Setup, you are ready to click on the Finish button. At any time during the setup you can click on the Back button to repeat a previous step. You can also use the Cancel button to jump out of the setup menu.

FIGURE 9.23 Angle measurement options.

FIGURE 9.24 Angle Direction options.

Starting from Scratch

The Start From Scratch button begins a new drawing with very minimal layout guidelines. You are asked only to choose between English and Metric units. This option is probably better suited for experienced users.

Using a Template

A template in AutoCAD is a drawing file with a predetermined set of standards and settings. Templates are available based on ANSI, ISO, DIN, JIS and architectural standards. Once you click on the Template button in the Setup dialog box, a screen appears with a listing of all the existing templates. An area to the right of the box allows you to preview the templates. The most obvious differences will be in the way the borders and title blocks are set up. Other values such as grid and snap settings, units and angle values, and text and dimensioning conventions will be less apparent to the eye. Notice that the template files are saved as .dwt files. You can create your own template files or modify existing ones using the Save As command.

Opening an Existing Drawing

The Windows environment makes opening an existing AutoCAD drawing a very familiar process. As always, you have several options. You can go to the File pull-down menu and click on Open, you can also simply type in the word **open** at the command line, or you can click on the icon for opening a file on the Standard Toolbar. The icon looks like an open file folder. The keyboard shortcut for opening an existing file is to press Ctrl + O.

Any of the methods just listed will put you directly into the Select File dialog box (see Figure 9.25). This allows you to search the existing files for the drawing you require. AutoCAD drawings should be saved as .dwg files and will display a red icon next to the file name. A single left-click with the mouse will provide you with a preview of the drawing in a window on the right side of the dialog box. Double-click to open the drawing. If you have trouble locating a file, you can utilize the Find File . . . or Locate buttons found toward the bottom right of the screen.

FIGURE 9.25 Select File dialog box.

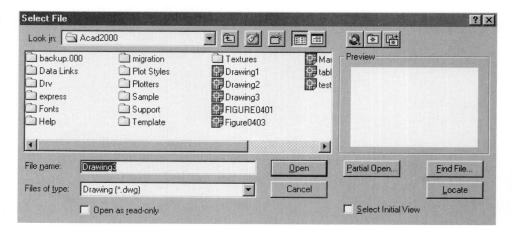

FIGURE 9.26 Save Drawing As dialog box.

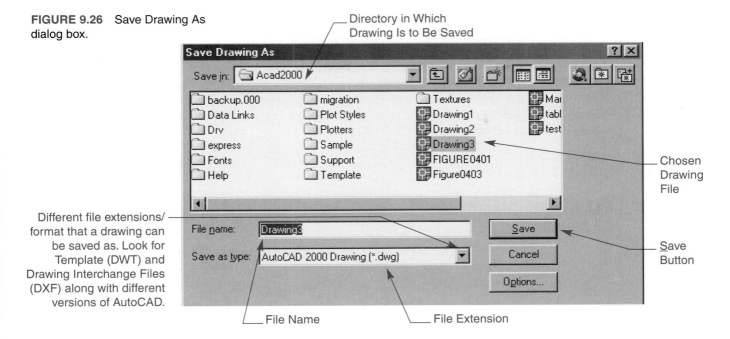

Directory in Which Drawing Is to Be Saved

Chosen Drawing File

Different file extensions/ format that a drawing can be saved as. Look for Template (DWT) and Drawing Interchange Files (DXF) along with different versions of AutoCAD.

Save Button

File Name

File Extension

Saving a Drawing

Because AutoCAD 2000 functions in the Windows environment, saving a drawing is a very straightforward process. A cardinal rule is to remember to save early and save often. There are basically two save commands, **Save** and **Save As**. Both appear under the File pull-down menu. The first time a drawing is saved, the Save As dialog box (see Figure 9.26) automatically appears on the screen no matter which command you choose. At this point you must select the drive and folder where you wish to save your drawing. Be sure to check with your instructor before saving any drawing to the hard drive, usually the C: drive. The Save command can also be accessed by left-clicking on the icon on the Standard Toolbar that looks like a floppy disk. Typing in the word at the command line will also work. The keyboard shortcut for saving a drawing is Ctrl + S. Once a drawing has initially been saved with the Save As screen, the dialog box does not reappear when the basic save is used. This is referred to as a qsave and assumes that everything will be saved according to the status quo.

AutoCAD drawings are typically saved as .dwg files. However, you are also given the option of saving your drawing as a Drawing Interchange File (.dxf) or template file (.dwt). AutoCAD 2000 allows you to save a drawing in a format compatible with several of the previous AutoCAD releases. So, for example, if your office has updated to the 2000 release but several of your clients are still using the R14 release, you can save a drawing in R14 to allow the clients to access the file on their own systems. A list of the formats in which an AutoCAD drawing may be saved and exported is shown below. These options are found in the File pull-down menu. Just select the Export suboption to get the list below:

- WMF—Windows Metafile (see WMFOUT)
- SAT—ACIS solid object file (see ACISOUT)
- STL—Solid object stereolithography file (see STLOUT)
- EPS—Encapsulated PostScript file (see PSOUT)
- DXX—Attribute extract DXF® file (see ATTEXT)
- BMP—Device-independent bitmap file (see BMPOUT)
- 3DS—3D Studio® file (see 3DSOUT)
- DWG—AutoCAD drawing file (see WBLOCK)

If you want to create a new version of a drawing without affecting the existing version, call up the original and then do a Save As under a different name. This will provide you with two files of the original. You can now edit one while leaving the other intact.

The AutoCAD Design Center is another useful tool. The Design Center is accessed with the Tools pull-down menu or by pressing Ctrl + 2. The Design Center allows you drag and drop existing drawings or portions of drawings into the file with which you are working.

9.6 Ending Your AutoCAD Session

Just as with the other commands, AutoCAD provides you with several options for ending your drawing session. Since AutoCAD 2000 runs in a Windows environment, you may close the program by clicking on the X button on the upper right of the screen. You may also type in **QUIT** or **EXIT** or select E_x_it from the _F_ile pull-down menu. If you have made no changes to the drawing, the program will immediately close down. If you have made changes, a dialog box will come up asking you whether you wish to save your drawing. At this time, you may also choose to cancel the close command.

REVIEW QUESTIONS

1. What does it mean when three dots appear next to a command on a pull-down menu?
2. Where should you look on the computer screen to determine which command AutoCAD is currently trying to execute?
3. What key should you press to access a listing of previously entered commands?
4. Describe a flyout menu.
5. List four ways you can communicate with the AutoCAD program.
6. What key will cancel a command while it is running?
7. Where should you go if you need a quick review of how a command works?
8. What function does the Undo command perform?
9. How many times in a row can you use the Redo command? What command must it follow?
10. Convert each of the following numbers to decimal, engineering, architectural, fractional, and scientific units.
    a. 21.5″
    b. 1′-7.25″
    c. 2′-1½″
    d. 16.75″
    e. 2.5E+01
11. What angle option is used on some mechanical as well as on some civil and architectural work?

EXERCISES

Exercises Using the Wizard
EXERCISE 9.1

Double-left-click on the AutoCAD icon on the Windows Desktop (default Windows screen). When the Startup dialog box opens, use the Wizard icon, which will offer two selections.

- Select Quick Setup and then select the OK button.
- Select the _A_rchitectural unit of measurement and then select the _N_ext> button.
- In the _W_idth: box, type 34′ . (This is the ¼″ = 1′-0″ equivalent of an 8.5″ real-size plotting sheet.)
- Left-click in the _L_ength: box and highlight the existing number, then type in 44′. (This is the ¼″ = 1′-0″ equivalent of 11″ real-size plotting sheet.) This setup is good for ¼″ = 1′-0″ scale.
- The setup is complete. Check with your instructor to see if it is all right to perform a Save As to save your drawing to a student directory on the hard drive. Use the name 9EX-1. To close the drawing, select _C_lose from the _F_ile pull-down menu.

EXERCISE 9.2

With the AutoCAD main screen still showing from exercise 9.1, select the File pull-down menu and then select New with a left click to begin a new drawing. Use a Wizard displays again. This time use the Advanced Setup option and select the OK button.

- At the Advanced Setup dialog box select Decimal units if it is not already highlighted, then select the Next>button.
- Select Decimal Degrees option if not already highlighted, and select the Next>button.
- At the next display, leave the East default selected and select the Next>button.
- Leave the next dialog box at the Counter-Clockwise selection.
- In the Area dialog display type in 36 at the Width: box, then highlight the Length: box and type 24. Now select the Finish button.
- The setup is now complete to draw at 1″= 1″(full scale) and 36″ × 24″ limits.
- Perform a Save As and name the exercise 9EX-2. Close the drawing using Close in the File pull-down menu.

EXERCISE 9.3

From the File pull-down menu, select the New option. When the Startup dialog box opens, use the Wizard icon, which will offer two selections.

- Select the Quick Setup and then select the OK button.
- Select the Architectural unit of measurement and then select the Next> button
- In the Width: box, type in 8.5′. (This is the 1″ = 1′-0″ equivalent of an 8.5″ real-size plotting sheet.)
- Left-click in the Length: box and highlight the existing number, then type in 11′. (This is the 1″ = 1′-0″ equivalent of 11″ real-size plotting sheet.)
- Perform a Save As to save your drawing to a student directory on the hard drive. Use the name 9EX-3. To close the drawing, select Close from the File pull-down menu.

Exercises Using a Template
EXERCISE 9.4

From the File pull-down menu select New. Select the Use Template icon to the left of the Wizard icon. When the selection is made, a list of existing templates is shown in the text display area. Use the arrow buttons to the right and scan through the existing templates. Select **Architectural, English units – named plot styles dwt** with a double left click.

- When this selection is made, an Architectural title block is loaded into the Paper Space/Layout1 environment. This is a 3′ × 2′ or 36″ × 24″ sheet size with a preloaded setup for your use.
- Notice in the left bottom corner a triangle with the W and the X inside it (see Figure 9.27). This symbol indicates the drawing is in a full-scale paper space environment. It is fine to put text in the title block at this stage but not to draw on the objects.
- To draw in the model space environment, move the cursor into the middle of the drawing and perform a double left click. Notice that the triangle disappears and the UCS (User Coordinate System) symbol is shown in the bottom left corner (see Figure 9.28). It is the normal symbol you get when you begin a new drawing from scratch.

FIGURE 9.27   Paper space icon.

FIGURE 9.28   UCS symbol.

Once you have activated model space, you can feel free to start drawing. In Appendix A on plotting, zooming in floating model space will be explained. When you need to get back to paper space, simply double-click with the cursor pulled over in the gray area off the layout sheet.

- You can save the drawing in paper space or model space. The process is the same. The trick is to watch the icons so you can click back and forth to the environment you want.

- Repeat exercise 9.4 using a different template. If you want to try something interesting, select a German Template (DIN) or a Japanese Template (JIS).

Exercises Starting from Scratch
EXERCISE 9.5

In the AutoCAD main menu, select the <u>N</u>ew command in the <u>F</u>ile pull-down menu. When the Create New Drawing dialog box opens, select the Start from Scratch icon. Use the default English (Feet and Inches) setting and left-click on the OK button. The environment comes up with the following setup:

- $12'' \times 9''$ drawing limits and the units set to inches.

Remember to do a Save As to give your drawing a name, and perform a Close to shut down the drawing.

Exercises Opening Existing Drawing
EXERCISE 9.6

In the AutoCAD main menu select the open folder icon in the lower bottom left corner of the graphics area. The Select File dialog box appears and shows the current directory in the <u>L</u>ook in: box. If the Acad 2000 directory is not listed, use the arrow button to the right and select it. In the listings below select the Sample subdirectory with a double left click (see Figure 9.29). At this point some sample drawings found in AutoCAD are listed.

- Select the Campus Dwg with a double left click.

This is one of the preloaded drawings in the AutoCAD sample directory. Scan through this directory and take a look at the different types of drawings. Open a few others to get some practice. Use the <u>C</u>lose option in the <u>F</u>ile pull-down menu to shut down the drawings one at a time.

FIGURE 9.29   The Sample AutoCAD directory.

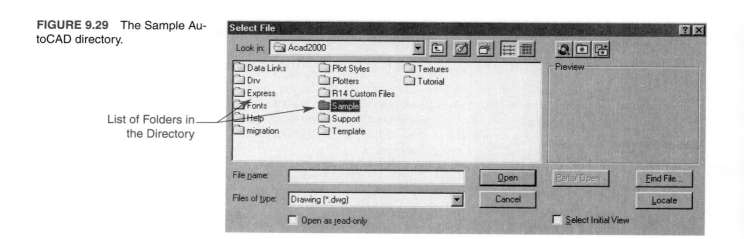

Exercise Creating Your Own Template
EXERCISE 9.7

Begin a new drawing by typing **NEW** at the command line.

- Select the Use a Wizard icon from the Create New Drawing dialog box, choose the Advanced Setup, and left-click on the OK button.
- Select Engineering units, then left-click on the Next> button.
- Choose the Surveyor angle settings, leave the Precision on N0dE, and left-click on the Next> button.
- Leave the direction for angle measurement set to East, and left-click on the Next> button.
- Select the Clockwise setting for the Angle Direction, then left-click on the Next> button again.
- Under the Area setting choose a Width: of 340′ and a Length: of 220′ and click the Finish button.

To save the drawing as a template file, type in **Save As**. At the File name: prompt, type Site1=20 to give the drawing a name. At the Save as type: prompt, select AutoCAD Drawing Template File [*.dwt] (see Figure 9.30). When prompted to Save in: the Template directory, type in Civil 11x17 to name the template (see Figure 9.31).

When prompted with a Template Description dialog box, keep the English Measurement, and click on the OK button (see Figure 9.32). The drawing setup you have just created is now a template and can be accessed when you begin a new drawing by using the Use a Template icon. Try starting a new drawing and see if you can find this template.

FIGURE 9.30 AutCAD template file

Template File

FIGURE 9.31   Civil template.

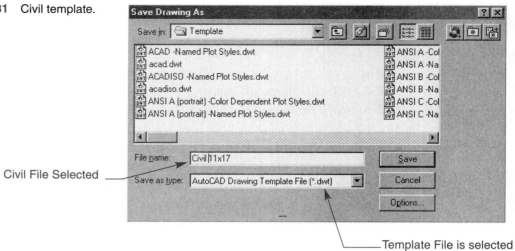

Civil File Selected ——

—— Template File is selected

FIGURE 9.32   Template Description dialog box.

Beginning to Draw

10.1 The Point Command

- Type **PO** or **POINT** at the command prompt and then press Enter (↵).
- Left-click on Point in the Draw pull-down menu. This will cause another menu to cascade down containing the options Single Point, Multiple Point, Divide, and Measure.
- Pick the Point icon on the Draw toolbar. It looks like a single dot.

Point
Icon

The **Point** command creates points within your drawing. These points are useful not only for marking a particular location but for editing purposes. Once you have accessed the POINT command, AutoCAD will ask you to Specify a point:. If you want to experiment with the command now, try left-clicking on a point anywhere on your graphics screen. Before this chapter is over, we will show you a more precise way to enter points. Pick Point and then Multiple Point on the Draw pull-down menu to draw several points without having to reselect the command. Multiple Point will remain active until you press the Esc button to exit the command. The **Point** icon will also allow you to draw multiple points. Typing in the command or selecting the Single Point option under the Draw pull-down menu will allow you to pick only one point.

You are also able to choose how you want your points to look. Go to the Format pull-down menu and select Point Style. Notice that Point Style is followed by three dots, so expect a dialog box to appear when you highlight it.

The Point Style dialog box (see Figure 10.1) offers 20 different looks or styles for your point. You can also size your points relative to the screen or in absolute units. Changing the point style changes *all* the points on your drawing, including the points you have already drawn, so you cannot have several different point styles within one drawing. You may have noticed that one of the point style boxes is blank. This option allows you to pick a point but not actually display the point on your drawing. This is useful for precise drawing and editing. You will hear more about this later in Chapter 13. In AutoCAD, a point is considered a node. This becomes important when you learn to use object snaps.

Note: The Point Style dialog box may also be accessed by typing in **DDPTYPE** at the command: line.)

Tip: The apparent size of the points on your screen may change as you use the Zoom command (see Section 11.2). You also need to use Regen for the style changes to appear on the screen (see Section 11.5).

Note: For an explanation of the Divide and Measure options of the Point command, see Section 13.7

Tip: To continue placing points on a drawing with repeating the Point command, choose the Multiple Point option on the Point cascade menu.

FIGURE 10.1 Point Style dialog box.

10.2 The Line Commands

Line
Icon

Note: If a letter is capitalized on the command line, you can use that letter as a shortcut to selecting that command rather than having to type out the complete word.

- Type **Line** or **L** at the command prompt and press Enter ⤶.
- Select <u>L</u>ine from the <u>D</u>raw pull-down menu.
- Pick the Line icon on the Draw toolbar. It looks like a single line with a red endpoint on each end.

Once you have selected the Line command by using one of the preceding methods, you are ready to begin drawing lines. Remember to check the command window to find out what AutoCAD expects of you. Once you enter the **Line** command, you will be asked to specify a first point. For now, you can do this by picking a point on the graphics screen with your left mouse button. From this point on you are given three options at each step. The default option is to specify the next point. Notice the words Close and Undo in the square brackets; these are your other two options. If you type in **Close** or **C** and press Enter⤶ instead of selecting a next point, AutoCAD will draw a line connecting the last point you entered to the first point selected. Take a minute and try out this option. If you accidentally choose a wrong point or if you change your mind, the Undo option will help you out. Type in **Undo** or **U** and press Enter⤶, and AutoCAD will erase the last line segment drawn. You can repeat this process for as many times as you have line segments to erase. But remember, you must stay in the Line command to exercise the Close and Undo options. Typing in **Undo** and pressing Enter⤶ directly after you have exited Line will erase all the lines drawn (see Section 9.4).

10.3 The Erase and Redraw Commands

Erase
Icon

Note: Sometimes you wish to use a command on more than one item at a time. When you choose these items to be acted on as a group, this is called a *selection set.*

- Type **ERASE** or **E** at the Command: prompt and then press **Enter**⤶.
- Select <u>E</u>rase from the <u>M</u>odify pull-down menu.
- Choose the Erase icon from the Modify toolbar. The icon looks like a pencil with an eraser on the end.

The **Erase** command may be one of the best tools in AutoCAD. It allows you to draw freely without worrying if you make a mistake or change your design. The first question AutoCAD will ask you after you have entered the Erase command is to select the objects you wish to erase. The program gives you several methods for doing this. You can select the object with a pick box, a window, a crossing, or a fence. We'll walk you through using each of the methods of selection. They will come in handy later when you begin to edit your drawings (Chapter 14). You can select multiple items within the same erase command. As you select the objects you wish to erase, they will be shown with a dashed line. Press Enter⤶ when you have finished selecting, and the objects will then be erased. If you find that was not what you wanted to do after all, you can use the Undo command to put the objects back.

Selecting Objects One at a Time with a Pick Box (See Figure 10.2)

As soon as the Erase command begins, your on-screen cursor will change from crosshairs to a pick box (□). Use your mouse to position the pick box over any object you wish to erase. A single left click on the mouse pad causes the object to be shown with dashed lines. You can pick as many objects as you want before pressing Enter⤶ and exiting the command. If you accidentally select the wrong object, type **U** at the Select Ob-

FIGURE 10.2 Selecting an object using a pick box.

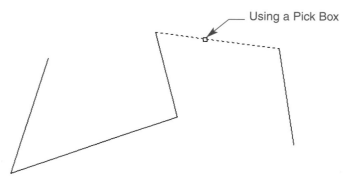

— Using a Pick Box

jects: prompt. The last object chosen will be taken out of the selection set. You can continue to use **U** to back you through all the objects you have chosen. As an object is taken out of the selection set, it will go back to its original configuration. If you use the Undo command after the Erase command has been executed, *all* the objects that were erased will be restored on the drawing.

Undo, Redo, and Oops Commands

AutoCAD offers several options for undoing a previously issued command. The **Undo** command works after any command (see Chapter 9, Section 9.3). It also works within the **Erase** command sequence (as just described). In both cases, the command may be used repeatedly to step you back through the work you have just done. If you go back too far, you can use the **Redo** command to take away the *last* Undo. But be very careful, Redo works only once, so if you have undone five commands, Redo will restore only the last of the five. Be careful not to accidentally reissue the Undo command by pressing the space bar or Enter ↵.

Some people prefer to use the **Oops** command with the **Erase** command sequence. The **Oops** command works after the **Erase** command has been executed to take away only the last **Erase**. The **Oops** command works only with **Erase**, **BLOCK**, and **WBLOCK** (see Chapter 19) commands. **Oops** cannot be used over and over again. Take a minute to experiment with using the **Undo** and **Oops** commands in conjunction with the **Erase** command.

Choosing a Window (see Figure 10.3)

When you are talking about selection sets, a **window** is a rectangular area outlined on the screen with a solid line. Everything that is completely contained within the window will be selected. You generate the window by using your cursor to pick (single click with the left mouse button) a point that is not on an existing object on the screen. The command line will then prompt you to Specify opposite corner:. *You must pick from left to right.* As you move your cursor you will see the rectangle being formed. Once you have selected your window, the command line will tell you how many objects were found within the rectangle you specified. Sometimes, no objects are found, and it will appear that nothing has happened unless you check the command bar. You may continue to add objects to your selection set by using another window or by using another method of selection.

Utilizing a Crossing (see Figure 10.4)

A **crossing** is similar to a window. You use your cursor to pick a rectangular box. The difference is that you select a crossing by *picking from right to left.* Everything that is either contained within the box or crosses the box will be selected. A crossing shows up on your screen as a dashed line. Notice the difference between the lines selected in Figures 10.3 and 10.4.

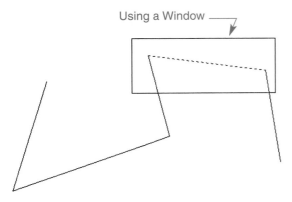

FIGURE 10.3 Selecting an object using a window selection.

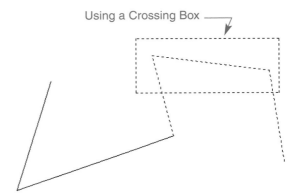

FIGURE 10.4 Selecting an object using a crossing box.

Employing an Irregular Window or Crossing (WP or CP) (see Figure 10.5)

Sometimes it is difficult to place everything within or on the boundaries of a rectangle. AutoCAD provides for this contingency by giving you the option of specifying an irregular window or crossing. Typing in **wp** at the Select Object: prompt and then pressing Enter↵ will place you in the **Window Polygon** command. The command line will prompt you to Specify first polygon point:. Then you will be asked to Specify endpoint of line or [Undo]. As you move your cursor to pick points, you will see a closed figure being formed. If you select a wrong point, simply type in **U** or **Undo** and press Enter↵, then return to selecting endpoints. When you are finished, press Enter↵. The objects chosen to be erased will be shown as dashed lines. You may continue to add to the selection set at this time or you may finish the command by pressing Enter↵.

The **Crossing Polygon** command works in the same manner as the Window Polygon command. Type **cp** at the Select Object: prompt and then press Enter↵. You will then be asked to select the endpoints of the lines making up your polygon crossing. These lines will show up as dashed lines to remind you that anything contained within or crossing the polygon will be selected.

Building a Fence (see Figure 10.6)

A **fence** is a little like a crossing box with the middle taken out of it. Only objects that cross the fence are selected. A fence does not necessarily form a closed figure. To get to the fence method of selection, type **f** at the command prompt asking you to specify or select an object. You will then be asked to pick the endpoints of the lines making up your fence. Just as with the other selection methods, you may use Undo to back out of any segment drawn. Just like a crossing, a fence shows up as a dashed line on your graphics screen.

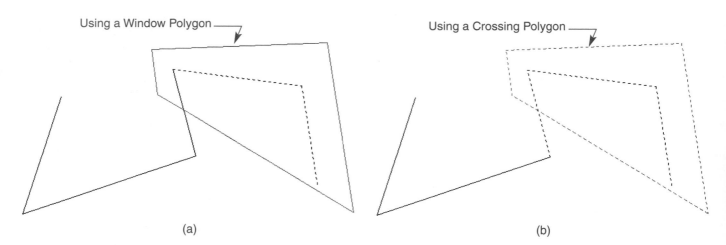

(a)   (b)

FIGURE 10.5   Selecting an object using (a) a window polygon; (b) a crossing polygon.

FIGURE 10.6   Selecting an object using a fence.

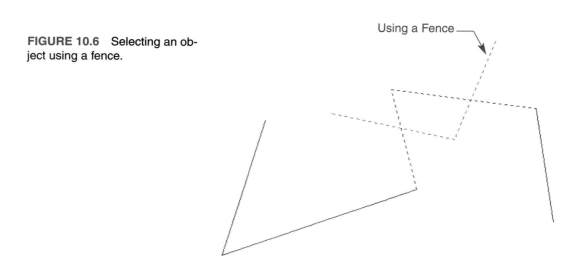

Selecting Objects that Are Too Close Together

Sometimes objects on the screen are so close together that it is difficult to pick the object you wish to select without also choosing an object you want to leave alone. If this happens, press the **Ctrl** button and then pick the location you are trying to select. AutoCAD will cycle through the objects in the vicinity. When you reach the one you want to choose, press Enter ↵.

10.4 AutoCAD Coordinate Systems

Picking points on a screen works just fine for some applications, but after a while you will need to draw with a little more precision. AutoCAD provides you with several methods of locating a point.

The Cartesian Coordinate System

Move your cursor around and notice that two of the three numbers on the status bar at the bottom of your screen change. If you move the cursor toward the left edge of the screen, the first number gets smaller. If you move the cursor toward the right edge of the screen, the first number gets larger. In the same way, moving the cursor toward the bottom of the screen makes the second number smaller. Moving toward the top of the screen makes the second number larger. The first number is the X-coordinate in the Cartesian coordinate system. The second number is the Y-coordinate. The third number is the Z-coordinate. It stays at zero because you are working in two dimensions. By default, you have been using Cartesian coordinates.

The **Cartesian coordinate system** (see Figure 10.7) provides you with a frame of reference for locating points. In this text we will be dealing only with two-dimensional drawing, so we will be discussing only X- and Y-coordinates. (The Z-coordinate remains zero until you switch to three-dimensional drawing.) All points are located based on their distance from a point called the **origin,** which is the intersection of two lines known as the X- and Y-axes. All points are given an X- and a Y-coordinate. The X-coordinate is the horizontal distance from the origin. The Y-coordinate is the vertical distance from the origin. The origin has (X,Y,) coordinates of (0,0). Any point to the right of the origin has a positive X-value, and any point to the left of the origin has a negative X-value. Any point above the origin has a positive Y-value, and any point below the origin has a negative Y-value. Looking at Figure 10.7, you can see that the X- and Y-axes divide the coordinate system into four sections called **quadrants**. Unless you specifically change the setup, AutoCAD automatically begins a drawing with the origin in the lower left-hand corner of your graphics screen. This setup provides for all the points shown on the screen to have positive X- and Y-values. You can input negative X- and Y-values, but you will have to change the screen view in order to see them.

When a command in AutoCAD asks you to specify a point, you now know how to use the Cartesian coordinate system to provide the absolute coordinates of that point. Always enter the X-coordinate first, followed by a comma, then the Y-coordinate. Press Enter↵ to proceed to the next step.

FIGURE 10.7 The Cartesian coordinate system.

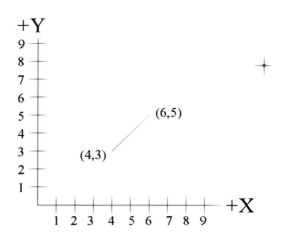

FIGURE 10.8   Drawing a line using coordinates.

Example: Cartesian Coordinates (see Figure 10.8)

Draw a line from point (4,3) to point (6,5)

Command: **L or LINE**↵
Specify first point: **4,3**↵
Specify next point or [Undo]: **6,5**↵
Specify next point or [Undo]: ↵
Command:

The Polar Coordinate System

The **polar coordinate system** (see Figure 10.9) specifies the location of a point with a distance and an angle. If you use **absolute polar coordinates**, the distance and the angle will be measured from the origin. Unless you specify otherwise, the angle will be measured in a counterclockwise direction from the X-axis. If you want to specify a point using polar coordinates, enter the distance first followed by an angle symbol (<) and the value of the angle.

Example: Polar Coordinates (see Figure 10.10)

Pick points using polar coordinates.

Command: **POINT**↵
Specify a point: **2<45**↵
Command: **POINT**↵
Specify a point: **2<30**↵
Command: **POINT**↵
Specify a point: **2<0**↵
Command: **POINT**↵
Specify a point: **4<45**↵

The Relative Coordinate System

The two systems we just discussed use absolute coordinates to specify points, but sometimes you don't know the absolute coordinate of a desired point. Sometimes all you know is where a point is located in reference to another point. It is just like giving directions to the local grocery store. You don't need to know the global lo-

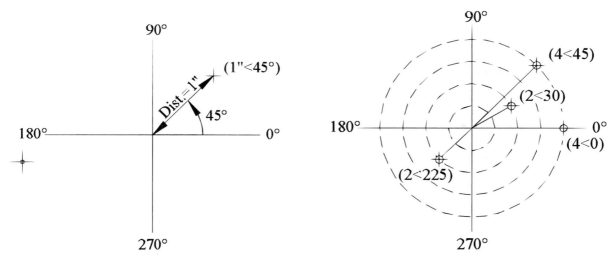

FIGURE 10.9   The polar coordinate system.

FIGURE 10.10   Specifying points using polar coordinates.

cation of the market in order to give someone directions. All you need to describe are the appropriate left or right turns to take starting from your house. That's the way relative coordinates work: you give AutoCAD directions based on the last point entered in the command. One of the nice things about relative coordinates is that they work with either Cartesian or polar coordinates. You indicate that you are using relative coordinates by placing the "@" symbol in front of your coordinates. Let's walk through a couple of examples using relative Cartesian and relative polar coordinates.

Example: Relative Cartesian Coordinates

Command: **LINE**↵

Specify first point: **2,3**↵   [You cannot use relative coordinates on the first point because AutoCAD would have no starting reference point.]

Specify next point or [Undo]: **@1,0**↵   [Go 1 unit in the positive X-direction and 0 units in the Y-direction from the last point (2,3); the new endpoint is (3,3).]

Specify next point or [Undo]: **@0,1**↵   [Go 0 units in the X-direction and 1 unit in the positive Y-direction from the last point (3,3); the new endpoint is (3,4).]

Specify next point or [Undo]: **@-1,0**↵   [Go 1 unit in the negative X-direction, 0 units in the Y-direction from the last point (3,4); the new endpoint is (2,4).]

Specify next point or [Undo]: **@0,-1**↵   [Go 0 units in the X-direction, 1 unit in the negative Y-direction from the last point (2,4); the new endpoint is (2,3)—back at the beginning.]

Specify next point or [Undo]: **@1,1**↵   [Go 1 unit in the positive X-direction, 1 unit in the positive Y-direction from the last point (2,3); the new endpoint is (3,4).]

Specify next point or [Undo]: ↵

See Figure 10.11 for the results of this input.

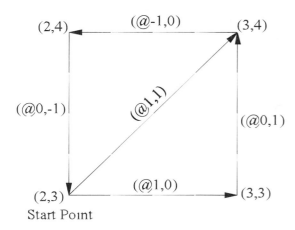

FIGURE 10.11   Relative Cartesian coordinates.

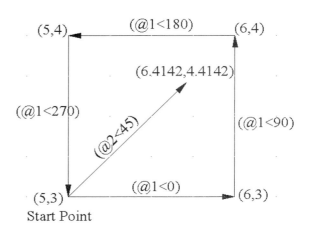

FIGURE 10.12   Relative polar coordinates.

Note: You can mix the methods of coordinate entry within one command. For example, you could input one endpoint in the line command using absolute Cartesian coordinates, the next endpoint with relative Cartesian, and the next with relative polar coordinates.

Example: Relative Polar Coordinates

Command: **LINE**⏎
Specify first point: **5,3**⏎   [Enter the first point with absolute coordinates or pick the point.]

Specify next point or [Undo]: **@1<0**⏎   [Place the new endpoint at a distance of 1 unit at an angle of 0° from point (5,3); the new endpoint will be (6,3).]

Specify next point or [Undo]: **@1<90**⏎   [Place the next endpoint at a distance of 1 unit at an angle of 90° from point (6,3); the new endpoint will be (6,4).]

Specify next point or [Undo]: **@1<180**⏎   [Place the next endpoint at a distance of 1 unit at an angle of 180° from the last endpoint of (6,4); the new endpoint will be (5,4).]

Specify next point or [Undo]: **@1<270**⏎   [Place the new endpoint at a distance of 1 unit at an angle of 270° from the last endpoint of (5,4); the new endpoint will be (5,3).]

Specify next point or [Undo]: **@2<45**⏎   [Place the new endpoint at a distance of 2 units at an angle of 45° from the last endpoint of (5,3); the new endpoint will be (6.4142,4.4142).]

Specify next point or [Undo]: ⏎

See Figure 10.12 for the results of this input.

10.5 The Units Command

- Type **units** at the command prompt
- Select Units … from the Format pull-down menu.

AutoCAD will accept coordinates in whatever Units format you are currently working with. You usually select the type of units during the setup phase of the drawing. If you wish to change the type of units that you are using, use the **Units** command. Once the command has been entered, the Drawing Units dialog box will appear on the screen (see Figure 10.13).

FIGURE 10.13 Drawing Units dialog box.

Note: Typing –UNITS at the command prompt will walk you through the Units command with a text window instead of a dialog box.

Just as during the initial drawing setup (Chapter 9), you can choose from architectural, decimal, engineering, fractional, or scientific units for displaying length. Angles can be displayed using grads, radians, surveyor's units, or degree/minutes/seconds. The precision of both length and angle measurements can be set using this command. Just as in the setup menu, you can change the direction and rotation used to measure angles.

REVIEW QUESTIONS

1. List three ways to access the **Point** command.
2. What procedure would you follow to change the way the points in your drawing look?
3. How many point styles can you have within one drawing?
4. Describe the difference between using the **Undo** command within the **Line** command and using the **Undo** command after the **Line** command has been completed.
5. What is a selection set?
6. What are the differences between using a window, a crossing, or a fence to specify a selection set?
7. Compare the Cartesian coordinate system with the polar coordinate system.
8. How do relative coordinates compare with absolute coordinates?
9. Can you use relative and absolute coordinates within the same command?
10. What command would you use to change from architectural to engineering units?

EXERCISES

EXERCISE 10.1

Draw Figure 10.14 three times using the following methods. Use full scale.
1. Absolute
2. Relative
3. Polar and relative

EXERCISE 10.2

Draw Figure 10.15 using the following methods.
1. Absolute
2. Relative

EXERCISE 10.3

Draw the shapes in Figure 10.16 using the pick point method.

FIGURE 10.14 Exercise 10.1.

FIGURE 10.14 Exercise 10.1.

FIGURE 10.15 Exercise 10.2.

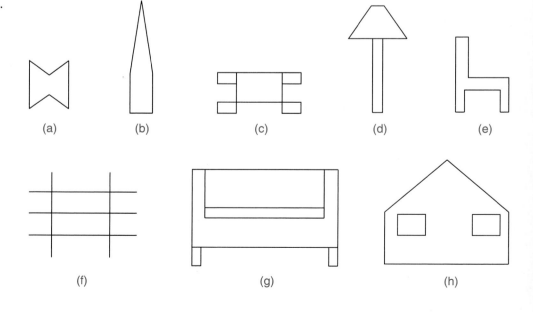

FIGURE 10.16 Exercise 10.3.

(a)   (b)   (c)   (d)   (e)

(f)   (g)   (h)

DRAWING ASSIGNMENTS

1. Draw the shapes in Figure 10.17 using full scale. Use the relative method. Save the drawing as 10-1.

2. Draw the shapes using full scale. This time use the polar method.

3. Draw shapes A, E, and F using full scale. This time use the absolute method. Each time you begin a new drawing, use 4,4 as the bottom left corner of the object.

4. Using the Multiple Point command, place nodes where the corners are formed on shapes B and D.

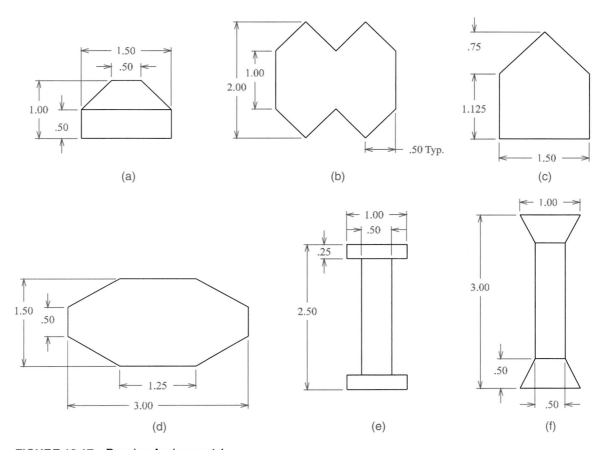

FIGURE 10.17   Drawing Assignment 1.

○ ○

View Modification

11.1 The Limits Command

- Type **Limits** at the command prompt and then press Enter ↵.
- Select Drawing Limits from the Format pull-down menu.

AutoCAD allows you to place limits on a drawing. These limits can be used as a frame of reference as you construct your drawing. Left-click on the Grid button at the bottom of the screen. The dots appear only on the area defined by the limits. When you use a Drawing Setup Wizard, you define the limits of your drawing by specifying the area that will be represented on your drawing. AutoCAD then effectively sets aside an area of the screen for you to draw in. The program assumes that the bottom left corner of the drawing will be at the coordinate (0,0), which by default is located at the bottom left corner of the graphics screen. The upper right corner will be at the coordinates defined by the numbers you choose at the area input in the dialog box. So if you input an area with a width of 12 and a length of 9 (see Chapter 9), the limits of your drawing will be defined by a rectangle with opposite corners of (0,0) and (12,9).

Note: Limits checking only checks on points that are entered as part of a command. This may still allow portions of objects such as circles to overlap the limits. See Section 13.2 for more information on the Grid command.

The **Limits** command allows you to change the limits of your drawing. Once you have accessed the command, the prompt will ask you to Specify lower left corner or [ON/OFF] <0.0000, 0,00000>: The default value is given in the brackets < >. This tells you the current setting of the lower left corner of your limit. At this point, you can type in a new set of coordinates or accept the current set by simply pressing the Enter ↵ key. Typing in **ON** or **OFF** will turn the limits checking either on or off. If limits checking is on, AutoCAD will not allow you to input points outside the limits. Typing **ON** or **OFF** will also finish the **Limits** command. If you still wish to change the boundaries of the limits, you must go back into the command. Once you have input the requirements for the lower left-hand corner of your limits, the command will ask you to Specify upper right corner <12.0000,9.0000>:. Again, the numbers within the brackets < > will give the current limits setting. Once you have entered coordinates (or accepted the established limit) for the upper right corner, AutoCAD will automatically change the Grid display if that command is activated.

Example: The Limits Command

Use the Quick Setup Wizard to create a new drawing with decimal units. Set the width at 15 and the length at 10.

Turn the Grid setting on with a spacing of 0.5 in both the X- and Y-directions.

Access the **Limits** command either with the pull-down menu or by typing **LIMITS** at the command prompt. Accept the default value or (0.0000,0.0000) for the lower left corner. Input a new value of (20, 15) for the upper right corner. Notice how the display changes.

Go into the **Limits** command and type in **ON** to activate the limit check. Now try to draw a line from (18,12) to (22,14). You should get a message telling you that the point is outside the limits. Go back into the **Limits** command and turn limit checking off. Now try to draw the line from (18,12) to (22,14). AutoCAD should now allow you to draw this line even though it is outside the limits shown by the grid. Notice that the grid remains at the limits even though limit checking has been turned off.

Save this drawing as "Limits" to use in experimenting with the **Zoom** command.

11.2 The Zoom Command

- Type **ZOOM** or **Z** at the command prompt and then press **Enter** ↵.
- Select Zoom from the View pull-down menu by left-clicking. This will cause another menu to cascade down containing a list of zoom options (Realtime, Previous, Window, Dynamic, Scale, Center, In, Out, All, Extents).

Zoom Icons

- Pick one of the Zoom icons from either the Standard toolbar or the Zoom toolbar. The Zoom icon looks like a handheld magnifying glass. Different symbols within the "glass" identify which type of Zoom command will be performed (see Figure 11.1). The Standard toolbar contains three Zoom icon buttons. One of the buttons has an arrowhead at the end of the handle of the magnifying glass. If you left-click on this icon and hold the mouse button down, a flyout menu will appear (see Figure 11.2). Still holding the mouse button down, move the cursor down until you reach the zoom option you wish to use. Releasing the mouse button will activate the Zoom command chosen.
- Without selecting an object, right-click in the graphics screen and choose Zoom from the menu that will appear. This will activate the Realtime Zoom command.

The **Zoom** command works like a microscope or a pair of binoculars to allow you to change your perspective on your drawing. You can zoom in to look at a closer view of your drawing or zoom out to "see" it from farther away. Just as looking through a pair of binoculars does not change the actual size of the players at a baseball game, using the **Zoom** command does not change any of the actual sizes of objects within your drawing; it just makes the objects look larger or smaller to you, so you can zoom in to see a small object on your drawing. You can draw lines or execute any of the AutoCAD commands on the screen shown after **Zoom** has been executed. If you **Zoom** back to the original screen, the new objects will be transferred at the correct size and proportions for the new screen.

AutoCAD provides you with several options for zooming. Let's take a moment to look at all the available options before experimenting with using the command.

FIGURE 11.1   The Zoom toolbar.

Window ____
Dynamic ____
Scale ____
Center ____
Extents
All
Out
In

FIGURE 11.2   The Zoom flyout menu.

Zoom All

At a minimum, the **Zoom All** command will display everything within the limits of your drawing. Even if you have drawn only a small object in the corner of your drawing area, the **Zoom All** command will zoom to the entire area covered by the limits. In addition, **Zoom All** will display any objects that have been drawn outside the limit area.

To continue with the ballpark analogy, if you set your limits to the size of the playing field, then the closest you could zoom in with Zoom All would be to a view that covered the entire playing field. If any home runs were hit out of the park, they could also be displayed using **Zoom All**.

Zoom Window

The **Zoom Window** command asks you to specify a rectangle by choosing the location of two opposite corners. The corners can be either picked with the left mouse button or keyed in with coordinates at the line. Once the rectangle is defined, AutoCAD zooms in as tightly as possible on that area of your drawing. Everything within the rectangle will be displayed as large as it can be displayed and still fit on the screen. One thing AutoCAD does not do is change the shape of the graphics screen display, so if you choose a rectangle that is not proportional to the screen, the program will display the contents of the screen plus whatever else fits within the graphics window to fill it up.

Returning once more to the ballpark analogy, **Zoom Window** allows you to define an area of the park such as first base and then zoom in tightly on that particular spot. You can see if the runner is really out or if the first base player missed the tag.

Zoom Extents

Zoom All and **Zoom Extents** are similar commands. Both display all the entities within the drawing. However, the area shown by **Zoom All** always includes the entire limits of the drawing. **Zoom Extents** shows only the area where objects have been drawn, so if you have used only a small section of your limits to draw in, **Zoom Extents** will fill the graphics screen with that section. If part of the limits area is blank, it will not be included in the display. Figure 11.3 provides a comparison between the two commands.

Zoom Previous

If you wish to go back to the way the screen looked before you used the **Zoom** command, **Zoom Previous** is the way to do so. The **Zoom Previous** command restores your screen to the previous view. It can be used up to 10 times to back out of several **Zoom** iterations.

Zoom Scale

The **Zoom Scale** command allows you to zoom relative to a value that you enter (see Figure 11.4). Entering a number greater than 1 will cause the display to zoom in tighter. In other words, the objects on the screen will look bigger. A number less than 1 will create a zoom out, and the objects will look smaller. There are three ways to enter a **Zoom Scale**. Entering a number as a scale factor will scale relative to the limits of your drawing. Entering a scale factor as a number followed by the letter *X* will scale the display relative to the view currently on your graphics screen. A scale factor made up of a number followed by the letters *XP* relates to paper space units (see Appendix A).

FIGURE 11.3 Comparison of Zoom All and Zoom Extents commands.

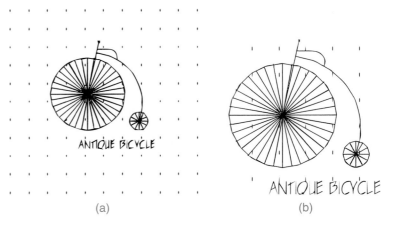

(a) (b)

FIGURE 11.4   Zoom Scale.

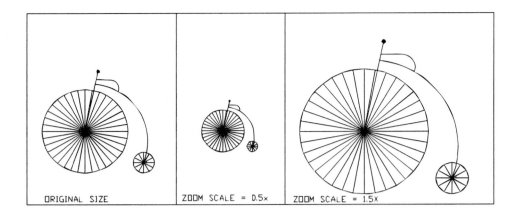

ORIGINAL SIZE   ZOOM SCALE = 0.5x   ZOOM SCALE = 1.5x

Zoom Realtime

Choosing the Zoom icon that looks like a magnifying glass with a plus (+) and minus (−) sign next to it places you in the **Zoom Realtime** command. The first thing you will notice is that your cursor now looks like the Realtime icon button. This is to remind you that Realtime Zoom is an interactive command. Press down and hold the left mouse button. As you guide the magnifying glass cursor up and down the screen the image will expand and contract. Unlike the other types of zooms, there is no abrupt change on the screen; the image changes smoothly as you move your mouse. If you reach the edge of your screen and still need to zoom more, release the mouse button and reposition the cursor on the other side of the screen, left-click, hold, and move the cursor again to zoom.

Zoom Center

The **Zoom Center** option asks you to Specify a centerpoint: and Enter magnification or height <current>:. The display then changes to a window defined by the chosen center point with a zoom value based on the magnification or height specified. The zoom magnification will decrease as the magnification number gets larger.

Zoom In

The **Zoom In** command has the same effect as using a **Zoom Scale** with a factor of 2X. The objects shown in the current view will appear to be twice as large. The effect takes place as soon as you select the icon or choose the command from the pull-down menu.

Zoom Out

The **Zoom Out** command is the opposite of the **Zoom In** command. The objects shown on the screen will appear at half the size of the previous display. **Zoom Out** has the same effect as a **Zoom Scale** with a factor of 0.5X.

Note: Once the Zoom command is entered at the command prompt a right click with the mouse will automatically give you a realtime zoom option. An additional right click will give you the Zoom shortcut menu (see Figure 11.5).

Zoom Dynamic

Zoom Dynamic is an interesting command. When you first select the command, the display changes to show all the parts of the drawing that you have generated. A blue dashed line is placed around the extents of the drawing, and a green dashed line indicates the area that was displayed when you entered the **Zoom Dynamic** command. A view box appears with a cross in the middle. You can move this box around with your mouse and left-click at the desired location. Now you can size the box by moving your mouse and left-clicking. This procedure can be repeated until you have framed in the exact area that you wish to choose for a zoom. Pressing **Enter.⌐** will execute the command.

Using an IntelliMouse

An **IntelliMouse** is a two-button mouse with a small wheel between the buttons. The buttons perform the same functions as a regular two-button mouse. In AutoCAD, the wheel can be used to **pan** or **zoom** without having to access the commands through the keyboard or the pull-down menu. The wheel rotates in discrete intervals that you feel as a click as you move the wheel. The default value for each movement or click is a **zoom** of 10%. (To change this value use the **Zoomfactor** system variable. The higher the number, the smaller the change will be.) Rotate the wheel forward or backward to **Zoom In** or **Out.** Press the wheel and then drag the mouse to **pan** across the screen.

FIGURE 11.5 The Zoom short-cut menu.

11.3 The Pan Command

- Type **PAN** or **–pan** at the command prompt.

- Select <u>P</u>an from the <u>V</u>iew pull-down menu. A menu will cascade out offering options for Real <u>T</u>ime, <u>P</u>oint, <u>L</u>eft, <u>R</u>ight, <u>U</u>p, and <u>D</u>own pans.

Pan
Icon

- Choose the Pan icon from the Standard Toolbar. The icon looks like a hand placed on top of a piece of paper.

The Pan icon provides a good visual image for the way the commands functions. Imagine that your entire drawing is like a piece of paper, and the graphics screen is like a window. The **Pan** command functions like a hand to move the "drawing" around in the "window." It does not change the size of the objects displayed, merely where they are located on the screen. So if you are zoomed in on a small portion of your drawing, you can use the **Pan** command to "move" the drawing around and see the parts that are not currently visible.

There are several ways to pan. Choosing the Real Time option will cause a hand to appear on the screen in place of the cursor. You can then use your mouse to move or pan the drawing around. Hold down the left button and move the mouse around until the drawing is in the position you desire. Typing in **PAN** or choosing the Pan icon from the toolbar places you in **Real Time Pan**. If you reach the edge of the screen and still need to pan some more, release the mouse button, reposition the mouse, and continue.

Typing in **–pan** or choosing the <u>P</u>oint option from the pull-down menu will allow you to pan by choosing a displacement. You will be provided with two command prompts. The first command prompt will ask you to Specify base point or displacement:. At this time you can enter either a specific point or the distance you want to pan the drawing. If you decide to specify a distance, use the same format as you would for a point entry. The pan will proceed just as though you had entered relative coordinates. Since the point and the displacement use the same format, AutoCAD will not know which you are entering until you answer the next command prompt. The second command prompt will read Specify second point:. If you wish to use the displacement option, press Enter↵, and the command will use the coordinates from the first command prompt as a displacement. If you want to use the point option, enter another point location. It will be as though you picked up the drawing at the first point and moved it to the second point. So if on the first entry you typed 2,3 and then pressed Enter↵ at the second prompt, AutoCAD would move the entire drawing 2 units in the X-direction and 3 units in the Y-direction. If you typed another set of coordinates such as 4,6, then AutoCAD would move the drawing from point (2,3) to point (4,6) or 2 units in the X-direction and 3 units in the Y-direction (see Figure 11.6).

Note: If your mouse has a wheel between the two mouse buttons, you can use this wheel to zoom and pan. The default value for each click of the wheel is 10%. You can change this variable with the Zoomfactor command.

The <u>L</u>eft, <u>R</u>ight, <u>U</u>p, and <u>D</u>own options provided in the Pan pull-down menu can be used to incrementally pan in the direction chosen.

FIGURE 11.6   Pan displacement.

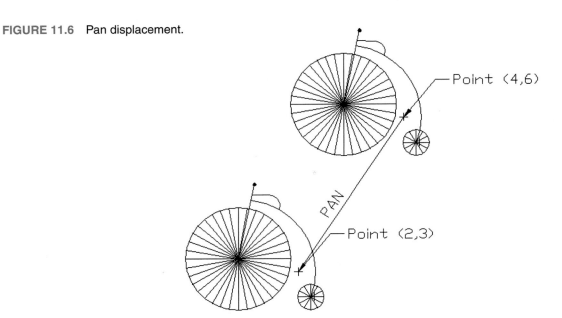

11.4 Drawing Scale

Architectural drawings use a wide variety of scales. There are two factors that determine how a drawing will be scaled:

- Paper or sheet sizes to fit the drawing for printing and plotting
- Readability for understanding the design

Paper can be manufactured in large sizes, but prints and plots need to be at a size that is convenient to carry. Most small printers have a standard size of 8½″ × 11″, which makes it easy to put in book form for a portfolio. The larger size sheets are given to contractors for carrying around to construction sites. A 24″ × 36″sheet size is fairly convenient for a contractor's needs. The following is a range of standard sizes for architectural drawings, but keep in mind that printers and plotters have some control on the sheet sizes. Rolls of paper come in preset widths that lend themselves to certain sizes to avoid wasting paper.

	Architectural Sheet Sizes (Full Size)			Mechanical Sheet Sizes		
	Length		**Width**	**Length**		**Width**
A-Size Sheet	12″	×	9″	11″	×	8½″
B-Size Sheet	18″	×	12″	17″	×	11″
C-Size Sheet	24″	×	18″	22″	×	17″
D-Size Sheet	36″	×	24″	34″	×	22″
E-Size Sheet	48″	×	36″	44″	×	34″

These sizes can be used in a wide range of fields. A 30″ × 42″ size is not uncommon to find in the architectural fields. The AutoCAD software will let you customize your sheet sizes according to your plotter's or printer's limitations.

Drawing Readability

Students tend to find full or real scale (1″ = 1″) the easiest to understand. This is the scale at which AutoCAD draws. (Of course, AutoCAD can plot a drawing to any scale that may be needed.) This scale is used in several disciplines, particularly mechanical drafting. Most of the parts drawn are fairly small and can be drawn at the real size and fit easily on typical sheet sizes.

FIGURE 11.7 Drawing of a partial site plan.

Now think about the types of drawings used in architecture.

- Site plans
- Landscape plans
- Foundation plans
- Framing plans
- Floor plans
- Elevations
- Roof plans
- Wall sections
- Building sections
- Interior elevation and details
- Door, window, and finish schedules

A site is one of the largest things anyone will ever draw (see Figure 11.7). Let's say you want to draw a site plan that is 200′ long by 100′ wide. Immediately you should understand that there is no way to view this drawing at full scale/real size on a monitor. Printing this drawing at full scale is also not feasible, so it is your job to manage the drawing so that it can be viewed on the monitor as well as plotted on a standard sheet size. One thing to remember is that the drawing must print out in a size large enough to be easily read and understood. Some typical scales for site plans and landscape plans are shown here.

$$1'' = 10'$$

$$1'' = 16'$$

$$1'' = 20'$$

$$1'' = 30'$$

$$1'' = 40'$$

$$1'' = 50'$$

$$1'' = 60'$$

$$1'' = 100'$$

Note: Information on reading these scales was covered in Chapter 2.

Now let's look at the drawings that go with a building or structure (see Figure 11.8).

A set of architectural drawings comprises an assortment of plan views as well as elevations. If a building measures 80' long by 35' wide, it has to be scaled down to fit on a standard size drawing sheet while still at a scale that can easily be read. Floor plans and exterior elevations generally use scales in the following ranges:

¼″ = 1′-0″ (most common for residential)

³⁄₁₆″ = 1′-0″

⅛″ = 1′-0″ (most common for large commercial projects)

If a small area of a plan needs blown up even further, a ⅜″ = 1′-0″ and ½″ = 1′-0″ are not uncommon.

The larger architectural scales are used for wall sections and other detailed drawings (see Figure 11.9). These drawings show a lot of assembly and materials that need to be as clear as possible to be read correctly. Large architectural scales are the following:

¾″ = 1′-0″

1″ = 1′-0″

1½″ = 1′-0″

3″ = 1′-0″

As shown in the various figures, a wide variety of scales are used in architectural drawings. Understanding scale usage will help ease you into scaling a drawing in AutoCAD.

Scaled Drawings in AutoCAD

An AutoCAD drawing must be scaled for the same reasons mentioned earlier in this section, largely so that the end product or drawing can be printed out at a readable scale on a standard sheet size.

The actual drawing is drawn and stored in the computer's memory. Today's computers have enough memory capability to draw almost any drawing at full scale. AutoCAD drawings are drawn to full scale but are adjusted for viewing on a monitor and printing on standard sheets of paper.

(a)

FIGURE 11.8 (a) Floor plan. (b) Elevation. Courtesy of Barker Cunningham Barrington Architects.
continued on next page

RIDGE VENT

EXISTING
ROOF LINE
BEYOND

SHINGLES TO
MATCH EXISTING

EXISTING BUILDING
BEYOND

TOP/BEARING PLATE
(MATCH ESISTING)

8'- 6 1/2"

FIN. FLOOR

E.I.F.S. CROSS
(SEE DETAIL 1, A24)

WEST ELEVATION

A
A23

Scale: 1/8" = 1'-0"

(b)

FIGURE 11.8   *continued*

Controlling the Scale in Model Space (See Appendix A on Plotting)

The **Limits** command setting is a useful tool for viewing a drawing to see if a certain scale will fit a standard sheet size. It is important to remember that the **Scale** command *is not* used to set scales in AutoCAD. It acts independently of the **Limits** command and will get you into a lot of trouble very quickly if you start using it to try and adjust scales in drawings.

The monitor is where a CAD operator views a drawing. Monitor sizes vary somewhat but setting up the limits of a drawing will allow you to see the whole drawing on the screen, even on a small one. Some examples for setting scales using limits follow.

COMPOSITE ROOF
SHINGLE
(MATCH EXISTING)

2X4 BLOCKING

TOP BEARING PLATE
(MATCH EXISTING)

MATCH
EXISTING

METAL GUTTER
& DOWN SPOUT

INSECT SCREEN
VENT

BRICK MOULD TO
MATCH EXISTING

BRICK VENEER

1/2" PLYWOOD
SHEATHING ON 6"
METAL STUDS @
16" O.C.

R-19 BATT
INSULATION

PRECAST CONC.
SPLASH BLOCK

FINISH FLOOR

2X4 SUSPENDED
CEILING TILE

SUSPENDED CEILING
(SEE FIN. SCHEDULE)

5/8" G.W.B.

BRICK TIES @ 16"
O.C. VERTICAL &
32" O.C. HORIZONTAL

8'-0"

FLOOR BASE
(SEE FIN. SCHEDULE)

WALL SECTION
① / A23   Scale: 3/4" = 1'-0"

FIGURE 11.9

Example 1

A floor plan is to be drawn at ¼″= 1′-0″ scale. The largest standard sheet size that your office plotter can handle is 24″ × 36″.

- Begin a new drawing and then select the Start from Scratch option when the Create New Drawing dialog box opens up. Left-click on OK.
- At the command line type in **Limits**.

Then when AutoCAD requests you to:

> Specify lower left corner or [ON/OFF] <0′-0″, 0′-0″>

Type **0,0** then AutoCAD command prompts you to:

> Specify upper right corner <1′-0″, 0′-9″>:

At this point type in **144′, 96′.**

Now, where did the 144′, 96′ come from? Here is how those numbers were found. We start with the scale needed: ¼″ = 1′-0″. This means that a ¼″ real size now represents 1′. There are a total of four (¼″) in one real inch.

¼″ + ¼″ + ¼″ + ¼″ = 1″ (therefore, 4′ are represented in one inch)

Now, we use that knowledge to adjust the sheet size, which is a standard 36″ × 24″ real size. Because each ¼″ represents one foot, and there are four quarter-inches in an inch, we simply multiply the sheet size by 4:

(4′ / 1″) × 36″ = 144′
(4′ /1″) × 24″ = 96′

Another method for calculating these numbers is to find the scale factor. To do this, divide the 1′ by ¼″.

(1′ / ¼″) = (12″ / ¼″) = 48

48 is the scale factor.

Then, take the desired sheet size of 36″ × 24″ and multiply 36″ by 48:

36″ × 48 = 1728″

Next, multiply 24″ by 48:

24″ × 48 = 1152″

The sheet size is now 1728″ × 1152″, but architectural scales are based on one foot, so convert the inches to feet by dividing them by 12″:

$$1728″ \times \frac{1\,\text{ft}}{12″} = 144′$$

$$1152″ \times \frac{1\,\text{ft}}{12″} = 96′$$

Thus, the limit of the upper right corner needs to be set to 144′, 96′ for this scale.

- Once the limits are set, do the following. At the command line use the **Grid** command and set the spacing at 2′ apart.

> Command: **Grid**
> Specify grid spacing (X) or [ON/OFF/Snap/Aspect] < >: **2′**

- Next, use the **Zoom** command and choose the **All** option by typing Z↵, then type A↵ at the command line.

Now you are looking at a grid that is set to your limits and desired sheet size. If your drawing starts getting close to the edges of the grid, you may need to go to a smaller scale.

If you do not want to use a grid but want to have a guide to see the sheet limits, then draw a rectangle with a lower left corner of 0,0 and an upper right-hand corner of 144′, 96′.

Example 2

A simpler way to set the scale follows. This time we will use a scale of ⅛″ = 1′-0″ with the same sheet size of 36″ × 24″.

- Begin a new drawing. Select the Start from Scratch option in the Create New Drawing dialog box and left-click on the OK screen button.

- Type in **MVSETUP** at the command line, then answer **No** to Enable paper space?

    Command: **MVSETUP**↵
    Enable paper space? [No/Yes] <Y>: **No or N**

At the command line, AutoCAD prompts you to pick your drawing units. Pick A for architectural.

    Enter Units type [Scientific/Decimal/Engineering/Architectural/Metric]:
        A↵

Now the screen displays a list of scale factors in the left column and the scales in the right column (see Figure 11.10). At the bottom left of this window, type in the scale factor you need. In this case, 96 for ⅛″ = 1′-0″.

    Enter the scale factor: **96**

Now you are prompted for the paper width. Enter the real size in inches. (AutoCAD converts to feet automatically for you.)

    Enter paper width: **36**↵

At the next prompt, it asks for the paper height, so type in 24.

    Enter paper height: **24**↵

As soon as the last number is entered, a rectangle appears showing you the limits or sheet outline automatically set at 288′, 192′.

FIGURE 11.10 MVSETUP screen.

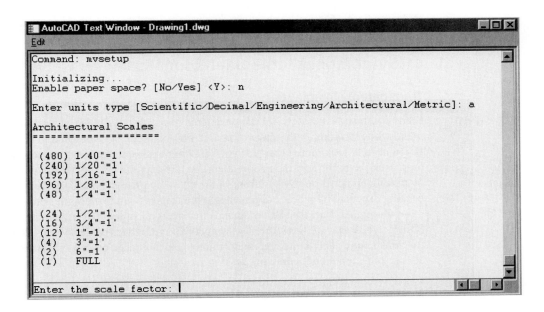

You are done. If you want a grid to display, pick 4 feet. This will work well at this scale. When typing in distances in architectural units, you can enter them as follows:

60″	inches
5′-0″	feet and inches with dash
5′0″	feet and inches without dash
5.5′	feet

These are the real sizes you are entering when drawing. The computer is drawing using real sizes at full scale. What you see on the monitor is the scale adjusted for your viewing.

When you zoom in and out on a drawing, you are constantly adjusting the viewing scale. To zoom to the limits of a drawing, use the Extents or All option.

MVSETUP

Using **MVSETUP** is a quick way to set up drawing specifications (see Figure 11.10). It does not show you all the scales that exist. You may have to calculate the scale factor yourself, using the following method.

If you want a scale factor for ⅜″ = 1′-0″, divide 1′ by ⅜″ to get the scale factor.

$$(\frac{1'}{\frac{3}{8}''}) = (\frac{12''}{\frac{3}{8}''}) = 32 \text{ scale factor}$$

When you use the MVSETUP command, you do not have to calculate the limits to a drawing. MVSETUP is not found in the Use a Wizard option in the Create New Drawing dialog box.

The two choices in the wizard setup are Advanced Setup and Quick Setup. If you choose to start a new drawing with either one of these options, at some point along the way you will need to calculate the limits. Both methods will ask you to enter your drawing area. You must enter a width and a length with the limits numbers converted to the desired scale, calculated as in Example 1. Learn to calculate limits to desired scales to make your life easier.

One thing to be aware of when using MVSETUP is that at the prompt

Enable paper space? [No/Yes] <Y>

answering No lets you customize your model space environment. Answering Yes will put you in the Paper Space Layout1 environment and give a list of options at the command line. Avoid going into paper space when you are just learning AutoCAD. Paper space is for the plotting environment and will be discussed later in Appendix A. The model space environment is for drawing and designing, so stay in model for now.

11.5 Additional Tools Useful for Modifying Views

Transparent Commands

Note: Using the **Undo** command will undo not only the command just executed but also any transparent commands used during the process.

Some commands in AutoCAD can be entered transparently, which means that you can execute a second command while working in the first command. For example, say you need to draw a line from a particular point. If you need to look more closely at your drawing to choose the location, you can transparently zoom in to that area, pick the point, and then zoom back out to select the next location. A command is entered transparently by putting an apostrophe (′) in front of the command name. AutoCAD indicates that a transparent command is being executed by placing double angle brackets (>>) in front of the action shown in the command prompt.

Zoom and **Pan** are two commands that are well suited to transparent usage. **GRID**, **SNAP**, and **Object SNAP** also work well transparently. Many other commands can also be used transparently. The rule of thumb for transparency is that the command cannot select objects, cannot create new objects, cannot cause regenerations, and cannot end a drawing session.

Regen, Redraw, and Blipmode

Some people feel more comfortable when a mark is placed at any location picked by the cursor. The command that activates this feature is called **Blipmode**. It places a temporary mark in the shape of a small cross wherever the cursor picks. If an object such as a line is erased, the blips will remain on the screen. To activate the blips, type in **BLIPMODE** and choose **ON**. If you get tired of having blips appear on your screen, type in **BLIPMODE** and then choose **OFF**.

The only way to remove the existing blips from your screen is to use a command that regenerates or redraws. Either **Zoom** or **Pan** will accomplish this. You can also activate the **Redraw** command. **Redraw** is like taking an eraser brush and cleaning up your drawing. It refreshes the display currently on the graphics screen. **Redraw** can be accessed from the View pull-down menu by typing in **REDRAW** at the command prompt, or by choosing the **Redraw** icon, which looks like the writing end of a pencil. **Regen** is another command that will clean up your drawing. **Regen** cleans up the current display as well as updating the database. Select Regen from the View pull-down menu or type in **Regen** at the command prompt.

The View Command

Sometimes you will find that you are repeatedly zooming and panning back and forth between the same views. In this case, it might be easier to give each of these views a name and identity so that you can call up that view whenever you need it. Typing in **VIEW** at the command prompt will bring up the View dialog box, where you can store each view with a name, location, coordinate system, and properties. You can also store orthographic and isometric views. Picking the New button will bring up the New View dialog box. This allows you to define the new view as what is currently displayed on the graphics screen or by picking a window for the view. If you choose the window option, the pick button will be activated. Click on this button to return to your drawing and choose a window. Once the window is selected you will be returned to the dialog box. View names may have up to 255 characters and may include any letters, numbers, or characters that are not already being used by Microsoft Word or AutoCAD. Blank spaces may also be inserted. Once a view is defined, all you have to do to select it is highlight the name in the View dialog box, click on the Set Current button and pick **OK**.

REVIEW QUESTIONS

1. By default, where is the coordinate (0,0) located on the graphics screen?
2. Will AutoCAD allow you to draw outside the limits set in the initial drawing setup? Is so, when and how?
3. What command would you choose to increase the apparent size of an object on the graphics screen?
4. Would a Zoom scale factor of 0.5X make an object appear larger or smaller on the graphics screen?
5. Does the **Zoom** command change the actual size of an object within a drawing?
6. Explain the difference between the **Zoom Extents** and the **Zoom All** commands.
7. Which command allows you to zoom interactively?
8. What is the purpose of the **Pan** command? Compare the **Pan** and **Zoom** commands.
9. What does a transparent command do? How do you make a command transparent?
10. List five commands that can be performed transparently.
11. Suppose you have activated the **Blipmode** so that marks are left on the screen everywhere that a point is picked. How can you get rid of the blips left on your screen?
12. Explain the purpose of the **View** command.

EXERCISES

EXERCISE 11.1

Locate the AutoCAD 2000 directory found in the Program files. Double-click on the Sample subdirectory to get a listing of drawings. Double-click on the Wilhome.Dwg to open it.

a. Zoom in on Fireplace Detail 1-A1. Use the View command, and under Named Views, select the New Button and name the view Fireplace, then select OK. Now perform a Zoom All.

b. Type **VIEW** at the command prompt and select the Fireplace view you just named. Pick the Set Current button, then select OK to bring the view back to the original position when you named it.

c. Zoom in on the floor plan and locate the kitchen sinks. Use Pan Real Time and pan to the right until you locate the other sink with the disposal.

d. Zoom to the stairs and find out how many risers are in the stairs.

e. Zoom in on the kitchen elevations and find the height of the countertop and ceiling in detail number 3.

EXERCISE 11.2

Open the Sample drawing named db_sample.dwg. Locate the following employees' cubical numbers.

Keith Jackson

Roxie Smith

Yolanda Torbati

John Feaster

Cintra Haque

Lars Sachsen

EXERCISE 11.3

Open the drawing named City map.dwg in the Sample directory. Look for the following:

a. The street closest to the Metrodome.

b. The river splitting the University of Minnesota.

c. Find the names of all the lakes on the map.

EXERCISE 11.4

Using the given scale factor of 96 for a scale of ⅛″ = 1′-0″ set the limits in feet for the following sheet sizes.

Y-value   X-value
a. 8½″ × 11″ sheet
b. 11″ × 17″ sheet
c. 18″ × 24″ sheet
d. 24″ × 36″ sheet
e. 36″ × 48″ sheet

EXERCISE 11.5

Using the given scale factor of 240 for a scale of 1″ = 20′, set the limits in feet for the following sheet sizes.

Y-value   X-value
a. 8½″ × 11″ sheet
b. 11″ × 17″ sheet
c. 18″ × 24″ sheet
d. 24″ × 36″ sheet
e. 36″ × 48″ sheet

EXERCISE 11.6

Using the given scale factor of 24 for a scale of ½" = 1'-0", set the limits in feet for the following sheet sizes.

Y-value   X-value
a. 8½" × 11" sheet
b. 11" × 17" sheet
c. 18" × 24" sheet
d. 24" × 36" sheet
e. 36" × 48" sheet

EXERCISE 11.7

Using the given scale factor of 4 for a scale of 3" = 1'-0", set the limits in feet for the following sheet sizes.

Y-value   X-value
a. 8½" × 11" sheet
b. 11" × 17" sheet
c. 18" × 24" sheet
d. 24" × 36" sheet
e. 36" × 48" sheet

EXERCISE 11.8

Using the given scale factor of 32 for a scale of ⅜" = 1'-0", set the limits in feet for the following sheet sizes.

Y-value   X-value
a. 8½" × 11" sheet
b. 11" × 17" sheet
c. 18" × 24" sheet
d. 24" × 36" sheet
e. 36" × 48" sheet

EXERCISE 11.9

Using the given scale factor of 48 for a scale of ¼" = 1'-0", set the limits in feet for the following sheet sizes.

Y-value   X-value
a. 8½" × 11" sheet
b. 11" × 17" sheet
c. 18" × 24" sheet
d. 24" × 36" sheet
e. 36" × 48" sheet

EXERCISE 11.10

Using the given scale factor of 600 for a scale of 1" = 50', set the limits in feet for the following sheet sizes.

Y-value   X-value
a. 8½" × 11" sheet
b. 11" × 17" sheet
c. 18" × 24" sheet
d. 24" × 36" sheet
e. 36" × 48" sheet

CHAPTER 12

○ ○

Creating Simple Geometric Entities

Note: For a review of the geometric terminology used in this chapter, see Chapter 4, Section 4.1.

Circle
Icon

12.1 The Circle Command

- Type **CIRCLE** or **C** at the command prompt.
- Select Circle from the Draw pull-down menu. This will cause a menu of options to cascade out (see Figure 12.1).
- Click on the Circle icon on the Draw toolbar. The icon looks like a circle with a red radius.

AutoCAD provides you with six options for drawing circles. The default option is that you specify a center point and a radius. Both of these inputs may be picked with the mouse or entered as coordinates. Notice that this is the first option listed on the Circle cascade menu (Figure 12.1). When you activate the Circle command, the prompt will read Specify center point for circle or [3P/2P/Ttr (tan tan radius)]:. This tells you that AutoCAD will assume that you are inputting a center point unless you type in the abbreviation for one of the other choices.

The other options are fairly straightforward. The decision on which one is best for your application will depend on the information you know about the circle and where you wish to place it. The Center, Diameter option is similar to the Center, Radius option except that you are asked to input the diameter of your circle instead of the radius. The 2 Point option asks you to specify two points that will define the diameter of the circle, which determines its location. The 3 Point option defines a circle that passes through three given points. Recall the manual construction process for this same process covered in Section 4.1. Makes you appreciate

FIGURE 12.1 Circle cascade menu.

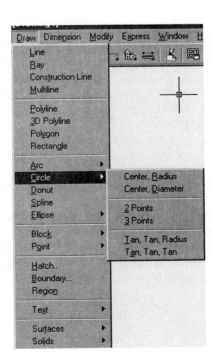

FIGURE 12.2   Circle selection options.

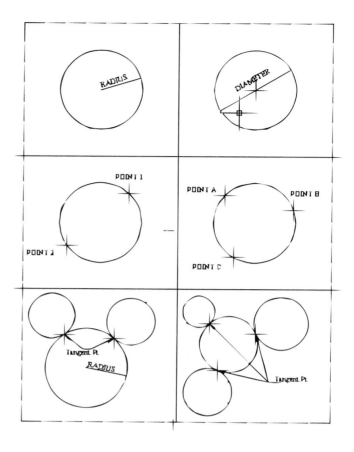

AutoCAD, doesn't it? For the Tan, Tan, Radius option you are required to input two tangent points that will be contained in the circle as well as the radius of the new circle. The Tan, Tan, Tan option is similar to the 3 Point option except that the three points are defined by three points of tangency (see Figure 12.2).

12.2 The Polygon Command

- Type **Polygon** or **pol** at the command prompt.
- Select Polygon from the <u>D</u>raw pull-down menu.
- Click on the Polygon icon on the Draw toolbar. The icon shows the shape of a pentagon (five sides).

Polygon Icon

The first prompt that appears once you activate the **Polygon** command is Enter the number of sides < >: The **Polygon** command allows you to draw regular polygons that have anywhere from 3 to 1024 sides. (The value shown within the angle brackets < > will be the default value based on the last time the command was used.) Once you have determined the shape of your polygon by picking the number of sides, you have the option of sizing and locating the figure either by specifying the center and the radius or by determining an edge.

The default option is to first choose the center point of the polygon. You may do this by picking a point with your mouse or by entering coordinates. Once you do this, you will be asked to Enter an option [Inscribed in circle/Circumscribed about circle]< I >:. This means you must decide whether you want your polygon constructed within the confines of the circle you will specify or around the circle (see Figure 12.3). The default value will initially be <u>I</u> for inscribed but will change to whatever was selected the last time the command was used. After you have entered either I for inscribed or C for circumscribed, you will be asked to Specify radius of circle:. Once the radius is entered, the polygon will appear on the drawing.

FIGURE 12.3 The difference between an inscribed polygon and a circumscribed polygon.

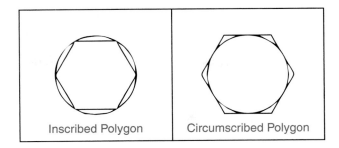

Inscribed Polygon   Circumscribed Polygon

12.3 The Arc Command

- Type **ARC or A** at the command prompt.
- Select <u>A</u>rc from the <u>D</u>raw pull-down menu. A cascading menu will appear with various input options (see Figure 12.4).
- Pick the Arc icon on the Draw toolbar. The icon looks like an arc with three red points shown on the endpoints and the center of the arc.

Arc
Icon

The **Arc** command is so versatile that it takes a little bit of experimenting to get used to it. The first step is to acquaint yourself with the various components of an arc (see Figure 12.5). You will find that once you begin needing the command, the choice of option will become obvious. Rarely do you have all the information about an arc. Your job is to find at least three pieces of data that can be used to input the arc.

Figure 12.6 illustrates each of the options available in the command. The 3 Point option is the default if you access the command through the Arc icon or by typing the command name. Unless you change the setup, arcs are usually created in a counterclockwise direction, so put some thought into choosing your Start and End points in options that require that input.

Note: You can use the space bar or the **Enter.⏎** key to make the endpoint of a previously drawn arc or line the starting point for a new arc.

The **Continue** option can be used to attach a new arc to the last arc or line drawn. The new arc will be tangent to the arc or line to which it is attached. If you wish to draw a series of continuing arcs, you can press the **Enter.⏎** button twice to reactivate the command and then indicate the Continue option. Figure 12.7 shows several ways this command can be utilized.

FIGURE 12.4 <u>A</u>rc command cascade menu.

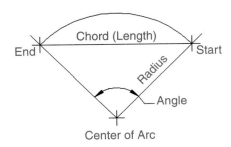

FIGURE 12.5 Components of an arc.

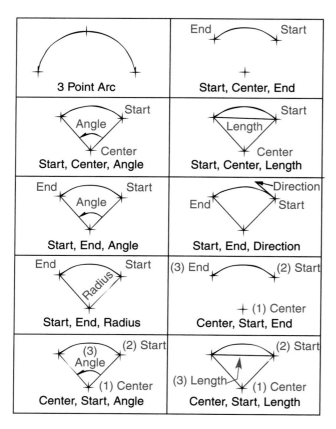

FIGURE 12.6 Examples of Arc input options.

FIGURE 12.7 Example of the Arc and Line Continue commands.

12.4 The Ellipse Command

- Type **ELLIPSE** or **EL** at the command prompt.
- Select <u>E</u>llipse from the <u>D</u>raw pull-down menu. A cascading menu will appear, offering three options: (1) <u>C</u>enter, (2) Axis, <u>E</u>nd, and (3) <u>A</u>rc.
- Pick the Ellipse icon from the Draw toolbar. The icon image is an ellipse with two red dots at quadrants of the ellipse.

Ellipse
Icon

Axis, Endpoint Option

An ellipse possesses a major and a minor axis (see Figure 12.8). The **Axis, Endpoint** option asks you to specify the endpoints of one axis of the ellipse. These endpoints may define either the major or the minor axis. AutoCAD then requests the distance from the center point of the first axis to the endpoint of the second axis. These three points will define your ellipse. As you experiment with the command notice that a preliminary ellipse appears as soon as you pick the first two endpoints. If you move the cursor you will see a line stretching from the center of the ellipse like a rubber band. As you move the cursor and stretch this rubber band, the preliminary ellipse will expand and contract depending on the location of your cursor. This feature lets you preview the ellipse you are defining. The ellipse does not actually exist in the drawing until you choose the final distance to the other axis (see Figure 12.9).

AutoCAD gives you the option of defining a Rotation instead of a distance in the last step. To take advantage of this option, you must type an **R** at the command prompt "Specify distance to other axis or [Rotation]:". To understand how this command works, visualize a circle. As you turn the circle away from you the circle begins to take on the appearance of an ellipse to your eye. The shape is determined by the way you view the object. In the first two steps of the **Ellipse** command, enough information is provided to pick one axis. If you choose the Rotation option, AutoCAD assumes that the information given is for the major axis,

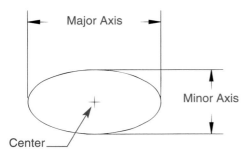

FIGURE 12.8 Components of an ellipse.

FIGURE 12.9 Axis, Endpoint option.

FIGURE 12.10 Ellipse rotation angles.

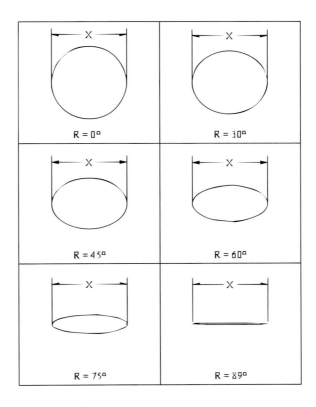

so at this point you have provided enough information to define a circle. Inputting a rotation angle will complete the information needed to define an ellipse. You tell AutoCAD how much to rotate the circle in order to construct the ellipse. A circle rotated 30° will create a 60° ellipse (see Figure 12.10).

Center Option

Another way to construct an ellipse with AutoCAD is to use the Center option. You can select this option from the menu that cascades next to Ellipse on the Draw pull-down menu. Otherwise, you will have to access this option by typing **C** at the command prompt "Specify axis endpoint of ellipse or [Arc/Center]:". AutoCAD will then ask you to Specify center of ellipse:. Once you have selected the center of your ellipse, you must specify the endpoint of one of the axes (see Figure 12.11). AutoCAD then asks for the distance to the other axis. You can input this value as a number or as a point location. As with the Axis, Endpoint option, you have the choice of choosing a rotation instead of a distance.

FIGURE 12.11 Center option for an ellipse.

FIGURE 12.12   Selection point for elliptical arcs.

Elliptical Arcs

Just as a normal arc is a portion of a circle, an elliptical arc is a portion of an ellipse. You can access this command by choosing the Arc option once you enter the **Ellipse** command. The following is the command sequence:

> Command: **ELLIPSE**
> Specify axis endpoint of ellipse or [Arc/Center]: **A**
> Specify axis endpoint of elliptical arc or [Center]: (Input the first axis endpoint.)
> Specify other endpoint of axis: (Input the second axis endpoint.)
> Specify distance to other axis or [Rotation]: (Input the distance for the second axis.)
> Specify start angle or [Parameter]: (Input the start angle.)
> Specify end angle or [Parameter/included angle]: (Input the end angle.)

If you access the command through the Draw pull-down menu, the sequence starts with the input of the first axis endpoint. Notice that this command as well as the next two follow a sequence almost identical with the Axis, Endpoint option for drawing an ellipse. This makes sense because at this point you are defining the ellipse which the arc will be part of. In fact, you will see the ellipse appear on the graphics screen, but do not worry because it is there only temporarily. Next, you will be asked for a start and an end angle. The part of the ellipse that is between these two angles is the part that will remain on the screen. Remember that these angles are not necessarily oriented like other angles in the program, with 0° being at due east. The start angle for an elliptical arc is oriented off the first endpoint of the first axis. A line between the center of the ellipse and the first endpoint of the first axis is considered to be at 0°. Angles are defined in a counterclockwise direction from there. Figure 12.12 shows an example of the selection points for an elliptical arc.

12.5 The Polyline Command

Pline
Icon

- Type **PLINE** or **PL** at the command prompt.
- Select Polyline from the Draw pull down menu.
- Choose the Polyline icon from the Draw toolbar. The icon looks like a curved line with three dots placed along the line.

A polyline is basically a line with personality. A polyline can have width. In fact, the width can change over the course of a polyline. A polyline can even change direction. All segments of a polyline do not even have to be straight; arcs may be included. When you draw a line using the **Line** command, each segment of the line picks as a separate entity. When you select a polyline, all segments react as one unit. This comes in very handy when you begin editing your drawings.

When you first enter the **Pline** command, you will see a message at the command prompt that is very similar to the way the **Line** command begins. The message asks you to Specify start point:. You can specify this start point either by entering coordinates (relative or absolute) or by picking a point with your cursor. From then on the command prompt begins to look a little different. The first difference you will notice is a message telling you the Current line-width. The default value will be whatever value was used the last time the command was accessed, so the first time you invoke the **Pline** command, the default line width will be zero. The next line to appear at the command prompt should read Specify next point or [Arc/Close/Halfwidth/Length/Undo/Width]:. If you are happy with all the settings, you can just keep choosing point locations until your polyline is complete, then press Enter⏎ to exit the command. If the linewidth is set at zero, the polyline will not look different from a series of lines drawn with the **Line** command. The difference will appear in editing the polyline.

If you want to draw something that does not look like a typical line, AutoCAD provides several options:

Specify next point or [Arc/Close/Halfwidth/Length/Undo/Width]:

Any of the options displayed within the square brackets can be selected by typing in either the complete word or the capitalized letter(s) of the option and then pressing Enter↵. Two of the options should look familiar—Close and Undo. These two choices work just like they do for the **Line** command. If you draw a segment that you are unhappy with, choose Undo (while you are still in the **Pline** command), and the last segment you drew will be removed. You can repeat this option as many times as you want to until you reach the beginning of the polyline. If you have drawn two or more segments and wish to close the object to the first chosen point, you may select the Close option by typing either **Close** or **C**.

The Width and Halfwidth options allow you to specify the width you wish the next segment of your polyline to have. Once you select the Width option (type **Width** or **W** at the command prompt), you will be prompted to input a starting and an end width. The segment can start at one width and taper down or up to another. The default width will be shown in angle brackets. The default for the starting width will be whatever was used the last time the **Pline** command was accessed. If you change the starting width, the default for the ending width becomes the same number. Once you have input the desired widths, you are free to choose another option or select the next endpoint for the line segment. Be very aware of the information displayed at the command prompt; this will keep you from having to use the Undo command as often. The Halfwidth option works just like the Width option. The only difference is that instead of inputting the full width of the polyline, you input the width from the centerline of the polyline to one outside edge. Thus, choosing the Width option and specifying a width of 0.5 will give you the same result as selecting a Halfwidth of 0.25. It just depends of which input is easier to provide.

Choosing the Arc option provides for a departure from the straight-line segments you typically associate with a line. After you type in **Arc** or **A** and press Enter↵, the command prompt will display the following message:

Specify endpoint of arc or
[Angle/Center/CLose/Direction/Halfwidth/Line/Radius/Second pt./Undo/Width]:

The Close, Halfwidth, Undo, and Width are the same options you encountered in the straight-line part of the command. If you wish to go back to drawing straight lines, choose the Line option. The remaining options have to do with constructing the arc segment. (see Section 12.4 for a review of the components of an arc.) The angle option (see Figure 12.13a) will prompt you to specify an included angle and then an endpoint. The command prompt for the Center option (see Figure 12.13b) will request the center and the endpoint of your arc. Inputting an arc segment with the Radius option (see Figure 12.13c) requires the radius of the arc and the endpoint of the arc. The Second pt. Option (see Figure 12.13d) prompts you to enter a second point of your arc and then the endpoint. Remember that the AutoCAD default is to construct arcs in a counterclockwise direction. Thus, for example, a positive included angle will be oriented from the start point to the endpoint in a counterclockwise direction. A negative included angle will be oriented clockwise from the start point of the arc segment.

FIGURE 12.13 Drawing arc segments with the Pline command. (a) Angle option. (b) Center option. (c) Radius option. (d) Second point option.

(a) Angle option: This option in the pline arc sequence lets the user specify the included angle that forms the arc.

(b) Center option: This option in the pline arc sequence lets the user specify the center point of the arc after supplying a starting point. A second point is needed to complete the arc sequence.

(c) Radius option: This option presets the value of the arc's radius automatically.

(d) Second point option: This option allows the user to simply pick the point where the arc will end.

Use the Length option to input a distance rather than a set of coordinates for the next point on the polyline. The next segment of the polyline will be drawn at the specified length at the same angle as the previous polyline segment. If the previous segment was an arc, the new segment will be drawn as a straight-line tangent to the arc.

EXAMPLE.   Using the Polyline command (Figure 12.14)

Command: **pline**
Specify start point: (Pick a point.)
Current line-width is **0'-0"**
Specify next point or [Arc/Close/Halfwidth/Length/Undo/Width]: **@1"<270↵**
Specify next point or [Arc/Close/Halfwidth/Length/Undo/Width]: **W↵**
Specify starting width <0'-0">: **0.125"** ↵
Specify ending width <0'-0 1/8">: **0↵**
Specify next point or [Arc/Close/Halfwidth/Length/Undo/Width]: **@0.5"<270** ↵
Specify next point or [Arc/Close/Halfwidth/Length/Undo/Width]: **W↵**
Specify starting width <0'-0">: **0↵**
Specify ending width <0'-0">: **0↵**
Specify next point or [Arc/Close/Halfwidth/Length/Undo/Width]: **@0.5"<270↵**
Specify next point or [Arc/Close/Halfwidth/Length/Undo/Width]: **A↵**
Angle/CEnter/CLose/Direction/Halfwidth/Line/Radius/Second pt/Undo/Width: **A↵**
Specify included angle: **90↵**
Specify endpoint of arc or [Center/Radius]: (Pick a point.)
Specify endpoint of arc or
    [Angle/CEnter/CLose/Direction/Halfwidth/Line/Radius/Second pt/Undo/Width]: **L↵**
Specify next point or [Arc/Close/Halfwidth/Length/Undo/Width]: **W↵**
Specify starting width <0'-0">: **0↵**
Specify ending width <0'-0 ">: **0.25"** ↵
Specify next point or [Arc/Close/Halfwidth/Length/Undo/Width]: **@.25"<0↵**
Specify next point or [Arc/Close/Halfwidth/Length/Undo/Width]: **@0.5"<0↵**
Specify next point or [Arc/Close/Halfwidth/Length/Undo/Width]: **W↵**
Specify starting width <0'-0 1/4">: ↵
Specify ending width <0'-0">: **0↵**
Specify next point or [Arc/Close/Halfwidth/Length/Undo/Width]: **@0.25"<0↵**
Specify next point or [Arc/Close/Halfwidth/Length/Undo/Width]: **@0.5"<0↵**
Specify next point or [Arc/Close/Halfwidth/Length/Undo/Width]: **A↵**
Angle/Center/Close/Direction/Halfwidth/Line/Radius/Second pt/Undo/Width: (Pick
    endpoint.
Angle/Center/Close/Direction/Halfwidth/Line/Radius/Second pt/Undo/Width: **L↵**
Specify next point or [Arc/Close/Halfwidth/Length/Undo/Width]: **@0.25"<90↵**
Specify next point or [Arc/Close/Halfwidth/Length/Undo/Width]: **W↵**
Specify starting width <0'-0">: **0.125"** ↵
Specify ending width <0'-0 1/8">: ↵
Specify next point or [Arc/Close/Halfwidth/Length/Undo/Width]: **@0.5"<90↵**
Specify next point or [Arc/Close/Halfwidth/Length/Undo/Width]: **W↵**
Specify starting width <0'-0 1/8">: **0.0↵**
Specify ending width <0'-0">: ↵
Specify next point or [Arc/Close/Halfwidth/Length/Undo/Width]: **CL↵**

FIGURE 12.14

Start Point

Editing Polylines

PEDIT is a special command used to edit polylines only. It also has the power to change lines into polylines, which allows the **PEDIT** command to be used on those converted lines.

Use the following command sequence to edit a pline:

- Type **PEDIT** or **PE** at the command prompt.
- Select Polyline from the <u>M</u>odify pull-down menu.
- Choose the PEDIT icon from the Modify II toolbar.

PEDIT
Icon

When you enter the command, you will be prompted to select a polyline:

Command: PE↵
PEDIT Select polyline:

You may choose only one polyline at a time with the pick box during this process. Once you have selected a polyline, the command line displays the suboptions of the **PEDIT** command:

Enter an option [Close/Join/Width/Edit vertex/Fit/Spline/Decurve/Ltype gen/Undo]:

The different suboptions perform the following tasks:

- **Close:** If an object made of polylines is open, then this suboption will draw a polyline from the first point drawn with the **PLINE** command to the last point drawn, closing the shape and forming a polygon (see Figure 12.15).
- **Join:** This suboption is used to join polylines together so they act as one object. This means that after a group of polylines is joined together they must be treated as one object. If you try to erase one polyline, they will all disappear because the first polyline has been joined to the others.
- **Width:** This option is used to edit a polyline's width. Type in the desired thickness (see Figure 12.16).
- **Edit Vertex**: This suboption allows the relocation of the polyline endpoint as well as some other vertex-related functions (see Figure 12.17).

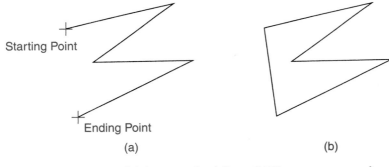

Starting Point

Ending Point

(a)   (b)

FIGURE 12.15 (a) A group of polylines. (b) The same group of polylines edited with The Close suboption of PEDIT.

FIGURE 12.16 A polyline whose width has been increased with the Width suboption of the PEDIT command

FIGURE 12.17 (a) A group of joined polylines. (b) The same group of joined polylines with the right outside corners moved in with the Vertex suboption of PEDIT.

(a)   (b)

FIGURE 12.18 (a) A group of joined polylines. (b) The same group of polylines with the Fit suboption of PEDIT applied. (c) The same group of polylines as in (a) With the Spline suboption of PEDIT applied.

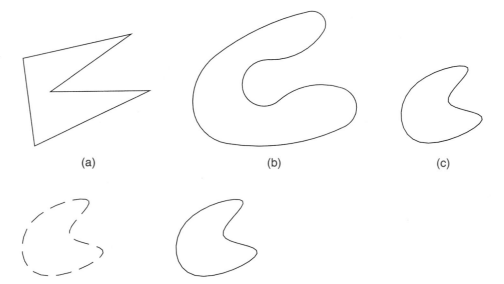

(a)   (b)   (c)

FIGURE 12.19 (a) A Spline curve with Ltype gen turned on. (b) The same curve with Ltype gen turned off.

(a)   (b)

- **Fit**: This suboption is used to change a polyline from a straight line into a curved line passing through the original endpoints (see Figure 12.18b).
- **Spline**: The spline suboption provides a smoother curve than the Fit option. The curve does not pass through the original endpoints of the polyline, so its shape is not restricted (see Figure 12.18c).
- **Decurve**: The Decurve option removes the curves on polylines that were constructed with the Fit or the Spline suboption.
- **Ltype gen**: Ellipses and hidden-line curves constructed with polyline suboptions such as Fit or Spline sometimes have a problem displaying the hidden linetypes around the curves. Ltype gen is a switch that when turned on helps display the gaps better when linetypes with spaces in between such as hidden, phantom, and centerlines are used (see Figure 12.19).
- **Undo**: This option takes back the previous PEDIT suboptions used while inside that command sequence.

Converting a Line into a Polyline

To change a line into a polyline, you must use the **PEDIT** command. Follow the same command sequence.

    Command: PE↵
    PEDIT Select Polyline: (Touch the line with the pick box.)

When you select the line, AutoCAD recognizes that it is not a polyline, and the following is shown at the command prompt.

    Object selected is not a polyline
    Do you want to turn it into one? <Y>

Ener Y at the command prompt for yes, and the line is converted into a polyline. You can then use the **PEDIT** command to edit the former line.

12.6 The Donut Command

- Type **DONUT** (or **DOUGHNUT**) or **DO** at the command prompt.
- Select Donut from the Draw pull-down menu.

The **Donut** command creates objects shaped like a doughnut. A **Donut** is actually constructed of two polyline arcs of a given width. Once you enter the command, you will be asked to Specify inside diameter of donut <current >:. Then you need to Specify outside diameter of donut <current >: (see Figure 12.20). Once

FIGURE 12.20 Components of a Donut.

Outside Diameter

Center

Inside Diameter

Note: The **Fill** command determines the way AutoCAD fills the body of the donut. In a large job, a solid fill may cause the regeneration of a drawing to slow. In addition, solid fill uses more ink. You may want to temporarily change the **Fill** setting during the preliminary stages of the drawing and have it solid only for the final output.

you have chosen the inside and outside diameters of the donut, you are free to choose a location for the center, either by picking with the cursor or inputting as coordinates. You can continue to keep choosing locations without exiting the command. When you have drawn as many donuts as you need, press Enter↵ to exit the command. Each time you access the command, AutoCAD will display a default value for the inside and outside diameters based on the previous time the command was used. If the inside diameter is set equal to zero, the command will create a filled circle.

12.7 The Rectangle Command

Rectangle Icon

- Type **RECTANGLE** or **rec** at the command prompt.
- Select Rectangle from the Draw pull-down menu.
- Choose the Rectangle icon from the Draw toolbar. The icon looks like a rectangle with a dot shown on opposite corners.

Drawing with the rectangle command is extremely simple. All you have to do is specify two points on opposite corners of the rectangle from each other, either by picking with the cursor or specifying by coordinates.

A figure constructed with the **Rectangle** command is considered to be a polygon made from polylines. As such it can be edited with **Pedit**. You can also construct a rectangle with chamfers, fillets, width, and several 3-D options.

REVIEW QUESTIONS

1. What are two ways to indicate the location of the center of a circle in AutoCAD? Must you know the location of the center in order to construct a circle?
2. If you have just finished drawing a circle, either of two keys will provide a quick shortcut back to the **Circle** command. Name these two keys.
3. What command should you use to draw a triangle?
4. Which would be larger—a polygon circumscribed or inscribed around a circle of the same diameter?
5. What information does AutoCAD require in order to construct a polygon?
6. Other than by selecting the Continue option, how could you continue an arc from the endpoint of a previously drawn line or arc?
7. Would you use the **Arc**, **Ellipse**, or **Polygon** command to draw an elliptical arc?
8. Discuss the differences between an object drawn with the **Line** command and an object drawn with the **Polyline** command.
9. What happens if you set the inside diameter of a **Donut** to zero?
10. List two commands that can be used to draw a square.
11. Other than the **Polyline** command, list three commands that draw objects using polylines.
12. Can an object drawn with the **Line** command be edited with the **Pedit** command?

13. What command should be used to fillet a polyline?

14. Which of the **Pedit** options allows you to change the width of various segments within a polyline?

15. What command would be used to create smooth curves that pass through the vertices of a polyline?

EXERCISES

EXERCISE 12.1
Draw the shapes in Figure 12.21 at full scale.

EXERCISE 12.2
Create two rugs using patterns consisting of two geometric shapes, one rectangular and the other elliptical.

EXERCISE 12.3
Create an elevation of a fireplace with a mantle. Use two geometric shapes in the design.

EXERCISE 12.4
Using the **Line** and **Arc** commands, draw the wood stud shading pattern in Figure 12.22 in plan view.

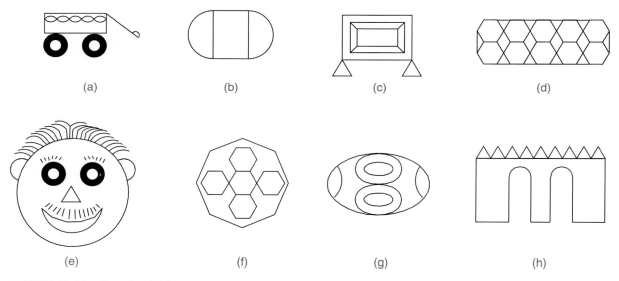

(a)   (b)   (c)   (d)

(e)   (f)   (g)   (h)

FIGURE 12.21   Exercise 12.1.

FIGURE 12.22   Exercise 12.4.

DRAWING ASSIGNMENTS

1. Draw the elevations in Figure 12.23 using full scale.
2. Draw the plans and elevations in Figure 12.24 at a scale of ½″ = 1′-0″. Set your limits so you can plot on an 11″ × 17″ sheet size.

(a)

Choose any dimensions that are not given and custom-design the rest of the cabinet

(b)

Divide the window into four equal sections and then divide the glass into four equal sections.

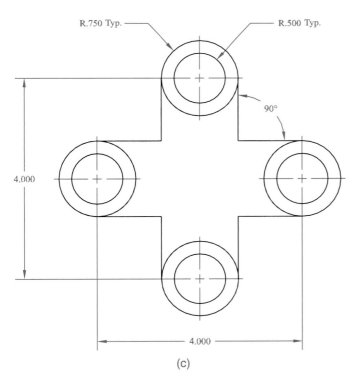

(c)

FIGURE 12.23 Drawing Assignment 1.
continued on next page

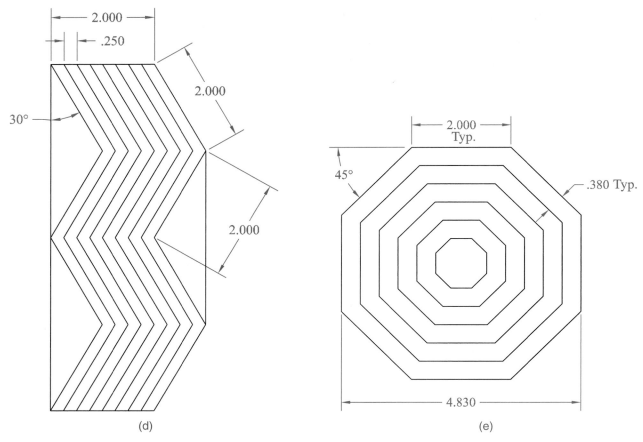

(d)

(e)

FIGURE 12.23 *continued*

FIGURE 12.24 Drawing Assignment 2.

CHAPTER 13

○ ○

Drawing Aids

Drawing quickly and accurately are skills a CAD operator must develop. AutoCAD provides many tools to speed up drawing time and make a drawing as precise as a calculator. Drafting on a drawing board quickly and accurately was a developed skill. All the manual equipment had human limitations built into them. Drawing with small scales and laying out construction lines with parallel bars and triangles to find intersections and corners always included some amount of error. This was accepted on the drawing board but now has been corrected using CAD software such as AutoCAD.

The terms *drawing aids* and *tools* have been used in AutoCAD for a long time. Mastering these commands and settings will increase your drawing speed and accuracy almost automatically.

The following commands will be covered in this chapter:

ORTHO

GRID

SNAP

Polar Tracking

OSNAP (Object Snap)

- Orthogonal or **ORTHO** controls vertical and horizontal alignment or 90° features. When this command is turned on, lines or objects can be drawn in a vertical or horizontal arrangement (see Figure 13.1). The ORTHO command restricts drawing and editing commands to function only in 90°or 270° (vertical) and 0° or 180° (horizontal) directions.
- The **GRID** command places small dots on the drawing screen as a guide to layout and drawing.
- The **SNAP** command gives the CAD operator the ability to move along and in between grids to precise increments.
- **POLAR Tracking** allows the user to see preset angles along with a distance in an on-screen text display. It is like an angle guidance system; however, it does not restrict you to drawing only with the preset angle.
- **OSNAP,** or **Object Snap** gives the AutoCAD operator the ability to lock onto or grab parts of a drawing based on its geometry, such as endpoints and the midpoint of shapes.

FIGURE 13.1 The Ortho option will allow commands to work only in the directions shown.

Vertical lines run 90° to 270°.

Horizontal lines run 0° to 180°

13.1 The ORTHO Command

A great many lines in architectural drawing are drawn vertically or horizontally. The ORTHO command forces the software to draw in this mode. The only angles that are allowed to be used when ORTHO is turned on are 0°, 90°, 180° and 270°. The ORTHO command is simple to set since it is an on or off setting found on the status bar at the base of the AutoCAD screen (see Figure 13.2).

Locating the ORTHO Command

There are several quick routes for turning ORTHO on and off.

- The F8 function key in the top row of the keyboard will toggle or switch ORTHO on and off. Just press it and watch the command line display whether it is on or off.
- The ORTHO on-screen button is at the bottom middle of the AutoCAD graphics window (see Figure 13.3).
- When the ORTHO command is turned on, the ORTHO button displays a line on the left side and top of the button giving the impression that the button is pushed in (see Figure 13.4). The Off position does not show these lines highlighted (see Figure 13.5).
- Type ORTHO at the command prompt.

Command: **ORTHO** ↵
Enter mode [ON/OFF]: *(Type in **On** or **Off**, then press the Enter ↵ key.)*

Button Locations on Status Bar at the Base of the Screen

FIGURE 13.2   Location of the ORTHO button on the AutoCAD status bar.

FIGURE 13.3   The status bar buttons.

Lines indicate that the
button in turned on.

The button is turned off.

FIGURE 13.4   ORTHO button on

FIGURE 13.5   ORTHO button off.

Note: Figure 13.6 is a good example of the rubber band effect on lines. It gives you a visual look at the path of the line before the final endpoint is selected.

FIGURE 13.6   Moving the cursor with ORTHO off.

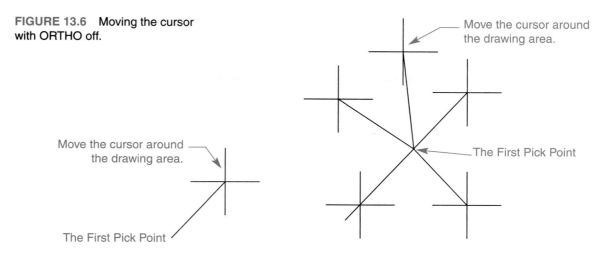

Example: Using the ORTHO Command

To see the direct effect of drawing with the ORTHO command, let's take a look at using the Line command with ORTHO turned off and then on.

Command: **LINE** ↵
LINE Specify first point: *(Left-click anywhere in the middle of the screen.)*

Now move the cursor around in a circular pattern. Notice that the line follows the cursor around wherever it goes (see Figure 13.6). Left-click to draw the line at any angle. The Off option allows lines to be drawn with the pick point method at any angle to which the cursor is moved.

Now let's set the ORTHO command to the On position and try the same thing using the Line command. Take a look at the screen while dragging the cursor around. Only vertical and horizontal lines appear, and when the second point is selected for the end of a line, what is drawn is vertical or horizontal (see Figure 13.7).

Obviously there are times when the ORTHO setting needs to be alternated between the On and Off options. If you need to draw lines at different angles other than vertical or horizontal turn it off. Note that you can turn it on or off in the middle of the Line command or other commands. If you are drawing only horizontal and vertical lines then leave ORTHO on (see Figure 13.8). The Grid and Snap Commands do have some control over Ortho. Their settings will determine how far the cursor needs to be moved before a line will change from the vertical direction to the horizontal.

Note: Watch the line follow the cursor movement when in the Ortho mode. Snap and Grid settings may be too restrictive for your needs so do not hesitate to turn them off.

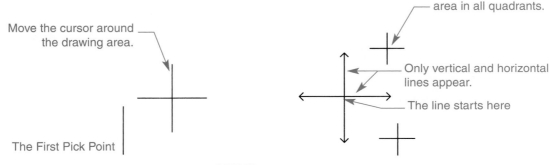

FIGURE 13.7   Moving the cursor with ORTHO on.

FIGURE 13.8 Drawing with ORTHO on and off.

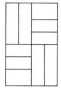

Turn ORTHO off to draw angles that are not vertical or horizontal.

Turn ORTHO on to draw vertical and horizontal lines.

Direct Distance

The ORTHO command must be turned on when using the **direct distance** method for drawing horizontal and vertical lines. Simply turn ORTHO on, then select the Line command. Pick the first or starting point, then pull the cursor in the direction the line should go. Then, instead of picking with the mouse or using another entry method, type in the distance needed at the command line and press Enter↵.

Some of the other commands that you will learn later such as Move and Copy can be used with OR-THO and direct distance as well.

13.2 The GRID Command

Setting up a grid as a drawing guide can be helpful when you are first learning how to use AutoCAD to draw lines. The grid will appear as a pattern of dots and will be located within the drawing limits. The grid dots can be switched on and off just like the ORTHO command. The grid dots will not print out. The grid dots are for laying out drawings and are not supposed to show up on the printout.

Locating the GRID Command

The **GRID** command is used to display a pattern of dots on the drawing screen.

- Type **GRID** at the command prompt.
- Under the Tools pull-down menu is a Drafting Settings option (see Figure 13.9). Just left-click on it, and the Drafting Settings dialog box will appear (see Figure 13.10).

FIGURE 13.9 Drafting Settings option selected on the Tools pull-down menu.

FIGURE 13.10 Drafting Settings dialog box.

FIGURE 13.11 GRID pop-up menu.

FIGURE 13.12 Grid spacing.

- The GRID button is found to the left of the ORTHO button on the status bar at the base of the Auto-CAD graphics area (see Figure 13.2).

To open the dialog box, right-click with the mouse cursor arrow on top of the GRID button. Left-click on Settings in the pop-up menu and the Drafting Settings box will appear (see Figure 13.11). Left-click on the Snap and Grid tab in the upper left corner of the dialog box. The Grid settings will appear on the upper right side. Left-click in the Grid X spacing and Y spacing boxes and type in the desired grid spacing (see Figure 13.12). The grid spacing will vary depending on the limits and drawing scale. One problem that occurs occasionally is that the grid spacing is too close together. When this occurs, a message, *Grid too dense to display,* will come up on the command line, and the grid will not show. When this happens, increase the spacing distance until the grid displays.

Turning the GRID On and Off

The GRID screen button can be turned on and off by left-clicking on it. The F7 function key on the top row of the keyboard will also toggle the GRID on and off. There are other ways to perform this function, but these two are the fastest methods.

13.3 The SNAP Command

The SNAP command works well with the GRID command. SNAP gives you the ability to move the cursor inside the grid pattern in precise increments. For instance, if a grid pattern is set to a 1′ spacing, then the snap can be set to a 6″ increment. This will cause the cursor to snap on the nearest 6″ increment as it moves across the grid, falling on the grid dots and halfway points (6″) between them (see Figure 13.13). This can be helpful if most of the lines being drawn are in 6″ divisions. If there were a lot of lines ending in 3″ increments, for example, then the snap could be set to 3″. The SNAP and GRID can be reset to different spacing in a drawing at any time.

Locating the SNAP Command

- Type **SNAP** at the command prompt.
- Select the Drafting Settings option under the Tools pull-down menu.

FIGURE 13.13 Using Snap with Grid.

FIGURE 13.14   SNAP pop-up menu.

- Select the on-screen SNAP button on the status bar at the base of the drawing area. A right-click on the SNAP button will pop up a small menu (see Figure 13.14). A left-click on Settings will open the Drafting Setting dialog box (see Figure 13.10). Once the dialog box is open, the Snap setting can be adjusted to the drawing needs.

Adjusting the Snap Settings

There are quite a few Snap settings in the Drafting Setting dialog box. Left-click on the Snap and Grid tab to find the Snap adjustments. Two areas are used to create Snap settings, Snap X spacing: and Snap Y spacing (see Figure 13.15), and Snap type and style (see Figure 13.16).

The Snap X and Snap Y settings control the movement of the snap increments in the X-direction (left to right) and the Y-direction (top to bottom). Just left-click in the box and type in the snap increments desired. When you select OK at the bottom of the Drafting Settings dialog box, the snap setting will take effect.

The Angle: snap setting will rotate the grid and the snap to the angle typed in at the box. Angle can be useful for drawing shapes turned or rotated at different angles (see Figure 13.17 with a 45° angle setting). Note that the X and Y grid and snap now work along this angle or rotation setting along with the ORTHO command. To change back to a 0 angle, replace the 45° angle with a 0. The grid returns to a rectangular alignment.

The X base and Y base settings control the origin of the grid and snap. Changing these settings repositions the grid and snap or shifts them to a new origin.

Settings in the Snap type and style area control the directional movement of the snap. For example, when the Grid snap radio button is selected along with the Rectangular snap, the snap moves along the rectangular shape of the grid (see Figure 13.18). If the Isometric radio button is selected, the snap changes from the X and Y rectangular pattern to the Iso snap mode. The grip and snap now are aligned to draw in an isometric drawing format. ORTHO will also work with this iso snap setting when turned on. After activating the Isometric snap and ORTHO modes, try drawing a line. Watch how the line moves as you move the cursor to pick a second point to complete the line. The cursor is limited to drawing only lines that fall along the isometric drawing format. Lines can be drawn only along iso axes set at 30°, 90°, 150°, 210°, 270° and 330° (see

FIGURE 13.15   Snap and Grid tab options from Drafting Settings dialog box.

FIGURE 13.16   Snap type and style options from Drafting Settings dialog box.

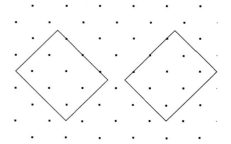

FIGURE 13.17   Using Angle snap.

FIGURE 13.18   Using Rectangular snap.

The snap moves along the grid in a rectangular pattern.

FIGURE 13.19   Using Isometric snap with ORTHO on.

The Grid and Snap Iso mode with the ORTHO on will draw lines using isometric angles only.

Figure 13.19). To change directions along the iso axes with the SNAP on, use the F5 function key or hold down the Ctrl key and the E key on the keyboard. Doing this will let you draw to all the iso axes. These settings can speed up isometric drawing tremendously. When it is time to draw a nonisometric line, just turn SNAP off.

Another valuable feature of the Isometric Snap is that when it is turned on the Ellipse command will display an Isocircle option. It is located in the Draw pull-down menu as an option in the cascade menu under Ellipse (see Figure 13.20). The Isocircle option is in the Axis, End selection. After left-clicking on the Axis, End option, look down at the command line. The command line will list the options in brackets [Arc/Center/Isocircle]. Type **I** and press the Enter↵ key to select the Isocircle option. Then you will be requested to pick a center. Use a left click or type in X and Y coordinates. Now, roll the mouse to drag out the ellipse. A defaulted radius size is set at the command line. Just type in the radius size or type a **D** for diameter, then specify a diameter value. Another choice to use the cursor to drag and left-click to draw the isocircle. Note the direction in which the isocircle is heading. It can be drawn in a horizontal position, left vertical, or a right vertical. Press **F5** to change the ellipse alignment before you select the diameter of the isocircle. Keep pressing **F5** until it falls on the correct isosurface, then type in the diameter value (see Figure 13.21).

The final option in the Snap type and style box is the Polar snap. Instead of using X and Y rectangular values as snaps, polar snap measures the snap distance along an angle. The Polar distance can be set in the box to the immediate left of Polar snap. The values will be displayed in the form Distance < Angle (Example: 2′ < 30°).

FIGURE 13.20   Ellipse, Axis End selected on the Draw pull-down menu.

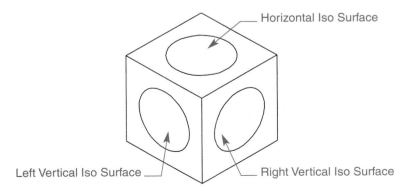

FIGURE 13.21   Iso surfaces.

FIGURE 13.22 Using polar snap.

Polar: 2'-0" < 30°

Example: Using Polar Snap

To see the effect of this setting, turn the Polar snap on and set a polar distance (see Figure 13.22). In our example, we used a 2′ distance at a ¼″ = 1′-0″ scale. The increment angle is set to 30°. Once these are set use the Line command.

    Command: **LINE** ↵
    LINE Specify first point: *(Pick any point.)*

Now, drag the cursor around the screen and click the **F10** function key (Polar Tracking On/Off switch), turning it to the On position. Look at the command line for the ON/OFF prompt to see when it comes on. While dragging the cursor around watch the polar snap values pop up on the screen when the increments are reached (see Figure 13.22). Every time a coordinate is found while dragging the cursor around the display pops up to let you know the polar value.

The SNAP command works hand in hand with the GRID command and is turned on and off just as easily as the grid. A left-click on the SNAP screen button on the status bar at the bottom center of the AutoCAD graphics screen turns the snap option on and off. The F9 function key also turns SNAP on and off.

In the beginning most students learn to use grids and snaps with most of their drawings. As a student progresses through AutoCAD and becomes more confident grids and snaps play a less prominent role in drawing.

13.4 Polar Tracking

- The Polar Tracking settings are found in the Drafting Settings dialog box, which, as shown previously, can be accessed through the Tools pull-down menu.
- A POLAR on-screen button is also located in the bottom center of the AutoCAD graphics screen to the right of the ORTHO button. Right-click on the POLAR button, then left-click on the Settings option. Left-clicking on the Polar Tracking tab in the Drafting Settings dialog box displays the screen shown in Figure 13.23. In the upper left corner is an On/Off switch for Polar Tracking. A left-click in the check box will turn it on and off from this dialog display.

In AutoCAD, polar is a designation for a distance value at a given angle. In the Line command when you used the Polar method, points were entered in the format (@Distance < Angle). Polar tracking works similarly to the Ortho option, but any angle increment can be set as a guide, not just 90° increments.

The Polar Angle Settings area is used to set up the tracking angle needed. The Increment angle: box lists some of the more commonly used angles. Left-click on the down arrow and scan through the selections. Angles are in degrees and can be set to the following selections: 5, 10,15, 18, 22.5, 30, 45, and 90. Left-click on the angle needed to select it, and it appears in the Increment angle: box.

If the Additional angles box is checked, then more angles can be added to the Increment angles. First, left-click on the New button and then type in the extra angle to be displayed. Use the New button to set more angles if needed. When the settings are in place, left-click on the OK button, and the angles will be seen in the polar display box (see Figure 13.24, where an additional angle of 33° was added).

There are two selections in the Object Snap Tracking Settings area. Object Snaps will be covered in more depth later on in this chapter, but we mention these two choices here. Basically, Object Snaps lock on to a wide variety of preset points such as endpoints of lines and tangents of circles. The tracking can be set to display the orthogonal only (90° angles) object snap tracking or the polar tracking, which tracks along preset polar angles.

FIGURE 13.23 Polar Tracking tab options.

FIGURE 13.24 Polar with additional angle of 33°.

FIGURE 13.25 Measuring with Absolute polar. Absolute always references 0° to the right.

FIGURE 13.26 Measuring with Relative polar. It refers to the last drawn line for its new 0° reference.

FIGURE 13.27 Setting angle increment value.

Tip: If you want the angle to measure every degree, left-click on the Polar Tracking tab. Highlight the angle in the Increment angle box, and then type **1** to make the tracking read every single degree increment (see Figure 13.27). Many CAD operators prefer this setting.

Finally, the Polar Angle measurement area controls the reference for the polar angle. The Absolute setting will use the current 0,0 location as a base for measuring angles (see Figure 13.25). A Relative to last segment setting will use the last segment drawn as the base 0,0 point (see Figure 13.26). This means that every time a new line is drawn, the 0 angle will move to the endpoint of the last segment drawn. Polar tracking is essentially a visual guidance system that gives the distance and angle readout before the line is drawn. It can be used very effectively on a drawing with a wide range of angled lines.

13.5 OSNAP (Object Snap)

One of the most valuable drawing tools is the Object Snap. Using the Object Snap is an exact method of grabbing and locking in on points that would be difficult to find using any other method in AutoCAD. You no longer have to rely on the precision of your hand to pick endpoints of a line. Always use OSNAP whenever possible. Being a beginner does not excuse anyone from not using them. The Object Snaps can lock in on the following:

- Endpoints of lines and objects
- Midpoints of lines
- Centers of circles
- Nodes, which are points placed on a drawing with some of these options: Point, Measure or Divide commands

- Quadrants of circles and ellipses (points at 0, 90, 180, and 270°)

- Intersections of lines and objects

- Extension will lock on the end of a line and float an extension with the cursor

- Insertion snaps to a predetermined insert point on any number of objects

- Perpendicular snaps 90° to a selected object or line

- Tangents of circles and arcs

- Nearest will snap to the first part of the object identified

- Apparent Intersection will lock in on where two lines that almost touch would intersect if they were extended to touch

- Parallel snap will draw a line parallel to an existing line

These are the basic explanations of what the Object Snaps can do. They will be easier to understand when examples are shown a little later on.

Object Snaps can be used in one of two ways. They can be activated manually each time they are needed, but it can be time consuming to have to activate an Osnap in the middle of a command. If an automatic setting is desired, then a Running Osnap can be set. When this is turned on, every time the cursor moves and encounters an Osnap condition, it automatically highlights it with a symbol. A left click will choose the highlighted Osnap. To override a current Running Osnap setting one time, simply manually pick the Osnap you desire to use, and it will supercede the running Osnap.

Turning on all the object snaps may seem like a good idea, but sometimes it provides too many options for a condition, and it will take a little time to separate out the correct one. As a general rule, look over your drawing and turn on the Running Osnaps that will be used frequently. The Running Osnaps are great to use. It takes just a little while to get used to them and how they work.

Setting OSNAPS

- Hold down the Shift key and right-click to display a list of OSNAPS (see Figure 13.28). Left-click on the desired selection and complete the command you are in.

- In the View pull-down menu left-click on the Toolbars... option to turn on an Osnap toolbar (see Figure 13.29). Scroll through the Toolbars options using the arrows on the right. Left-click on the box to the left of the Object Snap option (see Figure 13.30). The Object Snap toolbar will be displayed on the drawing screen (see Figure 13.31). When you lay the cursor arrow on top of an icon, a caption will appear identifying the symbol (see Figure 13.32). Left-click on the symbol to select the option.

FIGURE 13.28   List of Osnaps.

FIGURE 13.29   Toolbars selected on the View pull-down menu.

FIGURE 13.30   Toolbars dialog box.

FIGURE 13.31   Object Snap toolbar.

FIGURE 13.32   Intersection icon.

- Type **OSNAP** at the command prompt (OSNAP can also be set with a transparent command). Remember that Osnaps work while in a command. For instance, if a line had to be drawn from the endpoint of an object to the endpoint of a different object, the following sequence would be used:

Command: **LINE** ↵
LINE Specify first point: *(Select the Osnap Endpoint.)*

Touch near the object's endpoint and watch the yellow endpoint box light up when it is located, then left-click. The command line will now read:

Specify next point or [Undo]: *(Select the Osnap Endpoint again.)*

Touch near the endpoint of the second object, and when the yellow box is highlighted, left-click to select it.
A less preferred method of entering Osnaps is at the command line. The following abbreviations for each Osnap can be entered at the keyboard to activate it. The first three letters are used.

Osnaps Abbreviations

FRO—From a referenced base point

END—Endpoints of lines

MID—Midpoints of lines

INT—Intersections of lines

EXT—Extensions of lines

APP—Apparent intersections of lines

CEN—Centers of circles

NOD—Nodes generated by Point, Divide, and Measure

QUA—Quadrants of circles

INS—Insertion points from Block or other objects

PER—Perpendicular to a line or object

TAN—Tangent to circle, arc, or ellipse

NEA—Nearest grabs first point it sees

PAR—Parallel snaps to a line and then creates a parallel path for the line currently being drawn

Even when using the on-screen methods for activating Osnaps, look at the command line to make sure the correct selection was made.

Turning On the Running Osnaps

Running Osnaps are quickly accessed through the Drafting Settings dialog box. As shown earlier in this chapter, the Drafting Settings dialog box can be opened up using the Tools pull-down menu and left-clicking on Drafting Settings. Another quick way to get to the Drafting Settings dialog box is to go to the bottom center of the graphics area and right-click on the OSNAP button, then left-click on the Setting option that pops up (see Figure 13.33). Notice the alignment of the screen. The symbol that will appear in the drawing area when selected is on the left. The small check box in the middle is where you left-click to turn the Osnaps on and off. Study the symbols carefully. They are your on-screen aids for verifying that you are selecting correctly.

Also in this dialog box is a Select All button, which will turn on all the Osnaps. The Clear All button will turn all the Osnaps off. Try these buttons and watch for the checks to appear in the small squares.

FIGURE 13.33   Object Snap
tab options.

Turning Osnaps On and Off as a Group

Osnaps are needed the most when you are drawing lines with the pick point method. The other methods such as Polar, Relation, Absolute, and Direct Distance already have values inserted to complete the line. Conflicts will occur with these methods, so AutoCAD has some quick and easy switches for turning the Running Osnap mode on and off.

- F3 function key
- Left-click on the OSNAP button at the bottom of the graphics area
- Right-click on the OSNAP button, then left-click on the On or Off display

These are quick ways to toggle back and forth between different methods of drawing. Try each to see which one is easiest for you.

Using Osnaps on a Drawing

Osnaps start to work when a command has been requested such as Line or Circle. Here are some examples of each Osnap.

Example: From

In this example a 4″ rectangle has already been drawn (see Figure 13.34). Another rectangle needs to be drawn inside the existing one precisely .25 in all directions. The From Osnap works well in this case. Before starting, turn on the Intersection Running Osnap.

> Command: **REC⏎**
> Specify first corner point or [Chamfer/Elevation/Fillet/Thickened Width]:
>   **FRO**
> Base point: *(Move the cursor to the lower left corner and click when the intersection symbol appears (see Figure 13.35)).*
> Base point: <Offset>: **@.25, .25**
> Specify other corner point: **FRO**
> Specify other corner point: from Base point: *(Click on the intersection of the upper right corner (see Figure 13.36)).*
> Specify other corner point: from Base point: <Offset>: **@-.25,-.25** *(See Figure 13.37.)*

The end result should show a perfectly centered rectangle inside the 4″ rectangle.

FIGURE 13.34   **FIGURE 13.35**   **FIGURE 13.36**   **FIGURE 13.37**   Completed rectangle.

Example: Endpoint Osnap

In this example two lines have already been drawn, and we have started the Line command to draw another line across two of the endpoints of the existing lines (see Figure 13.38). We have turned on the Endpoint Running Osnap, and we have turned off Snap (F9), Grid (F7), and Ortho (F8) for all these examples.

Command: **LINE↵**
LINE Specify first point:

Touch the top half of the line on the left. When the endpoint box displays, left-click, and that endpoint is grabbed (see Figure 13.39).

Specify next point or [Undo]:

Move over to the line on the right and touch its top half until the endpoint symbol displays and then left-click (see Figure 13.40). The line has now been drawn from endpoint to endpoint (see Figure 13.41).

FIGURE 13.38   **FIGURE 13.39**   **FIGURE 13.40**   **FIGURE 13.41**

You Try It

Try this example for yourself: Draw two lines similar to Figure 13.38. Connect the endpoints on top with the line command using the endpoint Osnaps. Now connect the endpoints on the bottom without using the Osnaps; rely on your eyesight. After you're done, zoom in and see the difference in accuracy.

FIGURE 13.42

FIGURE 13.43

FIGURE 13.44   Example complete.

Example: Midpoint Osnap

In this example, a line will be drawn from the midpoint of an existing line to the midpoint of another existing line. Midpoint Running Osnap is turned on.

    Command: **LINE**↵
    LINE Specify first point:

Touch the line on the left-hand side. When the midpoint symbol appears, left-click, and the midpoint is grabbed (see Figure 13.42).

    Specify next point or [Undo]:

Move to the line on the right side and wait for the midpoint symbol to appear and perform another left click (see Figure 13.43). The line has now been drawn from midpoint to midpoint (see Figure 13.44).

Several other Osnaps work in a similar manner to the preceding ones. It is a matter of understanding the definitions and symbols (see Figure 13.45).

The following examples show perpendicular and parallel Osnaps in operation. They work a little differently.

FIGURE 13.45

⊗   A Node can be snapped to.

✕   The Intersection of two lines can be snapped to.

—   An Extension location can be snapped to.

⌐   An Insertion point from a block can be snapped to. (This Osnap lets you pass over an existing line in order to draw to a point that extends off the given line.)

⋈   The Nearest option can be snapped to. The Nearest option looks for the first point it finds.

FIGURE 13.46   **FIGURE 13.47**

Example: Perpendicular Osnap

In this example, there is an existing line and node. A new line will be drawn perpendicular to the existing one. Remember that the Node and Perpendicular Osnaps are turned on in this example.

Use the Line command, select the Node Osnap, and touch the point until the node symbol displays (see Figure 13.46).

Next, touch the existing line, and when the perpendicular symbol appears, left click to draw the line (see Figure 13.47). In this example the Osnap Tracking was turned on, so the word *perpendicular* is displayed.

Example: Parallel Osnap

In this example, there is an existing line along with a node. Start drawing a line from the node, and then touch the line with the cursor until the parallel symbol is highlighted (see Figure 13.48). When this happens move the cursor out below the point until the parallel tracking caption comes on, then left-click (see Figure 13.49). A parallel line will be drawn from the node. The node and parallel Osnaps need to be turned on in this example.

The final example will show some circle characteristics. The following Osnaps are used for circles: Tangent, Center, and Quadrant. In this example, the Tangent, Center and Quadrant Osnaps are turned on along with Osnap Tracking. A total of three circles are drawn.

FIGURE 13.48

FIGURE 13.49   Parallel example complete.

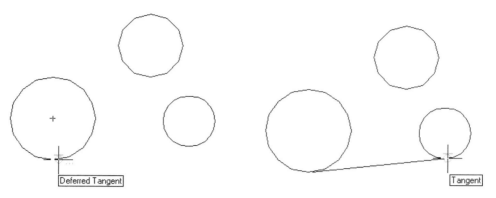

FIGURE 13.50   **FIGURE 13.51**

Example: Tangent Osnap

Using the Line command, and draw a tangent line at the bottom of two circles.

> Command: **LINE.⏎**
> Specify first point:

With only the Tangent Osnap On, touch the bottom of the big circle until the Deferred Tangent caption appears, then left-click (see Figure 13.50).

> Specify next point or [Undo]:

Go to the bottom of the circle on the right, and when the Tangent caption appears, left-click (see Figure 13.51). Press the space bar to exit the Line command.

Example: Center Osnap

Use the same example, but this time turn on only the Center Osnap option.

Use the Line command as before by touching each circle on its perimeter.

As you watch the Center caption appear, left-click, then move the cursor to the perimeter of the second circle (see Figure 13.52). When the Center Caption appears again, left-click (see Figure 13.53). Press the space Bar to cancel the Line command.

A line now appears between the exact centers of the circles (see Figure 13.54).

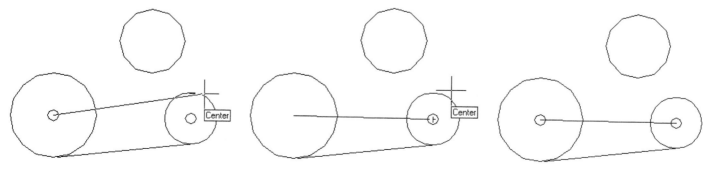

FIGURE 13.52   **FIGURE 13.53**   **FIGURE 13.54**

FIGURE 13.55

FIGURE 13.56

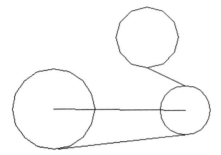

FIGURE 13.57

Example: Quadrant Osnap

Use the same example, but this time turn on only Quadrant Osnap.

Use the Line command and when it asks for the first point, touch the bottom of the top circle. When the Quadrant caption is displayed, left-click (see Figure 13.55).

Move the cursor to the circle on the right. Touch the top portion of the circle until the Quadrant caption appears, then left-click (see Figures 13.56 and 13.57).

Osnaps are an AutoCAD operator's best friend when it comes to drawing freely and quickly to exact points. They can be challenging in the beginning, but do not give up on them. Our examples utilized the Line command, but Osnaps work with modifying commands as well. Copying and Moving objects, just to name a few, are made much easier with Osnaps. Go back and draw out the examples and work them yourself, turning the running snaps on. Then do them again with the running snaps off. Pick the Osnap manually using the right mouse button while holding down the Shift key.

13.6 The List, ID, Dist, and Area Commands

Occasionally you will realize that you don't know the exact location of an object in your drawing, or you may be unsure of the layer (Chapter 16) on which something was placed. You may find that you need to know the distance between two points in a drawing or the area and perimeter of a portion of a drawing. AutoCAD provides several tools for answering these types of questions. Most of these tools are placed on the Inquiry toolbar (see Figure 13.58).

FIGURE 13.58 The Inquiry toolbar.

The List Command

List
Icon

- Type **LIST** or **LI** at the command prompt.
- Select Inquiry from the Tools pull-down menu. A flyout menu including List will appear.
- Pick the List icon from the Inquiry toolbar. The icon looks like a white sheet of paper covered with lines (or a list).

The List command provides a wealth of information about objects in a drawing. Once you enter the command you will be asked to select the objects about which you wish to inquire. You can use the List command on more than one object at a time. A list will be provided of each object's type and layer. In addition, the X-, Y-, and Z-coordinates will be provided based on the current User Coordinate System (UCS). If the object has a thickness other than zero, that information will be provided. Color, linetype, and lineweight are indicated as being set Bylayer or specific for that particular object.

The ID Command

(ID) Identification
Icon

- Type **ID** at the command prompt
- Select Inquiry from the Tools pull-down menu. A flyout menu including ID Point will appear.
- Pick the ID icon from the Inquiry toolbar. The icon looks like a thin yellow bar or ruler with the letters x,y,z above it.

The ID command provides the coordinate value of a location within the drawing. The coordinates are provided relative to the current User Coordinate System (UCS). Once you enter the command, select the point you wish to identify. Look at the command line to see the coordinates for that point. This new I.D. point has been set as a relative 0,0 coordinate.

The Dist Command

Distance
Icon

- Type **DIST** or **DI** at the command prompt.
- Select Inquiry from the Tools pull-down menu. A flyout menu including Distance will appear.
- Pick the Distance icon from the Inquiry toolbar. The icon looks like a thin yellow bar or ruler topped by a line with arrowheads on each end.

The Dist command enables you to determine the distance and angle between two given points in the drawing. Once you enter the command you will be prompted to pick your first point, then your second. Look at the command line for distance information.

The Area Command

Area
Icon

- Type **AREA** at the command prompt.
- Select Inquiry from the Tools pull-down menu. A flyout menu including Area will appear.
- Pick the Area icon from the Inquiry toolbar. The icon looks like a thin yellow bar or ruler topped by a figure shaped like a trapezoid.

The Area command calculates the area and perimeter of objects within your drawing. You can also use the command to calculate the area and perimeter of sections you choose to define. After you enter the area command, you will need to select Object subobtion then touch a polygon or circle and the area and perimeter information is displayed at the command line. You may also just pick the endpoints along the outside of the object instead of using the object suboption.

13.7 The Divide and Measure Commands

The Divide Command

- Type **DIVIDE** or **DIV** at the command prompt.
- Select Point from the Draw pull-down menu by left-clicking. A cascading menu will appear containing the options Single Point, Multiple Point, Divide, and Measure. Pick Divide.

The Divide command allows you to partition an object with a number of equally spaced points or blocks. These nodes do not actually break the object; they only distinguish locations on the object. Thus, for

FIGURE 13.59

The Divide command places nodes at the chosen intervals (5) along the selected line.

Note: Nodes will print out on the drawing. To remove them, type PD mode at the command line and set the value to 1. To see different node options go to the Format pull-down menu and select Point Styles for the displays.

example, if you pick the divided object as part of a selection set, the entire object will be chosen, not individual segments, but you can set Osnap to snap to any of the nodes defined by the Divide command.

Think back to the process for using manual drafting techniques to divide a line into equal sections (Chapter 4). This command accomplishes the same thing simply by your entering the command, selecting the object to divide, and specifying the number of divisions required. Imagine that you need to draw a checkerboard pattern (see Figure 13.59). Draw the lines defining the perimeter of the checkerboard area, then use the Divide command to define nodes (or points) along the perimeter lines dividing the lines into the number of spaces needed for the pattern. Then by turning on Node Osnap, you can easily draw the dividing lines by snapping to each node along the line. The Divide command can be used on arcs, circles, ellipses, elliptical arcs, polylines, and splines.

The Measure Command

Note: The nodes defined in the Divide and Measure commands may come in handy later in helping you define displacement for commands such as Copy (see Chapter 15).

The Measure command is similar to the Divide command. In the Divide command objects are divided with nodes whose spacing is determined by the overall length of the object. In the Measure command the spacing of the nodes is input within the command. For example, you could specify that nodes be placed every 2″ along the length of the object. AutoCAD will begin measuring from the end of the object closest to the pick point, so if your pick point for the object is closest to the left end of the object, the program will begin measuring from the left end. If you pick from the right, the measuring will begin from the right.

REVIEW QUESTIONS

1. Name three ways to turn Ortho on and off.
2. What are some of the drawbacks to drawing with the Ortho command on?
3. How does Ortho work with the Direct Distance point entry method?
4. How can the Ortho mode be changed to an Iso mode?
5. Name two ways to turn the Grid on and off?
6. What determines the overall area in which the grid dots are displayed?
7. How can the grid X spacing be set differently from the Y spacing?
8. If a grid is too dense to display, what can be done to fix this problem?
9. In how many different ways can the Snap command be activated?
10. Explain how the Snap command works with the Grid.
11. Right-clicking on the Snap button at the bottom of the drawing area will activate what?
12. Does the Snap turn off when the Grid is turned off?
13. How many different ways can the Polar Tracking be turned on and off?
14. How can the Polar Tracking be set to display at every 10 increments?
15. Make a list of all the Object Snaps and sketch the corresponding AutoSnap symbol.
16. Define a Running Object Snap.

17. How can the Drafting Settings dialog box be opened?

18. What kind of problems can occur when all the object snaps are turned on?

19. Can the Running Object Snaps be overridden?

20. What information does the List command supply? Make a complete list.

21. What function does the ID command serve?

22. What information does the Distance command provide?

23. List the command aliases for Distance and List.

24. Identify the function keys for the following:

    a. Grid

    b. Snap

    c. Ortho

    d. Isometric cursor switch

EXERCISES

EXERCISE 13.1

Set up a drawing environment with the following:

- Use ¼″ = 1′-0″ scale with limits of 0,0 and 34′,44′.
- Set up an X and a Y Grid of 1′.
- Set a Snap of .5″ with Rectangular snap on.
- Turn on the Endpoint and Perpendicular running Osnaps.
- Draw a rectangle 1′ inside the limits to form a border line.
- Using the Endpoint object snap, draw diagonal lines from corner to opposite corner to form an X.
- Save the drawing as 13EX-1.

EXERCISE 13.2

Using the setup in 13EX-1, do the following:

- Change the Rectangular Snap to the Isometric setting.
- Draw three iso circles in different corners with the Ellipse command: one in the horizontal plane direction, one in the left vertical plane direction, and one in the right vertical plane direction.
- Turn on the Center Osnap and draw a line from center to center on all the ellipses.
- Turn off the Center Osnap and turn on the Tangent Osnap. Try to draw tangent lines on the outsides of the ellipses. (Expect a little challenge. Tangents work well on circles but not so well on ellipses.)

EXERCISES 13.3

Open the 13EX-1 original drawing. Make the following changes.

- Turn on the Polar snap.
- Set Polar distance to 3′.
- Turn on Polar Tracking.
- Set the Increment angle to 45°.
- Set the Polar Angle measurement to Relative to last segment.
- Click on Track using all polar angle settings.

- With these settings watch the readouts on the screen and draw the following diamond-shaped boxes.
- Draw two diamonds with 6' sides.
- Draw one diamond with 12' sides.
- Save the drawing as 13EX-3.

EXERCISE 13.4

Using drawing 13EX-3, do the following:

- Turn on Midpoint Osnap and draw lines in the big diamond from the midpoint of a side to the midpoint of the opposite side.
- Turn on Perpendicular Osnap and draw lines from the midpoint of the sides perpendicular to the opposite sides in the small diamonds.

EXERCISE 13.5

Using different combinations of Osnaps redraw the drawings in Figure 13.60.

EXERCISE 13.6

Create a floor pattern that would fit in a 6″ × 6″ square. Use a minimum of two different geometric shapes.

FIGURE 13.60 Exercise 13.5.

DRAWING ASSIGNMENTS

1. Draw problems 13-1 through 13-8 in Figure 13.61 using the assigned scales. Set up the limits so that the drawings will fit on standard sheet sizes. Some dimensions are left off so that you may customize some of the drawings.

2. Use Polar Tracking to construct the drawing in Figure 13.62.

3. Set up AutoCAD to draw the objects in Figure 13.63 in isometric form.

4. Draw problems 13-7 and 13-8 from Figure 13.61 in oblique cabinet form, using a 30° angle for depth.

FIGURE 13.61   Drawing Assignment 1.

FIGURE 13.62 Drawing Assignment 2.

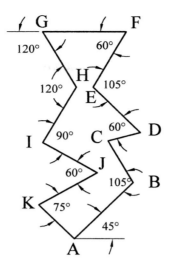

The lengths of the sides are as follows:
AB = 1.25
BC = .75
CD = .50
DE = 1.00
EF = 1.00
FG = 1.25
GH = 1.00
HI = 1.00
IJ = .94
JK = 1.01
KA = .75

13-10

13-11

13-12

13-13

13-14

13-15

13-16

FIGURE 13.63 Drawing Assignment 3.

CHAPTER 14

○ ○

Editing and Altering Entities

AutoCAD has many commands for editing or modifying existing entities or objects in a drawing. Learning to use such commands will make you faster and more efficient. The following editing commands will be demonstrated in this chapter (see Figures 14.1–14.3).

Commands

Trim

Extend

Break

Chamfer

Fillet

Stretch

Scale

Lengthen

Grips

Properties

Match Properties

FIGURE 14.1 The Modify toolbar.

FIGURE 14.2 Turning on the Modify toolbar.

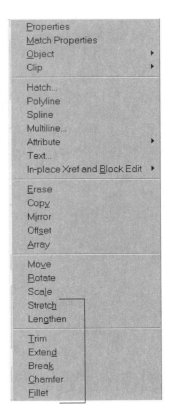

FIGURE 14.3 The Modify pull-down menu.

331

14.1 Using the Trim Command

Trim
Icon

- Type **TRIM** or **TR** at the command prompt.
- Select <u>T</u>rim from the <u>M</u>odify pull-down menu.
- Pick the Trim icon from the Modify toolbar.

The Trim command is used to clip off ends or overhangs of lines or objects. Figure 14.4 shows some situations where you could use the Trim command. The Trim command can remove only lines that touch or lap. Look at Figure 14.4 and think about what parts could be altered with the Trim command. Then look at Figure 14.5 to see if you came up with all these possibilities.

The Trim command is very easy to learn. The Trim command sequence would read as follows:

Command: **TR**↵
Select Objects: *(Select an edge.)*↵

*At this point you have two options to choose from when picking an edge.

Option 1

You can select a specific cutting edge by touching any line or lines with the cursor's pick box. (Do not touch the line you want to clip off first.) By touching the edge line you define where the trim will be made. To use a scissors analogy, the trim edge defines where the scissors will cut. After left-clicking on the cutting edge or edges, right-click to let AutoCAD know you are done picking cutting edges. Now, pick the lines to be removed with a left-click. As you pick these lines, they disappear (see Figure 14.6). Press Enter ↵ to exit the command.

Option 2

When the Trim command asks you to Select Objects: right-click to select all the lines as cutting edges (known as the *smart mode*). Now, select any lines that intersect with a left click, and they will be trimmed off.

- Try the example in Figure 14.6. Draw your own lines at any scale you want. Try both options.

> ### Tips for Working with Trim
>
> Sometimes lines look like they touch or intersect, but in reality they do not. If the lines are not trimming for you, try erasing them. This problem occurs every so often, so watch for it. Later you will learn about the Extend command (Section 14.2), which can also solve some trimming problems by making lines touch.
>
> Certain entities will not work with the Trim command. A Block Entity (see Chapter 19), for instance, will not allow trimming. One solution is to use the Explode command to break the block into individual lines and trim them.
>
> To Explode a Block, type in **X**↵ at the command line, then left-click on the object that is a block.

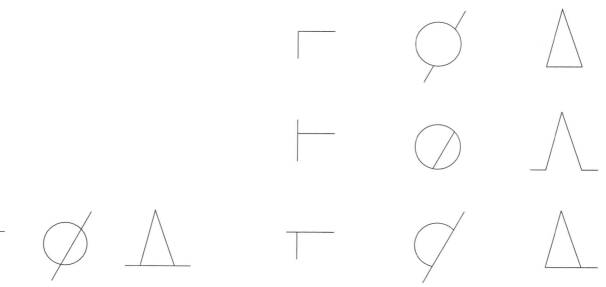

FIGURE 14.4   Shapes needing trimming.

FIGURE 14.5   Shapes showing how Trim can be applied in different ways.

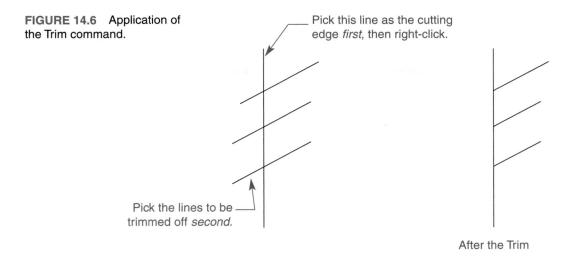

FIGURE 14.6 Application of the Trim command.

Pick this line as the cutting edge *first*, then right-click.

Pick the lines to be trimmed off *second*.

After the Trim

14.2 Using the Extend Command

- Type **Extend** or **EX** at the command prompt.
- Select Exten<u>d</u> from the <u>M</u>odify pull-down menu.
- Pick the Extend icon from the Modify toolbar.

The Extend command can be used to make lines intersect other lines. For example, in Figure 14.7 several lines stop short of another line. If you wanted the lines to touch the other line as shown in Figure 14.8, you would use the Extend command to do this.

External Icon

Using the Extend command is very similar to using the Trim command. The order in which you select lines is very important. Just as with the Trim command, you must select an edge or edges first in the Extend command, then you select the lines that must be extended. Use the following sequence for the Extend command:

At the command line type in **EX** or **EXTEND**.

Command line: **EX**⏎
Current settings: Projection = UCS Edge None
Select Boundary edges: *(Choose a boundary edge.)* ⏎
Select Objects:

*At this point you have the same two options you had in the Trim command.

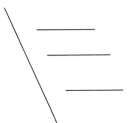

FIGURE 14.7 Lines to be extended.

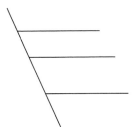

FIGURE 14.8 Extend example complete.

Option 1

Pick the edge to which you want other lines to extend and left-click on them, then right click. Now, touch the lines that need extending and left-click on them. They will extend as you select them.

Option 2

Right-click (smart mode) with the mouse . This automatically makes all lines on the drawing edges. After the right click the command line reads:

> Select object to extend or [Project /Edge /Undo]

Start left-clicking on the lines that need extending. When the extending is complete, press Enter ⏎.

Example: Using Extend

Draw a hexagon of any size you want, then draw two lines below the hexagon and one line inside the hexagon (see Figure 14.9). Use the Extend command. When it asks **Select Object:**, right-click.

    Left-click on the two vertical lines below the hexagon one at a time (see Figure 14.10). They should extend to the hexagon as you touch them.

    The horizontal line inside the hexagon can extend to two different edges, so it will require two separate picks. Left-click on the line on its left-hand side, and it extends to the left (see Figure 14.11). Now, click on the line's right side, and it extends to the right, touching the hexagon.

FIGURE 14.9   Lines to be extended.

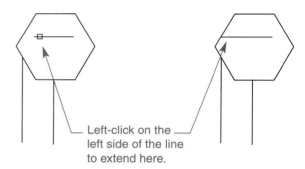

Left-click on the left side of the line to extend here.

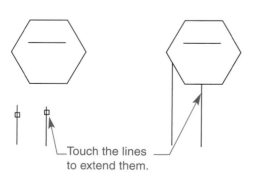

Touch the lines to extend them.

FIGURE 14.10   Application of the Extend command.

Left-click on the right side of the line to extend here.

FIGURE 14.11   Extend example complete.

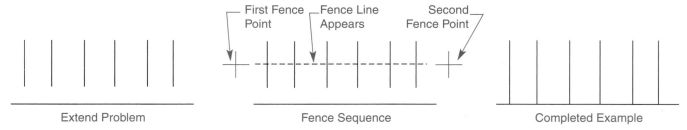

FIGURE 14.12 Using the Extend command with a fence.

Tips for Working with the Extend Command

1. If a line does not Extend, it may not have an edge directly in front of it. This will require you to either place an edge line in front of the line or use the Edge option found inside the Extend command.

2. As with the Trim command, some entities do not work with the Extend command. A Block will not read as an edge and will not let lines extend to it. Either Explode the Block or draw a line on top of the Block, then use the Extend command.

3. The crossing and window options will not work when selecting several lines to extend. You may use the Fence option to pick more than one line at a time. To use the Fence option, activate the Extend command, and select your edges as shown in the earlier examples. At the command line type F,

   Select Object to Extend or [Project/ Edge / Undo]: **F**⏎
   First Fence point:

   Pick a point on the far left side of the lines that need extending (see Figure 14.12). Now, drag the cursor to the right across your lines, and when you reach the other side, left-click to select a second fence point. Press Enter⏎, and the lines should extend all at once. (The Fence option also works with the Trim command.)

4. If you pick lines to Extend one at a time, you may type in **U** (for Undo) to take back the last line you extended. To undo as many lines as you need, just keep typing U. If you exit out of the command and then perform an Undo at the command line, the whole Extend command will be Undone.

14.3 Using the Break Command

- Type **Break** or **BR** at the command prompt.
- Select Break from the <u>M</u>odify pull-down menu.
- Pick the Break icon from the Modify toolbar.

Break
Icon

The two previous commands, Extend and Trim, required an edge for the commands to work. The Break command does not need an edge to function. It has a great deal more freedom and flexibility (see Figure 14.13).

Let's look at the command line sequence when the Break command is used:

Command: **BR**⏎
BREAK Select Object:

When the Select Object: line appears, the software is requesting you to pick a line or object to break. When you touch a line to be broken, the command line will then read:

Specify second break point or [First Point]:

FIGURE 14.13 Applications of
the Break command.

Examples of Use of the Break Command

Option 1

At this point AutoCAD has selected the object to be broken and marked the first point on the line to be broken.

You can then pick the second point on the line and have a piece of it erased (see Figure 14.14), or you can move completely off the line and left-click. The part of the line to the left of the first pick point will be removed (see Figure 14.15).

Option 2

If you wish to select a different first break point from the one AutoCAD selected, type in **F↵** after [First Point] and the command line will read

> Select first break point:

Now, select your first break point location by left-clicking on it. Next, you will be requested to pick the second break point on the object.

You can break only one object at a time with this command. Osnaps will work when selecting break points, so you can be very exact with the break locations. If you select a break point with the cursor off the object, then AutoCAD will find the nearest point along the object closest to the pick point.

Breaking an Object into Two Pieces without Erasing a Line

The examples so far have removed chunks or pieces from the objects. At certain times you will need to split an object in two and keep both sides. You can do this in one of two ways.

1. Make your first break point at the location where you want the split to occur. When AutoCAD asks for the second break point, type in the @ symbol. This will put the second break point in the same location as the first, thereby leaving no gap in the line.

2. You can use Osnaps to select your first and second break points at the exact same location. There will then be no gap, and the line will be split into two different lines, but leaving both sides intact (see Figure 14.16).

| Given Line | Second Break ⟋
 Point Selected | First Break
 Point Selected | End result after using <br> the Break command |

FIGURE 14.14 Application of the Break command.

| Given Line | Second Break ⟋
 Point Selected <br> off the Line | First Break
 Point Selected | End result after using the
 Break command with the <br> second pick point off the line |

FIGURE 14.15 Application of the Break command.

| Given Line | First and Second Break ⟋
 Point Selected at the
 Same Location | | End result after using the Break command at <br> the same break points. No gap is shown, but <br> the line is now in two pieces. (Try to erase one <br> side to prove it.) |

FIGURE 14.16 Application of the Break command.

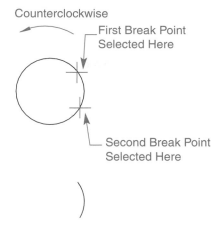

FIGURE 14.17 Breaking a circle.

Tips for Working with the Break Command

1. As with some of the previous editing commands, certain objects cannot be broken. A Blocked object must be exploded into individual lines before a Break command will work.

2. Many of the objects with which you are familiar can easily be broken; however, on certain round objects such as circles and ellipses the break points must be selected in a certain order because AutoCAD breaks in counterclockwise order by default (see Figure 14.17).

The command takes some getting used to at first. A little practice goes a long way.

Practice Example: Using the Break Command

Draw four circles of any size as shown in Figure 14.18. Follow the picking order given. Try to predict what shape will be left, then look at your end result after the command is finished. Did you anticipate it correctly? If not, try again.

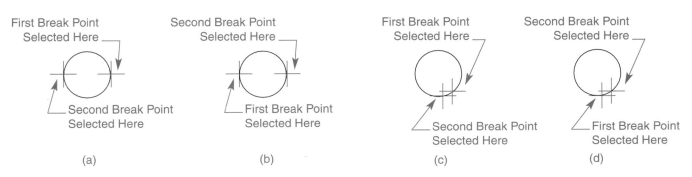

FIGURE 14.18 Practice example.

14.4 Using the Lengthen Command

Lengthen
Icon

- Type **LENGTHEN** or **LEN** at the command prompt.
- Select Lengthen from the <u>M</u>odify pull-down menu.
- Pick the Lengthen icon from the Modify toolbar.

The Lengthen command can alter the length of a line or arc in a variety of ways, depending on the need. Let's look at the command line sequence when the Lengthen command is used.

Command: **LEN** ↵
Select an object or [Delta / Percent / Total / Dynamic]:

If you select a line, the current length is displayed at the command line and returns you to the same prompt. The four options within the brackets give some flexibility in adjusting the length of a line or arc.

The Delta Option

The Delta option of selection works in the following way. Type **DE** and the command line shows:

Select an object or [Delta / Percent / Total / Dynamic]: **DE**↵
Enter Delta length or [Angle] < 0.000 >:

At this point typing a positive unit distance will increase the length of a line or arc, and a negative distance will shorten the objects. Right-click after entering a distance.

Select an object to change or [Undo]:

Just touch the object, and the line will change by the specified distance (see Figure 14.19).

Enter delta length or [Angle] < 0.000 >: **A** ↵
Enter delta angle <0>: *(Choose the desired angle.)*

Type in the angle desired, right-click, then select the arc to change.

Note: The Angle selection in the Delta option works on an arc by using an angle to add or subtract a length (see Figure 14.20):

Existing Line 2″ long

Existing Line 2″ long

Line becomes 3″ long

Line becomes 1″ long

A Delta length of 1 will add 1″ to the line length.

A Delta length of (−1) will subtract 1″ from the line length.

FIGURE 14.19   Application of the Delta option of the Lengthen command.

FIGURE 14.20   Lengthening an arc with the Angle suboption.

Original Arc

30°

A 30° segment is added.

The Percent Option

The Percent selection is used with a line's original length. The original length is used as a unit, and a percentage of that unit is applied to alter its size. For example, a line is drawn 4″ long. If the Percent option is set to 50, the line will be reduced by 50% or half its size:

$$4'' \times \frac{50}{100} = 2''$$

$$4'' \times \frac{1}{2} = 2''$$

If the same 4″ line was lengthened by 200%, its size would double:

$$4'' \times \frac{200}{100} = 2''$$

$$4'' \times \frac{2}{1} = 8''$$

Example: Using Percent

Draw a line 1″ long.
  Follow this selection sequence:

  Command: **LEN.**⏎
  Select an object or [Delta / Percent / Total / Dynamic]: **P**⏎
  Enter percentage length < 0.000> *(Enter desired percentage here. 200 is okay.)*
  Select an object to change or [Undo]: *(Pick the line or arc to be changed.)*
  The length of the line should double in size.

Total Option

The Total option changes the object to the distance that is set. For instance, if a line is originally drawn 2.5′ long, and the Total option is used in the Lengthen command, the command line will read:

  Command: **LEN**⏎
  Select object or [Delta / Percent / Total / Dynamic]: **T**⏎
  Specify Total length or [Angle]: *(Enter Value.)*⏎

If a value of 6′ is used, then when a line or arc is selected, its total length will be set to 6′.

Example: Total Option Using Angles

Instead of typing a value, type **A** for Angle, which will work on arcs. The command line will read:

Specify total angle <0>: *(Enter the angle value.)*⏎
Select object to change or [Undo]: *(Pick the arc.)*

If a value of 90° is used, the arc will be drawn as a quarter of a circle. Input 180° to draw a half circle (see Figure 14.21).

FIGURE 14.21 Lengthening an arc with the Total suboption.

Original Arc

An Angle value of 90° enlarges the arc.

An Angle value of 180° enlarges the arc.

Dynamic Option

The Dynamic option is used with the cursor. When this option is selected, the command line reads:

> Select an object to change or [Undo]: *(Pick a line or arc.)*
> Specify new end point:

Move the cursor around and watch the line float along with the cursor. The next point selected with a left click will lengthen the line to that location. You can just pick points, but the following two tips will help give you some control.

Tips for Working with the Lengthen Command

1. Osnaps can be used to snap to exact locations.

2. Direct Distance can be used. (Pull the cursor in the direction you want to draw, then type in the distance by which to lengthen, and press Enter↵.) The command works with Ortho turned off.

3. As in previous editing commands some entities cannot be lengthened, such as closed objects and Blocked objects.

4. Some of the angle options will have some restrictions on size. Choosing angles between 0° and 360° will solve most of those problems.

14.5 Using the Stretch Command

- Type **Stretch** or **S** at the command prompt.
- Select Stretch from the Modify pull-down menu.
- Pick the Stretch icon from the Modify toolbar.

Stretch
Icon

The Stretch command can be used on polygons and shapes with two or more connected lines. It basically performs some of the same functions as the Lengthen command, but Stretch works on more than a single line. Figure 14.22 shows some of the shapes that can be stretched.

With the Stretch command, there are only two methods of selecting objects: with a crossing box (**C↵**) or a crossing polygon (**CP↵**).

Crossing Boxes

By now you should have a good understanding of crossing boxes. Left-clicking and moving the cursor to the left gives you a crossing box. Make sure the box crosses or touches all the sides involved with the *Stretch* being performed (see Figure 14.23).

Pick the object to stretch, and right-click.

> Select Object: *(Pick objects with a crossing box.)*↵
> Specify a base point or displacement:

FIGURE 14 22   Application of the Stretch command.

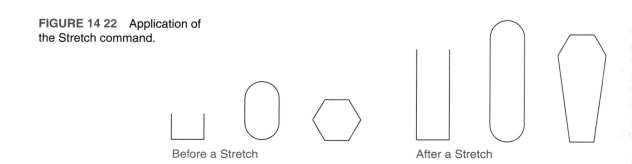

Before a Stretch   After a Stretch

FIGURE 14.23   Application of the Stretch command.

Pick with a Crossing Box

Select the Midpoint for Base Point

Second Point Selected

Completed Stretch

When a base point is requested, you must choose a point from which to reference the stretch. A midpoint or endpoint on the object will work fine for a base point even though picking anywhere will work.

Specify second point of displacement:

After picking a base point, select a second point to which to stretch the object. The distance between the base point and the second point determines how much the object will be stretched.

Crossing Polygon

Objects can also be selected with a crossing polygon (shown in Chapter 10). This option allows you to construct a shape by picking points and closing the polygon. Just make sure to cross or touch all lines involved with the stretch.

Tips for Working with the Stretch Command

1. Turn on ORTHO if you need the object to stretch vertically or horizontally.

2. The Direct Distance method works well for selecting the second point to which to stretch. Turn ORTHO on, pull the cursor in the direction the stretch should go, type in the distance needed for the stretch, and press Enter.⏎.

3. The majority of problems with the Stretch command involve trying to pick objects with some method other than a crossing box or polygon or selecting objects that cannot be stretched, like a circle or a Block.

14.6 Using the Scale Command

- Type **SCALE** or **SC** at the command prompt.
- Select Sca<u>l</u>e from the <u>M</u>odify pull-down menu.
- Pick the Scale Icon from the Modify toolbar.

Scale Icon

The Scale command is used to change the size of objects (see Figure 14.24). It is *not* used to change the scale of a drawing or its limits. For example, the Scale command is used to resize a table that has been drawn too large to fit in a room.

The Scale command sequence is as follows:

Command: **SC**⏎
Select Object: *(Pick objects.) (Use any selection method.)*
Specify base point: *(Pick a point from which the Scale can be referenced.)*
Specify scale factor or [Reference]:

FIGURE 14.24   Application of the Scale command.

Scale Factor of 1

Scale Factor of 2

Scale Factor of 2.5

For the scale factor, type in a numerical value and press Enter↵. Typing in 2↵ will double the size of a selected object. Drag the cursor to any point and click. The object will enlarge or shrink as the cursor is moved, much like the Dynamic option works in the Lengthen command.

Type **R**↵ to choose the Reference option. It lets you select a size or pick two points as a distance reference, then it scales proportionally based on the determined reference distance.

Example 1

Command: **SC**↵
Select objects: *Pick circle* ↵
Specify base point: *(Use Center Osnap.)*
Specify scale factor or [Reference]: **3**↵

The circle will triple in size (see Figure 14.25).

Example 2

Command: **SC**↵
Select objects: *Pick circle* ↵
Specify base point: *(Use Center Osnap.)*
Specify scale factor or [Reference]: *(Drag the cursor a distance outside the circle.)*

Watch the circle as the cursor drags, and left-click when the circle reaches the desired size (see Figure 14.26).

Example 3

Command: **SC**↵
Select objects: *(Select the circle.)*
Specify base point: *(Pick the center of the circle.)*
Specify scale factor or [Reference]: **R**↵
Specify reference length <1>: **.5** *(diameter of circle)*
Specify new length: **1.5** (see Figure 14.27)

Original Circle

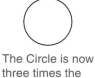

The Circle is now three times the original size.

FIGURE 14.25 Scaling a circle.

The circle will scale out to the cursor placement.

FIGURE 14.26 Scaling a circle with the cursor.

Original Circle with a .5″ diameter

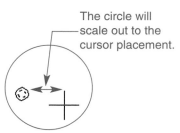

Circle after using the Reference option with a new diameter of 1.5″

FIGURE 14.27 Scaling a circle with the Reference option.

FIGURE 14.28 Scaling a circle with the Reference option and quadrants.

Use the 0° quadrant for your first reference point.

Use the 180° quadrant for your second reference point.

Before
Original Circle with a .5″ diameter

After
Circle after using the Reference option with a new diameter of 1.5″

Example 4

Command: **SC**↵
Select objects: *(Select the circle.)*
Specify base point: *(Pick the center of the circle.)*
Specify scale factor or [Reference]: **R**↵
Specify reference length <1>: *(Pick the 0° quadrant on the given circle.)*
Specify second point: *(Pick the 180° quadrant.)*
Specify new length: **1.5**↵ *(See Figure 14.28.)*

Tips for Working with the Scale Command

There are very few problems with the Scale command. Most entities can be scaled without any problem, including Blocks.

The biggest problem occurs when the Scale option is misused by individuals trying to adjust the drawing scale or limits with it. The Scale command will not change the limits environment; it is used to change an object's size, *not* its environment. The Limits command must be used to change limits.

14.7 Using the Chamfer Command

- Type **CHAMFER** or **CHA** at the command prompt.
- Select <u>C</u>hamfer from the <u>M</u>odify pull-down menu.
- Pick the Chamfer icon from the Modify toolbar.

Chamfer
Icon

A *chamfer* is an angled corner found between two lines or objects, such as at the corner of a table to eliminate a sharp point (see Figure 14.29). The command has a Trim mode that can be used to leave the intersection in place or to remove the intersection and show only the Chamfer (see Figure 14.30).

Chamfer does this to corners.

No Trim Option   Trim Option

FIGURE 14.29 Application of the Chamfer command.

FIGURE 14.30 Chamfering with and without the Trim option.

To use the Chamfer command, walk through the following steps. Type **CHA** at the command line.

Command: **CHA** ⏎
(TRIM Mode) = Current Chamfer Dist1 = 0.500, Dist2 = 0.500
Select first line or [Polyline / Distance / Angle / Trim / Method]

Take a look at the information in the command line. The second line gives you a list of current settings.

■ (TRIM Mode) means the Trim is on, and the intersection will be removed. This is the default setting.

■ The current chamfer distances are shown. Distance 1 (Dist1) is applied to the first line touched in the chamfer picking order. Dist2 is applied to the second line selected.

The last line in the command prompt lists the options from which to choose.

Select first line:

If the distances are OK, then simply click the two lines one at a time and the chamfer is performed (see Figure 14.31).

Polyline:

If the object being edited was constructed with polylines, then they must be chamfered with this option. Type **P⏎**, then click the polylines one at a time. This option can chamfer more than one corner at a time when performed on a closed polyline figure (see Figure 14.32).

Distance:

Note: Distance 1 and Distance 2 do not have to be the same number.

Type **D⏎** to change the values of the distance settings. The command sequence will look like this:

Select first line or [Polyline/Distance/angle/Trim/Method]: **D⏎**
Specify first chamfer distance <0.5000>: *(Select new distance for 1.)* ⏎
Specify second chamfer distance <0.5000>: *(Select new distance for 2.)* ⏎
Command: ⏎
Select first line or [Polyline/Distance/Angle/Trim/Method]:

Notice that after the second distance is set, you are returned to a blank command line. You must press **Enter⏎** or right-click to return to the Chamfer command so that you can start selecting the lines to chamfer.

Angle

Type **A⏎** to use an angle to determine the second chamfer point. The sequence looks like this:

Select first line or [Polyline/Distance/Angle/Trim/Method]: **A⏎**
Specify chamfer length on the first line <1.000>: *(Pick first distance.)* ⏎
Specify chamfer angle from the first line <0>: *(Type angle needed.)* ⏎
Command: ⏎

FIGURE 14.31   The Select first line option.

FIGURE 14.32   The Polyline option of Chamfer.

Notice again that after setting the angle, you must press **Enter↵** to return to the chamfer picking sequence. Just touch the first line and second line when the command line asks, and the chamfer will be drawn using the angle value instead of a distance for the second point.

Trim:

The Trim mode is set with this option by typing **T↵**.

> Select first line or [Polyline/Distance/Angle/Trim/Method]: **T↵**
> Enter Trim mode option [Trim/No trim] <Current Setting>:

Typing **N↵** will leave the intersection untrimmed.

- **Method:** This option allows you to jump back and forth between the Distance choice with its current setting and the Angle choice with its current settings. The command line sequence is as follows.

> Select first line or [Polyline/Distance/Angle/Trim/Method]: **M↵**
> Enter trim method [Distance/Angle] <Current setting>:

Select **D** to use the Distance method, or choose **A** to make an angle selection.

Tips for Working with the CHAMFER Command

Obviously, some shapes, such as circles and Blocks, will not chamfer. A common problem is that the distance and angle setting may be too large to work on small corners. If this happens you must change the chamfer settings or the size of the object.

14.8 Using the Fillet Command

- Type **FILLET** or **F** at the command prompt.
- Select Fillet from the Modify pull-down menu.
- Pick the Fillet icon from the Modify toolbar.

Fillet Icon

A **fillet** is a radius tangenting into two objects (see Figure 14.33). Fillet is a very frequently used command in AutoCAD because of its ability to automatically trim out edges. The picking sequence is very similar to that used with the Chamfer command. You must return to the command after selecting the radius of the fillet. Fillet also has a [Trim/No Trim] option, just like the Chamfer command.

Let's walk through the command line when the Fillet command is activated.

> Command: **F↵**
> Select first object or [Polyline/Radius/Trim]:

The Polyline and Trim options should be familiar to you; they are used in the same fashion as in the Chamfer command.

Polyline:

If lines or arcs are polylines, you must use this option to attach a fillet to them.

> Select first object or [Polyline/Radius/Trim]: **P↵**
> Select 2D polyline: *(Pick a Pline on a closed object.)*

FIGURE 14.33 Application of the Fillet command.

 Applied Fillet

 Applied Fillet

 Applied Fillet

FIGURE 14 34   The Polyline option of Fillet.   **FIGURE 14.35**   Fillet with and without Trim.

Make sure the polyline/Plines are touching, then select one Pline and the fillet is drawn. As in the Chamfer command, if the Polyline object is closed, then all the corners will get Fillets in a single selection (see Figure 14.34).

Trim:

This selection is the same as in the Chamfer command. Selecting **T** for Trim will remove the intersection, and the No Trim option will leave the intersecting lines untrimmed (see Figure 14.35).

Radius:

The Radius option allows you to change the fillet size. The following sequence shows how to select a new fillet radius.

         Command: **F**↵
         Select first object or [Polyline/Radius/Trim]: **R**↵
         Specify fillet radius <Current value>: *(Type new value.)* ↵
         Command: *(Press Enter↵)*
         Select first object or [Polyline/Radius/Trim]: *(Select first side.)*
         Select second object: *(Select second side.)*

Notice that you need to return to the Fillet command after choosing a new radius. Simply press Enter↵ or right-click to return to the Fillet command to start selecting the objects.

One very useful function of the Fillet and Chamfer commands is the ability to square off corners that stop short or overlap (see Figure 14.36). With the Fillet command just use a 0 radius and then follow through the normal sequence. Instead of a curve, a corner is formed.

Tips for Working with the FILLET Command

1. The most common problem with the Fillet command is using a radius that is too large. If this happens, the command line will let you know. Choosing a smaller radius is a solution.

2. Another problem is having the fillet go in the wrong direction at an intersection (see Figure 14.37). The Fillet will follow the counterclockwise selecting order; however, if there is not a clearly defined corner, you may need to break a line to dictate the path for the Fillet to follow (see Figure 14.38). Once the line is broken, it is easy to have the fillet go in the direction you need.

3. As in most of the editing commands, some things cannot be changed. Filleting a Block will not work without exploding the Block. As you try editing different entities you will develop an understanding of what will work well. (See Chapter 19 for more information about Blocks.)

FIGURE 14.36   Fillet with radius of 0.

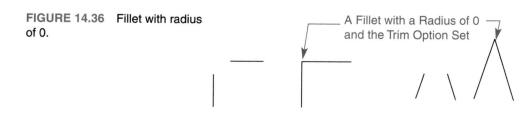

A Fillet with a Radius of 0 and the Trim Option Set

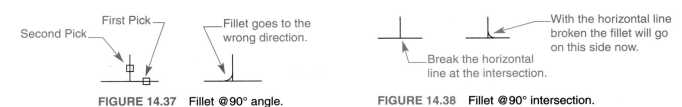

FIGURE 14.37   Fillet @90° angle.   **FIGURE 14.38**   Fillet @90° intersection.

14.9 The Basics of Using Grips Command

Note: If the fillet is placed on the wrong side try selecting the lines in a different order.

Usually, an AutoCAD user is first exposed to Grips when he or she accidentally turns them on by selecting an object without choosing a command. Grips are the small blue rectangles that appear on the drawing as a result (see Figure 14.39). The first reaction most people have is, How do I get rid of them? Pressing the Escape key twice will remove them.

Grips are an important editing tool. They are like little identification or definition points that are found at critical areas that make up the geometric shape of the object. If you draw a variety of shapes and activate the grips, you will find some of these characteristics.

Grips are found on endpoints and midpoints, and on tangents, centers, and quadrants. Grips can be in three different states: cold, warm, or hot.

1. A grip is considered *cold* when the hollow grip boxes remain on an object while the object is a continuous line. This object is not affected by what you do to entities with warm grips.

2. An object is in a *warm* grip mode when the objects selected are shown as a broken line. The grip boxes are still and remain hollow on the object. The objects selected will be affected if a grip is made hot (see Figure 14.40).

3. A *hot* grip is an active grip. A left click with the cursor over a warm or cold grip box will make it hot and active. The rectangle boxes, which are hollow and blue in the warm and cold states, now become solid red boxes. When a grip is hot, cursor movement will alter the object when shifted around. To make more than one grip hot, hold down the Shift key and left-click on as many grip boxes as needed. The more grips that are lit up, the more the grip option will affect the whole object (see Figure 14.41). Press the Esc key to change the state of the grips.

The next question most people ask is, What does an active grip do? Look at the command line when the grip is hot to see which function is active. The Grip command will default to the Stretch option.

STRETCH
Specify stretch point or [Base point/ Copy / Undo /Exit]:

Just move the cursor to any location and watch the line stretch there when you left-click. Osnaps can be used when moving a hot grip being stretched to an exact location (see Figure 14.42). This Stretch will work with single lines, unlike the other Stretch command introduced earlier in this chapter.

Grips can perform the following functions:

Stretch

Move

Rotate

Scale

Mirror

FIGURE 14.39   Grips.

FIGURE 14.40   Grips on multiple objects.

FIGURE 14.41   Hot grip.

FIGURE 14.42 Stretching using a grip.

Select an endpoint to stretch to.

Hot Grip

Completed stretch using a grip.

To access these selections, go through the following sequence to use the grips.

1. Left-click on an object.
2. Make a grip hot by left-clicking on top of the blue rectangular box.
3. Look at the command line, which is defaulted to Stretch. Press Enter↵ repeatedly to cycle through the other options. Look at the command line each time you press Enter↵ . Keep pressing until you reach the option you need.

The following are common options inside brackets. You have used most of these previously. Each of these will work with the Grip functions (Stretch, Move, Rotate, Scale, and Mirror).

Base point: Gives you a choice to locate a starting point for a base reference.

Copy: Will make a duplicate copy of the highlighted object.

Undo: Will take back the last grip placement used.

eXit: Exits the Grip command.

Reference: This option is found in Scale and Rotate. In Scale, it references a distance, then changes the scale base on a new assigned length. (See the Scale command found earlier in this chapter.) In Rotate, it references an angle you assign, then uses a second angle in combination to shift the rotation of a line.

The grips are like shortcuts to Stretch, Move, Rotate, Scale, and Mirror. They work very similarly to these commands accessed in the <u>M</u>odify menu. It is better to learn the basics of these commands, then come back and experiment with the grips options.

Some users do not like grips at all and turn them off. To do this, use the following sequence:

Command: **Grips**↵
Enter new value for Grips <1>: **0**↵

The ability to stretch and move objects quickly makes the grips a very useful tool. Be patient with the grips; they are a great tool to use.

14.10 The Properties Command

One of the most powerful editing tools in AutoCAD is the Properties command. It can change many features or characteristics of an object, such as the following:

Layers

Colors

Linetypes

Lineweights

Text

Geometry of shapes

FIGURE 14.43 Properties pull-down menu.

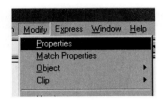

FIGURE 14.43 Properties pull-down menu.

- Type **PROPERTIES** or **MO** at the command prompt.
- Select Properties from the Modify pull-down menu (see Figure 14.43).
- Pick the Properties icon from the Standard toolbar.

Properties Icon

When the Properties command is activated, a dialog box appears and displays the characteristics that can be changed (see Figure 14.44). You can select the objects to be modified before activating the Properties command or immediately following. Left-click on the object to be altered, or use a window or a crossing box to activate the warm grips on an object. Depending on what is selected or highlighted, the options shown in the Properties dialog box will vary somewhat.

Two tabs that always appear at the top of the dialog box are Alphabetic and Categorized.

If the Alphabetic tab is chosen, then all the properties are put in alphabetical order (see Figure 14.45). The Categorized tab organizes the different property characteristics by groups or categories. As shown in Figure 14.44, the categories break down into areas such as General and Geometry. Notice the little boxes to the left with a minus sign in them. If you left-click on one, then that category is minimized and a plus symbol appears in the box (see Figure 14.46). Left-click on the plus symbol to restore the category.

The categories will change as the properties vary with different types of entities. Figure 14.47 shows an example of a new category when a string of text or lettering is selected for modification.

Notice that Text has its own category with its own unique properties. Each new entity you learn can have a different makeup and therefore may have its own individual category created. In the beginning, look for new categories to pop up.

FIGURE 14.44 Properties dialog box.

FIGURE 14.45 Properties displayed in alphabetic order.

FIGURE 14.46 The General options of the Categorized tab.

FIGURE 14.47   Text options of the Categorized tab.

FIGURE 14.47   Text options of the Categorized tab.

How to Use the Properties Command

To move through the Properties dialog box, left-click on the scroll arrows on the right. Once you find the property to change, left-click on the description to the left. After the description is highlighted, move the cursor to the right and pick on the current property setting. In the following example we will change the color from ByLayer to Cyan.

Example 1

1. Left-click on a line and activate the grips.
2. Activate the Properties command: **MO**↵
3. Left-click on the word Color in the dialog box (see Figure 14.48).
4. Left-click on the down arrow, then left-click on Cyan (see Figure 14.49).
5. The Cyan color now displays in the right column.
6. Close the Properties dialog box by left-clicking on the X in the upper right corner (see Figure 14.50).
7. Press the Esc key twice to turn off the grips. The line that was selected now has a cyan color.

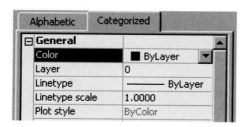

FIGURE 14.48   Properties Color option.

FIGURE 14.49   Changing color.

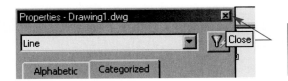

FIGURE 14.50 The Close button.

FIGURE 14.51 Geometry options.

FIGURE 14.52 Quick Select icon.

FIGURE 14.53 Quick Select dialog box.

The sequence just used in Example 1 is typical when changing properties of objects. Sometimes you may need to type in the change at the setting location on the right. Just highlight the entire box, then type in the new value (see Figure 14.51).

Making changes with the Geometry tab is best left to experienced CAD users who know the coordinate systems fairly well. As you gain some confidence you may want to start making modifications here.

The Quick Select button is found in the upper right corner of the dialog box (see Figure 14.52). It opens up the dialog box shown in Figure 14.53. It gives you a method of filtering through the selections quickly. It performs the same functions as the Properties box but focuses more on user-specified areas.

The Properties command is one of the more frequently used options in AutoCAD. You can use other editing commands to do some of the functions of Properties, but learning to use this command will give you a greater control over editing.

14.11 The Match Properties Command

- Type **MA** at the command prompt.
- Select <u>M</u>atch Properties from the <u>M</u>odify pull-down menu (see Figure 14.54).
- Pick the Match Properties icon from the Standard toolbar.

Match Properties Icon

The Match Properties command is used to quickly pick out the properties of an existing object, then to change the properties of other existing objects to match the properties of the first. It sounds complicated, but it is not. Here is an example of how it works.

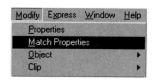

FIGURE 14.54 Match Properties selected in the Modify pulldown menu.

FIGURE 14.55 Three circles, one black, two blue.

FIGURE 14.56 Using the Match Properties command.

FIGURE 14.57 Example complete.

Example: Match Properties Command

In this example, three circles will be drawn. The first one will be black, and the other two will be cyan (see Figure 14.55).

Select Match Properties from the Modify pull-down menu.

Select source object:

Left-click on the black circle. A pick box and a paintbrush appear.

Select destination objects or [Setting]

Touch each cyan circle with the pick box and left-click each time. As you pick the circle its color changes to match the first one. Press **Enter** ↵ when you are done picking (see Figures 14.56 and 14.57).

Match Properties is quick and easy to use on all kinds of entities. When you get into Chapters 16 and 18 on Layers and Text, you will learn to like it a lot.

REVIEW QUESTIONS

1. How can the Modify toolbar be placed on the screen if it is turned off?
2. If a line does not Trim, what could be the problem?
3. List all the options inside the Grip command.
4. Explain the Trim/No Trim option in the Fillet and Chamfer commands.
5. How is the Lengthen command different from the Extend command?
6. How many options are found in the Scale command?
7. How do you activate grips?
8. When using the Stretch command, objects can be selected using only two methods. What are they?
9. What factors determine whether to use the Trim or Break command?
10. Why is Properties one of the more powerful editing commands in AutoCAD?
11. How does Match Properties work?
12. List the options inside the Chamfer command.
13. How can the Break command be used to break a line into two pieces without removing a portion?
14. Explain how the Break command selects the break points.

15. How do you remove the grip boxes from the AutoCAD screen?

16. List the command aliases for:

    a. Trim

    b. Extend

    c. Break

    d. Chamfer

    e. Fillet

    f. Stretch

    g. Lengthen

17. What are some problems that occur with the Extend command?

18. Explain the options inside the Lengthen command.

19. Draw a circle using any radius. Select the circle, then activate the Properties command. How many different changes can be made to the circle?

EXERCISES

EXERCISE 14.1

Draw a 2″ × 4″ rectangle. Place a chamfer on each corner using .25 on both distances.

EXERCISE 14.2

Draw a hexagon circumscribed around a circle with a 1.5″ radius using the Fillet command with a radius of .18. Fillet each corner.

EXERCISE 14.3

Draw a tick-tack-toe setup. Trim off all the lines that overhang so that all you are left with is one square block.

EXERCISE 14.4

Using the Properties command, change the color of the lines in exercise 14.1 to magenta.

EXERCISE 14.5

Draw the given example on the left in Figure 14.58 using .25″ spacing in between the horizontal lines. Use the Extend command to form 90° corners with the vertical line as shown on the right.

EXERCISE 14.6

Use the example in exercise 14.5 as the basic setup. Try the Lengthen command to force the horizontal lines to touch the vertical line. Use the Dynamic option along with Perpendicular Osnap.

EXERCISE 14.7

Draw a 3″ × 3″ square. Using the Stretch command change the shape to 3″ × 6″. Do it using the Direct Distance method with ORTHO turned on.

FIGURE 14.58 Exercise 14.5.

FIGURE 14.59   Exercise 14.8.

(a) Equilateral triangle   (b) The stretched triangle using grips   (c) The rotated triangle using grips   (d) The scaled triangle using grips

EXERCISE 14.8

Draw an equilateral triangle with the sides measuring 1.5″ (see Figure 14.59a).

    a. Use grips to make the right corner of the triangle the hot grip. Use the Stretch option and move the corner 1″ in the X-direction. Use Direct Distance with ORTHO on (see Figure 14.59b).

    b. Repeat the same sequence with the original triangle as in part (a), except use the Rotate option with a 30° rotation angle (see Figure 14.59c).

    c. Using the same basic triangle and gripping sequence, use the Scale option this time with a scale factor of 1.5 (see Figure 14.59d).

EXERCISE 14.9

Draw the shape shown in Figure 14.60a using a radius of .75″. Draw lines across the quadrants. Using the Break command, break the circle from 90° to 180° as well as from 270° to 0°.

EXERCISE 14.10

Draw the shape shown in Figure 14.61a. Break the lines in the middle of the circle.

(a) Before Breaking   (b) After Breaking   (a) Before Breaking   (b) After Breaking

FIGURE 14.60   Exercise 14.9.   **FIGURE 14.61**   Exercise 14.10.

DRAWING ASSIGNMENTS

1. Draw all the parts of Figure 14.62 with the assigned scales.

FIGURE 14.62 Drawing Assignment 1.
continued on next page

(a)
Scale: 1″ = 1″
Note: All chamfer distances
and fillet radii = .125″

(b)
Scale: 1″ = 1″

(c)
Scale: 1″ = 1″

(d)
Scale: 1″ = 1″

FIGURE 14.62 *continued*

Scale: ¼″ = 1′-0″

(e)

(f)

Scale: ¼″ = 1′-0″

(g)

Scale: ½″ = 1″

Moving and Duplicating Objects

15.1 The Move Command

Move
Icon

- Type **MOVE** or **M** at the command prompt.
- Select Mo<u>v</u>e from the <u>M</u>odify pull-down menu.
- Pick the Move icon from the Modify toolbar. The icon looks like two lines at right angles to each other with arrows on the ends of both lines.

The Move command relocates an object in your drawing. Unlike with the Pan command, once you move the object it goes to a different place on the drawing relative to the other objects drawn. The first step once you initiate the Move command is to Select objects:. You can move more than one object at a time. Select the objects with any of the selection methods you learned for the Erase command (Section 10.3). You can pick with the cursor, define a window or a crossing, or type **f** to use a fence. Once you have chosen all the objects you wish to move, press Enter⏎.

You should then see a command prompt asking you to Specify base point or displacement:. This is the part of the command where you begin to specify exactly how you want to move the object(s). Several methods are available. Think of trying to give directions to friends helping you move a couch. You might tell them to put the left corner of the couch in the northwest corner of the living room. In an AutoCAD drawing, you could do this by using OSNAP to pick the corner of the couch. (This would specify the base point.) Then when prompted for the second point of displacement, you would use OSNAP to pick the northwest corner of the room. Every object you selected initially would then be moved, with the objects staying in the same relative positions to one another. To continue the couch example—if you selected the couch as well as the pillows on the couch, they would all be moved together. Figure 15.1 shows the sequence for executing this command.

You may also enter coordinates for the base point and second point of displacement, using either absolute or relative coordinates, or you may use the Direct Distance method of entry. The base point does not have to be located on any of the objects being moved (see Figure 15.2). The two points you select simply provide the program with a relative displacement for your object(s).

Now suppose you know that you want your couch moved 2′ toward one wall and 3′ toward the other wall. You can input this information in AutoCAD by using the displacement option. When the command prompt asks you to Specify base point or displacement:, type in the displacement you need. In this case, you would type in **@2,3**. Press **Enter**⏎ at the next prompt, Specify second point of displacement or <use first point as displacement>:. This tells AutoCAD to use the values input in the previous step (2,3) as relative X- and Y- coordinates for displacement. The objects selected will be moved 2 units in the positive X-direction and 3 units in the positive Y-direction (see Figure 15.3).

(a) Original Placement

(b) Select Objects

Base Point

Window is used to select the couch first.

Second Point of Displacement

(c) Move

FIGURE 15.1 Application of the Move command

(a) Original Placement

(b) Select Objects, Begin Move

Base Point

Second Point of Displacement

(c) Move Complete

FIGURE 15.2 Moving an object with a base point not located on the object.

FIGURE 15.3 Moving an object with relative displacement.

New Location after Move

Original Placement

3 Units

2 Units

15.2 The Copy Command

- Type **Copy** or **CO** or **CP** at the command prompt.
- Select Cop<u>y</u> from the <u>M</u>odify pull-down menu.
- Pick the Copy icon from the Modify toolbar. The icon displays a circle at the top left with an arrow pointing to two overlapping circles at the bottom right.

Copy
Icon

The Copy command works very much like the Move command, so it is important to understand the differences before you begin using the commands. When you Move an object, the object disappears from its original location and becomes established at the new location. The Copy command leaves the original object in the same location and makes one or more copies in a new location. You can copy more than one object at a time using any of the selection options provided by AutoCAD. You specify where to place the copied item using the same procedures for specifying base points or displacement as you do for the Move command.

Take a moment to look over the Copy command sequence:

Select objects:
Specify base point or displacement, or [Multiple]:
Specify second point of displacement or <use first point as displacement>:

The sequence is almost identical with the Move command sequence with the exception of the Multiple option. If you wish to make more than one copy of an object, type **M** then press **Enter.**↵ at that point in the command sequence. The command prompt will then again ask you to Specify base point: When you start specifying second points, you can make multiple copies without having to reenter the command. When you have made all the copies you want, press **Enter.**↵ to exit the command (see Figure 15.4).

(a) Original

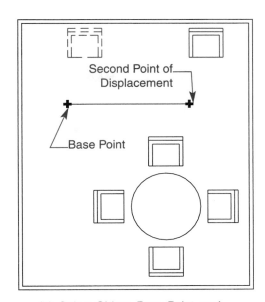

(b) Select Object, Base Point, and
Second Point of Displacement

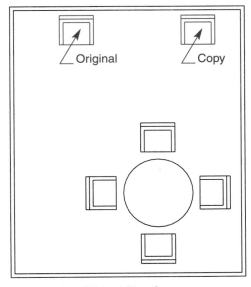

(c) Original Plus Copy

FIGURE 15.4 Application of the Copy command.

15.3 The Mirror Command

- Type **MIRROR** or **MI** at the command prompt.
- Select Mirror from the Modify pull-down menu.
- Pick the Mirror icon from the Modify toolbar. The icon has two triangles mirrored around a thin red line.

Mirror
Icon

When Alice walked through the mirror into Looking Glass Land, everything was exactly the same as the "real" world, only opposite. Sometimes you need to create that same effect in a drawing. The Mirror command allows you to create a mirror image of any object(s) in your drawing. This is a great tool. For example, if you have a section of your drawing that is perfectly symmetrical, you can draw half of the item and then use Mirror (see Figure 15.5).

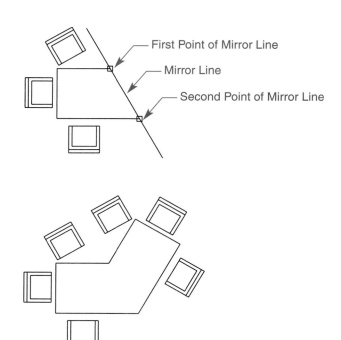

FIGURE 15.5   Application of the Mirror command.

FIGURE 15.6   Example of an angled mirror line.

Once you enter the Mirror command, the first step is to select the objects you wish to mirror. The command prompt displays the message Specify first point of mirror line, then you are asked to Specify second point of mirror line:. You are defining where the mirror is to be situated. If you select two points that define a line 4′ from the original object, the mirrored object will be constructed at a distance 4′ from the mirror line or 8′ from the original object. If the mirror line is at an angle relative to the original object, the mirrored object will be constructed at an angle to the original (see Figure 15.6).

Note: Try turning the ORTHO on when mirroring objects in a vertical or horizontal alignment.

The final question before the Mirror command is executed is Delete source objects? [Yes/No]<N>:. If you do not delete the source objects, the original objects selected at the beginning of the command will be left in place, just as they were before you entered the Mirror command. If you answer yes to this question, the original objects will be deleted from your drawing and only the mirrored objects will appear. Notice that the default answer, shown in the angled brackets, is N for no. Simply pressing **Enter⏎** and accepting the default will leave your original object in place along with the new mirrored object.

15.4 The Offset Command

- Type **OFFSET** or **O** at the command prompt.
- Select Off**s**et from the **M**odify pull-down menu.
- Pick the Offset icon from the Modify toolbar. The icon shows two irregularly shaped objects, one inside the other. The inside shape is red.

Offset
Icon

The Offset command is useful for creating parallel lines or concentric circles, arcs, and ellipses. When used with an existing line, the Offset command generates a copy of the line at a specified distance away (see Figure 15.7a). When used with an arc, a circle, ellipse, or polygon, the Offset command generates a new entity of the same basic shape as the original at the specified distance away (see Figure 15.7b). For example, if you use the command to create concentric circles, choosing an offset toward the inside of the circle will create a smaller circle centered inside the original circle. Choosing an offset toward the outside of the circle will create a larger circle around the original circle.

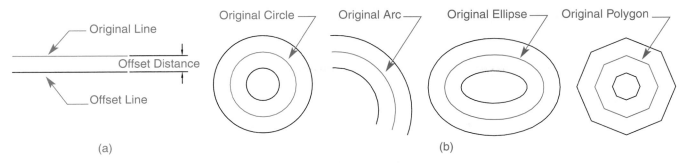

FIGURE 15.7   Using the Offset command on a line, arc, circle, and ellipse. Offsets may be placed on either side of a line or object.

Take a moment to look over the offset command sequence.

Specify offset distance or [Through]<Through>:
Specify second point:
Select object to offset or <exit>:
Specify point on side to offset:

The first steps in the command deal with setting the offset distance. Two options are available for setting this distance. You can simply input a number indicating the distance that you want placed between the objects being offset. If you do this, the request for a second point does not appear. The other option is to utilize the **Through** option, which asks you to specify two points that will define the offset distance.

Once the offset distance is set, you are ready to begin selecting objects to offset. At this point your cursor changes from crosshairs to a small square. Offsets are performed on one entity at a time, so the only method of selection allowed is to choose the object with the pick box. As soon as the object is selected Auto-CAD displays it as a dashed line. If you are paying attention, this should prevent you from offsetting the wrong object. If you are having trouble picking an object, you may need to use a transparent Zoom (see Chapter 11, Section 11.5) to get "close" enough to select the desired entity.

AutoCAD will repeat the last two steps of the command until you press **Enter⏎** (or Esc or the space bar) to exit the command sequence. You can continue to offset as many times as you need. You can even offset from an object that has just been created. Of course, the offset distance will remain the same. To change the distance you must exit and reenter the command.

Note: The Offset command cannot be used with 3D objects or faces.

Offset works with 2D polylines as well. A polyline offsets as a single entity, so if you select a rectangle that has been created with the Pline or Rectangle command, the entire rectangle will offset. If the rectangle was constructed with four separate line segments, you will have to offset each line separately. In addition, the offset will be exactly the same length as the original lines, so you will need to trim or extend them to obtain a perfect rectangle. Figure 15.8 illustrates these differences.

FIGURE 15.8   Using the Offset command on a Pline rectangle versus a rectangle made of separate lines.

(a) Figure Drawn with Rectangle Command (Polyline) then Offset

(b) Figure Drawn with Line Command then Offset

15.5 The Rotate Command

Rotate
Icon

- Type **ROTATE** or **RO** at the command prompt.
- Select <u>R</u>otate from the <u>M</u>odify pull-down menu.
- Pick the Rotate icon from the Modify toolbar. The icon contains a circular line with an arrow showing a clockwise direction.

The Rotate command allows you to rotate items within your drawing. You can select several items at once using any of the selection methods including the pick box, a window, a crossing, or a fence. The objects will be rotated around a base point that you select. This base point can be on one of the objects, or it can be totally removed from the objects. Object snaps (OSNAP) can be very useful in selecting this base point. Figures 15.9 and 15.10 show examples of using the Rotate command with different base points.

(a) Original Location

(b) Select Objects and Base Point

(c) Location after 45° Rotation

FIGURE 15.9   Using the Rotate command with the base point on an object.

(a) Original Location

(b) Select Objects and Base Point

(c) Rotation

(d) Location after 45° Rotation

FIGURE 15.10 Using the Rotate command with the base point away from an object.

Take a moment to look over the Rotate command sequence.

Command: **ROTATE**
Current positive angle in UCS: ANGDIR=counterclockwise ANGBASE=0
Select objects:
Specify base point:
Specify rotation angle or [Reference]:

As soon as you enter the command AutoCAD displays the current settings for constructing angles. In this example, the angle direction (ANGDIR) is set at counterclockwise while the base angle (ANGBAS) is set at zero. These are the default values. They can be changed either when you set up the drawing or separately during the course of the session. When the command line prompts you to select the objects to be rotated, the cursor changes to a pick box. As you pick items to be rotated they will appear on the screen as dashed lines. When you have chosen all the objects you wish to rotate, press Enter↵ to indicate that you wish

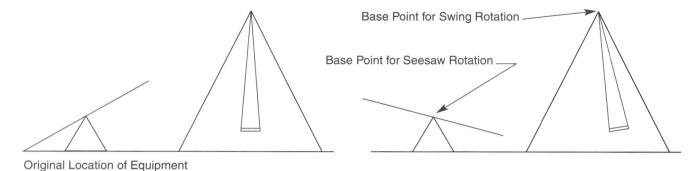

Base Point for Swing Rotation

Original Location of Equipment

FIGURE 15.11   Application of the Rotate command.

to proceed to the next step. Now you are ready to specify a base point. This is the point about which all the objects selected will be rotated. The objects rotate about this point as a group; their positions relative to each other do not change. The last step of the process is to specify a rotation angle (or reference angles). The direction and basis for the angles will be based on the information displayed at the beginning of the command. The following example walks you through using the command. You will want to experiment with using the command on your own. Make sure you understand the difference between the Move command and the Rotate command.

Example: The Rotate Command

Step 1.   Use a Wizard to Start a New Drawing. Use the Quick Setup with Decimal Units and an area of 8.5 × 11. Use the Zoom Extents commands to zoom to the limits of your drawing. (If you want to "see" the Limits on your screen, turn the GRID on.)

Step 2.   Use the Line command to draw figures similar to the playground equipment shown in Figure 15.11a. Feel free to utilize any other commands that make drawing the figure easier for you.

Step 3.   Use the Rotate command to tilt the seesaw −45° and swing +10°. Rotate the seesaw about the top point of the triangle (the fulcrum). Rotate the swing around the pivot point at the top where the two supports come together.

15.6 The Array Command

- Type **ARRAY** or **AR** at the command prompt.
- Select <u>A</u>rray from the <u>M</u>odify pull-down menu.
- Pick the Array icon from the Modify toolbar. The icon displays four square boxes in a rectangular array.

Array Icon

Like most of the other commands in this chapter, the Array command has the potential to save a lot of drawing time. The command takes an object (or several objects) and makes copies that are placed in an ordered pattern. The pattern may be either rectangular or polar.

Rectangular Array

Choosing the rectangular array option will copy your objects into a regularly spaced arrangement of rows and columns. The following command sequence is used for a rectangular array.

Command: **ARRAY**
Select objects:
Enter the type of array [Rectangular/Polar]<R>:
Enter the number of rows (---)<1>:
Enter the number of columns (| | |):
Enter the distance between rows or specify unit cell (---):
Specify the distance between columns (| | |):

Both the rectangular and the polar arrays start out by prompting you to select objects. These objects can be chosen using any of the normal selection methods such as windows, crossings, or fences. You can select one object or several to array. When you have included all the entities required, press Enter↵ to indicate that you are ready to proceed to the next step, which is selecting the type of array. If you want to construct a rectangular array, type in **R** and press Enter↵. The letter in the angle brackets indicates the default setting from the previous time the command was used. If the angle brackets already contain an *R*, you can simply press Enter↵ to accept the default option.

Now you must indicate the number of rows and columns you wish to have in your array. You can have an array with one row *or* one column, but you cannot have an array with one row *and* one column. In other words, either the number of rows or the number of columns must be greater than 1. This makes sense because a 1 × 1 array would leave you with the original object and no copies, so the command would accomplish absolutely nothing. In case you have trouble remembering the directions in which direction rows and columns run, AutoCAD provides you with a handy reminder in the command line. Rows run horizontally, so the program puts three horizontal dashes inside parentheses as a reminder. Likewise, columns run vertically, so three vertical dashes are shown.

Note: If you have only one row, the prompt will ask you to specify only the distance between columns.)

Once you have selected the number of rows and columns, the next prompt to appear is to determine the distance between the rows. You can do this in one of two ways. One way is to directly enter a number, which will be the distance between each row plus the length of the object being arrayed. So, for example, if you were arraying a rectangle, the distance between rows would be from the top of one row to the top of the next row (see Figure 15.12). The command assumes that the objects selected will be in the lower left corner of the array. If this configuration is not what you have in mind, you can place a negative sign in front of the distance between rows to indicate that the array should be constructed downward instead of upward. The distance between columns works in much the same way (see Figure 15.12). If you input a negative number for the column distance, the array will be constructed to the left of the original object(s) instead of in the default direction to the right.

2 Row × 3 Column Rectangular Array
Distance between Rows = 1.75
Distance between Columns = 1.25

FIGURE 15.12 Determining the distance between rows and columns in an array.

The other way to indicate the distance between rows in an array is to specify a unit cell. A **unit cell** is a rectangle that you define by specifying two points at opposite corners. You can identify the unit cell either by picking the corners with the cursor or by entering a set of absolute or relative coordinates. If you use the cursor, a window will appear after the first point is picked. This window serves to show you the tentative size of the window at the present cursor location. The cell is not actually defined until you pick a second point. It is important to realize that the unit cell defines only *distance*. It does not define *location*. Because the unit cell has length as well as width, the program uses the cell to define the distance between the columns as well as between the rows. Thus, if you utilize this option, the command line will not prompt you to specify the distance between columns.

Example: Rectangular Array—Table and Chairs

Arrays are very useful in architectural drawings. Drawing multiple seat layouts in movie theaters, churches, and school classrooms becomes a snap. Look at Figure 15.13, which shows a rectangular array of a table and chair. Draw your own table and chair using your own dimensions and make a similar array. Use a ¼″=1′-0″ scale with 5 columns and 4 rows.

Polar Array

Instead of arraying an object (or objects) into a configuration of rows and columns, the polar array command constructs a circular pattern of objects around a central point (see Figure 15.14). The command sequence starts off just like the rectangular array by prompting you to select objects. You have to indicate that you wish to construct a polar array by typing in **P** and then pressing Enter↵. Take a moment to look over the command sequence.

```
Command: array
Select objects:
Enter the type of array [Rectangular/Polar]<R>:
Specify center point of array:
Enter the number of items in the array:
Specify the angle to fill (+=ccw,- =cw)<360>:
Rotate arrayed objects?[Yes/No]<Y>:
```

FIGURE 15.13   A rectangular array.

FIGURE 15.14   A polar array.

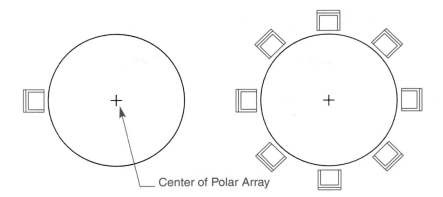

Center of Polar Array

Think of the center point of a polar array as the center of a clock face. All the objects in the array will be constructed in positions relative to this point. The center point can be chosen using coordinates or by picking with the cursor. The number of objects in the array is the final number once the array is complete, so the original object should be included in this count. If, for example, you enter **4** as the number of objects in the array, your final polar array will include four objects—the original plus three copies. The next step in the process allows you to choose the angle that you want your array to include. A polar array does not have to go around a complete circle (or 360°). The prompt reminds you that positive numbers will indicate a counter-clockwise (ccw) angle, whereas negative numbers indicate a clockwise angle (cw). The last decision you must make is whether to rotate the objects being arrayed. If you accept the default value, which is Yes, the items will be rotated around the center point (see Figure 15.15a). If you type **NO↵** at the prompt, the items will be displayed in the exact same position as the original (see Figure 15.15b).

FIGURE 15.15   Effect of rotating on a polar array.

Center of Array

Center of Array

(a) 360° Polar Array with Objects Rotated

(b) 360° Polar Array with Objects Not Rotated

REVIEW QUESTIONS

1. Can you move more than one object at a time?

2. Is it possible to use relative coordinates to specify the displacement for an object?

3. What is the difference between the Move command and the Copy command?

4. What option would you utilize to copy an object several times without exiting and reentering the Copy command?

5. When you Mirror an object in your drawing are you always left with both the original and the mirrored image? Explain your answer.

6. Give a short explanation of the Offset command.

7. How do the Move and Rotate commands differ? How are they similar?

8. Explain how OSNAPs can be helpful when moving and duplicating objects.

9. Think of two examples in which the Array command could be used on a drawing. Give an example for both polar and rectangular arrays.

10. If you are drawing a rectangular array in which the objects are 3″ tall and need a 1″ space between each object, what value should you use for the distance between the rows?

EXERCISES

EXERCISE 15.1

Draw the table and chairs shown in Figure 15.16. Use an overall size of 3′ × 6′ for the table and a 10″ radius for the outside circle of the chairs. Use the figure as a typical layout and size for a restaurant's dining room. Take a 30′ × 60′ room and put as many tables in it as possible using a spacing of 5′ between chair backs and walls. Use a scale of ¼″ = 1′-0″. Use a Limits setup of 0,0 and 68′,44′.

EXERCISE 15.2

Draw a circle with a 2″ diameter. Using the Array command array the line 10 times using a polar array. Choose the midpoint of the line as a base point and use a 180° angle to make three copies of the tree (see Figure 15.17).

EXERCISE 15.3

a. Draw a rectangle to enclose the four trees of exercise 15.2 (see Figure 15.18a).

b. Move each tree and place the centers at the corners of the rectangle (see Figure 15.18b).

FIGURE 15.16   Exercise 15.1.

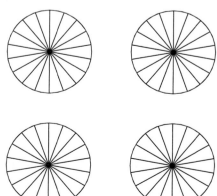

FIGURE 15.17   Exercise 15.2

c. Rotate the entire drawing at a 45° angle using the center of the bottom left circle (see Figure 15.18c).

d. Draw a vertical line to the right of the shape. Use the endpoints of the line as a reference for a Mirror command. Mirror the entire shape to the right side leaving the original objects in place (see Figure 15.18d).

e. Using the Offset command, Offset the circle .50 inside and outside the originals (see Figure 15.18e).

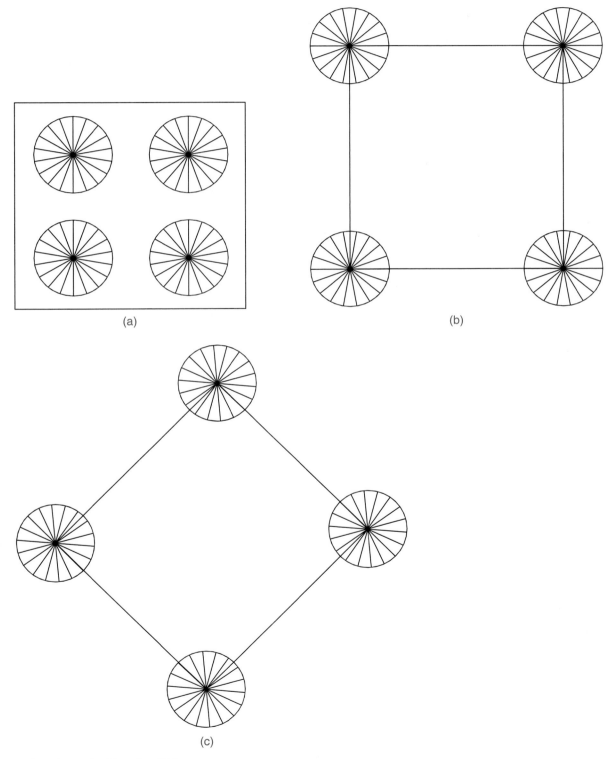

(a)

(b)

(c)

FIGURE 15.18 Exercise 15.3
continued on next page

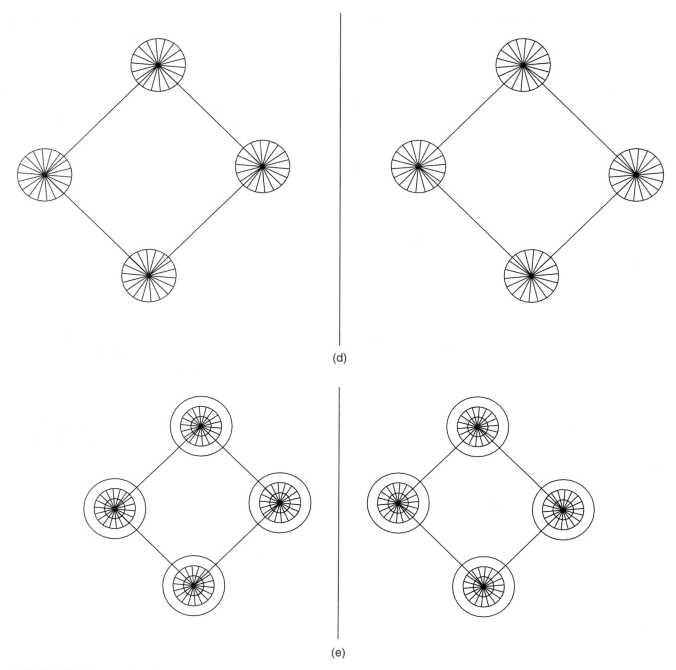

(d)

(e)

FIGURE 15.18 *continued*

EXERCISE 15.4

Using the Polygon command, draw a hexagon circumscribed around a circle with .75″ radius. Create the shape seen in Figure 15.19.

FIGURE 15.19   Exercise 15.4

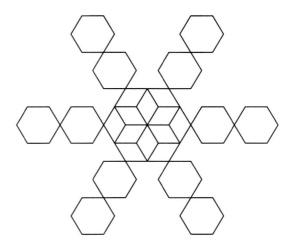

DRAWING ASSIGNMENTS

1. Draw the door elevation in Figure 15.20 using a scale of ⅜″ = 1′-0″. Use an offset of 2″ for the panels.

2. Draw the window elevation in Figure 15.21 using a scale of ⅜″ = 1′-0″. Divide the window into four equal sections, then divide the glass into four equal sections. Use an offset of 2″ for the panels.

3. Draw the deck in Figure 15.22 at a ¼″ = 1′-0″ scale. The deck has 6″-wide deck boards. Create some plants around the perimeter.

4. Draw the elevation in Figure 15.23 at a scale of ¼″ = 1′-0″.

5. Draw the two-bedroom apartment shown in Figure 15.24 at a ¼″ = 1′-0″ scale. Set limits at 0,0 and 68′,88′ (17″ × 22″ plotted sheet). Mirror the plan to create a duplex. Use 4½″-thick interior walls with 6″ exterior walls.

6. Draw the front side and rear elevations to the duplex in assignment 5. Use a ¼″ = 1′-0″ scale.

Door Elevation

FIGURE 15.20   Drawing Assignment 1.

Window Elevation

FIGURE 15.21   Drawing Assignment 2.

Deck Plan

FIGURE 15.22   Drawing Assignment 3.

Elevation

FIGURE 15.23   Drawing Assignment 4.

Two-Bedroom Apartment

FIGURE 15.24   Drawing Assignment 5.

Layers

16.1 Why Use Layers?

First, let's talk about what layers are, then we'll move on to why you might use them. Layers are a way to group together parts of a drawing that have some logical connection with one another. Each layer can be assigned a different color, linetype, and lineweight. Each layer can be viewed by itself or with a group of other layers. When you initially set up a drawing, AutoCAD provides you with a single layer. This is the only layer that is absolutely required. As long as the drawings remain simple, one layer may be all that you will need, but as you become more proficient with the program, you may find yourself looking for tools to organize your information.

Think of layers as a series of transparent overlays used for presentation on an overhead projector. Each overlay relates to the others but can also be shown alone. Science teachers in elementary school use a set of overlays to teach children about the human body. Placed one on top of another, the overlays show systems of a human body. Overlays are a good way to show the relationships among the various parts of the body, but it is also helpful to peel off layers and study each system separately. Layers work the same way in AutoCAD. You can group objects in your drawing based on common characteristics. For example, on a house plan you could put the walls on one layer, the dimensions on another, and the text on another. The electrical, plumbing, and HVAC could also be placed on separate layers. The interior designer could create a furniture layout on a separate layer. Since you can choose which layers to display, the designer might choose not to show the electrical and mechanical layers while working on the drawings. In addition, several different furniture layouts could be produced and then placed on separate layers. Because AutoCAD allows you to choose which layers are plotted, several layouts could be printed without erasing and starting over each time.

In the same way, a landscape designer could use layers to create several landscape designs. The initial drawing might contain all the information provided for the site plan. The designer could then create a layer for an initial landscape plan. Another layer could be created for plantings to be added over a 5-year period. Another alternative would be to place all trees on one layer, shrubs on another, and base plantings on another. AutoCAD allows each layer to be displayed and printed in separate colors, linetypes, and lineweights. These options can help bring clarity to your drawings.

16.2 Accessing the Layer Properties Manager

- Type **LAYER** or **LA** at the command prompt.
- Select <u>L</u>ayer from the <u>F</u>ormat pull-down menu.
- Click on the Layer icon on the Object Properties toolbar. The icon shows a stack of papers.

Layer
Icon

Once you have accessed the Layer Properties Manager (see Figure 16.1), you have a variety of options from which to choose. The next few sections of the text describe how to take advantage of the choices available.

FIGURE 16.1 Layer Properties Manager showing default layer.

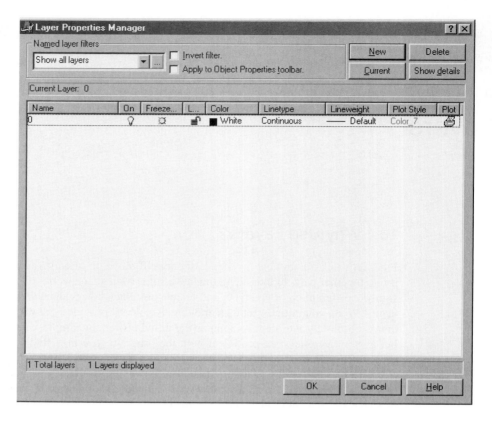

16.3 Naming and Creating New Layers

The first time you enter the Layer Properties Manager, only one layer, named 0, will be shown (see Figure 16.1). This is the default layer that is automatically created when you start a new drawing. This is the only layer required by AutoCAD, and it cannot be purged or renamed.

You can create additional layers in your drawing by picking the New button in the Layer Properties Manager dialog box. A new layer listing will appear highlighted on the screen with the name of the layer outlined with a box (see Figure 16.2). AutoCAD defaults to numbering the layers; however, you can use up to 255 characters to create your own names. Letters, numbers, and certain special characters such as spaces can be used. If you use an invalid character (such as ,.∧":?=`) the program will let you know immediately with a polite message.

Layers can be based on a number of different systems. For simple drawings, it may be easiest to group layers by color and linetype. For more complex drawings, layers may be determined by the function of the objects in the layer. Notice as you create new layers that the layers are listed using alphanumeric sorting. Numbered layers are listed first, followed by an alphabetical listing of the additional layers.

Once you have entered a new layer, you can make it current by highlighting the layer and picking the Current button. Once a layer is current, any new objects drawn will be placed on that layer until another layer is selected as current. The exception to this rule is objects being edited using some of the modify commands such as Match Properties or Properties. If the program uses an existing object to construct a new entity, the new entity will be placed on the same layer as the existing one. Different colors are often assigned to different layers as a visual clue of an object's affiliation.

Several layer names can be entered at one time without having to choose the New button between each layer. Simply type in the new layer name followed by a comma each time. When you are finished entering new layer names press Enter↵ or pick OK if you are finished with the Layer Properties Manager.

16.4 Layer Properties

Color

The default color for AutoCAD is white. Objects will be shown as white on a screen with a black background. This does not mean that the lines will be invisible if you are using a white background for your screen. With a white background, the lines are shown as black. In the same way, any layers plotted on white paper will be drawn in black.

Note: To highlight a layer, left-click in the name area for that particular layer.

Note: In the releases prior to Auto-CAD 2000, names could not be longer than 31 characters and could not contain spaces. If you save a drawing from AutoCAD 2000 in the format of an earlier release, the program will automatically shorten the layer names and replace any spaces with underscores (_).

Note: AutoCAD will create a layer called Defpoints when certain commands are used. Leave this layer alone. This is *not* a layer for you to use

FIGURE 16.2 Layer Properties
Manager with New layer being
created.

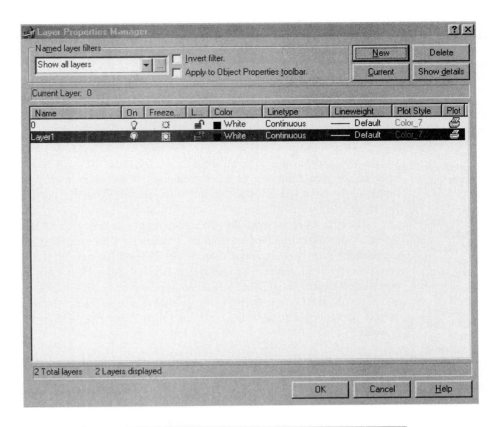

FIGURE 16.3 Select Color dialog box.

Note: The ACI
number will appear
in the Color: text box
once the color has
been chosen. Once
you have selected a
color, pick OK to exit
the Select Color Dia-
log box. The new
color for the layer
should now be dis-
played in the Layer
Properties Manager.

To select the color for a layer, highlight the layer and left-click on the color displayed. The Select Color dialog box will appear on your screen (see Figure 16.3). Layer colors are coded by name and by number. You can
select a color by picking it directly from the display or by entering the name or number in the Color: text box.

The number of colors available will depend on the graphics card and the monitor of your system. Seven
standard colors as well as several gray shades are displayed at the top of the Select Color dialog box. The
numbers assigned to each color are as follows:

1   Red

2   Yellow

3   Green

4   Cyan

5   Blue

6   Magenta

7   White

Linetype

Unless you decide otherwise, all lines drawn by AutoCAD will be of the continuous type. Notice that the linetype for your default layer 0 is Continuous. If you wish to change the linetype for a layer, you need to highlight the layer and left-click on the Linetype column to display the Select Linetype dialog box (see Figure 16.4).

The first time you open this dialog box only one linetype will be displayed. The standard linetypes are stored in an external file named acad.lin. Storing the files externally allows you to load only those linetypes required for your specific application. If the linetype you wish to use is not displayed in the Select Linetype box, pick the Load… button to activate the Load or Reload Linetypes dialog box (see Figure 16.5). The linetypes available are listed along with their appearance and a brief description. Highlight the linetype desired and pick OK. Back in the Select Linetype dialog box, highlight the linetype desired and pick OK again. The correct linetype should now appear in the Layer Properties Manager. Pick OK once again to return to your drawing.

Color is most often assigned BYLAYER or BYBLOCK, which means that all the objects in a particular layer or block are the same color. You can use the Properties command to modify the color of single objects within a layer; however, we do not recommend this.

Note: The gaps and spaces found on different linetypes (hidden, center, and phantom) may appear as continuous lines if the Ltscale (Linetype scale) is set incorrectly for the current drawing scale. The default Ltscale is set at 1 when a new drawing is started from scratch. A good practice is to set the Ltscale as you choose what drawing setup is needed for the drawing scale to be used. See Appendix B for typical Ltscale settings.
To change a Ltscale setting is easy. At the command line type in the following:
Command: LTS ↵
LTSCALE Enter new linetype scale factor <1.0000>:
At this point just type in the desired value for your drawing scale. This value is good for all the lines on the drawing. To change a single line's Ltscale, you must use the Properties command, which is described in Chapter 14.

FIGURE 16.4   Select Linetype dialog box.

FIGURE 16.5   Load or Reload Linetypes dialog box.

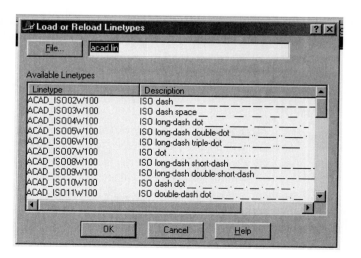

Note: An ISO library of linetypes is available by picking the File . . . button in the Load or Reload Linetypes dialog box and selecting acadiso.lin (see Figure 16.6). The ISO linetypes are identical in the acad.lin and acadiso.lin files. The difference lies in the non-ISO linetypes. These are scaled up by a factor of 25.4 to convert them from inches into millimeters.

ACAD_ISOO2W100	ISO dash	————————————————
ACAD_ISOO3W100	ISO dash space	— — — — — — — —
ACAD_ISOO4W100	ISO long-dash dot	——————————————
ACAD_ISOO5W100	ISO long-dash double dot	——————————————
ACAD_ISOO6W100	ISO long-dash triple dot	——————————————
ACAD_ISOO7W100	ISO dot	· · · ·
ACAD_ISOO8W100	ISO long-dash short-dash	——————————————
ACAD_ISOO9W100	ISO long-dash double-short-dash	——————————————
ACAD_ISOO10W100	ISO dash dot	——————————————
ACAD_ISOO11W100	ISO double-dash dot	——————————————
ACAD_ISOO12W100	ISO dash double-dash	——————————————
ACAD_ISOO13W100	ISO double-dash double-dot	——————————————
ACAD_ISOO14W100	ISO dash triple-dot	——————————————
ACAD_ISOO15W100	ISO double-dash triple-dot	——————————————
BATTING	Batting	
BORDER	Border	— — · — — · — — ·
BORDER2	Border (.5x)	– – · – – · – – · – – ·
BORDERX2	Border (2x)	—— —— · —— —— ·
CENTER	Center	—— — —— — —— —
CENTER2	Center (.5x)	— – — – — – — –
CENTERX2	Center (2x)	——— — ——— —
DASHDOT	Dash dot	— · — · — · — ·
DASHDOT2	Dash dot (.5x)	– · – · – · – · – · – ·
DASHDOTX2	Dash dot (2x)	—— · —— · —— ·
DASHED	Dashed	— — — — — — —
DASHED2	Dashed (.5x)	– – – – – – – – – –
DASHEDX2	Dashed (2x)	—— —— —— ——
DIVIDE	Divide	— · · — · · — · ·
DIVIDE2	Divide (.5x)	– · · – · · – · · –
DIVIDEX2	Divide (2x)	—— · · —— · ·
DOT	Dot	· · · · · · · · · ·
DOT2	Dot (.5x)	··············
DOTX2	Dot (2x)	· · · · · · ·
FENCELINE1	Fenceline circle	—○——○——○——○——○—
FENCELINE2	Fenceline square	—□——□——□——□—
GAS_LINE	Gas line	—GAS——GAS——GAS——GAS——GAS——GAS——GAS—
HIDDEN	Hidden	— — — — — — — —
HIDDEN2	Hidden (.5x)	----------------
HIDDENX2	Hidden (2x)	—— —— —— ——
HOT_WATER_SUPPLY	Hot Water Supply	—HW——HW——HW——HW——HW——HW—
PHANTOM	Phantom	——— — — ——— — —
PHANTOM2	Phantom (.5x)	— – – — – – — –
PHANTOMX2	Phantom (2x)	——— —— —— ———
TRACKS	Tracks	+++++++++++++++++++++++
ZIGZAG	Zigzag	∿∿∿∿∿∿∿∿∿∿

FIGURE 16.6   AutoCAD linetype library of standard, ISO, and complex linetypes.

Lineweight

AutoCAD 2000 is the first release to allow weight or thickness to be assigned to objects that were not poly-lines. The default Lineweight is set at 0.01″ or 0.25 mm. To change the lineweight, highlight the layer and pick the lineweight column. The Lineweight dialog box should appear (see Figure 16.7). The available lineweights are based on those most commonly used in drawing (see Figure 16.8). The width varies from 0.00 mm to 2.11 mm. The original as well as the new lineweight will be shown in the area near the bottom of the dialog box.

FIGURE 16.7   Lineweight dialog box.

Alphabet of Lines for Architectural Drawing

Thicker/Wide lines
Line width around 1/32″ or about the same
width as a 0.7-mm drawing pencil

Thin lines
Line width around 1/64″ or a little wider
than a 0.3-mm pencil

Visible or Object Line
Thick continuous line

Cutting-Plane Line
Thick line with 1/4″ segments
and 1/8″ gaps

Viewing-Plane Line
Thick line with 1/8″ segments
and 1/16″ gaps

Short Freehand Break Line
Thick rough line drawn freehand across short distances

Long Break Line
Thin line with jagged Z-shape
that varies in size depending on
space limitations

Hidden Lines
Thin line with 1/8″ segments
and 1/16″ gaps

Center Lines
Thin line with 1/8″ segments
and 1/16″ gaps

Section or Hatch Lines
Thin continuous line

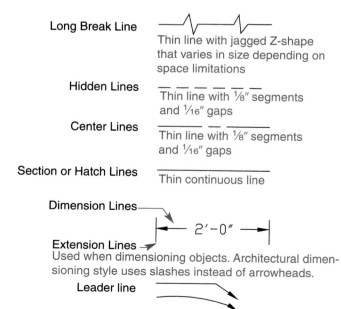

Dimension Lines

Extension Lines
Used when dimensioning objects. Architectural dimensioning style uses slashes instead of arrowheads.

Leader line
Used when pointing to
parts of a drawing

FIGURE 16.8   Alphabet of lineweights.

16.5 On/Off, Freeze/Thaw, and Locking Layers

Turning Layers On and Off

Note: To regener-
ate a drawing type
Regen at the com-
mand line. At times
AutoCAD will auto-
matically perform a
regeneration after a
command. A Regen
command will recal-
culate the screen, re-
freshing and sharp-
ening the lines and
shapes.

Looking at the Layers Properties Manager dialog box (see Figure 16.9) you will notice that the first column after the Name is designated On and contains a column of light bulbs. If the bulb shows yellow, the layer is turned on. If the bulb is gray, the layer is off. The light bulb toggles between off and on as you pick it with the cursor.

If the layer is turned off, the objects within that layer will not be displayed on the screen and will not show up on a plot. However, the objects can still be affected by certain editing techniques. For example, if you enter the Erase command and select the All option, the objects in the layers that are turned off will still be erased. If you Regen your drawing, the layers that are turned off will still be regenerated.

Layers are often turned off to avoid confusion on a crowded screen. Sometimes you wish to plot only certain features of a drawing. For example, a floor plan drawing will not always have the electrical information plotted.

Freezing and Thawing Layers

The third column in the Layers Properties Manager dialog box is entitled Freeze…. The layers displaying a yellow sun under this column are considered *thawed*. The layers displaying a white snowflake are *frozen*. Frozen layers are not displayed on the screen, nor are they plotted. In addition, frozen layers cannot be edited or regenerated. Freezing a layer may speed up system performance in a very complex drawing. The Freeze/Thaw icons can be toggled just like the On/Off icons by picking on the icon.

Locking and Unlocking Layers

The fourth column in the Layers Properties Manager dialog box in entitled L… for Lock. The icons displayed in this column are either closed or open padlocks. The locks can be toggled open and shut by picking the icon. If a layer is locked (padlock closed), the objects on the layer will be visible on the screen but Auto-CAD will not allow you to edit or change them. New objects can be added to the layer.

This option is particularly useful in situations where several people will be using the same drawing file. Layers can be locked to ensure that they are not inadvertently changed.

FIGURE 16.9 Layers Properties Manager showing layers.

16.6 Managing Layers

Deleting a Layer

The remaining two buttons displayed in the Layers Properties Manager dialog box are the Delete and the Show details buttons. Highlighting a layer and then selecting the Delete button will remove that layer from the drawing. AutoCAD will not allow you to delete Layer 0, the current layer, or any layer containing objects.

The Show details Option

The Show details button toggles with the Hide details button. The Show details button works only when a layer is highlighted. It displays basically the same details about color, linetype, and lineweight displayed in the upper level but with pull-down menus to allow you to make any necessary changes to the layer (see Figure 16.10). You can also access the On/Off, Freeze/Thaw, and Lock/Unlock options with this button.

Changing the Name of a Layer

To change the name of a layer, highlight the layer and pick the Name column. A box will then appear around the current name. Type in the new name and press Enter↵. Pick OK to accept the change and exit the dialog box. The only layer you cannot rename is the default Layer 0.

Shortcuts for Modifying Layers

You can select several layers at one time by holding down the Shift key as you pick the layers. If you continue to hold the Shift key down while you highlight two layers that are not adjacent to each other, the layers in between the two picked will also be selected.

Pressing the Ctrl key also lets you pick several layers at once. The Ctrl key allows you to pick layers that are not adjacent to one another without also selecting the layers in between.

Right-clicking while you are in the Layers Properties Manager will bring up a shortcut menu. Figure 16.11 shows the options available for managing your layers with this menu.

FIGURE 16.10   Layer Properties Manager showing details.

FIGURE 16.11   Layers shortcut menu.

Select here to view your layers.

FIGURE 16.12   Object Properties toolbar.

The Object Properties Toolbar

The Object Properties Toolbar (see Figure 16.12) makes it easier for you to manage your layers. The first icon on the toolbar looks like a stack of papers, with the bottom paper in the pile being yellow. This is the Make Object's Layer Current icon. Select a particular object in your drawing. Click on the icon. The current layer will now be set to the layer of the selected object.

The next icon on the toolbar is the Layers icon. It looks like a stack of white papers. Picking this icon will bring up the Layers Properties Manager. The first window in the toolbar provides a pull-down menu of all the layers in the drawing. The layer being displayed will be the current layer in the drawing. You can pull down the list and highlight a different layer to make it current.

16.7 Using AutoCAD Design Center to Import Layers

- Select AutoCAD DesignCenter from the Tools pull-down menu.
- Pick the AutoCAD DesignCenter icon from the Standard Toolbar. The icon looks like a calculator with multicolored buttons.

Design Center Icon

The AutoCAD DesignCenter allows you to import features of previous drawings into the current drawing. One of the features you can import is the layers defined in a previous drawing. Not only does this save time, since you do not have to create all those new layers, but it leads to consistency between drawings. Once you have activated the command, the DesignCenter will appear on the left side of the graphics screen. A list of blocks, layers, and other features of the drawing such as dimension and text styles will be displayed. To import one of these features into the current drawing, simply drag and drop the information with your cursor.

REVIEW QUESTIONS

1. What is a layer? What purpose do layers serve in a drawing?
2. Where would you go to create a new layer in your drawing?
3. How many layers are required by AutoCAD?
4. What is the default linetype and the default color in AutoCAD?
5. Do all objects within a layer have to be the same color and linetype?
6. What does it mean to freeze a layer? How does this differ from turning a layer off?
7. Can you erase a line in a locked layer?
8. What procedure would you follow to change from working in one layer to working in another layer?
9. If you realize that you have drawn a line while working in the wrong layer, what can you do to put the line on the correct layer? (You may need to refer to Chapter 14.)

EXERCISES

EXERCISE 16.1

A floor plan of a house is to be drawn and layers need to be set up. Your task is to set up a drawing with the following layers and characteristics.

- Create a layer named Text. Set the color to Red and use Continuous linetype.
- Create a layer named Wall. Set the color to White and the linetype to Continuous along with a lineweight setting of .35 mm.
- Create a layer named Overhead Cabinets. Set the color to Cyan and the linetype to Hidden.
- Create a layer named Ceiling Line. Set the color to Blue and the linetype to Hidden (2X).
- Create a layer named Cabinet. Set the color to White and the linetype to Continuous.
- Create a layer named Appliances/Fixture. Set the color to Magenta and the linetype to Continuous.

Save the drawing and name it 16EX-1.

EXERCISE 16.2

In this exercise lay out a kitchen plan using the exercise 16.1 layer setup. Here are some minimum guidelines for the plan:

- Use a $\frac{3}{8}'' = 1'-0''$ scale.
- Use a rectangular plan with approximately 225 square foot layout.
- The total perimeter distance between the refrigerator, stove/oven, and the sink should be between 18′ and 22′.
- Recess part of the ceiling.
- Overhead cabinets need to be 12″ deep.
- Counters need to be 25″ deep.
- Use a 4½″ wall thickness
- If you need some ideas on kitchen layouts, refer to the *AIA Graphic Standards* or the *Interior Graphic Standards*.

Match the layers with the correct objects when you draw them. Save the drawing as 16EX-2.

EXERCISE 16.3

Construct some interior elevations of the kitchen plan in exercise 16.2. Use the following guidelines.

- Use 16EX-1 layers.
- Use ⅜″ = 1′-0″ scale.
- The counter height should be 36″ above the floor line.
- The bottom of the overhead cabinets should be 54″ above the floor line.
- Use a 4″ recessed base and a 4″ countertop base.
- Create a new layer and name it Shelves. Make the color Cyan and the linetype Hidden.

Draw the shelves in the Cabinet elevations with the new layer.

DRAWING ASSIGNMENT

1. Redraw the plan view in Figure 16.13 at a ¼″ = 1′-0″ scale. Use the following settings for the drawing. Layers to create:

Layer Name	Color	Linetype	Lineweight
WALLS	White	Continuous	.7 mm
TEXT	Red	Continuous	Default
DIMENSION	Blue	Continuous	Default
Rod	Cyan	Hidden	Default
Fixtures	Blue	Continuous	Default
Appliances	Green	Continuous	Default
Cabinet and Shelves	Blue	Continuous	Default

Set Ltscale to 35.

2. Draw two interior elevations for the Master Bath plan found in Figure 16.13. Create a layer for walls, dimensions, and fixtures. Research bathroom information in the AIA Graphic Standards to get accurate sizes.

FIGURE 16.13   Drawing Assignment 1

CHAPTER 17

Dimensioning

○ ○

Dimensioning on the drawing board seemed to take as much time to do as the drawing itself. Planning the layouts, constructing the guidelines, and finally placing the correct dimensions in their desired locations was very time consuming. There is no comparison when it comes to dimensioning with AutoCAD.

One thing AutoCAD does not automatically do is dimension to office standards or practices. Learning to dimension using the same standard as everyone else in an office or classroom takes a little practice time and guidance. Check with your instructor or office manager for dimensioning guidelines. Knowing the system will help cut down on early errors. The speed of placing and editing dimensions in AutoCAD will enhance the learning process. A little bit of patience when planning dimensions and learning the ropes goes a long way toward making an excellent looking drawing.

It does take time initially to set up a dimensioning style that works for each type of drawing required. The advantage to all this dimension planning and setup is that once you create a style you can use it again on different drawings, either by putting it into a saved template or dragging and dropping it from the Design Center.

Another advantage to dimensioning with AutoCAD is that it is much easier to control office dimensioning standards. A copy of the office's standard dimensioning styles can be saved for each computer, so there is no excuse for anyone not to use them. All offices strive for consistency on drawings; it makes the drawings look better and eliminates confusion when reading them.

In this chapter learning about dimensioning with AutoCAD is broken into three parts:

1. Creating architectural dimension styles and settings
2. Placing dimensions on a drawing
3. Editing dimensions on a drawing

The AutoCAD software has gone through quite an evolution when it comes to dimensioning. In the early stages of AutoCAD, all the settings (variables) had to be input by typing on the keyboard. Remembering what all the different settings did without any visual aids was a major task, but now most of the dimension variables show an example of how the dimensions will look when a setting is adjusted.

17.1 Creating Dimension Styles

This section will show how to create architectural dimension styles.

Figure 17.1 shows the Dimension Style Manager dialog box, which is where the AutoCAD 2000 dimension styles are created.

The Dimstyle command

- Type **Dimstyle** or **D** at the command prompt.
- Select <u>D</u>imension Style from the F<u>o</u>rmat pull-down menu (see Figure 17.2).
- Click on the Dimension Style icon on the Dimension toolbar (see Figure 17.3).
- Select <u>S</u>tyle from the Dime<u>n</u>sion pull-down menu (see Figure 17.4). To turn on the Dimension toolbar select T<u>o</u>olbars . . . from the View pull-down menu (see Figure 17.5).

Dimension Style
Icon

387

FIGURE 17.1   Dimension Style Manager dialog box.

FIGURE 17.2   Dimension Style selected on the Format pull-down menu.

FIGURE 17.3   Dimension toolbar.

    The Toolbars dialog box appears (see Figure 17.6). To turn on the Dimension toolbar simply left-click in the box to the left of Dimension. Left-click on the Close button on the Toolbars dialog box to close the toolbar selection. (Do not close the Dimension toolbar, only the Toolbar dialog box.) The Dimension toolbar will remain as seen in Figure 17.3.

    Planning what the dimensions should look like will help in the long run, and creating a standard style to use will save time. The settings demonstrated will be for architectural use.

Helpful Hints

1. Create a separate layer for dimensions.
2. Adjust dimensioning settings to make the text height and tick sizes appear and plot at the correct size. See Solutions 1 and 2 on page 390 (also see Figure 17.34).

FIGURE 17.4 Style selected on the Dimension pull down menu.

FIGURE 17.5 Toolbars selected on the View pull-down menu.

FIGURE 17.6 Toolbars dialog box.

Select here to turn on the Dimension Toolbar.

Desired Architectural Settings

- Use a text height of ⅛″ if the drawing is at full scale.
- Use ⅛″ ticks instead of arrows at full scale.
- Place text above a continuous dimension line.
- Use a ¹⁄₁₆″ (full scale) origin gap. (Gap off the object before the extension line begins.)
- Use a baseline spacing of ⅜″ (at full scale).
- Use a fraction height scale of .75.

For instance, let's say a 50′ line needs to be dimensioned. When this line is dimensioned, the ⅛″ text and ticks will be too small and will not display well because the limits are set for a ¼″ = 1′-0″ scale. There are two approaches to selecting scales and sizes.

Solution 1

Leave the sizes in the full-size or real height or size setting and change the Scale for Dimension Features to fit a ¼″ = 1′-0″ scale by dividing ¼ inch into 1 foot, or 12 inches:

$$\frac{12''}{.25''} = 48$$

This calculation can be performed the same way for any scale. The 48 would be the number used in the Scale for Dimension Features box. (Where to do this will be shown a little later.)

Solution 2

Leave the Scale for Dimension Features at 1 and change the sizes to what they should be in the scale you wish to use. Thus, a ⅛″ dimension text height in a ¼″ = 1′-0″ scale would need to be set to 6″ high. The height is calculated by using the scale factor and multiplying it by the ⅛″ desired height:

$$\text{Scale Factor} \quad \frac{1'}{\frac{1}{4}''} = \frac{12''}{.25''} = 48$$

Scale Factor	Real Size	Text Height Setting
48	× ⅛″	= 6″

For further information on this topic, refer to Appendix A.

Opening the Dimension Style Manager

At the command line type in **DIMSTYLE** or **D** and press Enter↵. The Dimension Style Manager dialog box appears. Left-click on the <u>N</u>ew . . . button on the right side of the dialog box. The Create New Dimension Style dialog box opens up (see Figure 17.7). At the <u>N</u>ew Style Name: text box type in a name for a style to be created. We will use Arch-1 for our example. Once the name is typed, select the Continue button in the lower left corner of this display box. Another dialog box, which is the heart and soul of the dimension settings, opens up with the heading New Dimension Style: Arch-1 (see Figure 17.8). There are six major tabs across the top of the box for the following settings:

- Lines and Arrows
- Text
- Fit
- Primary Units
- Alternate Units
- Tolerances

FIGURE 17.7 Create New Dimension style dialog box.

FIGURE 17.8 New Dimension
Style dialog box.

Lines and Arrows Tab

When the Lines and Arrows option is selected with a left click, the following five areas appear (see Figure 17.9): a graphic illustration in the upper right-hand corner, Dimension Lines, Extension Lines, Arrowheads, and Center Marks for Circles.

1. The **graphic illustration** shows a drawing and dimensions. As changes are made to the settings the dimensions change to show the effects of the new settings.

2. **Dimension Lines** can be changed in the following ways:

FIGURE 17.9 Lines and Arrows
tab menu.

Tab for Lines and Arrows

FIGURE 17.10 Example of an extension line.

FIGURE 17.11 Baseline spacing.

FIGURE 17.12 Suppression of dimension lines and ticks.

- **Colors** for dimensions can be changed ByLayer, ByBlock, or by individual colors found in AutoCAD.
- **Lineweights** can also be altered by using the arrow to the right of the text box to access the desired setting. (The Display Lineweight setting must be turned on in the Lineweight Setting dialog box under the Format pull-down menu in order to generate lineweight changes.)
- **Extend beyond ticks** allows the extension lines to be set above architectural tick marks with a positive value. Values of ¹⁄₁₆″ to ⅛″ are acceptable (see Figure 17.10).
- **Baseline spacing** sets a standard space between dimensions when they are stacked on top of one another (see Figure 17.11).
- **Suppress** will cut off the first or second dimension lines and ticks when they are not desired. For example, you would use Suppress when you dimension from an existing dimension and you do not want to duplicate the line and tick that already exists (see Figure 17.12).

3. **Extension Lines** are the lines that extend from the object being dimensioned (see Figure 17.10). They can be changed in some of the same ways that dimension lines get altered. Color, lineweight, extension beyond ticks, and suppression of lines are changed in exactly the same way as for the dimension lines; however, baseline spacing is replaced with an Offset from origin setting (see Figures 17.13 and 17.14). This controls the gap between the object being dimensioned and the start of the extension line (see Figure 17.15).

4. **Arrowheads** and tick marks can be changed by selecting options in the text boxes (see Figure 17.16).

Check Here to Suppress

FIGURE 17.13 Dimension Lines options.

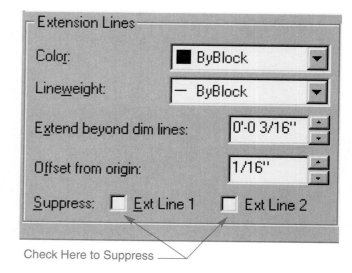

Check Here to Suppress

FIGURE 17.14 Extension Lines options.

FIGURE 17.15 Offset from origin option.

FIGURE 17.16 Arrowheads options.

FIGURE 17.17 Example of a leader.

FIGURE 17.18 Types of center marks.

FIGURE 17.19 Center mark options for circles.

The first and second options control how the dimensioning symbol will be displayed. A wide assortment of arrowheads, tick marks, dots, and just about anything found in the various drafting fields is provided. Left-click on the arrows to the right to check them out. We will select the Architectural tick for architectural drawings.

The Leader option will need to be a closed filled arrowhead. Leaders are used for notes and dimension circles (see Figure 17.17). The size of the dimensioning ticks and arrowheads is specified in the Arrow size: box. The minimum size used should be ⅛″.

5. **Center Marks for Circles**—This box has two controls in it to mark the center of circles: Type: and Size:. See Figure 17.18 for the Type options. The size control to the right adjusts the size of the mark or line setting. Most architectural drawings consistently use the None option (see Figure 17.19).

Text Tab

The Text Tab consists of four areas (see Figure 17.20): the graphics display, Text Appearance, Text Placement, and Text Alignment.

FIGURE 17.20 Text options.

Text Tab

FIGURE 17.21 Text appearance options.

1. The **graphics display** shows how the changes affect the dimension settings and is located in the upper right corner. As you make changes look at the graphics display and make sure this is the way your dimensions should look.

2. **Text Appearance**—This box has five settings that control the text aspects (see Figure 17.21).

- **Text style** lets you change font styles for the dimension text. Left-clicking on the down arrow will display font styles that have been loaded. Left-clicking on the box with three periods in it will bring up the Text Style dialog box and let you pick a style name and font style. (This is discussed in Chapter 18.)

- The **Text color** box allows you to set the color of the text or coordinate it with a ByBlock or By-Layer selection. We recommend selecting the ByLayer option, placing the color in the layer controls.

- **Text height** needs to be set in this box. The minimum plotting height needs to be ⅛″ for full-scale drawings. If you want to dimension a drawing at a scale other than full, then leave the height at ⅛″ and change the scale factor in the Scale for Dimension Features located under the Fit tab to match the Limit settings.

- The **Fraction height scale** is based on a proportion of the text height. A factor of .75 works well for architectural drawings. This factor will reduce the height of the numerator and denominator text to three-fourths of the height of the text height setting.

- The final option is the **Draw frame around text box**. A left click in the box will turn it on. It is used mainly in mechanical drafting, so leave it unchecked for architectural work.

3. **Text Placement** – Three options are located in this display (see Figure 17.22).

- The **vertical** setting offers four choices, as seen in Figure 17.23. The **above** selection is commonly used in architectural work; however, a few individuals use the Centered option in some residential drawings (see Figure 17.24).

- The **Horizontal** option can be set to *Centered* for most architectural drawing styles and can be adjusted later if needed. The function of this variable is to shift the text along the dimension line (see Figure 17.25). There is a lot of flexibility here, but stick with Centered and use the grips to move the text around if editing is needed later.

FIGURE 17.22 Text placement options.

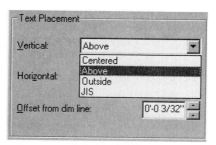

FIGURE 17.23 Vertical text placement.

FIGURE 17.24 The Above and Centered options.

FIGURE 17.25 Horizontal options.

FIGURE 17.26 Offset from dimension line.

FIGURE 17.27 Text alignment options.

The text is always aligned with the bottom of the sheet.

FIGURE 17.28 Unidirectional alignment. (Horizontal)

FIGURE 17.29 Aligned with dimension line setting. Text above line is used for Architectural drawings.

- The **Offset from dim line** is used to set the gap between the text and the dimension line (see Figure 17.26).

4. **Text Alignment**—There are three selections from which to choose in this box (see Figure 17.27).

- The **Horizontal** setting will keep the text in a position known as *unidirectional*. Figure 17.28 shows this type of alignment, which is used primarily in mechanical drafting.
- The **Aligned with dimension line** setting is more typically used in architectural drawing. The text will shift with the dimension lines, as shown in Figure 17.29.
- The final option is the international **ISO Standard**, which is used in most countries outside the United States and Canada.

Fit Tab

As text is placed on a drawing, everything can get crowded. The Fit menu gives you some choices when tight conditions arise (see Figure 17.30).

As in the previous menus, a graphics screen is situated in the upper right corner. Four other areas are displayed in this menu.

1. Fit Options is the largest display area. This box lets you pick how to handle the condition stated at the top of the display (see Figure 17.31). When there is not enough space between extension lines to fit the arrows and text inside them, then what should AutoCAD do with text and arrows?

FIGURE 17.30   Fit options.

Fit Tab —

FIGURE 17.31   Fit Options menu.

One thing to remember is that if ticks or slashes are being used, it will not matter. They look the same and are equally spaced on the inside and outside of the extension lines. The choices are as follows:

- Either the text or the arrows, whichever fits best
- Arrows
- Text
- Both text and arrows
- Always keep text between ext lines
- Suppress arrows if they don't fit inside the extension lines

Whichever option is chosen, it is easily edited later. Placing the text outside and using a leader to point back between the extension lines is a common architectural practice (see Figure 17.32). Selecting the *Text* setting will generate this option.

2. The **Text Placement** display area has three options from which to choose (see Figure 17.33). It goes into effect when the text is not in the default position. AutoCAD will place the text in one of three ways:

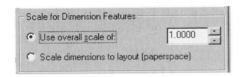

FIGURE 17.32 Using a leader with dimension text.

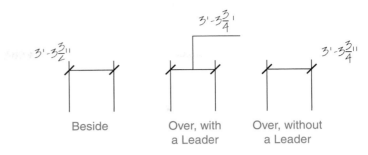

Beside   Over, with a Leader   Over, without a Leader

FIGURE 17.33 Text placement options.

FIGURE 17.34 Scale for Dimension features options.

- <u>B</u>eside the dimension line
- <u>O</u>ver the dimension line, with a leader
- Over the dimension line, with<u>o</u>ut a leader

3. A **Scale for Dimension Features** area is found directly below the graphics or drawing example (see Figure 17.34).

As shown in the figure, there are two choices. The option **Scale dimensions to layout (paper space)** is used if the drawing is to be placed into the paper space environment later. (See Appendix A, Plotting: Dimensioning in Floating Model Space.)

The option **Use overall <u>s</u>cale of** is used when dimensioning is done in the model space environment. For example, if model space scale or limits are set to a scale of ¼″ = 1′-0″ and you want to leave the text setting at the real scale, such as ⅛″ for text height and ticks, then you must insert a scale factor here to match the drawing scale. For ¼″ = 1′-0″ it would be 48.

To find the scale factor for a given scale see Figure 17.35. This method will work for any desired scale.

4. The **Fine Tuning** display area has two options (see Figure 17.36).

- **Place text manually when dimensioning**—Checking this box on will allow you to move the cursor around and drag the floating text to various positions (see Figure 17.37). Once you find the right location a left click will apply the dimension.
- **<u>A</u>lways draw dim line between ext lines**—This setting when checked on will always generate a dimension line between the two extension lines. Having both these boxes turned on works very well with architectural drawings.

$$\text{Scale } ¼″ = 1′-0″ \quad \text{Scale Factor} = \frac{1′}{.25″} \text{ or } \frac{12″}{.25″} = 48$$

$$\text{Scale } 1″ = 1′-0″ \quad \text{Scale Factor} = \frac{1′}{1″} \text{ or } \frac{12″}{1″} = 12$$

FIGURE 17.35 Calculating scale factors.

FIGURE 17.36 Fine tuning options.

FIGURE 17.37   Placing text with the cursor.

Cursor on the left   Cursor in the center   Cursor on the right

FIGURE 17.38   Primary Unit menu.

Tab for Primary Units

Primary Units Tab

This group of settings pertains to unit displays and controls (see Figure 17.38).

   1. **Linear Dimensions** is the largest display area with seven settings.

   ■ Unit format—There is a list of formats for each drafting profession (see Figure 17.39).

Scientific—uses exponential forms

Decimal—uses inches or milimeters for mechanical drafting

Engineering—uses feet for civil drafting

Architectural—uses feet and inches for architectural drafting

Fractional—uses whole numbers and fractions only

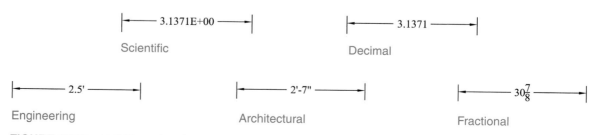

FIGURE 17.39   Unit Format options.

FIGURE 17.40 Precision menu.

Horizontal   Diagonal   Not Stacked

FIGURE 17.41 Fraction format options.

- **Precision**—You may select the accuracy with which the text should be displayed. The architectural choices range from $0'-0''$ to $0'- 0\frac{1}{256}''$ (see Figure 17.40).

- **Fraction format**—The style of fractions can be set to one of three ways (see Figure 17.41). The diagonal reads very well and fits in with the architectural style.

- **Decimal separator**—When decimal units are selected, the decimal (.) in a number (2.75) can be altered to a comma (2,75) or an empty space (2 75). For architectural drawing this is not an option and is ignored.

- **Round Off**—This setting allows you to determine whether the dimension text will display to the nearest $\frac{1}{16}''$, $\frac{1}{8}''$, or any increment of $\frac{1}{16}$th. Leave it at zero to get an exact value.

- **Prefix**—If a text display in front of the dimension is desired, it can be typed in at the prefix box, for example, FIELD VERIFY $100'-0'$

- **Suffix**—This setting applies text after the dimension, for example, $10'-0'$ C.O.

2. **Measurement Scale**—This area is dedicated to adjusting dimension readings based on scale changes (see Figure 17.42). Let's say a full-scale drawing is too big to fit on a standard sheet size, so you draw the objects in the drawing at half scale to get a good fit on the sheet. Just because the objects are drawn at half size does not mean the dimensions should read half; they must read and show the real size on the drawing. In this case the Measurement Scale can be set to 2 to show the correct dimension. It measures the half scale then doubles the size. The **Apply to layout dimensions only** box can be checked on to apply this process to the layout/paper space environment.

3. **Zero Suppression** for linear dimensions is found in the bottom left corner. When checked on with a left click this setting will remove zeros from dimension text as follows:

Zero Suppression for Architectural Units

- Leading off shows $0'-8''$

- Leading on shows $8''$

- Trailing off shows $1'-0''$

- Trailing on shows $1'$

Notice that the zero disappears when the suppression is activated. Most architectural drawings should be set with the Leading suppression checked on and the Trailing suppression checked off.

FIGURE 17.42 Measurement Scale options.

4. **Angular Dimensions**—Angle dimension settings are input in this area, which is located in the bottom right corner below the graphics area (see Figure 17.43).

The *Units format* sets the units for the angles. Angles can be displayed in the following units:

- Decimals   30.75°
- Degrees, Minutes, Seconds   30° 45′ 30″
- Gradians   100g
- Radians   3r

Most individuals are familiar with degrees. See Chapter 4 for a review of angle units. The *Precision* box allows you to select the accuracy with which the dimension should display.

Setting	Angle Reading
0	30
.0	30.0
.00	30.00

Zero Suppression for angles is in the bottom right corner. This setting affects angle values only.

Zero Supression	Angle Reads
Leading on	.5
Leading off	0.5
Trailing on	30
Trailing off	30.00

Two more menus used in the Dimension Style dialog box are the Alternate Units menu and the Tolerances menu. When selected they appear as shown in Figures 17.44 and 17.45.

These two menus are pretty much ignored for architectural drawings. They are heavily used in other drafting fields, but almost never in architectural work.

Practice and experiment in order to learn how to use the settings optimally. It will help to watch the graphics display to see how the changes are affecting the dimensions. Another helpful thing to do when learning to create styles is to start from scratch every so often even though you can put a style in a template or copy it over from one drawing to the next.

Dimension Style Manager

Let's take another look at the Dimension Style Manager dialog display (see Figure 17.46). A list of dimension styles is displayed in the <u>S</u>tyles: box. The styles you create through the <u>N</u>ew. . . button are found here along with AutoCAD's default Standard styles. Once a style is listed here you can use it by highlighting it

FIGURE 17.44 Alternate Units menu.

FIGURE 17.45 Tolerances menu.

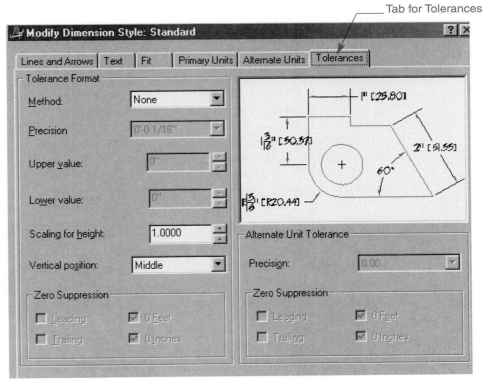

with a left mouse click, then moving the cursor to the Set Current screen button and left-clicking there. If you need to change a style, highlight the style you want to change with Set Current, then left-click on Modify. The Modify Dimension Style dialog box will appear, which looks exactly the same as when you create a new style. The same optional settings are available in the six menus: Lines and Arrows, Text, Fit, Primary Units, Alternate Units, and Tolerances.

Editing or making changes to an existing style instead of making a new style is exactly the same as in the New setup. Make any necessary changes in the settings, then click on the OK button to activate the new settings.

FIGURE 17.46   Dimension Style Manager dialog box.

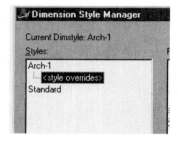

FIGURE 17.47   Override display.

The <u>O</u>verride... button gives you the ability to make a temporary change to the current style setting. To use the override command make the desired style current, then left-click on the <u>O</u>verride... button. The override dialog display appears with the six standard menus for dimension variable settings that you have seen before. Make your changes and pick OK when you are finished. Notice in the <u>S</u>tyles: listing that the override is listed as a branch off the original style (see Figure 17.47).

Close the Dimension Style Manager display, and the override changes will take effect when dimensions are applied to a drawing. When it is time to return to the original style, left-click on that style and then left-click on the Set Current button. An AutoCAD Alert box appears and lets you know that the override settings will be discarded if the OK button is selected (see Figure 17.48).

If you wish to keep the overrides and the original style, then create a New style using the override changes. That way it will be possible to switch back and forth between the two styles without deleting any settings.

The <u>C</u>ompare... button will display dimension variable settings. At the top of the Compare Dimension Styles dialog box are two text boxes where you can select styles and compare them with other existing styles (see Figure 17.49). The screen lists the Description and the Variable in the DIM mode and the setting of this variable in both styles. Only two styles can be compared at a time.

FIGURE 17.48   AutoCAD alert.

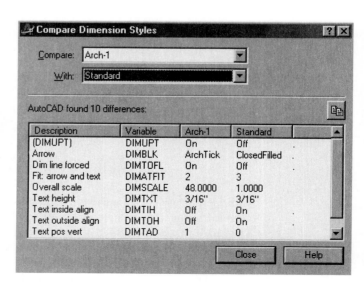

FIGURE 17.49   Compare Dimension Styles dialog box.

Dimension Variables (DIM)

In early AutoCAD releases, dimension variable settings were typed in at the command line. There were no icons or displays to help the user set up dimension styles. It took a lot of time and a great memory to set the DIM variables in those days. These variables still exist, and we are going to show them to you with the current dimension boxes. Select the Help pull-down menu on the standard AutoCAD screen and left-click on the first option (AutoCAD Help F1). Under the Contents pull-down double-left-click on the Command Reference option. Next, double-left-click on the suboption, Dimension Variables Quick Reference. This is the best place to look when checking out the DIM variables.

If you want a taste of the pre-Windows AutoCAD era left-click on the Dimension Styles button. Notice that there is a written description along with the variable abbreviation (see Figure 17.50). It is easy to see that setting dimension variables was a real memory game. This screen also included standard DIM variable settings for:

ANSI—American National Standards Institute

ISO-25—International Standards Organization

DIN—Deutsche Industrie Norm

JIS—Japanese Industrial Standard

Use the scroll bars to the right and scan through all the variables. Sixty-four (64) DIM variables are listed here, and it is a real challenge to remember what each one does. Today's AutoCAD gives you a choice of using dialog boxes and icons instead of typing these DIM variables.

We need to look at one more option in this Help screen menu. Use the Back button at the top of the screen to return to the Dimension Variables Quick Reference (see Figure 17.51). Now, left-click on the Dimension System Variable button and check out the screen that appears (see Figure 17.52).

Use the Maximize button in the top right corner of the screen to display the entire visual. What a great index or reference! The screen displays the pictures and dialog boxes along with the DIM variables. Use the scroll bars and scan through completely. Use this help screen whenever dealing with DIM variable settings for quick answers.

Now that we have shown you how to set up the appearance of dimensions, it is time to learn how to place them on a drawing. This is the fast, fun part of dimensioning.

FIGURE 17.50 Dimension Style Variables.

Dimension Style Variables

Variable	Description	ANSI	ISO-25	DIN	JIS
DIMADEC	Decimal places for angular dimensions	0	0	0	0
DIMALT	Alternate units selected	Off	Off	Off	Off
DIMALTD	Alternate unit decimal places	2	4	2	2
DIMALTF	Alternate unit scale factor	25.4000	0.0394	0.0394	0.0394
DIMALTRND	Alternate unit rounding value	0.0000	0.0000	0.0000	0.0000
DIMALTTD	Alternate tolerance decimal places	2	4	2	2

FIGURE 17.51 Location of the Back button.

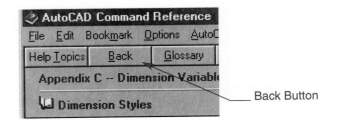

Back Button

The following illustrations show how the dimension system variables are organized on tabs in the New Dimension Style dialog box. Although not shown, these system variables are organized the same way on the Modify Dimension Style and Override Dimension Style dialog boxes.

FIGURE 17.52   Dimension System variables.

17.2 Placing Dimensions on a Drawing

You can physically put dimensions on a drawing in a variety of ways. The primary method is to use the mouse. The two ways most preferred are through the Dimension pull-down menu and the Dimension toolbar.

The Dimension pull-down menu can be opened with a left click to show all the following options (see Figure 17.53).

- **QDIM**—Quick dimensioning applies dimensions fast to individual selections or a group selection. Dimensions are applied on a straight alignment (see Figure 17.54).

- **Linear**—Linear dimensioning is used when a dimension is needed between two points or between two given lines or objects. Dimensions are applied on vertical or horizontal lines (see Figure 17.55).

- **Aligned**—The Aligned option is used to place a straight-line dimension on an angled line (see Figure 17.56).

FIGURE 17.53   Dimension pull-down menu.

FIGURE 17.54   QDIM.

FIGURE 17.55 Linear dimensioning.   FIGURE 17.56 Aligned dimensioning.

- **Ordinate**—Ordinate dimensioning does not use arrows or ticks but instead references from a (0,0) coordinate and uses an extension line (see Figure 17.57).
- **Radius**—Radius dimensioning is applied to circles or arcs, measuring from the center to the outside (see Figure 17.58).
- **Diameter**—Diameter dimensioning is applied to circles or arcs, measuring across the circle or twice the radius (see Figure 17.59).
- **Angular**—The Angular option is used to dimension angles. Pick the two lines that make up the angle, and you can place the dimension on the drawing in a variety of ways (see Figure 17.60).
- **Baseline**—The Baseline option is used to datum dimensions. Establish a datum line with a linear dimension first, then you can use the baseline option with multiple picks (see Figure 17.61).
- **Continue**—The Continue option strings dimensions in a straight line, also known as a *chain*. The first dimension must be placed with the Linear option (see Figure 17.62).

FIGURE 17.57 Ordinate dimensioning.

FIGURE 17.58 Radius dimensioning.

FIGURE 17.59 Diameter dimensioning.   FIGURE 17.60 Angular dimensioning.

The first point picked is the datum.

The baseline or datum reference is on the left side.

Use the Linear command for the first dimension.

Use the Continue command for the other dimensions.

FIGURE 17.61 Baseline dimensioning.

FIGURE 17.62 The Continue option.

Line Setting

Mark Setting

None Setting

FIGURE 17.63 The Leader option.

FIGURE 17.64 Center mark options.

- **Leader**—The Leader option generates an arrowhead with a leader line plus an MTEXT option for notes (see Figure 17.63).
- **Tolerance**—The Tolerance option is for geometric tolerancing in mechanical drawings and is not used in architectural work at all, so we will not include it in our discussion.
- **Center Mark**—This selection places center ticks and lines on circles and arcs depending on the setting in the Dimension Style Manager (see Figure 17.64).

Some remaining options (Oblique, Align Text, Override, and Update) are used for editing dimensions after they have been placed on the drawing and will be explained later in this chapter. The Style option was demonstrated earlier to show how to create styles and set variables. Any of these dimension options can be activated with a left-click on the Dimension pull-down menu.

The Dimension Toolbar

Using the on-screen Dimension toolbar is another popular way of placing dimension options on the screen. The toolbar will stay on the screen until it is closed, which is a shorter, quicker way to access commands. The Dimension toolbar can be turned on by left-clicking on the View pull-down menu and then left-clicking again on Toolbars at the bottom (shown earlier in this chapter). Check the Dimension box selection and close the Toolbars dialog box (see Figures 17.65 and 17.66).

FIGURE 17.65 Toolbars dialog box.

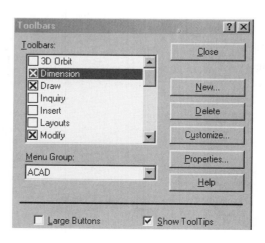

FIGURE 17.66 Dimension toolbar.

Dimension

List of the Dimension Styles

Linear
Aligned
Ordinate
Radius
Diameter
Angular
Quick Dimension
Baseline
Continue
Quick Leader
Tolerance
Center Mark
Dimension Edit
Dimension Text Edit
Dimension Update

FIGURE 17.67 Linear Dimension icon.

Linear Dimension

Notice in the Dimension toolbar in Figure 17.66 that the options are the same as in the pull-down menu version. If you forget what a button does, just put the mouse arrow on top of the icon for a few seconds, and the description will appear just below the icon (see Figure 17.67).

The lone drawback to using the toolbar is that it takes up some room on the drawing screen. It is a floating toolbar and can easily be moved around if you hold down the left-click button while in the dark blue shaded area of the toolbar with the cursor and drag it across the screen. If dragged far enough to the left or right the toolbar will align vertically (see Figure 17.68). Aligning a toolbar is a matter of preference. If too much of the screen is being covered up, turn it off and use the pull-down menu instead.

FIGURE 17.68 Aligning the toolbar vertically.

Using the Linear Option

Dimensioning with the Linear option can be done in two ways. Once you have selected the command, look at the command line. It reads:

Command: **dimlinear**
Specify first extension line origin or <select object>:

Option 1: *<select object>*

Note: The Direct Distance method can be used for placing dimension.

The option in the brackets <select object> is the default. Just press **Enter⏎** or right-click to accept the default option. Notice that the cursor changes into a small rectangular box (pick box). When this box appears, just touch the line to be dimensioned (see Figure 17.69). Next, roll the mouse above or below the object. The dimension text, dimension line, ticks, and extension line will follow the cursor around. Place the dimension by left-clicking when the desired location is reached. Alternately, pull the cursor in the direction the dimension should go and type in the distance you want the dimension line to be placed away from the object (see Figures 17.70 and 17.71).

Option 2: *Specify first extension line origin*

Using the other option at this command line, pick the ends of the line or object to be dimensioned. Using object snaps, grab the endpoint of the line on one side, then the endpoint of the other side (see Figure 17.72). Once you have chosen the second point the dimension appears and can be placed in the same manner as in the previous example in option 1 (see Figure 17.73).

Both of these methods show the following text options at the command line that can be used by typing them in at the command line.

[Mtext/Text/Angle/Horizontal/Vertical/Rotated]

Typing **Mtext** will bring up the Multiline Text Editor, where the text can be altered or changed. The angle brackets (<>) found in the text area represent the current dimension value. You can type notes in front of it or behind it, and they will show up with the dimension after you select the OK button and place the dimension on the drawing. Typing Text will allow you to replace the current dimension text at the command line.

The other four choices (Angle, Horizontal, Vertical, and Rotated) deal with different alignments and positions. Go ahead and try a few of these options. Once in a while you might need one of these.

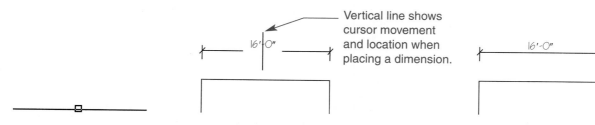

FIGURE 17.69 Selecting line to be dimensioned.

FIGURE 17.70 Dimension placement by moving the cursor.

FIGURE 17.71 Completed dimension.

FIGURE 17.72 Picking line endpoints.

FIGURE 17.73 Completed dimension.

FIGURE 17.74   Aligned dimension.

FIGURE 17.75   Circle dimensioning with the Radius option.

Using the Aligned Option

The Aligned option is for dimensioning along an angled line or surface (see Figure 17.74). The Aligned option works in the same way as the Linear feature. Both option 1, selecting the object, and option 2, picking the endpoints of the object, will work in the same way. The following three options become available in the command line after the object is selected.

[Mtext/Text/Angle]

These choices also work identically with those of the linear command.

The Ordinate option is not used in architectural drawing. It is normally found in some electronic fields. It is easy to use—just pick a point and the dimension text and extension line are placed on the drawing.

Using the Radius and Diameter Options

Dimensioning with the Radius or Diameter option is similar to using the Aligned option. Select Radius, and the command line will read:

Command: **dimradius**
Select arc or circle:

Touch the circle that needs dimensioning with the pick box, and the dimension will appear, ready to be positioned. Place the dimension in the desired location with the mouse, and left-click to apply it to the drawing (see Figure 17.75). The command line will also allow you to change the dimension with the standard options [Mtext/Text/Angle]. To use these choices make sure to select them between selecting the circle and applying the text to its final position.

Hint for Radius and Diameters

Set up a separate dimensioning style to be used when dealing with circles. It is desirable to use arrowheads along with horizontal text. It may be desirable to use the Leader command to dimension circles and arcs.

Using the Angular Option
Dimensioning angles gives you three choices for picking objects (see Figure 17.76).

1. You can select two lines that form an angle.
2. You can select an arc.
3. You can select a vertex of an angle along with the endpoints of the angle.

The [Mtext/Text/Angle] option will appear again in the command line for additional modifications of the text if desired.

FIGURE 17.76   Dimensioning with the Angular option.

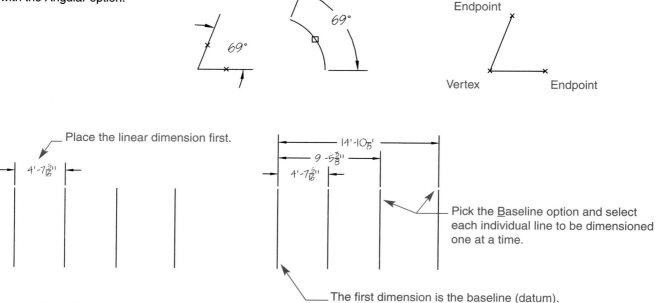

FIGURE 17.77   Baseline dimensioning.

Using the Baseline Option

The Baseline will work once a base or datum is established. This means that another dimension such as a linear dimension must be placed first. Pick the lines in sequence so they stack properly (see Figure 17.77). Baseline dimensioning is seldom used in architectural drawings, but occasionally a variation of it may be used.

Using the Continue Option

Dimensioning along a straight line is a common practice on architectural drawings. The process is much like using the Baseline command: a reference such as a linear dimension is needed before the Continue command will work. Then it becomes a matter of picking each individual line (see Figure 17.78). Watch the dimension appear as you pick.

Using the Leader Option/Quick Leader

Leaders are used to call out dimensions or notes and point to their location. Select the Leader option, also known as Q leader, in the Dimension pull-down menu, and the command line will show:

> Specify first leader point or [Settings] <Setting>:

Press Enter⏎ to open the Leader Settings dialog box, which contains three pull-down menu tabs (see Figure 17.79).

FIGURE 17.78   Using the Continue option.

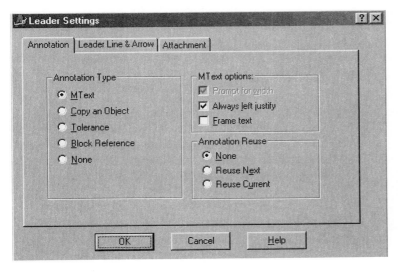

FIGURE 17.79 Leader annotation menu.

FIGURE 17.80 Leader help

Annotation

The settings in the Annotation menu will allow Mtext to work with the Leader option to generate notes at the same time. The Always left justify option will align the text on the left-hand side. One useful help feature is the question mark in the upper right corner. Left-click on it, then pick the option you have a question about. A description or definition will appear, to aid you (see Figure 17.80).

Leader Line & Arrow

This menu tab does quite a bit. The Leader Line can be set to draw a straight line or a curved spline (see Figure 17.81). The Number of Points box will let you set how many points can be used to draw the leader line (see Figure 17.82).

You can set different types of arrowheads here along with choosing typical angles on the leader lines. Leaving them at Any angle will give you more flexibility when laying out dimensions.

Attachment

The Attachment pull-down tab lets you decide how the leader will intersect with the text (see Figures 17.83 and 17.84).

FIGURE 17.81 Leader Line & Arrow menu.

The line can change direction four times.

The line can change direction twice.

Leader Set to 4-Point Option

Leader Set to 2-Point Option

FIGURE 17.82 Using the Number of Points option.

FIGURE 17.83   Attachment menu.

FIGURE 17.84   Leader Mtext.

The Leader Settings are fairly easy to use. One setting that CAD operators change often is the <u>N</u>one option at the bottom of the menu under the Annotation tab (see Figure 17.79). This option is used when no text is wanted with the leader. The text may already have been created and the leader is needed.

When the <u>N</u>one option is set you can just left-click to draw the leader, and the Mtext option will not appear while the leader line is placed on the screen. The <u>N</u>one option can be used when a large number of notes and leaders are needed. It can be faster to place the notes on the drawing continuously with the AutoCAD Text commands and add the leaders to the notes later.

Using Mtext with the leader is fairly simple. Click on the <u>M</u>Text option in the Annotation pull-down tab, and click on <u>N</u>one under Annotation Reuse selections. These choices will activate the Mtext option each time the leader command is used. After the leader is drawn, the command line will read:

Enter first line of annotation text <Mtext>:

At this point you can type in the note or press Enter↵ to bring up the Multiline Text Editor (see Figure 17.85). Just type in the note and left-click on the OK button, and the note will appear with the leader. If the same note and leader needs to be repeated, click on Reuse Ne<u>x</u>t, and each time the leader command is used the previous note or text will be repeated automatically (see Figure 17.86).

FIGURE 17.85   Multiline Text Editor dialog box.

FIGURE 17.86   Reuse Leader option.

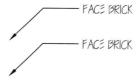

Using the Center Mark Option.

The Center Mark command is fairly simple to use. The Center Mark command is found in the Dimension pull-down menu. Left-click on the Center Mark option and then left-click, touching the circle or arc. If it does not work, check the center mark settings in the Dimension Style's Lines and Arrows menu to make sure the Line or Mark choice is set. If the None option is set, then the center mark will not be shown. Set the Mark option, select the OK button, close the dialog display, and retry the Leader command again.

Using Quick Dimensions (QDIM)

The Quick Dimension command can apply dimensions to a drawing with tremendous speed. It can work in two different ways when selected:

1. You can pick individual lines one at a time and generate a group of dimensions in the defaulted Continuous mode (see Figure 17.87). Right-click after selecting the last line, then drag the dimension line into position and left-click to place the string of dimensions.

2. When selecting lines to be dimensioned, use a crossing box and touch every line that needs a dimension (see Figure 17.88). After selecting the lines with the crossing box, drag the dimension line into position and left-click when ready. This is a great new feature in AutoCAD that makes dimensioning faster than ever.

QDIM Options

After you have selected the lines or objects and it is time to place the dimension line, take a look at the command line in the lower left corner:

Specify dimension line position, or
[Continuous/Stagger/Baseline/Ordinate/Radius/Diameter/datum Point/Edit]
    <Continuous>

You can select these choices by typing them in at the command line. Figure 17.89 gives examples of each.

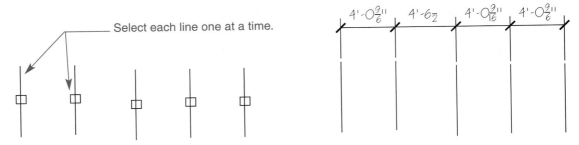

FIGURE 17.87   Quick Dimensioning picking one line at a time.

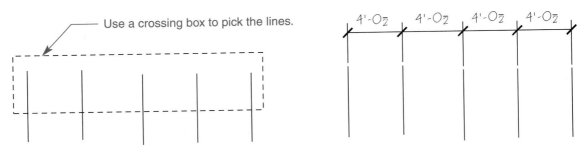

FIGURE 17.88   Using a crossing box to Quick Dimension.

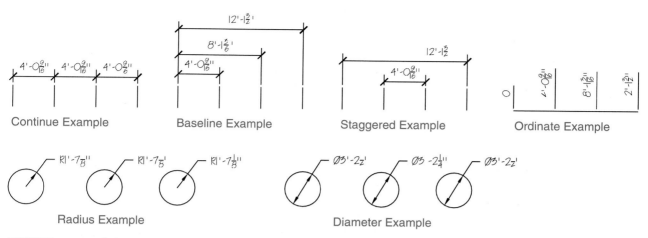

FIGURE 17.89 Quick Dimension Options.

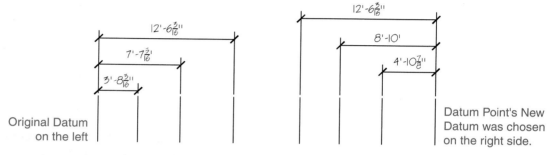

FIGURE 17.90 Using a datum point.

The datum Point option can be used with the Baseline option. The datum Point for the Baseline is established by the order in which lines are selected. However, the datum point can be changed by using the datum Point and picking a new location for the datum (see Figure 17.90).

The Edit option is the final selection in this list of options. When chosen it displays Xs on all the lines that were selected to be dimensioned (see Figure 17.91). The purpose here is to change the dimension locations that were originally selected. A Remove option is the default setting. A left-click with the cursor placed on top of an X causes the X to disappear and to be removed from the original selection. The Add option is activated by typing **A** and pressing Enter↵. A left-click can place a new X, which will be included in the dimension selection (see Figure 17.92). Once you are finished making the selections, exit with a right-click, then left-click where the dimensions are to be placed (see Figure 17.93). The dimensions will show up where the Xs were left on the drawing.

Edit option places an X on the selected lines.

FIGURE 17.91 Using the Edit option.

FIGURE 17.92 Editing options.

FIGURE 17.93 Dimensions edited.

17.3 Editing Existing Dimensions

You have many choices when it comes to changing dimensions after they are placed on a drawing. When a dimension is put on a drawing, it is a Block and is treated as one object. It is edited differently than a string of text or a line. A dimension can be edited by two methods:

1. The dimension can be left as a Block and altered with the some of the following choices.

- Grips
- MO—Properties
- DIMTEDIT—Dimension Text Edit
- DIMEDIT

2. A dimension can be Exploded or have its DIMASO (Associative Dimensioning) cut off (prior to dimensioning).

Both the options in number 2 have consequences and should be used only in rare cases. When these options are used the dimension is no longer a block, and the individual pieces must be dealt with as single entities.

Editing Dimensions with Grips

Grips are a great dimension editing tool. The following grips options are available: Stretch, Move, Rotate, Scale, Mirror, and Copy.

To activate the grips, left-click on the dimension block (the command line should be clear). Little boxes should show up all along the dimension. These are the warm grip boxes. Next, put the cursor on the middle box near the dimension text, and left-click when the box changes color. The box becomes solid and is considered a hot grip (see Figure 17.94). That means it is ready to perform a Grip option.

The default option is the Stretch. Watch what happens when you move the mouse in all directions (see Figure 17.95).

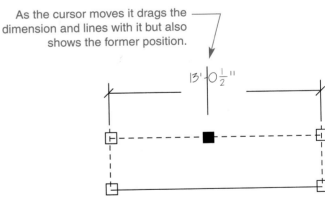

As the cursor moves it drags the dimension and lines with it but also shows the former position.

Hot Grip Active on the Dimension

FIGURE 17.94   Hot grip on dimension.

FIGURE 17.95   Stretching lines and dimensions with grips.

FIGURE 17.96   Moving lines and dimensions with grips.

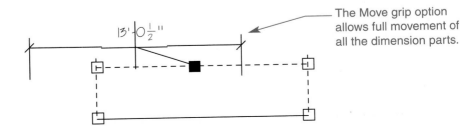

The Move grip option allows full movement of all the dimension parts.

The Grips Stretch option helps shift text around in crowded areas. To change to the Move option hold the Shift key down and press Enter↵ once (see Figure 17.96). The Stretch and Move options are used frequently to edit dimensions. To cycle through the Grip options continue holding down the Shift key and pressing Enter↵

Example

Draw a dimension anywhere with any variable settings. Using the grips, experiment with the Stretch and Move options.

The Stretch option works very well for moving dimensions around for better fits. When you are done, hit the Esc key twice to turn the grips off. Once will take you from warm grips to cold and twice will turn off the grips completely.

Editing Dimensions with Properties Command

The most powerful editing tool in AutoCAD is the **Properties** command because it gives you access to a great many choices. Normally it is the first option used because it can do so much at one time. For instance, turn on the grip boxes on an existing dimension (do not make the grip hot), then activate the **Properties** command.

Properties
Icon

- Type **MO** at the command prompt.
- Select **Properties** from the Modify pull-down menu (see Figure 17.97).
- Pick the **Properties** icon from the Standard Toolbar.

Figure 17.98 shows all the settings that can be changed under the Alphabetic pull-down menu tab. All the Dimension Variables are listed there for editing dimensions. Left-click on the Categorized pull-down menu tab, and the dimension settings are grouped in their six main categories (see Figure 17.99). Click on the + signs to open them. Also, notice the other options under General.

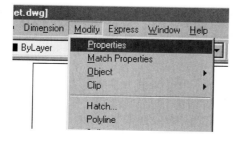

FIGURE 17.97 Modify pull-down menu.

FIGURE 17.98 Alphabetic tab menu.

FIGURE 17.99   General menu under Categorized tab.

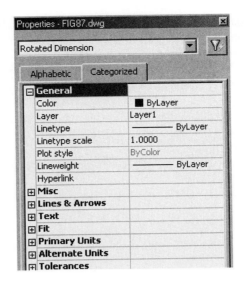

To make changes left-click on the written description, and when it is highlighted left-click on the value to be changed to the right. Type in the new values, and when the change is made close the Properties dialog box and click the Esc key twice.

Editing Dimensions with Dimension Edit (DIMEDIT) and Dimension Text Edit (DIMTEDIT)

The **DIMEDIT** and **DIMTEDIT** commands are used for changing dimensions. Each has a different function. **DIMEDIT** changes the text in the dimension Block.

- Type **DIMEDIT** at the command prompt.
- Select the **DIMEDIT** icon from the Dimension toolbar.

DIMEDIT
Icon

The following choices in **DIMEDIT** are shown at the command line:

[Home/New/Rotate/Oblique] <Home>

Type in the suboptions. Press Enter↵ for the Home suboption, which will place the text in its default position in the middle of the dimension line (see Figure 17.100).

The New suboption will allow you to change the text value using the Mtext Editor (see Figure 17.101).

The Rotate suboption will ask you to specify an angle for the dimension text. The example in Figure 17.102 used a 30° angle.

The Oblique suboption will change the angle of the extension lines (see Figure 17.103).

Before Home   After Home

FIGURE 17.100   Home suboption of DIMEDIT to change the text position.

Before New   After New

FIGURE 17.101   New suboption of DIMEDIT to change the text.

FIGURE 17.102   Rotate suboption of DIMEDIT.

FIGURE 17.103   Oblique suboption of DIMEDIT.

DIMTEDIT has some similarities to the Grip option and DIMEDIT. It can adjust the location of the text and dimension line like a stretch grip, but it also will reposition the text along the dimension line.

DIMTEDIT
Icon

- Type **DIMTEDIT** at the command prompt.
- Select the **DIMTEDIT** icon from the Dimension toolbar.

At the command line the following suboptions are shown.

[Home/New/Rotate/Oblique] <Home>

There are no new options in this command, just a different set of combinations.

Edit DIM Text Value DDEDIT

- Type **DDEDIT** at the command prompt.

Using this command brings up the Multiline Text Editor for changing text values. Just type in **DDEDIT** at the command line, press Enter↵, and select the dimension text with a left click.

There are other offshoots to these commands, but the following are some of the most beneficial in the beginning. The Update command is an important one. When modifications to dimension settings or variables are made, sometimes they will not take effect until the Update command is used. The <u>Up</u>date option is at the very bottom of the Dime<u>n</u>sion pull-down menu. Select it and then touch the dimension to be updated. Do not expect the Update to work on all the commands. It has limitations just like the other editing commands, and it may take several combinations to get the desired layout.

Editing Dimensioning Command with DIMASO

- Type **DIM** at the command line and press Enter↵, then type DIMASO and press Enter↵ again.

Associative Dimensioning, also known as the DIMASO variable, controls the dimension block or unit. The dimension is defaulted to the DIMASO On setting, which makes the dimension one unit or block. This means that if you tried to erase a tick mark by itself, the whole dimension, being one unit,would be erased totally. Turning the DIMASO off before applying the dimension to the drawing will insert it in individual pieces. Each part of the dimension can then be edited separately as lines and text (see Figure 17.104).

The **DIMASO** variable can be changed at the command line:

Command: **DIM**↵
Dim: **DIMASO**↵
Enter new value for dimension variable <ON> OFF↵

At this point type the setting desired and press Enter↵, then press the Esc key.

5'-10¾"   Dimension text and line are
          now individual pieces.

          Extension line and tick marks
          are individual pieces.

FIGURE 17.104   Associative dimensioning turned off.

Tips for Using DIMASO Turned Off

When DIMASO is turned off, the normal dimension editing commands will not work on the split-up dimension. For example, the following will not work:

- Dimension Edit
- Dimension Text Edit
- Gripping as a unit
- Updating, Overriding, Modifying as a Unit

You must then manually edit every piece. This is a major drawback, but sometimes this is the only option to get what is needed. Use this as a last option.

Another drastic option is Exploding a dimension unit. This will also split up the dimension into pieces. The same problems will exist after an Explode; a lot of the most powerful dimension editing tools will be wasted.

Tips for Efficient Dimensioning

1. Create an architectural style that works well for horizontal and vertical dimensions.
2. Create a style to switch to when placing dimensions on circles and pointing with leaders. (Use arrows instead of ticks, and set the text to the horizontal position.) Save Dimension Styles on a template drawing.
3. Always use Osnaps when dimensioning.
4. Turn on DIMUPT. (Place text manually when dimensioning.)
5. Create a layer just for dimensions.
6. Use **DIMASO** off and Explode only after all other editing features have failed.

REVIEW QUESTIONS

1. List the different methods used to open the Dimension Style Manager dialog box.
2. What does the Scale for Dimension Features control?
3. List the six major Tabs found in the New Dimension Style dialog display.
4. Where is the setting that changes the arrowheads to tick marks located?
5. What setting will help when dimensions are too crowded together?
6. How should the Zero Suppression be set for architectural drawings?
7. What does the Override command do?
8. What do the following abbreviations stand for?
   a. ANSI
   b. ISO-25
   c. DIN
   d. JIS
9. Sketch an example of an aligned dimension, baseline dimension, and continue dimensioning.
10. How does the Quick dimensioning work?
11. Which dimension setting has a Spline option in it?

12. What are four ways to edit existing dimensions?

13. What options are found in the DIMEDIT command and what do they do?

14. DIMASO controls what function?

15. DIMUPT can be used to control what?

16. At what point should a dimension be exploded and why?

EXERCISES

EXERCISE 17.1

Begin a new drawing from scratch and create a Dimensioning Style for a ¼″ = 1′-0″ scale drawing with the following settings.

In the Lines and Arrows tab:

- Name the New Style .25 Arch.
- Set the Extend beyond dim lines to 1/16″.
- Set the Arrowheads 1st and 2nd to Architectural Tick.
- Set Arrow size to .125.

In the Text tab:

- Set Text style to City Blueprint.
- Set Text height to .125.
- Set Fraction height scale to .75.
- Set Text Placement Vertical to Above and Horizontal to Centered.
- Set Text Alignment to Aligned with dimension line.

In the Fit tab:

- Under Scale for Dimension Features set Use an Overall scale of: to 48
- Under Fine Tuning turn on both Place text manually when dimensioning and Always draw dimline between ext lines.

In the Primary Units tab:

- Under Linear Dimensions set Unit format to Architectural.
- In the Zero Suppression box to the left, remove the check from the Trailing 0 Inches.

Perform a Save As and name the drawing 17EX-1.

EXERCISE 17.2

Begin a new drawing from scratch and create a Dimensioning Style for a ½″ = 1′-0″ scale drawing with the following settings.

In the Lines and Arrows tab:

- Name the New Style .5 Arch.
- Set the Extend beyond dim lines to ⅛″.
- Set the Arrowheads 1st and 2nd to Architectural Tick.
- Set Arrow size to .18.

In the Text tab:

- Set Text style to City Blueprint.
- Set Text height to .125.
- Set Fraction height scale to .5.
- Set Text Placement Vertical to Above and Horizontal to Centered.
- Set Text Alignment to Aligned with dimension line.

In the Fit tab:

- Under Scale for Dimension Features set use an Overall scale of: to 24.
- Under Fine Tuning turn on both Place text manually when dimensioning and Always draw dimline between ext lines.

In the Primary Units tab:

- Under Linear Dimensions set Unit format to Architectural.
- In the Zero Suppression box to the left remove the check from the Trailing 0 Inches.

Perform a Save As and name the drawing 17EX-2.

EXERCISE 17.3

Begin a new drawing from scratch and create a Dimensioning Style for a 1″ = 1′-0″ scale drawing with the following settings.

In the Lines and Arrows tab:

- Name the New Style 1 Arch.
- Set the Extend beyond dim lines to 1/16″.
- Set the Arrowheads 1st and 2nd to Closed Arrows.
- Set Arrow size to .18.

In the Text tab:

- Set Text style to Country Blueprint.
- Set Text height to .18.
- Set Fraction height scale to .75.
- Set Text Placement Vertical to Above and Horizontal to Centered.
- Set Text Alignment to Aligned with dimension line.

In the Fit tab:

- Under Scale for Dimensions Features set Use an Overall scale of: to 12.
- Under Fine Tuning turn on both Place text manually when dimensioning and Always draw dimline between ext lines.

In the Primary Units tab:

- Under Linear Dimensions set Unit format to Architectural.
- In the Zero Suppression box to the left remove the check from the Trailing 0 Inches.

Perform a Save As and name the drawing 17EX-3.

EXERCISE 17.4

Begin a new drawing from scratch and create a Dimensioning Style for a ⅛″ = 1′-0″ scale drawing with the following settings.

In the Lines and Arrows tab:

- Name the New Style .125 Arch.
- Set the <u>E</u>xtend beyond dim lines to 1/8″.
- Set the Arrowheads 1<u>st</u> and 2<u>nd</u> to Architectural Tick.
- Set Arrow s<u>i</u>ze to .125.

In the Text tab:

- Set Text st<u>y</u>le to Country Blueprint.
- Set Text heig<u>h</u>t to .125.
- Set Fraction <u>h</u>eight scale to .85.
- Set Text Placement <u>V</u>ertical to Above and Hori<u>z</u>ontal to Centered.
- Set Text <u>A</u>lignment to Aligned with dimension line.

In the Fit Tab:

- Under Scale for Dimension Features set Use an Overall <u>s</u>cale of: to 96.
- Under <u>F</u>ine Tuning turn on both <u>P</u>lace text manually when dimensioning and <u>A</u>lways draw dimline between ext lines.

In Primary Units Tab:

- Under Linear Dimensions set <u>U</u>nit format to Architectural.
- In the Zero Suppression box to the left remove the check from the <u>T</u>railing 0 <u>I</u>nches.

Perform a Save As and name the drawing 17EX-4.

DRAWING ASSIGNMENTS

1. Using the Architectural Dimensioning setup of exercise 17.1 draw and dimension drawings shown in Figure 17.105.
2. Create an Architectural Dimensioning style that will work for ³⁄₁₆″ = 1′-0″ (64 Scale Factor). Draw and dimension the elevations in Figure 17.106 with the style you created.
3. Using the duplex drawing created in Chapter 15, add dimensions to it. Use the dimensioning style created in exercise 17-1.
4. Dimension the duplex drawing from Chapter 15.

FIGURE 17.105 Drawing Assignment 1.

BATHROOM PLAN

Scale: 1/ 4" = 1'- 0"

(a)

Use a 4″ thickness for your walls. Research
the dimensions that are not given to you.
Look in the *Architectural Graphic Standards*
or a manufacturer's catalog.

MASTER BATH PLAN

SCALE: 1/ 4" = 1'-0"

(b)

KITCHEN PLAN

SCALE: 1/ 4" = 1'-0"

(c)

Use a wall thickness of 3.5″. Research typical sizes of
cabinets, and use those dimensions.

Garage Elevation
Scale: ³⁄₁₆″ = 1′-0″

Building Elevation
Scale: ³⁄₁₆″ = 1′-0″

FIGURE 17.106   Drawing Assignment 2.

Using AutoCAD Text Commands

Architectural working drawings tend to contain a good deal of text. The more technical a drawing is the more notes are needed for explaining details. In the days of board drawing, hand lettering was extremely time consuming even for the fastest drafters.

In computer-aided drawing the art of lettering has been turned into more of an exact science. Each CAD drawing can have the exact same lettering style no matter how many different people work on the same drawing. Being consistent is a must in drafting, and with CAD it is very achievable.

Typing and editing text are big advantages on a CAD project. Even someone who is a fairly slow typist can place and revise text faster than a drafter who is hand lettering a drawing.

The term *text* in CAD has replaced what was once called *lettering*. This chapter is broken into three sections:

1. Creating Text Settings and Formats
2. Placing Text on a Drawing
3. Editing and Modifying Existing Text on a Drawing

18.1 Creating Text Settings and Formats

Here are some guidelines to use when setting up text formats. A minimum ⅛″ (.125″) text height should be set for architectural notes. Some architectural firms will even bump up this height to ³⁄₁₆″ (.18″) if there is a possibility that the drawings will be reduced in size at some point. Titles on drawings should be set to a minimum of ¼″ (.25″) (see Figure 18.1). When text appears in paragraph form the spacing between the sentences should be half the text height (see Figure 18.2).

The drawing scale can affect the text height and needs to be carefully planned. To set the text height, take the scale factor and multiply it by the text height as if it were at the full plotting size. See the examples in Figure 18.3. Understanding how this works will help set the right text height correctly each time a drawing is done at a different scale.

FIGURE 18.1 Text height.

GLASS BLOCK WALL FLOOR TO THE CEILING.

Notes ⅛″ Height

FIRST FLOOR PLAN

Notes ¼″ Height

FIGURE 18.2 Text spacing.

4″ FACE BRICK WITH 1/2″
GYPSUM BOARD PAINTED
WITH FLAT FINISH.

Spacing between sentences and paragraphs should be half to two-thirds the text height. This is done automatically in the AutoCAD Text commands.

FIGURE 18.3 Setting text heights.

Setting Text for ¼″ = 1′-0″ Scale

If the drawing is to be drawn at a scale of ¼″ = 1′-0″, calculate the text height as follows:

1. Divide the 1′ by the ¼″ of the scale to find the scale factor:

$$\frac{1'}{\frac14''} = \frac{12''}{.25''} = 48 \qquad \text{48 is the scale factor needed.}$$

2. Multiply the desired text height of ⅛″ for notes by the scale factor of 48:

⅛″ × 48 = 6″   This will be the text height for your notes.

Use the same format to find text height for ¼″ titles:

¼″ × 48 = 12″   This will be the text height for your titles.

Setting Text for 1″ = 1′-0″ Scale

If a wall section is to be drawn at a scale of 1″ = 1′-0″, calculate the text height as follows:

1. Divide the 1′ by the 1″ of the scale to find the scale factor:

$$\frac{12''}{1''} = 12 \qquad \text{12 is the scale factor needed.}$$

2. Multiply the desired Text height of ⅛″ for notes by the scale factor of 12:

⅛″ × 12 = 1.5″   This will be the text height for your notes.

Use the same format to find text height for ¼″ titles

¼″ × 12 = 3″   This will be the text height for your titles.

The Text Style Command.

- Type **DDSTYLE** or **ST** at the command prompt.
- Select Text <u>S</u>tyle from the F<u>o</u>rmat pull-down menu (see Figure 18.4).
- Pick <u>S</u>tyle from the Dimension pull-down menu.

The Text Style dialog box appears, where you can make some selections concerning text appearance (see Figure 18.5).

FIGURE 18.4 Text <u>S</u>tyle selected on the F<u>o</u>rmat pull-down menu.

FIGURE 18.5 Text Style dialog box.

 THE FLOOR PLAN   NAꟼ ꓤOOⱢꟼ ƎHT

FIGURE 18.6 Upside-Down text.   **FIGURE 18.7** Backwards text.

T
H
E

F   FLOOR   FLOOR
L   Width Factor   Width Factor
O   Set at 2   Set at .5
O
R   **FIGURE 18.9** Setting text width.

P
L
A   *THE BEST OF THE BEST*   THE BEST OF THE BEST
N   Oblique Angle Set to 23°   Oblique Angle Set to −23°

FIGURE 18.8 Vertical text.   **FIGURE 18.10** Oblique text.

The **Effects** section has five options that alter how basic text can look.

- **Upside down**—Left-click on the little boxes to the left of the words to activate the settings. If this option is activated, the text will appear upside down when placed on the screen (see Figure 18.6).

- **Backwards**—This setting will cause the text to appear from right to left (see Figure 18.7).

- **Vertical**—This setting will cause the text to run vertically on the drawing instead of the standard horizontally (see Figure 18.8).

- **Width Factor**—Left-click in the box to the right of the words, and type in the width factor desired. The normal or default setting for text is 1. Increasing this number will widen the text, and reducing it will compress it (see Figure 18.9).

- **Oblique Angle**—Left-click in the box to the right of the words and change the default setting of zero by typing in a new angle setting. Changing this setting will give the letters a slant or slope (see Figure 18.10). A positive angle slopes the text to the right. (A slope between 0 and 23 is acceptable in some fields of drafting.) A negative angle is not acceptable for any drafting field.

Creating Style Names and Fonts

As an AutoCAD user, you can create a name for any style that you customize. Do so by left-clicking on the New... option in the Style Name section. The New Text Style dialog box pops up (see Figure 18.11). Type in the Style Name desired and left-click on the OK screen button. The new name is placed in the style name list. Left-click on the arrow to the left of the New... button and check the list for the new style name just created. Select the new style name to make it the current one.

With the new name current, it is easy to pick out a font or lettering style for it. Left-click on the arrow found under the Font Name option (see Figure 18.12).

AutoCAD has a wide range of fonts. Scroll down with the arrows in the Font Name: text box to see all the styles loaded that can be selected. Two common architectural styles are City Blueprint and Country Blueprint. Find the City Blueprint and left-click on the words to select it.

In the lower right corner of the dialog display the Preview box shows you what this font style looks like. Other font controls are found to the right of the font name. Some fonts may have additional choices in the Font Style box. For instance, the Times New Roman font has four choices in this box: Bold, Bold Italic, Italic, or Regular.

The height setting box is found just to the right of the Font Style text box. This is where the height can be set if desired. Notice that the default height is set to 0. If this setting is used, then every time the text com-

FIGURE 18.11   New Text Style dialog box.

FIGURE 18.12   Choosing a font.

Remember to calculate the text height based on the drawing scale.

mands are requested, the program will automatically ask/prompt you for a height to be used. This works well if you are changing text height frequently on the drawing. Another benefit to using a 0 setting is that font height will not override the text height setting for dimensions when those are in place.

It is also possible to Rename and Delete style names in the Text Style dialog display. Left-click on the style name to highlight it and then Rename or Delete it.

The best order to set up your lettering is as follows:

1. Select a new style name.
2. Select a font to be used.
3. Choose a font height.
4. Select any other setting desired for this style.
5. Make sure to left-click on the Apply... box or the font settings will not hold.
6. Left-click on the Close button to close the Text Style dialog box.

Deciding on a Font to Use

AutoCAD has an extensive number of fonts with an extreme range of styles. Choosing a style for the right job is a matter of purpose. When you are looking for a font for architectural or interior technical drawings, clarity and legibility must play a major factor in selection. An architectural drawing should also have a certain flair or artistic style that separates it from other drawing fields. Three good fonts in AutoCAD that fit these characteristics are CityBlueprint, CountryBlueprint, and Stylus BT. Stay away from fonts that are difficult to read on working drawings. These three work well.

Fonts for special usage such as logos and title blocks may shift to the more extreme fonts. A logo is a company symbol or trademark with a design that is intended to get attention or make a statement about a company. Businesses want something their clients will recognize and remember.

18.2 Placing Text on a Drawing

Lettering can be placed on a drawing using a variety of methods, which are split into two categories: single line text and multiline text.

The DTEXT Command

- Type **DTEXT** or **DT** at the command prompt.
- Select Text from the Draw pull-down menu, then select Single Line Text from the cascade menu to the right (see Figure 18.13).

FIGURE 18.13 Text, Single Line Text selected on the Draw pull-down menu.

FIGURE 18.14 Angled text.

The command prompt line then reads:

Specify start point of text or [Justify/Style]

At this point you have three choices.

1. You can pick a text starting point by left-clicking once, and the single line of text will begin there running from left to right, after you supply it with two more bits of information.

   Check out the command line. If the text height was set to 0 in the initial text style settings as discussed in the previous section, then you are being asked to pick a height for that line of text. Next, the command line will prompt you for an angle to incline the text. The 0° angle is the default, but it can easily be changed here by typing in a new value (see Figure 18.14, which shows a 45° example).

2. Look at the original command line after typing in **DT**. You may choose what is inside the brackets [Justify/Style].

   Typing **JUSTIFY** or **J** will give you the following options in the command line: [Align/Fit/Center/Middle/Right/TL/TC/TR/ML/MC/MR/BL/BC/BR].

   The Align option can be selected by typing **A** ↵. Then you will be asked to pick a first text point and a second text point using the mouse's left-click button and the cursor. Once you do this and start typing, the software will do whatever it needs to do to place the text between the two points. This includes expanding and shrinking text sizes in all directions.

   The Fit option will do the same thing as Align; however, you can set the height to remain the same, so at least it will be consistent (see Figure 18.15).

   It is more acceptable to use the following options, as they do not distort the letter sizes.

Note: Avoid using the Align and Fit settings on technical drawings. They are too inconsistent.

Options	Shortcut Keystrokes
Center	C (press Enter ↵)
Middle	M (press Enter ↵)
Right	R (press Enter ↵)

THE KEY TO ARCHITECTURAL DRAWING IS BEING CONSISTENT AND ACCURATE   THE KEY TO ARCHITECTURAL DRAWING IS BEING CONSISTENT AND ACCURATE

Example of the Align DTEXT Option   Example of the Fit DTEXT Option

FIGURE 18.15   Align and Fit options.

FIGURE 18.16   Center option.   FLOOR PLAN DETAIL

Example of the Center Option

The Center option will start where you left-click and place the text center bottom of the text (see Figure 18.16). Other choices inside the Center option are Height and Rotation angle. The command sequence appears as follows:

Align/Fit/Center/Middle/Right/TL/TC/TR/ML/MC/MR/BL/BC/BR:
Center point *(Pick a point with your left mouse button.)*
Height <current setting> *(Type new setting.)*
Rotation angle <0>: *(Type your angle.)*
Text: *(Type your text.)*

The Middle option is almost identical with the Center option except that the starting point is in the middle of the letters, not at the bottom. See Figure 18.17 for a comparison of the letter locations around the starting point.

The Right option is a right-side justify. This causes the text to align on the right-hand side where the initial starting point was selected (see Figure 18.18).

The rest of the options are abbreviated. The abbreviations represent the starting point and general text alignments (see Figure 18.19).

(TL) TOP LEFT

(TC) TOP CENTER

(TR) TOP RIGHT

(ML) MIDDLE LEFT

(MC) MIDDLE CENTER

(MR) MIDDLE RIGHT

(BL) BOTTOM LEFT

(BC) BOTTOM CENTER

(BR) BOTTOM RIGHT

The choices are many, so check with your instructor or office manager for the classroom or office standards.

FIGURE 18.17   Middle option.   ⎯ Middle point

FLOOR PLAN DETAIL

Example of the Middle Option

FIGURE 18.18   Right justification.   THERE ARE SEVERAL PLAN VIEWS
FOUND IN ARCHITECTURAL DRAWINGS ⎯ Right side lines up
AND RELATED ENGINEERING DRAWING

Example of Right Justification

Indicates the start or initial pick point.

WALL SECTION
Top Left

WALL SECTION
Top Center

WALL SECTION
Middle Right

WALL SECTION
Top Right

WALL SECTION
Bottom Left

WALL SECTION
Middle Left

WALL SECTION
Bottom Center

WALL SECTION
Middle Center

WALL SECTION
Bottom Right

FIGURE 18.19 Justification options.

3. The last choice at the DTEXT command line is style.

Specify start point of text or [Justify/Style]:

If you type **S↵**, then you can change the font style name to a different selection if it has been previously created in the Text Style setting. If you type **?↵** at the prompt, then you can access a list of the created styles by pressing Enter↵ again at the <*> prompt. An advantage to using **DTEXT** is that you see the text on the screen as it is being typed.

The MTEXT Command

The multiline text option is used to generate a lot of text in paragraphs or sentences. It is not seen as it is typed on the drawing. The multiline command has its own dialog display box for the text (see Figure 18.20).

- Type **MTEXT**, **MT,** or **T** at the command prompt.
- Select Text from the Draw pull-down menu, then select Multiline Text... from the cascade menu to the right (see Figure 18.21).
- Select the Multiline Text icon from the Draw toolbar.

A

MTEXT
Icon

The command line then prompts you to pick a first corner with the left mouse button. Once you have done this the command shows a variety of choices:

Specify first corner: *(Pick any point.)*
Specify opposite corner or [Height/Justify/Line Spacing/Rotation/Style/Width]

FIGURE 18.20 Multiline Text Editor dialog box.

FIGURE 18.21 Text, Multiline Text... selected on the Draw pull-down menu.

Dragging the cursor and performing another left click will pop up the Multiline Text Editor dialog box. (see Figure 18.20).

The Character tab is open, which shows the following options:

■ Selecting font styles

■ Selecting a height for text

■ Underscoring or underlining (U)

■ Selecting colors for the text

■ Picking a symbol

The Symbol choices include Degrees, Plus/Minus, and Diameter (see Figure 18.22). The Other... option brings up a Character Map of symbols unique to the font style that is selected (see Figure 18.23).

To use a symbol from the chart, left-click on one, then move the mouse arrow to the Select button and left-click. Next, move to the Copy button and left-click on it, then left-click on the Close button. Finally, insert the symbol by right-clicking and then choosing Paste with a left click.

If the Properties tab is selected, the following set of options pops up (see Figure 18.24).

■ Style

■ Justification

■ Width

■ Rotation

FIGURE 18.22 Symbol options.

FIGURE 18.23 Character map.

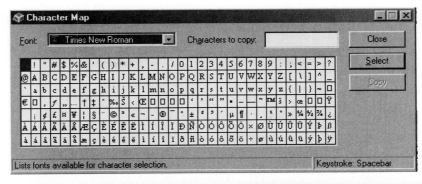

FIGURE 18.24 Multiline Text Editor.

The Line Spacing tab will open two line spacing settings to control the distance between text lines stacked on top of one another. The Final/Replace tab can be used to scan the text for editing.

There are four screen buttons on the right-hand side of the dialog display.

- The **OK** button puts the text on the drawing and exits the Text Editor.
- The **Cancel** button terminates the text in the mline text area and exits the Text Editor.
- The **Import Text...** button allows you to search and bring in text from another program or file and use it in this drawing.
- The **Help** button displays the help screen for MTEXT.

The multiline text editor is preferred by most CAD operators; however, keyboard options are available. Look at the command sequence again after typing **MTEXT** and selecting the starting corner. You can type in the options shown at the command line prompt:

[Height/Justify/Line Spacing/Rotation/Style/Width]

All these options have just previously been shown. They are found in the dialog boxes, but sometimes a fast CAD operator can use a single keystroke for making changes instead of going into the dialog box. Once you have selected the command by typing the first letter and pressing Enter↵, the Multiline Text Editor pops up ready for you to type.

18.3 Editing and Modifying Existing Text

Once you have placed text on a drawing and exited the DTEXT or MTEXT options, you must use special editing commands to make changes. **Properties** and **DDEDIT** are two excellent text editing commands used in AutoCAD (see Figures 18.25, 18.26, and 18.27).

The Properties Command

Properties Icon

- Type **PROPERTIES** or **MO** at the command prompt.
- Select **Properties** from the Modify pull-down menu (see Figure 18.28).
- Pick the **Properties** icon from the Modify toolbar.

The DDEDIT Command

DDEDIT Icon

- Type **DDEDIT** or **ED** at the command prompt.
- Select Text from the Modify pull-down menu (see Figure 18.29).
- Pick the **Edit Text** icon from the Modify II toolbar.

FIGURE 18.25   Properties tab options.

FIGURE 18.26   Edit Text dialog box for single-line text.

FIGURE 18.27   Multiline Text Editor dialog box.

FIGURE 18.28   Properties selected on the Modify pull-down menu.

FIGURE 18.29   Text... selected on the Modify pull-down menu.

When selecting text to edit, you have a choice of either picking and highlighting the DT text string or MTEXT paragraph first and selecting DDEDIT (ED) or DDMODIFY (MO) second, or picking the editing commands first and selecting the text second. It is purely a matter of preference. In both cases the Text Editor dialog box will open ready for changes.

Text Tips

The DDEDIT command shows a blinking vertical bar so you can locate where the changes are being made. Use the keyboard's four arrow keys to maneuver around the text, or just place the mouse arrow at the desired location and left-click to get the blinking bar. Once you have changed the text, make sure to select the OK button to keep the changes.

Modifying with Properties has a lot more options than just editing text, but it is the most powerful and commonly used editing AutoCAD command. When dealing with text, make sure that you have selected the text with a window or by left-clicking on part of it in order for the Text options to open in the Properties dialog box. When it opens, go to the right of the vertical line down the middle and select what is to be edited. In the Contents group of text to the right, you may need to select a box with three little dashes to open the full text editor window. After making the changes, make sure to close the Properties dialog display by left-clicking on the X in the little box in the upper right-hand corner. To turn off the grips (the little blue boxes that show up when clicking on objects and entities) press the Esc key on the keyboard twice.

The MTEXT command will have many symbols to pick from in its setup. In contrast, only a few symbols can be generated in DTEXT, such as:

%%% will show a % symbol

%%U will underline text if used before the text

%%D will add an angle degree symbol

%%O will draw a line above the letters if used before the text

%%C will generate a diameter symbol

Note: the symbols will not appear until you press Enter↵ twice or once followed by pressing the Esc key.

The command called **QTEXT** is used to display a rectangular box where the text will be located. Just type in **QTEXT** at the command line and then type **ON**.

Command: **QTEXT↵**
Enter node [ON/OFF] <OFF> **ON**

This setting is used to reduce the amount of memory that text uses for a drawing; therefore, if there is a lot of text on a drawing, then turning **QTEXT** on will speed up the computer. To get the letters back, just turn **QTEXT** off and follow it with the **Regen** command. The Regen performs a recalculation of the screen and will bring the text back.

Another feature in AutoCAD is the spelling check, which is located under the Tools pull-down menu. Select Spelling and left-click on top of the text and it will scan the text for misspelled words. This spell checker works similarly to ones that are found in word processing software packages. If a spell check of the whole drawing is desired, just type **ALL↵**, then press Enter↵ when the Select objects prompt appears at the command line, and every piece of text will be checked.

Example: DTEXT

In this example we will create a new style name called Arch1 and pick a font style called CountryBlueprint from the Font Name selection. The text height will be set to 1/4″ (.25″) with a Width Factor set to .75. The text to be typed:

AutoCAD® 2000 HAS A WIDE
RANGE OF FONT SYTLES.

Right after the text is placed on the drawing with the **DTEXT** command, then it will be changed using **Properties (MO)** to the following:

- Text height of 1/8″ (.125″)
- Width Factor of (.9)
- Obliquing angle of 15°

Begin by selecting Text Style from the Format pull-down menu (see Figure 18.30), which will open up the Text Style dialog box (see Figure 18.31).

Left-click on the New box to activate the New Text Style dialog box and type in Arch1. Left-click on the OK box to return to the Text Style display, and left-click on the arrow in the Font Name text box. Two new arrows appear, and when you left-click on either one it will start moving through the different fonts (see Figure 18.32). When you come to CountryBlueprint left-click on it to select it (see Figure 18.33). Make sure the setting in the Height box is at 0, which will force the **DTEXT** command to ask you for a text height when it is used later. Left-click in the Width Factor text box and set the Width Factor to .75. The settings are complete, so left-click on the Apply button, then on the Close button (see Figure 18.34).

To start the **DTEXT** command type in **DT** at the command line and press Enter↵.

Command: **DT** ↵

Next, left-click near the middle of the graphics screen when the command line reads as shown in Figure 18.35. The command line will then show a current text height. Type in the .25 height desired after the colon.

Specify height <Current Height Shown Here>: **.25**↵

Press Enter↵ when the next command prompt comes up displaying a default rotation angle of 0.

Specify rotation angle of text <0>: ↵

The command line now prompts you to enter the text desired. At this point type in your text.

Enter text: **AutoCAD® 2000 HAS A WIDE** ↵
Enter text: **RANGE OF FONT STYLES** ↵
Enter text: ↵↵ (press Enter↵ twice)

The DT command is complete, and the text appears on the screen as shown in Figure 18.36.

To edit the existing text, let's use the **PROPERTIES** command to make the changes. Pick both lines of text with a crossing window until the blue grip boxes appear, then type in **MO** at the command line.

Command: **MO**

The Properties box will appear displaying the Text options (see Figure 18.37).

Left-click on the height setting on the right side of the box, and change it from .25 to .125. Next, left-click on the width factor, highlighting the .75 setting, and change it to .9. Finally, change the Obliquing setting from a 0 slope to a 15° slope (see Figure 18.38).

When you are finished, close the Properties display by left-clicking on the small X in the upper right corner. The text is now displayed with the new changes (see Figure 18.39). Press the Esc key twice to turn off the grip boxes.

FIGURE 18.30 Text Style selected on the Format pull-down menu.

FIGURE 18.31 New Text Style dialog box.

FIGURE 18.32 Font style options.

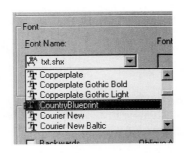

FIGURE 18.33 Font style highlighted.

FIGURE 18.34 CountryBlueprint font style selected.

```
DTEXT
Current text style:  "ARCH1"  Text height:  0.2500
Specify start point of text or [Justify/Style]:
```

FIGURE 18.35 Command line text.

AutoCAD 2000 HAS A WIDE
RANGE OF FONT STYLES

FIGURE 18.36 Text display.

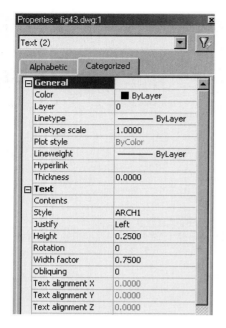

FIGURE 18.37 Text options.

FIGURE 18.38 Obliquing option in the Properties dialog box.

AutoCAD 2000 HAS A WIDE RANGE OF FONT STYLES

FIGURE 18.39 Text with grips.

Example: MTEXT

In this example we will create a new style name called Interior and pick a font style called City-Blueprint. The text height will be ½″ (.5″) with a Width Factor of 1.25. Using the MTEXT (MT or T) command we will type the following:

> The lobby will have a brick tile floor with a 4″ base. A semi-gloss paint for all gypsum board walls. The counter will have a glass bock exterior face.

Once we exit the **MTEXT** command, we will use a DDEDIT to change the wording in the text. Begin by typing in **STYLE** or **ST** at the command line.

Command: **ST** ↵

The Text Style dialog display immediately pops up. Use the <u>N</u>ew... button to create a <u>S</u>tyle Name called Interior by typing it in when the style1 is highlighted. Left-click on the OK button, and the new style name will appear. In the <u>F</u>ont Name box use the arrow to scroll through the list of the AutoCAD font styles. When you find the CityBlueprint font, select it by left-clicking on it. Left-click in the Heigh<u>t</u> box and type in a text height of ½″ (.5″). Left-click in the <u>W</u>idth Factor box and change the setting to 1.25. When you are done click the Apply button, then Close. The settings should look like Figure 18.40 before closing.

To start using **MTEXT**, type **MT** at the command line.

Command: **MT**

Left-click in the lower left corner for the Specify first corner, then move the mouse to the upper right corner and click again. The Multiline Text Editor dialog box opens, and you can begin typing. The screen should look like Figure 18.41 when the text is complete.

Left-click on the OK button, and the text is placed on the drawing.

To start editing the paragraph (words only) type DDEDIT or ED at the command line:

Command: **ED**

The command prompt requests a selection, so the text on the drawing must be highlighted/selected for editing. Once you have done this the Text Editor dialog box opens. Now, place the cursor inside the text area and make changes from the keyboard after a left click (see Figure 18.42 for the new text).

FIGURE 18.40 Text Style dialog box.

FIGURE 18.41 Multiline Text editor.

FIGURE 18.42 Multiline Text Editor with changes.

These two examples combined some basic skills to place text on a drawing. The problems at the end of the chapter will give you some more practice getting used to the commands.

REVIEW QUESTIONS

1. How are lettering styles set up in AutoCAD?

2. What happens when the text height is set to 0?

3. Explain the difference between DTEXT and MTEXT.

4. List the options found in the Justify selection in the DTEXT command.

5. How can symbols be used inside the MTEXT command?

6. Qtext displays letters in what format?

7. Name three ways to edit existing text.

8. What are the aliases for the following commands?

   a. Properties

   b. DDEdit

   c. MTEXT

   d. DTEXT

9. How are the following symbols generated with DTEXT?

   a. Percent symbol

   b. Underlined text

   c. Diameter symbol

   d. Degree symbol

10. What effect will an Obliquing angle cause on the text?

11. A Width Factor of .5 will do what to a letter?

12. What are some of the factors considered in selecting a font style for architectural working drawings?

EXERCISES

EXERCISE 18.1

Start a **New** drawing **Starting from Scratch** and create a Text Style with the following settings:

- Set <u>S</u>tyle Name as Int1.
- Set Font St<u>y</u>le to Country Blueprint.
- Use a .75 <u>W</u>idth Factor.
- Set Heig<u>h</u>t to .5″.

Type the following using MTEXT:

DRAWING INDEX
A-1 SITE PLAN
A-2 FLOOR PLAN
A-3 ELEVATIONS
A-4 WALL SECTION
A-5 INTERIOR DETAILS

Save the drawing as 18EX1.

EXERCISE 18.2

Edit the drawing 18EX1 with the following changes:

- Change the letter height to .25 for every line except DRAWING INDEX.
- Change the <u>W</u>idth Factor on all letters to .5.
- **Save** changes as 18EX2.

EXERCISE 18.3

Start a **New** drawing with the **Use a Wizard's** Quick Setup. Use **Architectural Unit**, then set a 34′ width and 44′ length. Create a Text Style with the following settings:

- Set Style Name as INT2.
- Set Font Style to City Blueprint.
- Use a 5° Oblique Angle.
- Set text Height to 6″

Type the following paragraph using the MTEXT command:

Before deciding on an office chair, it is important to understand the CAD operator's habits. If the operator will be in the chair eight to ten hours a day, then the desired comfort level may be high.

Save the drawing as 18EX3.

EXERCISE 18.4

Use the title block shown in Figure 18.43 from Chapter 3.

- Create a New Style and use the Times New Roman font.
- Draw the title block for an 8.5″ × 11″ sheet at full scale.
- Place the text in the title block area using the sizes specified on the sheet.

Save the drawing as 18EX4.

EXERCISE 18.5

Create a title block of your own for a sheet set to limits of 0,0 lower left corner and 144′, 96′ upper right corner. Make sure to use an 8′ left-hand margin (equivalent to 2″) and 4′ margins (equivalent to 1″) on the three remaining sides. Check some of the templates for some ideas.

FIGURE 18.43 Title block.

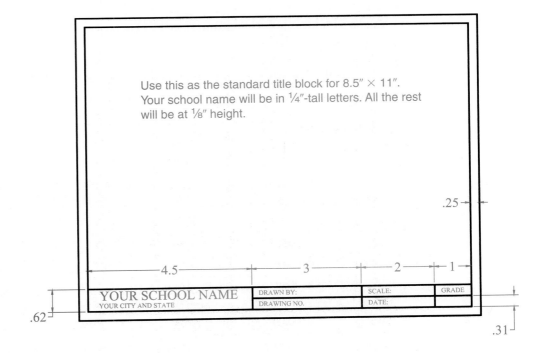

DRAWING ASSIGNMENTS

1. Using the Door Schedule in Figure 18.44 as a guide, make a version of your own. Put it on an 8.5″ × 11″ sheet at full scale.

    - Use three text heights:

        .25 large letters

        .18 medium letters

        .125 small letters

    - Make sure the text fits comfortably between the lines both vertically and horizontally. Use guidelines to place the text on the schedule. Turn the guidelines' layer off when the schedule is complete.

2. Using the Window Schedule in Figure 18.45 as a guide, make a version of your own. Put it on an 8.5″ × 11″ sheet at full scale.

    - Use three text heights:

        .25 large letters

        .18 medium letters

        .125 small letters

    - Make sure the text fits comfortably between the lines both vertically and horizontally. Use guidelines to place the text on the schedule. Turn the guidelines' layer off when the schedule is complete.

3. Using the Finish Schedule in Figure 18.46 as a guide, make a version of your own. Put it on an 8.5″ × 11″ sheet at full scale.

    - Use three text heights:

        .25 large letters

        .18 medium letters

        .125 small letters

    - Make sure the text fits comfortably between the lines both vertically and horizontally. Use guidelines to place the text on the schedule. Turn the guidelines' layer off when the schedule is complete.

4. Design three different logos for the following businesses.

    a. Architectural firm
    b. Interior design firm
    c. Landscape design firm

5. Use the logos in assignment 4 to design business cards for each firm. Include a company name, address, phone number, fax number, and E-mail address. The cards should be 3.5″ × 2″.

FIGURE 18.44 Drawing Assignment 1.

DOOR SCHEDULE			
MARK	SIZE	TYPE	REMARKS
1	3^0 X 7^0 X $1\frac{3}{4}$"	PANEL WOOD	SOLID CORE
2	2^8 X 6^8 X $1\frac{3}{4}$"	FRENCH	S.C. W/ FIXED GLASS
3	3^0 X 6^8 X $1\frac{3}{4}$"	FLUSH	SOLID CORE
4	2^8 X 6^8 X $1\frac{3}{4}$"	DUTCH	SOLID CORE
5	2^8 X 6^8 X $1\frac{3}{8}$"	PANEL	HOLLOW CORE
6	2^6 X 6^8 X $1\frac{3}{8}$"	PANEL	HOLLOW CORE
7	2^2 X 6^8 X $1\frac{3}{8}$"	LOUVERS	H.C. PANTRY DOORS
8	2^8 X 6^8 X $1\frac{3}{8}$"	PANEL	HIDDEN-POCKET
9	4^0 X 6^8	LOUVERS	FOLDING CL UNIT
10	9^0 X 7^0	PANEL WOOD	GARAGE DOOR
11	3^8 X 6^8	PANEL	H.C. HIDDEN-POCKET CL DOORS

FIGURE 18.45 Drawing Assignment 2.

WINDOW SCHEDULE			
MARK	SIZE	TYPE	REMARKS
A	10" x 6'-10"	SIDE LITE	WD. & BRICK JAMB
B	1'-10" x 4'-9"	FIXED	WD. & BRICK JAMB
C	2'-6" x 6'-6"	D.H.	WD. & BRICK JAMB
D	3'-6" x 4'-9"	D.H.	PICTURE WINDOW IN BREAK. RM.
E	5'-1" x 5'-6"	PICTURE	WD. & BRICK JAMB
F	2'-6" x 2'-0"	HORIZON	WD. & BRICK JAMB
G	5'-1" x 2'-6"	HORIZON	WD. & BRICK JAMB
H	1'-10" x 2'-6"	D.H.	WD. & BRICK JAMB
I	3'-6" x 2'-6"	HORIZON	WD. & BRICK JAMB
J	3'-6" x 1'-6"	DECOR	W/ 3'-6" x 3'-0" FIXED GLASS BELOW

FINISH SCHEDULE

ROOM NAME	FLOORS					BASE			WALLS			CEILING	REMARKS
	Oak Flooring	Carpet	Concrete	Ceramic	Linoleum	Wood - 6" High	Ceramic	Wood - 4" High	Ceramic Tile	Gyp Board Wall Cover	Gyp Board Painted	Gyp Board Painted	
ENTRY & FOYER	●					●					●	●	
LIVING ROOM		●				●					●	●	
DINING ROOM	●					●					●	●	
FAMILY ROOM		●						●			●	●	
KITCHEN & BREAKFAST	●							●	●			●	
BEDROOMS		●						●			●	●	
CLOSETS		●						●			●	●	
BATHROOMS				●			●		●	●		●	TILE STOPS 40" ABOVE FLR. LINE
MECH. & SHOP			●								●	●	
GARAGE			●								●	●	
MUD ROOM					●			●			●	●	

FIGURE 18.46   Drawing Assignment 3.

Learning to Create Blocks and WBlocks

One of the real pleasures of using AutoCAD is the ability to reuse existing information. AutoCAD commands can transfer images within a single drawing or from one drawing to another. The smallest of elements or an entire drawing can be put together as a unit using various methods.

The goals of this chapter are to show you how to use the Block and Wblock commands. These commands will be broken down into the following parts:

1. Creating Blocks and Wblocks.
2. Inserting Blocks and WBlocks into drawings.
3. Editing Blocks.

19.1 Creating Blocks and WBlocks

The Block Definition dialog box can be accessed in the following ways.

- Type **BLOCK** or **B** at the command prompt.
- Select the <u>M</u>ake flyout option of Bloc<u>k</u> in the <u>D</u>raw pull-down menu (see Figure 19.1).
- Pick the Block icon from the Draw toolbar.

Block
Icon

Once you are in the Block Definition dialog box, use the following sequence when making a Block (see Figure 19.2).

FIGURE 19.1   Block, Make... selected on the Draw pull-down menu.

FIGURE 19.2   Block Definition dialog box.

445

FIGURE 19.3   Object selected.

FIGURE 19.4   Midpoint of sofa.

1. Name the Block. (This example will be called Sofa.) Type the name in the Name text box.
2. Left-click on the Select Objects screen button.
3. The Block definition box will close. Select the objects or items on the drawing that need to be included in the Block (see Figure 19.3).
4. Once you have selected all the lines on the Sofa, right-click to return to the Block definition screen. Left-click on the Pick point screen button.
5. The original drawing screen reappears and waits for you to pick a reference or insertion point. Choose a point. Osnaps are recommended when doing this. We will choose the midpoint on the front of the sofa (see Figure 19.4).
6. As soon as the Midpoint is selected, the Block Definition dialog box reappears. Left-click on the OK screen button and the Block creation is finished.

Several options exist in the Objects area of the dialog box:

- The **Retain** option will leave the block object in its original position and form.
- **Convert to Block** will leave the original object, but it will be a block and will act as one unit if selected.
- **Delete** will remove the original object from the drawing.
- The **Quick Select** selection will give you some additional options to filter in or remove components from the blocks (more for the advanced user) (see Figure 19.5).

In the Base point area of the dialog box the Pick point screen button is used for identifying where the block is to be inserted. Another method is to pick the insertion point by typing in the X, Y, and Z coordinates (see Figure 19.6). Either method will get the job done. It just depends on what information is available at the time.

The bottom half of the Block Definition dialog box has four choices. The Preview icon area lets you create an icon or picture to be included in a preview. This is the default setting that can be turned off by left-clicking on the Do not include an icon radio button. A text description can be associated with the block definition and will display in the area where it is typed. The final option is Insert units (see Figure 19.7). It will assign a unit value to which the block is scaled when it is dragged from the AutoCAD Design Center.

Insert unit contains the following options: Unitless, Inches, Feet, Miles, Millimeters, Centimeters, Meters, and Kilometers.

Depending on the environment any of these could be needed. In the architectural environment, drawings are normally done in inches or feet, but Unitless will adjust sizes to fit the different scaled environments.

FIGURE 19.5   Objects options.

FIGURE 19.6   Base point options.

FIGURE 19.7   Preview icon options.

The WBLOCK Command.

■ Type **WBLOCK** at the command prompt.

A Wblock is different from a Block in the following way. The W in the command stands for Write. By definition, a Wblock writes a file name or creates a drawing file. In the previous releases of AutoCAD, a Wblock was the best method for inserting Blocks from one drawing environment into another. When a Wblock is created, it gets a .dwg file extension, for example, Sofa.dwg. A Block, on the other hand, does not get a file extension and therefore is part of the original drawing in which it was created. The only way to transfer a Blocked unit from its original drawing to a brand new drawing is through the AutoCAD Design Center.

Take a look at the Write Block dialog box and note some of the differences between it and the Block Definition display (see Figure 19.8).

The Source area has radio button options for Block, Entire drawing, and Objects.

These are the choices you make when creating a Wblock.

1. A block can be made into a Wblock and is given a file extension.

2. An entire drawing can be a Wblock. (Any drawing with a .dwg file extension can be inserted whether or not it was created with the Write Block command or was saved as a normal drawing.) With the **Wblock** comand you can select what item you want to reuse instead of taking the whole drawing as a unit.

3. You can select individual objects to make up the Wblock.

The Destination area in this dialog box contains the File name text box where the Wblock is named. Use the same rules as when naming a new drawing or saving a drawing. The Location text box lets you save the Wblock to a particular directory or to a floppy disk. The Insert units box serves the same purpose as in the Block Definition dialog display.

As you can see, making Blocks and Wblocks will take a little bit of practice to learn the sequence. Read through the steps as you learn to make your own Blocks.

FIGURE 19.8 Write Block dialog box.

FIGURE 19.9   **Three blocks.**

Chair   Table   Sofa

19.2 Inserting Blocks and WBlocks into Drawings

This first example will demonstrate how to insert Blocks from an existing drawing into a new drawing using AutoCAD 2000's Design Center. The following example will have three blocks that have previously been created using the same steps explained in the first part of this chapter. The three Blocks are of a chair, a table, and a sofa (see Figure 19.9). After blocking each object separately, we will save the drawing and give it the name **oblocks**.

Example

Close the drawing named oblocks and start a new drawing by left-clicking on the File pull-down menu and then left-clicking on the New option. Using the Wizard in the Create New Drawing dialog box, select the Quick Setup option and click OK (see Figure 19.10).

The Quick Setup dialog box opens. Choose the Architectural option and left-click on the Next button. Set the width to 34′ and the length to 44′ and then left-click on the Finish button at the base of the dialog box. This drawing is the one we will drag the blocks into.

Now left-click on the Design Center icon (see Figure 19.11). It is on the Standard Toolbar between the Zoom Previous icon and the Properties icon.

The Design Center dialog box opens up split into two screens (see Figure 9.12). The left screen is basically the Exploring option showing all the directories and folders. The right side shows a detailed listing of what has been selected in the left screen. In this example we scanned through the files to find the oblocks.dwg stored in the user/Blockchapter folder. A double left click on the Blockchapter folder, followed by a double left click on the oblocks.dwg generated Figure 19.13.

The right-hand screen displays the components of this drawing (see Figure 19.14). A double left click on the Blocks icon produces the three Blocks that exist in this drawing (see Figure 19.15).

To move a copy of the Blocks into the new drawing, left-click on the chair block icon seen in Figure 19.15 and hold down the left mouse button (see Figure 19.16). While holding the button down roll the mouse out of the Design Center area and drag it into the new drawing area. Once in this area simply let go of the mouse button, and the Block appears (see Figure 19.17).

Repeat the left-click, hold, and drag method on the sofa and the table to place them into the new drawing (see Figure 19.18).

FIGURE 19.10   **Create New Drawing dialog box.**

FIGURE 19.11   Design Center icon.   **FIGURE 19.12**   Design Center dialog box.

FIGURE 19.13   Design Center showing oblocks open.

FIGURE 19.14   Blocks folder.

FIGURE 19.15   Chair, sofa, and table in Design Center.

Left-click holding down the button.
Then roll the mouse up, dragging the
sofa into the other drawing above.

FIGURE 19.16   Sofa highlighted in Design Center.

Dragged in from the Design Center

FIGURE 19.17   Dragged sofa in Design Center.

FIGURE 19.18   Dragged sofa, chair, and table in Design Center.

At this point, a copy of the Blocks has been placed on this drawing, and the blocks are now part of this drawing and can be used again without going through the Design Center. The Insert command (discussed in the following section) can now be used on the Block in a new drawing.

Using the Insert Block Command

This command will let you place Blocks or Wblocks on a drawing.

Insert Icon

- Type **DDINSERT** at the command prompt.
- Select Block from the Insert pull-down menu (see Figure 19.19).
- Pick the Block icon from the Draw toolbar.

The Insert dialog box appears (see Figure 19.20). The Name box lists all the Blocks that are part of the current drawing (see Figure 19.21). Currently the chair, the sofa, and the table are the Blocks that were copied from oblocks.dwg. Pick the Block you want to use and left-click on the OK screen button. That Block appears on the drawing and can be dragged by rolling the mouse around. (Notice that the cursor is pointing to the base point that was chosen in the original Make Block option.)

This point is locked in, and the only way to change the base point is to make another Block and choose a different base point at a new location. To place the Block on the drawing, just left-click, and the block will be placed. For a precise placement, use the Osnaps to lock in on an endpoint, intersection, or wherever the Block is desired. Another way to place the Block is to check the Specify On-screen button and type in the co-ordinates at the X, Y, and Z text boxes (see Figure 19.22). Keep in mind the units of the drawing and also that

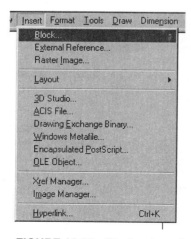

FIGURE 19.19   Block selected on the Insert pull-down menu.

FIGURE 19.20   Insert dialog box.

FIGURE 19.21   Insert text box.   **FIGURE 19.22**   Insertion point options.

the X- and Y-coordinates are for two-dimensional drawings. The Scale display area has a few choices for the CAD operator.

Specify On-screen will default the Block scale to the command line if this option is checked. At the command line the display shows:

Specify insertion point or [Scale/X/Y/Z/Rotate/PScale/PX/PY/PZ/PRotate]:

These options will do the following:

- **Scale** will set a uniform scale for X, Y, and Z.
- **X** will change the X-coordinate scale.
- **Y** will change the Y-coordinate scale.
- **Z** will change the Z-coordinate scale.
- **Rotate** will set a rotation angle to turn the Block.

The rest of the options preceded by a **P** are a repeat of the previous options with the following exception: The **P** stands for preview. It allows you to preview the scale before it gets inserted in the drawing. The sequence at the command line goes like this.

1. Type in **PX** to preview and select an X scale.
2. Specify a preview X scale factor.
3. Pick an insertion point on the drawing while looking at the Block's preview scale.
4. After the pick enter the scale again or change it to something else. A Y scale factor will also be available.

There is also a **Rotation** option in the dialog box. Checking the box marked Specify On-screen will initiate a sequence at the command line that will ask you for a rotation angle. Specifying an Angle setting will automatically rotate the block to a predetermined angle. A setting of 45° would turn the sofa as shown in Figure 19.23.

Left-clicking on the Explode box in the lower left corner will break up the Block cell into individual lines and pieces.

The Insert command also inserts Wblocks. Because Wblocks are basically drawing files with extensions, they will not be listed where the Blocks are shown in the Name text box. You must left-click on the Browse... screen button located to the right of the Name box. Browsing is like using the exploring option. The Select Drawing File dialog box opens, and you can scan through all the directories and folders and find where the Wblock was saved (see Figure 19.24). In this example a drawing named CIRCLES.dwg is highlighted.

FIGURE 19.23   Sofa rotated.

FIGURE 19.24   Select Drawing
File dialog box.

The Preview area on the right-hand side gives you a peak at the highlighted drawing file. When you find Wblock, left-click on the Open button, and you return to the Insert box. Left-click on the OK button and then left-click in the drawing area when it opens to place the Wblock on the drawing. All the options work the same for the Blocks as for the Wblocks.

Note: Block and Wblock existed before the Windows Copy and Paste commands. A new student to AutoCAD might try to use these because they are more familiar to them. This method of copying and pasting between different drawings will work, but it does not have the scale control or other options of the Block command. You may find the scale change a drawback to using copy and paste options.

The Minsert Command

■ Type in **MINSERT** at the command prompt.

A Minsert may be desired when a rectangular array is needed to insert many blocks in a rows-and-columns pattern. The Minsert command is very similar to the Insert command, with a couple of exceptions. It has an Array option, and MINSERT cannot be exploded into separate parts. Minsert is not used very much, so you will not find it in a toolbar or a pull-down menu; it must be typed in at the command line.

Command: **MINSERT**
Enter block name or [?] <Table>:

Type in the block name or a question mark to get a list of the existing blocks and make a selection. If you want to Minsert a Wblock, type the exact location of the file in the computer. For example, if a Minsert is required for a drawing named Door1.dwg that is in a directory labeled DoorElevation, then type in DoorElevation/Door1.dwg at the command line, and the computer will search the path and find the Wblock.

Command: MINSERT
Enter Block name or [?]: DoorElevation/Door1.dwg

Layering Tips for Blocks and Wblocks

Even though a Block or a Wblock acts as one unit or a cell, they can have different characteristics within that cell. A wide variety of lineweights, colors, and linetypes may be found in a Block. Good layer management can help keep the Block properties intact after the Insert or Minsert command is completed. Plan out the layers and properties that will make up the Block before it is created.

■ Do not use Layer 0 (zero) as part of your Block. It will not hold the properties you establish when inserted if another layer is current during the insertion process. The Block takes on the properties of the current layer.

■ When a Block is inserted into an existing drawing and the Block's layer names match some in the existing drawing but have different properties, the existing drawing will dominate and change the properties of the Block layers to match its own.

■ You may use layer 0 for a block if you want the block to assume the properties of the current layer when inserted.

Example of Insertion Problems with Layer

A Block with a layer named Chair that has a red color and a Hidden linetype is inserted into another drawing. This drawing already has a layer named Chair, but the color and linetype assigned are Blue and Continuous. What is going to happen? The Block will insert, but the Block properties will change to a blue color and a continuous line type.

Set up your Blocks with special layer names that do not repeat in any other drawings or Blocks. This should keep your Blocks from becoming chameleons.

Redefining a Block

If a Block has been inserted into a drawing many times and it needs to be revised, redefining it is a good time-saver. The process is easy. Make the necessary changes to one of the existing blocks on the drawing. When the changes are complete, go through the Block command again. Name the edited Block the same name as the old Block. AutoCAD will ask if the Block should be redefined. Click on the Yes button. Watch the other existing Blocks update themselves. If the original block disappears, use the Oops command to get it back. Do not use the Undo command because it will not keep the created Block.

19.3 Editing Blocks

A Block cell acts as one unit or element, so it is easy to change a Block as a whole. Blocks can be edited to a certain extent. Some of the Block properties are easy to change. Layers, colors, and linetypes can be modified using the Properties command, as demonstrated in Chapter 14.

Note: The Explode command does not work on the Minsert command.

Trying to change an individual part of a Block separately from the rest of the unit is a problem. To do this, you must disassemble the Block cell with the Explode command. The pieces can then be altered individually. Remember that all the parts act separately now and must be edited one at a time.

An exploded cell can be put back together by going through the steps of making a Block again. Early planning to get your Block in the correct format so that little or no editing will be required later is the best way to go. Another way to handle changes ahead of time is to make several Blocks with the changes in the different Blocks. Create a library of Blocks with all the possible changes already made before using the Make Block command. Add new Blocks to your master drawing library as needed.

REVIEW QUESTIONS

1. Explain the difference between the Block and Wblock commands.
2. How do you start the Wblock command?
3. How do you make a Block?
4. What are the four choices in the Block Definition dialog box?
5. How can the AutoCAD Design Center be of benefit when dealing with Blocks?
6. In what toolbar will you find the Insert Block icon?
7. How does Exploding affect Blocks and Wblocks?
8. What options are available in Minserting a Block?
9. How can inserted Blocks and Wblocks be edited in AutoCAD?
10. Why should you avoid using layer 0 on components of a Block?
11. Explain some of the problems that occur with layers when a Block or Wblock is inserted into another drawing.

EXERCISES

EXERCISE 19.1

Draw the bathroom fixtures shown in Figure 19.25a and make them into Blocks. Name the Blocks shower, toilet, sink, and tub. Save the drawing and name it Bath. Next, start a New drawing using architectural drawing units and set the drawing limits to (0,0) lower left corner and (34′, 44′) in the upper right corner. Draw the given master bath plan in Figure 19.25b.

Use the AutoCAD Design Center on this first exercise. Open it and find the drawing named Bath in the left-side area. Once you find it, keep opening it until the Block drawings appear. Use the drag-and-drop method to complete the drawing shown in Figure 19.25c. Save this drawing as Bath1.dwg.

EXERCISE 19.2

Begin a new drawing. Set up architectural units with limits at (0,0) in the lower left corner and (34′, 44′) in the upper right corner. Use the Browse option of the Insert Block command to find the drawing name Bath1.dwg created in exercise 19.1. Insert it into your new drawing. Mirror the Wblock so the drawing looks like Figure 19.26. Save this drawing as Bath2.dwg.

Draw the fixtures, not the titles or dimensions.

(a)

Note:
1. Use a 4″-thick wall.
2. Use a 30″-wide window with a
   6″-thick frame.
3. Use a 30″-wide shower door
   and a 32″-wide entry door.

(b)

(c)

FIGURE 19.25   Exercise 19.1.

FIGURE 19.26   Exercise 19.2

FIGURE 19.27   Exercise 19.3

Minsert Layout for 19.3

EXERCISE 19.3

Open drawing Bath2.dwg. Explode the Wblock, make a copy of the toilet, and drag it to the bottom of the sheet. Make a new Block of the toilet at the bottom. Minsert the new toilet block. Set the scale to 1.5 and change the rotation angle to 90°. Enter 2 rows and 2 columns with a distance between the rows and columns of 5′ as shown in Figure 19.27.

DRAWING ASSIGNMENTS

Use the following figures as a guide for creating some of the furniture blocks for the assignments. Add new furniture as needed. Research sizes in the *Architectural Graphic Standards*.

1. The furniture in Figure 19.28 is in 3-D form. Make a plan view of each piece of furniture from its 3-D drawing. After each piece is drawn make a Block for each individual one. If you desire more choices, research the sizes and create your own. Once the Blocks are complete, label them with text and print them on individual title block sheets at a ¼″ = 1′-0″ scale.

2. The duplex drawing you created in Chapter 15 needs a furniture layout. Freeze the dimension layer you created in Chapter 17 and create a furniture layer. Using the AutoCAD Design Center, take the furniture created in assignment 1 and place the pieces in the duplex drawing. Be sure to put the blocks on the furniture layer. Use an 11″ × 17″ sheet size for the duplex drawing.

3. Draw the given master bedroom and bath in Figure 19.29 at a ¼″ = 1′-0″ scale. Provide a furniture layout for the bedroom. This time create a wallboard (17″ × 11′-4″) at the head of a king-size bed.

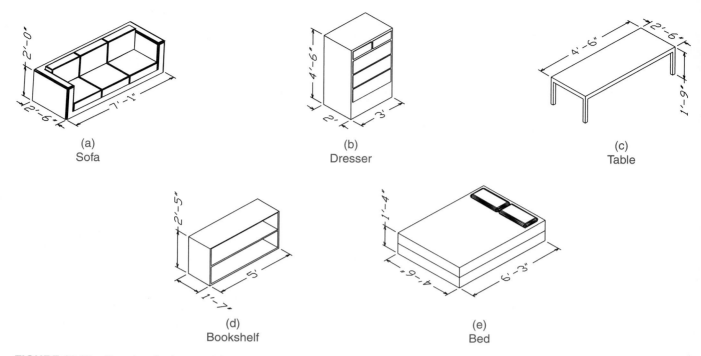

(a)
Sofa

(b)
Dresser

(c)
Table

(d)
Bookshelf

(e)
Bed

FIGURE 19.28   Drawing Assignment 1.

FIGURE 19.29   Drawing Assignment 3.

SECOND-FLOOR MASTER BEDROOM AND BATH

Scale: 1/4" = 1'-0"

Insight into Plotting and Paper Space

Most individuals who have used a computer have printed a copy of something. Once the basic printing settings are established the process is quite easy. Plotting a drawing in AutoCAD tends to be more challenging. Some of the principles are the same as when printing in other software packages, but in AutoCAD 2000 the options seem endless.

AutoCAD 2000 plotting is very powerful and loaded with options. Many training centers and schools offer classes in plotting alone. As with the rest of this book our aim is to introduce you to the basics of AutoCAD plotting and printing. We will explain concepts and walk through a basic plot in this appendix.

Model Space, Layout/Paper Space, and Floating Model Space

It is possible to plot in model space as well as in the Layout format. Some AutoCAD users do not use the Layout plotting environment (known as the Paper Space environment in earlier releases of AutoCAD). The Layout format is a bit of a different world with its own set of guidelines but is not always necessary for plotting. We will start by defining the different environments, then we will explain how to choose a plotting environment.

Model Space

Model space is the drawing and designing environment. When you see the UCS icon on the drawing screen, as shown in Figure A.1, your drawing is in model space or floating model space, which is explained a little later. There are very few limitations on drawing in this environment, but model space is a single environment where everything is handled the same way. Placing text, dimensions, and a title block in this world means tying them to the limits or scale set up in this environment.

Layout/Paper Space

The Layout/Paper Space environment enhances your ability to plot using multiple options. The icon in Figure A.2 is showing that Paper Space is being used. This format allows two different environments to coexist (see Figure A.3). For instance, a title block can be placed in the layout at a full scale of 1″ = 1″ in paper space. Inside that title block a window or, in AutoCAD terms, a viewport can be opened to display a drawing from model space at any desired scale. This is called *floating model space,* as shown n Figure A.4. In this world you can jump back and forth between paper space and model space by double-left-clicking outside the viewport to switch to paper space. Likewise, double-left-clicking inside the viewport will place you in floating model space.

A viewport is analogous to a TV screen that can be used as one large screen or has the ability to be split into smaller ones. Viewports can be created in the Model Space or in the Layout/Paper Space option.

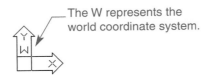

The W represents the world coordinate system.

FIGURE A.1 UCS icon.

FIGURE A.2 Paper space icon.

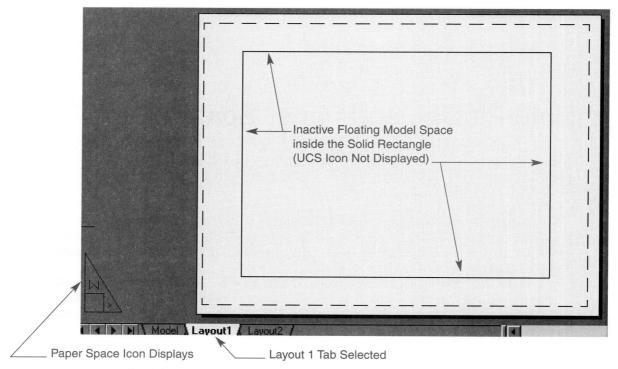

Inactive Floating Model Space
inside the Solid Rectangle
(UCS Icon Not Displayed)

Paper Space Icon Displays   Layout 1 Tab Selected

FIGURE A.3   Layout1 tab selected.

Thick Viewport Line in Floating Model Space

Active Floating Model
Space (UCS Displayed)

Inactive Paper Space
No (PS) Icon Displayed

FIGURE A.4   UCS in floating model space.

■ To create viewports type **VPORTS** at the command prompt. The Viewports dialog box appears (see Figure A.5).

Any number of viewport alignments are found under the Standard viewports heading. Figure A.6 shows the result of choosing the *Four: Equal* option. The screen is split into four equal spaces.

FIGURE A.5   Viewport dialog box.

FIGURE A.6   Viewports four equal spaces.

— Right-click on
Layout Tab

FIGURE A.7   Layout2 selected.

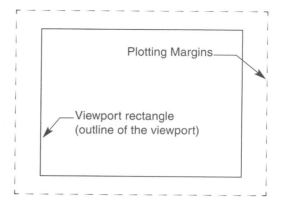

FIGURE A.8   Components of Layout screen.

Viewports in model space are generated immediately after you select the alignment and press the OK button in the dialog box. Creating viewports in the Layout environment takes an extra step.

If you select a Layout tab at the bottom of the drawing screen, a single viewport window is automatically cut into the paper space environment. Two Layout tabs (Layout1 and Layout2) are the default in paper space. Each can represent a different viewport to the same drawing. If you need a customized viewport or layout, right-click on either Layout tab (see Figure A.7). Left click on the New layout selection, and a new layout is created.

Sometimes you might need multiple viewports in a single layout. A quick and easy way to do this is to left-pick on the viewport rectangle (while in paper space) located on the inside of the broken rectangle that represents the margins (see Figure A.8). Once you have selected the viewport rectangle, press the Delete key on the keyboard to eliminate the single viewport. Now you can use the Viewports command to create multiple ports in a layout. There are fewer alignments to choose from in paper space and the defaulted fit window option will require you to cut the floating model space viewport opening in paper space. After you select the alignment the command line prompts you to Specify the first corner: of the viewport window. Left-pick inside the plotting margins in the lower left corner. Move the cursor to the upper right corner, staying inside the dashed margin, left-pick again, and the viewport will be placed in the Layout/Paper Space environment. Paper space is active or current at this time. Simply double-left-click inside the viewport in which you wish to draw, and the viewport becomes active in floating model space. This may be more than you want to know at this time, but viewports play a major part in deciding whether to plot in model space versus layout/paper space. The advanced AutoCAD user will use the Viewports command while in paper space. It will enable the user to use paper space scaling and to hide lines in the different viewports, which is discussed later.

Should the Drawing Be Plotted Using a Layout or in Model Space?

Model space has the following plotting limitations:

1. The title block must be drawn to the same limits or scale as the rest of the drawing.
2. Only the current viewport can be printed in model space.

The Layout/Paper Space environment has the following plotting features.

1. A title block can be placed in paper space at full scale. A floating viewport can be placed inside the title block. The floating viewport can be set to different scales using the Zoom XP Option.

   For instance, make the floating model space viewport active by double-left-clicking in the middle of the viewport rectangle. At the command line use the following sequence:

Command: **ZOOM**↵
Specify corner of window, enter a scale factor (nX or nXP), or
   [All/Center/Dynamic/Extents/Previous/Scale/Window] <real time>: 1/48 XP

For a ¼″ = 1′-0″ scale type **1/48 xp**. This is how scales are set in floating model space. It does not matter what the limits settings were in the original model space. The Zoom XP command must be used to set up

1/24 XP or ½" = 1'-0" in these viewports

1/48 XP or ¼" = 1'-0" scale in this viewport

FIGURE A.9 Three viewports using different scales.

FIGURE A.10   Layer Properties Manager dialog box.

a scale to plot everything inside that viewport to that scale. The title block should be outside the viewport rectangle. This is a full-scale paper space area. Double-left-click outside the viewport rectangle to set the paper space active, and plot the drawing and title block together using full scale.

Tips for Dimensioning in Floating Model Space

■ Create a dimension layer for each individual viewport. Use that layer when dimensioning in that viewport.

Note: When a dimension is placed in its desired viewport, it also shows up in the other viewports. When a dimension shows up in a viewport in which it was not created, a scaling problem can occur when that viewport is zoomed to a different scale. The dimension size is not proportional to that viewport, so it will need to be removed from the viewport in which it was not created. To do this you must hide that layer with that viewport active. You can do this using the layer Properties Manager (see Figure A.12).

2. Multiple viewports can be plotted at the same time with different scales in the same layout. This means that a single layout can contain one viewport showing the whole floor plan at ¼″ = 1′-0″ (1/48 XP) scale along with two other viewports of the same drawing blowing up a plan view of the kitchen and bathroom at a larger scale (see Figure A.9).

3. Lines may be removed or hidden in one viewport but remain visible or displayed in another viewport. Remember that whatever is drawn in the active floating viewport will be drawn in the inactive ones also.

For example, dimensions could be added to a drawing in one viewport but would not be needed in other viewports. To remove the dimensions from a particular viewport make it active or current, then open the Layer Properties Manager dialog box. On the far right-hand side is an Active heading where each layer can be frozen in that selected viewport if desired (see Figure A.10).

Dimensioning in Floating Model Space via Paper Space

A powerful feature to use in paper space is the paper space scaling of dimensions. This is an automatic adjustment that can be turned on while you are dimensioning in floating model space. DIMSCALE can be set to work in real model space as well. A DIMSCALE of 48 would be used in model space to plot ¼″ = 1′-0″. DIMSCALE is calculated in the same way as the scale factor (see Appendix B for different scale factors, and "Drawing Scale" in Chapter 11).

As discussed earlier in this appendix, a single drawing floating in model space can have different viewports or layouts with independent scales in each. A viewport is scaled with the Zoom XP option, as shown earlier.

In the Dimension Style dialog box, the Fit tab has the **Scale dimensions to layout (paper space)** selection (see Figure A.11). This must be selected for paper space scaling of dimensions floating in model space.

Turning this option on will force the DIMSCALE to adjust with the Zoom XP each time it is used. Make sure that the Zoom XP is set correctly before dimensioning. If the Zoom function is changed, the dimension sizes will adjust to the new zoom factor.

Example: Paper Space Dimension

A house floor plan is split into two separate viewports. One is scaled with the **Zoom** command at 1/48 XP for a ¼″ = 1′-0″ scale to view the whole drawing while the other viewport is scaled at 1/24 XP for a ½″ = 1′-0″ scale to blow up the kitchen area.

Dimensions placed in the 1/48 XP scaled viewport will have the DIMSCALE automatically set when that viewport is active. When the other viewport is active, dimensions can be placed in that viewport and the 1/24 XP scale will force the DIMSCALE to automatically fit that scale. See Note.

FIGURE A.11   Scale dimensions to layout (paper space) button.

To be turned on in paper space when dimensioning in the floating model space mode.

FIGURE A.12   Layer Properties Manager dialog box.

The AutoCAD Training Centers introduce viewports and paper space usage in a student's Level II training. The training is more advanced and takes some time to learn. Do not get overwhelmed by this information in the beginning. There are still a few professionals who shy away from using it.

The reasons for choosing a plotting environment are fairly straightforward: If you do not need to

- plot at different scales in a viewport,
- plot multiple viewports on the same sheet, or
- hide lines in one viewport but not in another,

then plotting a drawing in model space may be the best choice if you have a title block for every sheet size and scale used.

Plotting in AutoCAD 2000

In previous AutoCAD releases, there were minimal upgrades and features to learn about plotting. Release 2000 plotting has much more power and many more settings for the user to learn. It can seem overwhelming even to those who have experience in early releases, but AutoCAD provides support in learning to plot.

FIGURE A.13 Fast Track to zlotting option of the Help dialog box.

Fast Track to Plotting is loaded with all kinds of help. Instructions with audiovideo support can be accessed through the AutoCAD Help pull-down menu (see Figure A.13). Go through the Fast Tracking to Plotting before attempting your first plot. It is not important that you understand everything about plotting. The best teacher when it comes to plotting is experience, but the Fast Track crash course will give you some preparation and background before attempting to plot.

Getting Ready to Plot a Drawing

Check the following with your instructor before trying to plot.

1. Find out what plotter is configured in your lab.
2. Find out what page or sheet sizes are available in that plotter.
3. Figure out the scale in which your drawing should be plotted.

- Layout/Paper Space scaling is controlled by the Zoom command while in floating model space. The individual viewport must be activated before the Zoom command can be used for XP scaling. The following sequence is used to input a scale of ¼″ = 1′-0″, which has a scale factor of 48.

  Command: **ZOOM**↵
  Specify corner of window, enter scale factor (nX or NXP), or
  [All/Center/Dynamic/Extents/Previous/Scale/Window] <real time>: **1/48 XP**

- The model space scale for plotting the drawing can be set in the Layout Settings tab in the plotting sequence. As a guide, use the same scale that you created with the limits or wizard setup.

4. Determine which environment (Model Space or Layout/Paper Space) will be best for your drawing to be plotted in. Practice plotting in both environments for the experience.
5. Check with your instructor to verify your printable area. Each printer/plotter has a dead zone around the perimeter that is determined by the plotting device. Make sure your border and title block will be inside the printable area.

Plotting a Drawing in Model Space

To plot the entire drawing, start by zooming to the limits of your drawing while in model space.

1. To choose the Plot command, do one of the following:

- Left-click on the Plot icon on the Standard Toolbar.
- Select Plot from the File pull-down menu.
- Type **Plot**↵ at the command line.

Note: If the Fast Track to Plotting dialog box appears, close it by choosing the No option.

The Plot dialog box appears (see Figure A.14).

2. Left-click on the Plot Device tab first to bring up the options found in this tab (see Figure A.15).

Plot Settings Tab

Arrow Used to Show Sheet Sizes

Plot Scale Options

Plot Area Selection

Click Here to Center a Model Space Plot

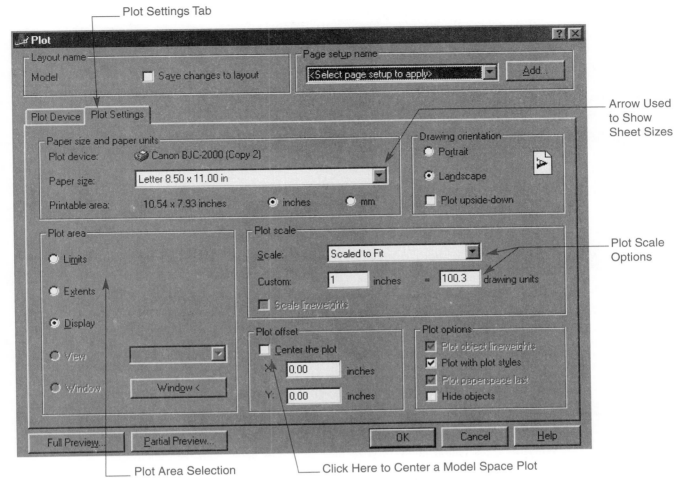

FIGURE A.14 Plot dialog box.

FIGURE A.15 Plot Device tab options.

Plot Device Tab

Arrow Used to Choose a Plotter

Used to Select Style Tables

Edit Styles

- In the **Plotter configuration** area select the plotter to be used by using the down arrow on the right.
- In the **Plot style table (pen assignments)** area, choose a plot style name. It is OK to choose the **Default R14 pen assignments.ctb** or **acad.ctb** when just starting out and learning the plotting sequence.

3. Left-click on the Plot Settings tab and make the following selections (see Figure A.14):

Note: The paper size must be supported by the plotter/printer chosen or a warning will display on the screen.

- In the Paper size and paper units area, choose a paper size for printing and then pick inches or mm (millimeters) for the units of the drawing to be plotted in.
- In the **Drawing Orientation** area choose from the following alignments:

Po<u>r</u>trait

La<u>n</u>dscape

Plot upside-down

Watch the small graphic window to the right to check the alignment visually.

- The **Plot area** options include the following choices:

Note: Use the **Limits** choice to plot the whole defined area of your drawing setup.

Li<u>m</u>its—This will plot the limits that have been established on the drawing.

E<u>x</u>tents—This will plot only all the objects in the drawing with no respect to the limits.

<u>D</u>isplay—This will plot only what is seen or displayed on the screen.

<u>V</u>iew—Views created with the **View** command previously can be selected to be plotted.

<u>W</u>indow—This button allows you to pick an area/window with the cursor and mouse or by typing in coordinates forming a rectangular shape.

- The **Plot scale** area is where you set the desired plotting scale to plot a model space drawing to a scale (see Figure A.16). Two choices are available:

<u>S</u>cale – There are 31 scale choices, ranging from mechanical to civil engineering to architectural. **Scaled to Fit** and **Custom choices** are also available (see Figure A.15).

Scaled to Fit will adjust the drawing to fit in the plotting area. This creates some very unorthodox scales and should be used only when the scale is not a factor.

Custom – This choice allows you to set any desired scale in the Custom text boxes (see Figure A.17).

FIGURE A.16   Plot scale choices.

FIGURE A.17   Plot scale for customizing.

■ Set the **Plot offset** area to **C**enter the plot for model space plotting (left-click in the box).

4. After picking the settings, it is time to preview what the plot will look like. At the bottom left corner of the Plot dialog box are two Preview buttons:

Partial Preview—This selection shows the plotting area in relation to the selected paper size. It also will display warnings when a plotting problem exists. A partial preview will not display objects in the drawing.

Full Preview—This option shows all the objects that will be printed as well as the outline of the paper size. Any part of the drawing not shown in the preview will not print.

5. If the full preview looks acceptable, right-click and choose plot. If you select Exit instead, then the screen returns to the Plot dialog box. Choose the OK button at the bottom right of the Plot dialog screen to execute the plot. If you click Cancel, then the standard AutoCAD screen returns.

Plotting from a Layout or Paper Space

Layout plotting works a little differently, but it really is just a matter of understanding paper space and how to scale floating model space inside paper space.

If you chose a template from the Startup dialog box when you began your drawing, then a Layout/Paper Space environment was automatically created for you. If the drawing was done in model space, then you must select the Layout1 tab at the bottom of the graphics screen. When you click on the Layout1 tab, the Page Setup dialog box appears, and you will need to make some choices similar to those in model space plotting.

1. Left-click on the Plot Device tab (see Figure A.18).

■ Choose the plotter.

■ Choose a Plot style (pen assignments).

FIGURE A.18 Plot Style Table R14 pen assignments.

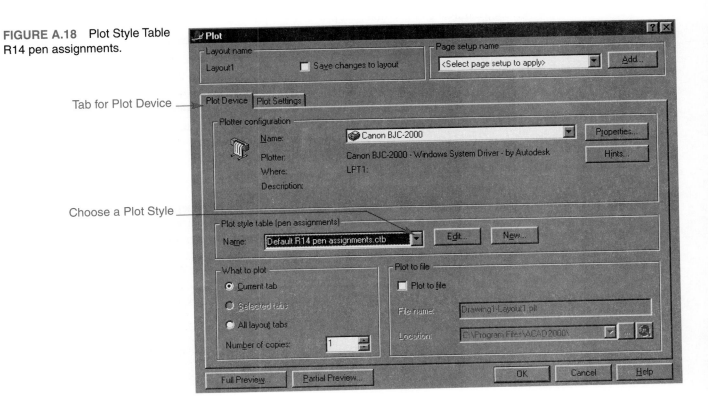

FIGURE A.19   Scale to
lineweight for plotting.

Check to scale lineweights for plotting. ——

2. Left-click on the Plot Settings tab and make a few more choices (see Figure A.19).

- Choose a paper size that works well with your drawing.
- Notice your printable area. It can be displayed in inches or millimeters.
- Check the drawing orientation area just as in the previous model space example.
- Notice that the Plot area is set to Layout. This is because you are intending to plot from the Layout/Paper Space option, so leave this setting alone.
- In the Plot scale area you have choices similar to the ones found in model space. Use 1:1 scale typically for your paper space plot scale. Left-click in the Scale lineweights box to turn it on so that lineweights will be scaled in proportion to the plot scale (see Figure A.19).
- Click the OK button at the bottom of the Plot dialog box to exit the layout/page setup.

Tips   The paper
space portion of your
drawing, which typi-
cally contains a title
block and border, is
drawn at 1″ = 1″.
This is the reason for
setting the plot scale
to 1:1 for Layout/Pa-
per Space plotting.

Inside the Viewport Window

Remember that viewport lines exist within the Layout mode. A viewport separates paper space from floating model space. Inside the viewport's rectangular lines is floating model space, a window to a different world, analogous to a glass bottom boat looking into the sea. You draw and design in model space. It is active when you double-click inside the viewport rectangle and the UCS icon appears (see Figure A.20).

The final step before exiting floating mode space is to scale it. The Zoom command is one way to do this, using the scale factor for your desired scale. Suppose you wanted floating model space to plot at ¼″ = 1′-0″ scale (scale factor of 48). Type the following at the command line to set this environment:

Command: **ZOOM**↵
Specify corner of window, enter scale factor (nX or NXP), or
[All/Center/Dynamic/Extents/Previous/Scale/Window] <real time>: **1/48 XP**

Exit floating model space by double-clicking outside the viewport rectangle.

FIGURE A.20 Floating model
space identification.

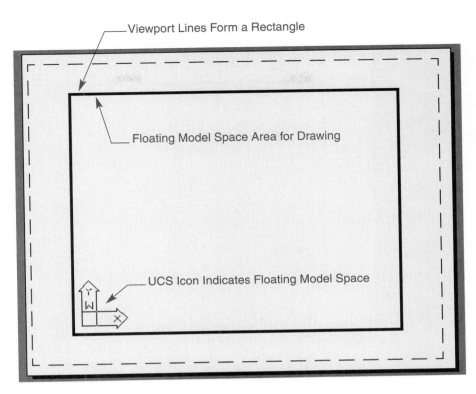

Outside the Viewport Window

Outside the viewport rectangle and inside the dashed rectangle is where you need to use a full-scale environment. The drawing's border lines and title block should be placed in here. If you selected a template with a title block and border from the Create a New Drawing dialog box when you first began a drawing, notice that its position is outside the viewport lines. This is where the full-scale world exists. If you want to bring in your own full-scale title block and border, use the Insert command to import a drawing file (.dwg) or import it from another drawing as a Block using the AutoCAD Design Center. Recall that you can draw and place text there at their real sizes. Make sure the paper space icon is displayed when you are working with the full-scale environment (title block and border) (see Figure A.21).

Previewing a Plot

Once the floating model space and the Layout/Paper space environments are set, it is time to preview the plot. Make sure the paper space icon is present on your screen to plot the whole layout. Select the Plot command to begin. Settings reappear in the Plot dialog box that were made when the Layout button was first used. This time, however, there are two buttons at the bottom left corner of the screen for plot previews.

- Partial Preview—Lines representing the plotting area (dashed line) and paper size (continuous line) will appear on the screen. None of the drawing appears for you to see. Partial preview will also display warnings of possible problems with the plot being previewed.
- Full Preview—This option shows the drawing that will be plotted. Look at the screen picture very carefully to make sure everything on the drawing will be printed. Right-click to access the following choices:

- **Exit**—This choice takes you back to the Plot dialog box.
- **Plot**—This choice executes the plot.
- **Pan**—This selection lets you hold the left mouse button down and pan around the drawing.
- **Zoom** (default)—Holding the left mouse button down and moving the magnifying glass up and down will adjust the zoom.

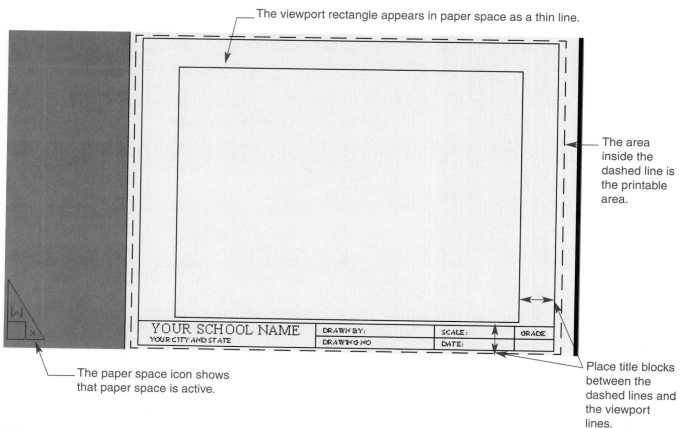

The viewport rectangle appears in paper space as a thin line.

The area inside the dashed line is the printable area.

YOUR SCHOOL NAME
YOUR CITY AND STATE

DRAWN BY:
DRAWING NO

SCALE:
DATE:

GRADE

Place title blocks between the dashed lines and the viewport lines.

The paper space icon shows that paper space is active.

FIGURE A.21   Paper space identification

- **Zoom Window**—This choice lets you define a zoom window by holding down the left mouse button to start the window and releasing it to complete the zoom window.
- **Zoom Original**—Returns the screen to the original size when the preview button was selected initially.

Choose the Plot option to execute the plot.

Settings for Sheet Sizes and Limits (Architectural and Civil Engineering Drawings)

Architectural Settings

Scale	Scale Factor	Paper Space Zoom Factor	Text Height ⅛″ ³⁄₁₆″ ¼″	LTSCALE
¹⁄₁₆″ = 1′-0″	192	¹⁄₁₉₂ XP	24″ 36″ 48″	96
¹⁄₃₂″ = 1′-0″	128	¹⁄₁₂₈ XP	16″ 24″ 32″	64
⅛″ = 1′-0″	96	¹⁄₉₆ XP	12″ 18″ 24″	48
³⁄₁₆″ = 1′-0″	64	¹⁄₆₄ XP	8″ 12″ 16″	32
¼″ = 1′-0″	48	¹⁄₄₈ XP	6″ 9″ 12″	24
⅜″ = 1′-0″	32	¹⁄₃₂ XP	4″ 6″ 8″	16
½″ = 1′-0″	24	¹⁄₂₄ XP	3″ 4.5″ 6″	12
¾″ = 1′-0″	16	¹⁄₁₆ XP	2″ 3″ 4″	8
1″ = 1′-0″	12	¹⁄₁₂ XP	1.5″ 2.25″ 3″	6
1½″ = 1′-0″	8	⅛ XP	1″ 1.5″ 2″	4
3″ = 1′-0″	4	¼ XP	.5″ .75″ 1″	2
1″ = 1″	1	¹⁄₁ XP	.125″ .188″ .25″	.5

* LTSCALEs are approximate and should be used as an initial starting value and adjusted as needed.

Architectural Limits for Different Sheet Sizes

Scale	Sheet Size 11″ × 8.5″ (X,Y)	Sheet Size 12″ × 9″ (X,Y)	Sheet Size 17″ × 11″ (X,Y)	Sheet Size 18″ × 12″ (X,Y)	Sheet Size 24″ × 18″ (X,Y)	Sheet Size 36″ × 24″ (X,Y)
¹⁄₁₆″ = 1′-0″	(176′,136′)	(192′,144′)	(272′,176′)	(288′,192′)	(384′,288′)	(576′,384′)
³⁄₃₂″ = 1′-0″	(117′-4″,90′-8″)	(128′,96′)	(181′-4″,117′-4″)	(192′,128′)	(256′,192′)	(384′,256′)
⅛″ = 1′-0″	(88′,68′)	(96′,72′)	(136′,88′)	(144′,96′)	(192′,144′)	(288′,192′)
³⁄₁₆″ = 1′-0″	(58′-8″, 45′-4″)	(64′,48′)	(90′-8″, 58′-8″)	(96′,64′)	(128′,96′)	(192′,128′)
¼″ = 1′-0″	(44′,34′)	(48′,36′)	(68′,44′)	(72′,48′)	(96′,72′)	(144′,96′)
⅜″ = 1′-0″	(29′-4″, 22′-8″)	(32′,24′)	(45′-4″, 29′-4″)	(48′,32′)	(64′,48′)	(96′,64′)
½″ = 1′-0″	(22′,17′)	(24′,18′)	(34′,22′)	(36′,24′)	(48′,36′)	(72′,48′)
¾″ = 1′-0″	(14′-8″, 11′-4″)	(16′,12′)	(22′-8″, 14′-8″)	(24′,16′)	(32′,24′)	(48′,32′)
1″ = 1′-0″	(11′,8′-6″)	(12′,9′)	(17′,11′)	(18′,12′)	(24′,18′)	(36′,24′)
1½″ = 1′-0″	(7′-4″, 5′-8″)	(8′,6′)	(11′-4″, 7′-4″)	(12′,8′)	(16′,12′)	(24′,16′)
3″ = 1′-0″	(3′-8″, 2′-10″)	(4′,3′)	(5′-8″, 3′-8″)	(6′,4′)	(8′,6′)	(12′,8′)
1″ = 1″	(11″,8.5″)	(12″,9″)	(17″,11″)	(18″,12″)	(24″,18″)	(36″,24″)

Civil Engineering Settings

Scale	Scale Factor	Paper Space Zoom Factor	Text Height ⅛″ ³⁄₁₆″ ¼″	LTSCALE
1″ = 10′	120	¹⁄₁₂₀ XP	15″ 22.5″ 30″	60
1″ = 20′	240	¹⁄₂₄₀ XP	30″ 45″ 60″	120
1″ = 30′	360	¹⁄₃₆₀ XP	45″ 67.5″ 90″	180
1″ = 40′	480	¹⁄₄₈₀ XP	60″ 90″ 120″	240
1″ = 50′	600	¹⁄₆₀₀ XP	75″ 112.5″ 150″	300
1″ = 60′	720	¹⁄₇₂₀ XP	90″ 135″ 180″	360
1″ = 100′	1200	¹⁄₁₂₀₀ XP	150″ 225″ 300″	600

Civil Engineering Limits for Different Sheet Sizes

Scale	Sheet Size 11″ × 8.5″ (X,Y)	Sheet Size 12″ × 9″ (X,Y)	Sheet Size 17″ × 11″ (X,Y)	Sheet Size 18″ × 12″ (X,Y)	Sheet Size 24″ × 18″ (X,Y)	Sheet Size 36″ × 24″ (X,Y)
1″ = 10′	(110′,85′)	(120′,90′)	(170′,110′)	(180′,120′)	(240′,180′)	(360′,240′)
1″ = 20′	(220′,170′)	(240′,180′)	(340′,220′)	(360′,240′)	(480′,360′)	(720′,480′)
1″ = 30′	(330′,225′)	(360′,270′)	(510′,330′)	(540′,360′)	(720′,540′)	(1080′,720′)
1″ = 40′	(440′,340′)	(480′,360′)	(680′,440′)	(720′,480′)	(960′,720′)	(1440′,960′)
1″ = 50′	(550′,425′)	(600′,450′)	(850′,550′)	(900′,600′)	(1200′,900′)	(1800′,1200′)
1″ = 60′	(660′,510′)	(720′,540′)	(1020′,660′)	(1080′,720′)	(1440′,1080′)	(2160′,1440′)
1″ = 100′	(1100′,850′)	(1200′,900′)	(1700′,1100′)	(1800′,1200′)	(2400′,1800′)	(3600′,2400′)

○ ○

Typical Furniture Sizes

Note: Furniture comes in a wide variety of shapes and sizes. The furniture sizes provided here are merely representative of typical furniture and fixture dimensions. In your design work you may want to use more specific dimensions gleaned from actual measurements, furniture catalogs, or other professional resources.

Bedroom Furnishings

Bed Sizes

Twin*	39″W × 75″, 80″, 84″H
Double*	54″W × 75″D
Queen*	60″W × 80″, 84″D
King*	76″W × 80″, 84″D

Mattress Depths*

Innerspring	5½″ – 6½″ H
Foam	4″ – 7½″ H
Box spring	5½″ – 9″ H

The average height of a bed equals the depth of the mattress and box spring plus the height of the frame above the floor. The headboard or footboard may also extend above the mattress.

Bassinet	26″W × 39″D
Infant Crib*	30″W × 50″, 52″D
Junior Crib	33″W × 54″, 47″D

These dimensions are for typical mattress sizes. Inclusion of a headboard and/or footboard may increase the size of the bed unit.

Night stand	18″W × 18″D × 24″H (square)
	16″ Ø × 16″ H (round)
Dresser	72″W × 20″D × 29″H (low)
	37″W × 20″D × 54″H (high)
Chest	48″ × 22″D × 29″H

Kitchen and Dining Room Furnishings and Fixtures

Standard Base Cabinets	6″, 12″–45″ in 3″ increments, 49″ W × 24″ D × 34½″ H
	(Typical counter height including countertop = 36″.)
Standard Wall Cabinets	12½″-13″ D
	36″, 39″, 42″ W × 12″ H
	30″–42″ W (in 3″ increments) × 15″ H
	24″–42″ W (in 3″ increments) × 18″ H
	15″–36″ W (in 3″ increments) × 24″
	12″–36″ W (in 3″ increments) × 30″
Cooktop	12″–48″ W × 18″–22″ D × 2″–3″ H
Dishwasher	23″–24″ W × 23¹¹⁄₁₆″–26¼″ D × 33½″–34½″ H
Freestanding Range/	19½″–40″ W × 24¼″–27½″D × 35⅛″–36⅛″ H
Oven Combination	
Microwave Oven	23″ W × 17″ D × 15″ H
Oven	21″–24½″ W × 21⅛″ × 24″ D × 23½″ × 26⅞″ H
Refrigerators	
Top freezer	28″–32¾″ W × 28¾″–31⅝″ D × 66″ H
Side-by-Side	30½″–35¾″ W × 29½″–32⅞″ D × 64″–68⅞″ H
China Cabinets	2′8″–3′8″ W × 1′2″–1′9″ D × 5′6″–6′0″ H
Dining Room Tables*	
Boat Shaped	3′5″–6′0″ W × 8′0″–20′0″ L × 28″–29″ H
Rectangular	2′6″–6′0″ W × 5′0″–28′0″ L × 28″–29″ H
Round	3′6″–10′0″ D × 28″–29″ H
Square	3′0″–5′0″ × 28″–29″ H
Dining Chairs	1′6″–1′9″ W × 1′6″–1′10″ D × 2′10″–3′3″ H
	Remember to provide space to move chairs in and out to sit at the table.
Sideboard	4′0″–5′0″ W × 1′8″–2′0″ D × 3′2″ H

Living Room and Family Room Furnishings

Armchairs	2′2″–2′6″ W × 2′0″–2′4″ D × 3′0″–4′0″ H
Club Chairs	2′4″–2′10″ W × 2′4″–2′10″ D × 3′0″ H
Coffee Tables	3′0″–3′6″ W × 2′0″–3′0″ D × 1′6″ H
	3′0″ Ø × 1′6″ H
End Tables	1′8″–3′0″ W × 1′8″ D × 1′6″–1′8″ H
	1′6″–2′0″ Ø × 1′6″ H
Folding Chairs	1′4″–1′7″ W × 1′6″–1′8″ D × 2′4″–2′6″ H
Loveseat	6′0″–6′8″ W × 2′8″–3′0″ D × 2′6″–2′9″ H
Ottoman	2′0″ W × 2′0″ D × 1′4″ H
Piano	
Grand	4′10″ × 5′8″
Upright/Spinet	4′6″–5′9″ W × 1′9″ D
Side Chairs	1′4″–2′0″ W × 1′6″–2′8″ D × 2′4″–3′0″H
Sofa	7′6″–9′0″ W × 2′8″–3′0″ D × 2′6″–2′9″ H
Wingback Armchairs	2′4″–2′10″ W × 2′4″–2′10″ D × 3′0″–4′0″ H

Office Furniture

Bookshelves	$2'0''$–$4'0''$ W $\times$ $11''$–$1'2''$ D $\times$ $2'6''$–$7'0''$ H
Computer Cart	$3'0''$ W $\times$ $1'8''$ D $\times$ $2'6''$ H
Desks	
Double Pedestal	$4'7''$–$7'0''$ W $\times$ $2'6''$–$2'9''$ D $\times$ $2'4''$–$2'6''$ H
Kneehole Desk	$2'6''$–$3'6''$ W $\times$ $1'6''$–$1'10''$ D $\times$ $2'6''$ H
Secretary	$2'8''$–$3'8''$ W $\times$ $1'6''$–$1'10''$ D $\times$ $6'2''$–$7'2''$ H
Desk Chairs	$1'8''$–$2'4''$ W $\times$ $1'6''$–$2'8''$ D $\times$ $2'11''$–$4'0''$ H
Floor Lamps	$1'4''$–$1'6''$Ø $\times$ $4'10''$–$5'9''$ H
File Cabinets	$1'3''$–$1'6\frac{1}{4}''$ W $\times$ $26\frac{1}{2}''$ D $\times$ $2'5''$–$5'0''$ H
Returns	$1'3''$–$1'8''$ W $\times$ $1'11''$–$4'0''$ D $\times$ $2'1''$–$2'3''$ H

Landscape Symbols

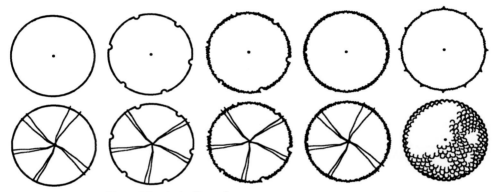

Various Deciduous Trees Simple to Complex

Various Coniferous Evergreen Trees
Simple to Complex

Boulders

Various Palm Trees

Various Cactus

Hexagon Pavers

Square Pavers

Various Ground Coverings

Brick Pavers

Stone Pavers

Fraction and Decimal Conversions

Divisions of an inch by Fractions

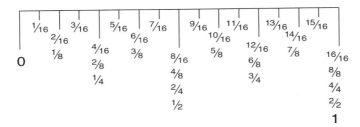

Divisions of an inch by 1/16″ only

Divisions of an inch by 1/8″

Divisions of an inch by 1/4″ and 1/2″

Fraction	Decimal Equivalent (to Four Places)
1/16	.0625
1/8	.1250
3/16	.1875
1/4	.2500
5/16	.3125
3/8	.3750
7/16	.4375
1/2	.5000
9/16	.5625
5/8	.6250
11/16	.6875
3/4	.7500
13/16	.8125
7/8	.8750
15/16	.9375
1	1.000

Index

Z